LEADING CHANGE

in Multiple Contexts

Concepts and Practices in
Organizational, Community,
Political, Social, and Global
Change Settings

Gill Robinson
HICKMAN

University of Richmond

y

Los Angeles | London | New Delhi
Singapore | Washington DC

For information:

SAGE Publications, Inc.
2455 Teller Road
Thousand Oaks, California 91320
E-mail: order@sagepub.com

SAGE Publications India Pvt. Ltd.
B 1/I 1 Mohan Cooperative
   Industrial Area
Mathura Road, New Delhi 110 044
India

SAGE Publications Ltd.
1 Oliver's Yard
55 City Road
London EC1Y 1SP
United Kingdom

SAGE Publications Asia-Pacific Pte. Ltd.
33 Pekin Street #02-01
Far East Square
Singapore 048763

Printed in the United States of America

Library of Congress Cataloging-in-Publication Data

Hickman, Gill Robinson.
Leading change in multiple contexts: concepts and practices in organizational, community, political, social, and global change settings/Gill Robinson Hickman.
    p. cm.
Includes bibliographical references and index.
ISBN 978-1-4129-2677-5 (cloth)
ISBN 978-1-4129-2678-2 (pbk.)
   1. Leadership. 2. Social change. 3. Organizational change. I. Title.

HM1261.H53 2010
303.48′4—dc22   2009002579

This book is printed on acid-free paper.

09   10   11   12   13   10   9   8   7   6   5   4   3   2   1

Acquisitions Editor:	Lisa Cuevas Shaw
Editorial Assistant:	MaryAnn Vail
Production Editor:	Catherine M. Chilton
Copy Editor:	Cheryl Duksta
Typesetter:	C&M Digitals (P) Ltd.
Proofreader:	Doris Hus
Indexer:	Diggs Publication Services
Cover Designer:	Gail Buschman
Marketing Manager:	Christy Guilbault

Brief Contents

Detailed Contents

Acknowledgments

I wish to thank the many colleagues, students, and family members who have contributed to the completion of this book. Specifically, I would like to thank the students in my Leading Change classes at the Jepson School of Leadership Studies who helped to shape the content and format of this text through their use of and comments on the initial draft manuscripts; the current Dean of the Jepson School, Sandra Peart, and former interim Provost of the University of Richmond, Joseph Kent, for granting me time to complete *Leading Change*; and former Dean of the Jepson School, Howard Prince, for giving me the opportunity to develop and teach the course that led to this book. I am forever grateful to the two academic coordinators of the Jepson School, Cassie Price and her successor, Tammy Tripp, for their many months of reference checking and technical editing, their endless patience, and their consistently congenial dispositions.

My deep appreciation goes to my longtime colleague and friend Richard (Dick) Couto, an eminent scholar and cocontributor to Chapters 1 and 5 and sole contributor to Chapter 7; to Sarah Hippensteel Hall and Marti Goetz for their experience, insight, and scholarship as cocontributors to Chapter 5; and to Rebecca Todd Peters for her superb scholarship, global perspective, and creativity as cocontributor to Chapter 10. A most special thank you to James MacGregor Burns, my mentor, colleague, friend, and role model, for writing the epilogue: "Leading Intellectual Change: The Power of Ideas." Your intellectual leadership has inspired me and numerous scholars and students of leadership studies all over the world, and for that we are exceedingly appreciative.

I am most thankful to the editors and staff of Sage Publications for their expertise, support, and care during the writing and publication of this book, especially Lisa Cuevas Shaw, MaryAnn Vail, and the late Al Bruckner. You serve as exemplars of the best in publisher-author relationships.

I am grateful to Wang Fang, a wonderful colleague and friend, whose intellect and sage advice about the book I fully respect and appreciate. Finally, I owe a special debt of gratitude to my husband, Garrison Michael Hickman, who provided infinite support and laughter; kept me motivated, fed, and supplied with coffee; and graciously read every word of the manuscript.

Introduction

Leadership brings about real change that leaders intend.

—Burns (1978, p. 414)

The St. Luke Penny Savings Bank: A Change Vignette

The first female bank founder and president in the United States, Maggie L. Walker, led an unprecedented change to establish an African American–owned bank where people could combine their economic power to purchase homes, start businesses, and educate future leaders. Virginia banks owned by Whites in the early 1900s were unwilling to accept deposits from African American organizations or accept the pennies and nickels saved from the meager incomes of African American workers. Inadvertently, the discrimination by White bankers spurred Walker to study Virginia's banking and financial laws and enroll in a business course with the aim of opening a bank (Stanley, 1996). In a 1901 speech before the African American fraternal organization the Independent Order of St. Luke, she said, "Let us have a bank that will take the nickels and turn them into dollars" (Walker, 1901).

Walker and her associates formed the St. Luke Penny Savings Bank in 1903, with opening-day receipts totaling $9,430.44. By 1913, the bank's holdings had grown to more than $300,000 in assets. The Penny Savings Bank survived the Great Depression, whereas many other banks across the United States failed. It merged with two other banks in 1930 and was renamed Consolidated Bank & Trust. The bank still exists today and continues to pursue the founder's purpose of economic self-reliance for African Americans.

Purpose, Concepts, and Practices

The story of Maggie Walker and the founding of the St. Luke Penny Savings Bank provide a focus for examining the concepts involved in leading change in multiple contexts. *Leading change* is a collective effort by participants to intentionally modify, alter, or transform human social systems. Certainly, Walker and her colleagues were involved in an intentional, goal-focused change effort. Research and publications on leading change typically center on how to lead change successfully in organizations, often with an emphasis on practices. The establishment of an African American–owned bank in the early 1900s conforms to the typical focus of change. Yet the focus on the practices of leading organizational change is only one part of the story. Figure I.1 illustrates the connections among key factors involved in leading change and identifies several change contexts, including organizational, community, political, global, and social action. Leading change is ignited by purpose, influenced by context, and linked by concepts and practices of both leadership and change, which function jointly to create new outcomes.

The founding of St. Luke Penny Savings Bank provides an introduction to how the factors in Figure I.1 work together. Moving from the inside of Figure I.1 outward, it is apparent that the Penny Savings Bank came about because of a steadfast commitment to a compelling purpose. Most often, the purpose of leadership is change—change in human conditions, social structure, dominant ideas, or prevailing practices in one context or several. Walker articulated the purpose most eloquently: "Let us put our moneys together; let us use our moneys; let us put our money out at usury [interest] among ourselves, and reap the benefit ourselves" (Miller & Rice, 1997, pp. 66–68).

Several concepts and practices of change apply to the Penny Savings Bank example. The founding and operation of the bank involved strategic change (actions to achieve a competitively superior fit between the organization and its environment; Rajagopalan & Spreitzer, 1997). Its long history of sustained operation illustrates theories of change, such as life cycle—stages in the bank's functioning from initiation to growth to maturity to decline to revitalization) and teleological (step-by-step change based on goals and purpose) and dialectical change (conflict, negotiation, compromise, and resolution; Van de Ven & Poole, 1995), such as the firing of its officers in 2003.

In the area of community change, the purpose and focus of the bank demonstrate concepts of community empowerment or social power (i.e., actions by a community to control its own destiny; Speer & Hughley, 1995) using practices of community development (i.e., mobilization of resources by the community; Kretzmann & McKnight, 1996), social capital development (i.e., social networks and the associated norms of reciprocity; Putnam, 2000), and economic development. Walker's stature in the business community and her personal convictions allowed her to become involved in social change or social movements. She cofounded civil rights organizations to fight racial injustice in the South, including the Richmond branch of the National Association for the Advancement of Colored People (NAACP) and the Richmond Council of Colored Women, and she became an active member of the National Urban League and the Virginia Interracial Committee, among others. Through these organizations, Walker was able to participate in social change that illustrates theoretical concepts of rational choice (strategies to transform social structures) and resource mobilization (actions taken by social movement organizations) (Garner & Tenuto, 1997).

Walker exhibited several concepts of leadership in action during her quest to bring about organizational, community, and social change. Her speeches clearly

FIGURE I.1   Leading Change in Multiple Contexts

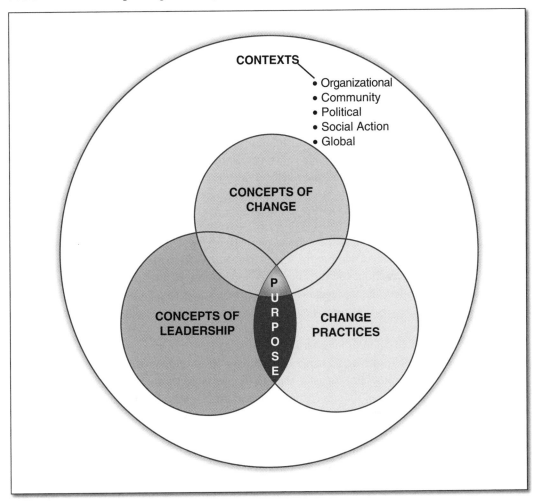

exemplified her charismatic leadership style through strong rhetorical skills and the ability to create an uplifting vision in the hearts and minds of followers (Hughes, Ginnett, & Curphy, 2009, p. 637). She was a capable transactional leader (Burns, 1978) who, as president of the Penny Savings Bank, provided an exchange of valued things between the bank and the community. For example, the bank accepted small deposits of hard-earned cash from customers in exchange for providing a source of consolidated funds to build homes and businesses. Walker's initiative intended "real change" in the sense that James MacGregor Burns's (1978) concept of transforming leadership connotes. By 1920, the Penny Savings Bank had helped members of the community purchase 600 homes. Walker made loans to African American–owned businesses and started a department store and weekly newspaper, the *St. Luke Herald*. These businesses employed many members of the Jackson Ward area who, in turn, were able to support themselves, their families, and their community.

Context, the setting or environment in which change takes place, matters a great deal, along with larger contextual elements of history, culture, and society. Wren (1995) explained the significance of larger contextual elements to leadership:

> Leaders and followers do not act in a vacuum. They are propelled, constrained, and buffeted by their environment. The effective leader must understand the nature of the leadership context, and how it affects the leadership process. Only then can he or she operate effectively in seeking to achieve the group's objectives. . . . First—beginning at the most macro level—are the long-term forces of history (social, economic, political, and intellectual); the second sphere of the leadership context is colored by the values and beliefs of the contemporary culture; and finally, at the most micro level, leadership is shaped by such "immediate" aspects of the context as the nature of the organization, its mission, and the nature of the task. (p. 243)

Many historical and cultural elements are evident in the St. Luke Penny Savings Bank vignette. Long-term forces of history—from slavery, to the Civil War, to Reconstruction, and then Jim Crow segregation—led to the context that generated the leadership of Maggie Walker and many others, who in turn helped create a self-sufficient society for African Americans that paralleled European American society in the South.

In addition to long-term forces, immediate contexts—organizational, community, political, social change, and global—affect leading change in significant ways. The purpose and focus of leading change in each context varies, as indicated in Table I.1, even though change in one context (social or community) may lead to or call for change in another (political). The way in which authority is granted to constituted leaders to bring about change in organizations is different from the authority of elected officials to affect change in local, state, or federal government. Leaders in each context are chosen by different means (elected vs. appointed) and they serve different constituencies (the electorate/public vs. boards and stockholders).

Context also influences concepts and practices of leadership, even though leadership concepts and practices tend to be adaptable and effective in different settings. For example, Maggie Walker was able to use charismatic, transactional, and transforming leadership to bring about change successfully in organizational, community, and social action contexts. The same concept or form of leadership may be used in different contexts but affect very different groups and bring about different outcomes. Charismatic, servant, transactional, and invisible leadership, for example, can be used in organizational, political, social change, and community contexts. Yet these forms of leadership affect different groups (employees, constituents, underrepresented groups, or local citizens/community members), and they are intended for different purposes. Leading global change may require transcending boundaries (by identifying what makes us all human), whereas some new social movement leadership may entail creating new identities (the new Right or Left) that separate groups. Although the Penny Savings Bank provides an illustration of leading change in an organizational context, this example also demonstrates the interdependent nature of change and its impact across several contexts—organizations, community, and social activism (social movement).

TABLE I.1 Contextual Influences on Leading Change

	Contexts				
	Organizational	**Community**	**Political**	**Social Change**	**Global**
Purpose of change	To alter the form, quality, or state of an organization to meet challenges and opportunities in the internal or external environment	To advance or protect rights, health, and well-being of civil society/members in communities	To confront situations in which policy must be formulated, promulgated, and executed	To give voice to specific causes in order to correct injustices, counter or resist social conditions, or pursue and create new possibilities for society	To address large-scale transnational or transcultural problems, create new opportunities, develop or alter global governance structures
Participants in change process	Positional leaders (private, public, NGO sectors), informal leaders, members/employees of the organization	Community/citizen leaders, community members, NGO leaders and members	Elected officials, advocacy groups, the public	Nonconstituted leaders, activists, NGO leaders and members	Positional leaders (international agencies, and corporations), government officials, NGO leaders and members
Source of authority to lead change	Legitimate/positional authority, shared authority, informal or referent power	Self-agency or social power	Constituted/legal authority (elected officials), social power (advocacy groups)	Social power and legitimate authority (NGOs, movement organizations)	Negotiated agreements or contracts (private sector), legal authority (governing bodies), social power (NGOs)
Affected groups	Stakeholders: employees, customers, investors, and community members	Community members/citizens	Constituents, specific industries and organizations	Groups seeking justice or humane treatment	Transnational society (nation-states, civil society, corporations, international agencies)

The efforts of Maggie Walker and her colleagues to lead change in the Jackson Ward community led to many significant outcomes. In addition to establishing a bank to serve the financial needs of the African American community, Walker and her associates helped to create a self-reliant and thriving community with its own banks, businesses, jobs, homes, and social and economic capital. Members of the community were able to use these resources to establish civil rights organizations, which contributed to the ultimate downfall of segregation in the South.

The intent of this book is to bring together many concepts and practices of change and leadership from various disciplines and connect them to leading change in the five different contexts. The introduction to each context begins with a vignette about actual circumstances, like the founding of St. Luke Penny Savings Bank, to help illustrate concepts and practices in each context, and concludes with an application and reflection that allows readers to analyze other real-life situations using information from the chapter. These vignettes and applications provide examples of each context featured in the text and give readers a sense of how leading change differs in every setting. The book is divided into five parts. Part I, which has only a single chapter, deals with conceptual views of leadership. Part II consists of three chapters devoted to the organizational change context, given that more research and publications have been generated about leading change in organizations than in the other contexts. Part II includes five applications and reflections that represent several types of organizations. In Parts III–V, community, political, social, and global change contexts are examined separately for analytical purposes. Three chapters examine situations in which leading change in one context involves advocating or initiating change in another context because, in reality, change in one context almost invariably generates some form of change in at least one other context. These interactions across contexts commonly produce change in both settings. It is difficult to bring about long-term community or social change, for instance, without ultimately generating public-policy change that authorizes or inhibits specific actions. Few long-term gains in civil rights or environmental protections would be possible without significant policy changes in these areas.

Leading change is almost always a complex, long-term, and challenging endeavor. Yet it is one of the most central processes to the study and practice of leadership. I hope that this book will help its readers understand concepts and practices involved in leading change and inspire each reader to make a meaningful difference in some aspect of life in communities, organizations, politics/public policy, society, or the world.

References

Burns, J. M. (1978). *Leadership.* New York: Harper Torchbooks.

Garner, R., & Tenuto, J. (1997). *Social movement theory and research: An annotated bibliographical guide.* Lanham, MD: Scarecrow Press.

Hughes, R. L., Ginnett, R. C., & Curphy, G. J. (2009). *Leadership: Enhancing the lessons of experience* (6th ed.). Boston: McGraw-Hill.

Kretzmann, J., & McKnight, J. P. (1996). Assets-based community development. *National Civic Review, 85*(4), 23–29.

Miller, M. M., & Rice, D. M. (1997). *Pennies to dollars: The story of Maggie Lena Walker.* North Haven, CT: Linnet Books.

Putnam, R. D. (2000). *Bowling alone: The collapse and revival of American community.* New York: Touchstone.

Rajagopalan, N., & Spreitzer, G. M. (1997). Toward a theory of strategic change: A multi-lens perspective and integrative framework. *Academy of Management Review, 22,* 48–79.

Speer, P. W., & Hughey, J. (1995). Community organizing: An ecological route to empowerment and power. *American Journal of Community Psychology, 23,* 729–774.

Stanley, B. N. (1996, February 13). Maggie L. Walker. *Richmond Times Dispatch,* p. B6.

Van de Ven, A. H., & Poole, M. S. (1995). Explaining development and change in organizations. *Academy of Management Review, 20,* 510–540.

Walker, M. L. (1901). *An address to the 34th annual session of the right worthy grand council of Virginia, Independent Order of St. Luke.* Retrieved August 19, 2004, from http://www.nps.gov/malw/speech.htm

Wren, J. T. (1995). *The leader's companion: Insights on leadership through the ages.* New York: Free Press.

PART I

Conceptual Perspectives on Leading Change

Introduction

Prior to writing this book, I participated with several leadership scholars in a project known as the General Theory of Leadership (GTOL), led by James MacGregor Burns, George (Al) Goethals, and Georgia Sorenson. Our mission, as conceived by Burns, was to develop an integrative theory of leadership—in his words, "to provide people studying or practicing leadership with a general guide or orientation—a set of principles that are universal which can be then adapted to different situations" (Managan, 2002). Though the group did not produce a general theory of leadership, at the conclusion of the project "the members of the group decided that the most productive way to proceed was to create a volume of essays designed to capture, to the best of our ability, the nuances of 3 years of scholarly debate and discussion" (Wren, 2006, p. 34). This effort resulted in a book titled *The Quest for a General Theory of Leadership* (referred to as the Quest) (Goethals & Sorenson, 2006).

Congruent with my scholarship and teaching interests, and in anticipation of writing *Leading Change in Multiple Contexts*, I worked with a group (consisting of Richard Couto, Fredric Jablin, and myself) that would write the Quest chapter on change. The greater part of that chapter is included in this introduction to provide the conceptual perspective from which I consider leading change.[1] As indicated by the Quest editors, this perspective:

take[s] issue with the "Newtonian, mechanistic and old science" view of a leader or leaders initiating change and instead offer[s] a complex net of co-arising historical, economic, group and environmental factors that ebb and flow, push and pull, to collectively birth change. Using a constructionist approach [the view that humans construct or create reality and give it meaning through social, economic and political interactions] as opposed to an essentialist one [the view that social and natural realties exist apart from our perceptions of reality and that individuals perceive the world rather than construct it], they deftly demonstrate the interpenetrating and complex nature of leadership in action. (Goethals & Sorenson, 2006, p. xvii)

This viewpoint does not presume that "conditions change merely because a group of people wants them to change. . . . social reality is subject to historical conditions that can either foster or hinder change beyond any single person's or group's ability to effect change" (Hickman & Couto, 2006, p. 153).

The next section presents a vignette from the early civil rights movement in the United States and describes the actions taken by Barbara Rose Johns and the student leaders at Moton High School in protest of injustices committed by Prince Edward County Virginia School Board officials. The analysis that follows identifies and examines elements that contributed to change in this case, with the hope of illuminating elements that may be useful for understanding change across contexts.

Note

1. I wish to thank Wang Fang for her recommendation concerning this chapter.

References

Goethals, G. R., & Sorenson, G. L. J. (Eds.). (2006). *The quest for a general theory of leadership*. Cheltenham, UK: Edward Elgar Publishing.

Hickman, G. R., & Couto, R. A. (2006). Causality, change, and leadership. In G. R. Goethals & G. L. J. Sorenson (Eds.), *The quest for a general theory of leadership* (pp. 152–187). Cheltenham, UK: Edward Elgar Publishing.

Managan, K. (2002, May 31). Leading the way in leadership: The unending quest of the discipline's founding father, James MacGregor Burns. *Chronicle of Higher Education*, *48*(38), A10–12. Retrieved October 26, 2008, from http://newman.richmond.edu:2511/hww/results/results_single_ftPES.jhtml

Wren, J. T. (2006). Introduction. In Goethals, G. R. & Sorenson, G. L. J. (Eds.), *The quest for a general theory of leadership* (p. 34). Cheltenham, UK: Edward Elgar Publishing.

CHAPTER 1

Causality, Change, and Leadership

Gill Robinson Hickman and Richard A. Couto

Barbara Rose Johns

As a junior at Robert R. Moton High School in Farmville, the county seat of Prince Edward County, Virginia, Barbara Rose Johns knew that the segregated, all-Black school that she attended in 1951 was separate but certainly not equal. She saw the same markers of inequality familiar to African American school children and their parents throughout the South at the time: textbooks handed down from the White students and, most of all, overcrowded facilities. In Johns's case, a school built in 1939 to serve 180 students instead housed 450 students. The school accommodated some of the overflow students in three buildings hastily erected in 1949. Built of 2 × 4s, plywood, and tar paper, they were dubbed "shacks" or "chicken coops."

At the constant prodding of the Moton PTA and its president, the Reverend L. Francis Griffin, pastor of the First Baptist Church, the all-White school board offered regular assurances but no action on a new high school for African American children. Progress slowed and the assurances became so broad that in April 1951, the school board suggested that the Moton High School PTA not come back to the school board's meetings. Johns shared her concerns about the poor facilities and her frustration with the board's delaying tactics with her favorite teacher, Inez Davenport. Davenport replied, "Why don't you do something about it?"

AUTHORS' NOTE: This chapter is an excerpt from "Causality, Change, and Leadership," by Gill Robinson Hickman and Richard A. Couto. In *The Quest for a General Theory of Leadership* (pp. 152–187), by George R. Goethals & Georgia L. J. Sorenson (Eds.), 2006, Cheltenham, UK: Edward Elgar Publishing. Copyright © 2006 by Edward Elgar Publishing. By permission of Edward Elgar Publishing, Inc. This chapter includes the invaluable contributions of our late colleague and friend, Fredric M. Jablin, who provided his seminal insights during the conceptualization and outlining phase of this project.

So Johns did. During a 6-month period she enlisted student leaders a few at a time to take action themselves. Finally on April 23, 1951, following the PTA's failed efforts, the students put their plans in motion. They started by luring M. Boyd Jones, the African American principal of the school, away from the premises with a false alarm about students making trouble at the bus station. He had received such complaints before and was anxious to put a stop to whatever was going on. As soon as he left, Johns and the other student leaders sent a forged note to every classroom calling for a school assembly at 11:00 a.m.

When the students and teachers arrived in the auditorium, the stage curtain opened on Johns and other student strike leaders. She asked the two dozen teachers to leave, and most of them did. She then laid out the already well-known grievances and said that it was time for the students to take matters into their own hands by striking. No one was to go to class. If they stuck together, she explained, the Whites would have to respond. Nothing would happen to them, because the jail was not big enough to hold all of them. Principal Jones returned to school to find the student assembly in full swing. He pleaded with the students not to strike and explained that progress on the new school was being made. Johns asked him to go back to his office, and he did.

Flush with their initial success, the student strike committee asked Rev. Griffin to come to the school that afternoon and give them some advice. They asked him if the students should ask their parents' permission to strike. The African American adult population in Prince Edward County was "docile" in the view of Rev. Griffin, who had spent time trying to organize an NAACP chapter in the county. He suggested that the matter be put to a vote, which ultimately determined that the students should proceed without getting their parents' approval. At Griffin's urging, Johns and Carrie Stokes, student body president, wrote a letter to the NAACP attorneys in Richmond asking for their assistance.

The next afternoon the strike committee met with the superintendent of schools, T. J. McIlwaine, who was serving a fourth decade in that position. He represented the softer side of Jim Crow—accepting things as they were and doing his best to be fair and evenhanded in a system of injustice and oppression. At the meeting, the opposing sides hardened their stances. McIlwaine insisted on African American subordination and made numerous promises—assuring the students that much had already been done and that more would be done in time. He also previewed a gauntlet of reprisals—warning the students that unless they went back to class, the teachers and the principal would lose their jobs. The students left dismayed by McIlwaine's elusive and evasive manner but encouraged by their performance in the confrontation. They had held their own in the face of White power.

On Wednesday, 2 days into the strike, NAACP attorneys Oliver Hill and Spottswood Robinson III came by to talk with the strike leaders and their supporters in response to the letter they had received from the students. Both Hill and Robinson were high-profile civil rights lawyers who regularly engaged in lawsuits. They had studied at Howard University, a training ground for advocacy lawyers, and had joined the network of African American lawyers working to redress racial inequality across the country. On the state and national level, the premise of the NAACP's advocacy had been that as long as *Plessy v. Ferguson* was the law of the land, the government had to make equal what it insisted remain separate. They had already won several lawsuits for equal pay and facilities around the state of Virginia. Hill had even won a case for equal salaries for Prince Edward County teachers before World War II.

Hill and Robinson were not encouraging on this day, however. They and other NAACP members had grown tired of equalization suits, which although plentiful, only succeeded in changing the subordination of African Americans teachers and students at the margins. They were interested in shifting their strategy to confront school desegregation directly and were paying close attention to a case from Clarendon County, South Carolina, that was moving toward the U.S. Supreme Court. In fact, when Hill and Robinson stopped to speak to the Farmville student strike organizers, they were en route to Pulaski County, Virginia, to determine if the plaintiffs in a case there were willing to transform their suit from equalization to desegregation. They counseled the students to go back to class.

The students, however, were adamant in their refusal to end the strike. Impressed by their determination and not wanting to dampen their spirits, Hill and Robinson offered to help if the students would agree to return to school and change their case from one of equalization to one of desegregation.

The next evening, April 26, 1,000 students and parents attended a mass meeting in Farmville. The secretary of the state NAACP urged the parents to support their children. Without parental support, he said, the NAACP would not initiate what it knew would be a long, hard suit that would require considerable endurance. Initial assessments suggested that 65% of parents supported the students and the NAACP intervention; 25% opposed it; and 10% had no opinion. No opponents spoke that night.

On April 30, the school board sent out a letter signed by Principal Jones, urging parents to send their children back to school. The strange wording, which stated that Jones and the staff "had been authorized by the division superintendent" to send the letter, suggested that Jones was acting under duress. Rev. Griffin, however appreciative of Jones's difficult position, nevertheless understood that the principal's prestige and authority could influence many parents to change or waver in their support of the strike and court action. Consequently, Griffin sent out his own letter calling for another mass meeting on Thursday, May 3, and underscoring the significance of what the students were trying to accomplish: "REMEMBER. The eyes of the world are on us. The intelligent support we give our cause will serve as a stimulant for the cause of free people everywhere" (Smith, 1965/1996, p. 58). John Lancaster, Negro county farm agent, helped Griffin get out the mass mailing.

On May 3 Hill and Robinson petitioned the school board for the desegregation of the county's schools. The meeting that night took the form of a rally and served as a real turning point. J. B. Pervall, the former principal of Moton High School, spoke in favor of the standard of equality but not integration and gave many people in the packed church reason to pause and reassess what they were supporting. The NAACP officials attempted to regain the momentum, but it was Barbara Johns who succeeded in restoring the crowd's support. She reminded members of the audience of their experience and the students' action. In concluding, she effectively recounted the many small and large insults suffered by African Americans in the history of race relations, challenging Pervall with unmistakable metaphors of White oppression and Black accommodation to it. She admonished the huge gathering: "Don't let Mr. Charlie, Mr. Tommy, or Mr. Pervall stop you from backing us. We are depending on you" (Smith, 1965/1996, p. 59). Rev. Griffin took the cue and asserted Pervall's right to speak but implied cowardice of anyone who would not match the students' courage and back them. The students consented to return to school on Monday, May 7. Hill and Robinson promised that they would file suit in federal court unless the school board agreed to integrate by May 8.

The Walkout Becomes a Federal Case

On May 23, one month after the strike, Robinson followed through on the NAACP's promise in light of the board's inaction and filed suit in federal court in Richmond, Virginia, on behalf of 117 Moton students. In *Davis v. County School Board of Prince Edward County* he argued that Virginia's law requiring segregated schools be struck down as unconstitutional. The attorney general, looking at the facts, counseled that an equalization suit was indefensible for the state but integration was too radical a remedy. The state immediately began improving the facilities in an effort to render the suit moot.

The prestigious Richmond law firm Hunton, Williams, Anderson, Gay, & Moore represented the school board. Two senior partners, Archibald Gerard Robertson and Justin Moore, prepared a vigorous defense of segregation. During the 5-day trial, which began on February 25, 1952, they argued a very familiar defense of poor facilities for African American children: to each according to the taxes that they pay. The poverty of African Americans meant a low tax base among them and thus a generous White subsidy of their schools.

Robinson and Hill presented a now-familiar cast of witnesses who discussed the psychological impact of segregation. Moore rebutted one witness for the plaintiffs specifically for his Jewish background and the others for their unfamiliarity with the mores of the South. Moore ridiculed educator and psychologist Kenneth B. Clark for his research methods and overreaching conclusions. During Moore's cross-examination of Clark, Moore and Hill clashed vehemently—and just short of physically—over Moore's contention that the NAACP and Hill himself stirred up and fomented critical situations. The passions of this exchange portended events to come.

The court found unanimously for the school board. The students and their parents were disappointed, given their honest, albeit idealistic, belief that they would win because their cause was just. Robinson and Hill were neither surprised nor disappointed; they were now prepared to appeal to higher courts. *Davis v. School Board* reached the Supreme Court in July and joined with other school desegregation cases for argument on December 8, 1952.

The drama of a local school strike reaching the U.S. Supreme Court was not over, although many of the original actors in the school strike had exited the stage. Barbara Rose Johns left Farmville soon after the strike. Her family, concerned for her safety, sent her to Montgomery, Alabama, to live with her uncle Rev. Vernon Johns, minister of the Dexter Avenue Baptist Church. The education board fired Boyd Jones, and he and his new wife, Moton High School teacher Inez Davenport, also moved to Montgomery so he could attend graduate school. Ironically, the couple became members of the Dexter Avenue Baptist Church.

The arguments of December left the Court with the task of deciding the legality of school desegregation and possibly the constitutionality of *Plessy v. Ferguson*, the 1896 decision that found separate but equal to be constitutional. A divided Court, with at least two dissenting votes, was ready to overturn *Plessy* but sought a stronger majority. Justice Felix Frankfurter bought some time for the Court by developing a set of remaining questions, and the Court asked that the case be reargued on October 12, 1953. In the interval Chief Justice Fred Vinson died and Earl Warren, former governor of California, replaced him as the new chief justice. Warren worked to gain a consensus among his fellow justices, who had become deeply divided during Vinson's tenure regarding civil liberties in the McCarthy era. Firmly opposed to the constitutionality of *Plessy v. Ferguson*, Warren relied on diplomacy and compromise in language to make it possible for the Court, including a hospitalized member, to render a unanimous decision on May 17, 1954. The Court ruled that school segregation was unconstitutional and that separate-but-equal could not be applied to schools.

Local Authorities and Their Reactions

The Court's decision engendered a severe backlash in the South, particularly in Prince Edward County and other parts of Virginia. As long as the courts did not set a remedy for segregation, one of Warren's compromises, segregation remained the de facto practice in Prince Edward County and other parts of the South. In 1956 the courts finally ordered desegregation but still did not set a timetable for it. Prominent Virginia politicians and editors invoked the theory of interposition—the right of state government to position itself between the federal government and those otherwise bound by its laws. They called for "massive resistance" in much the same way that Johns had, certain that they could avoid punishment for noncompliance with the new federal law by presenting a united front. Extremists promised to put an end to public schools rather than integrate them.

Reprisals and resistance hit Prince Edward County particularly hard. On the personal side John Lancaster lost his job as Negro county farm agent and Rev. Griffin, besieged by every creditor, was left penniless. His wife suffered a nervous breakdown as a result of the stress. On the policy side the Prince Edward County Board of Supervisors had been providing funding for the public schools one month at a time as long as the schools remained segregated. But in 1959 the federal appeals court ordered Prince Edward County and the rest of Virginia to desegregate its schools in September. In response, the board of supervisors did not allocate any funds for public schools. Instead it provided tuition assistance to students desiring to attend all-White private schools that had been established in the county in the event of court-ordered integration. The county's public schools remained closed until 1964, perhaps offering the most radical example of massive resistance on the local level in the nation.

For the 5 years the public schools were closed, the NAACP litigated for public funding of integrated schools. African American residents established learning centers for their children. A few families were able to send their children to live with relatives outside the county where they could attend public schools.

New tensions arose in the African American community. Attorneys for the NAACP sought a legal remedy rather than a local remedy that they feared might undermine their case. Intent on having the courts decide the controversy, the NAACP did not want the learning centers to approximate the quality of school instruction and steadfastly avoided a compromise with officials that would lead to the reopening of the public schools. African Americans heeded the NAACP's advice and began to register to vote in an effort to vote local authorities out of office rather than submit to them.

By 1960 Prince Edward County had gained notoriety and came to represent what needed to be changed in the South. It attracted organizations other than the NAACP and more direct action protest: Black Muslims supported separate and better schools; the Sit-In Movement inspired direct action; and the Student Non-Violent Coordinating Committee sent in organizers to plan boycotts as well as to tutor the children locked out of their schools. Griffin managed to bridge the gap between the increasingly "old" efforts of NAACP litigation and the "new" methods of movement organizing. He supported the latter in the county even as he became president of the NAACP statewide. Ironically, the "new" movement tactics of direct action had an exemplar: a school boycott organized in 1951 by high school junior Barbara Rose Johns.

Analytical Elements

What elements contributed to change in this case? Are these elements present in organizational, community, political, and other social contexts? In this section we explore these questions by proposing several analytical elements that may be useful for understanding this case and others.

Causality

Accounts of leadership often reduce causality to a limited set of factors. This enables us to portray leadership as links in a chain of cause and effect, such as when we credit Clinton's fiscal policies with the prosperity of the 1990s or a CEO with the turnaround of a company, without considering the many other factors that played a part in these outcomes. In the case of Prince Edward County, Barbara Johns's leadership undeniably influenced school desegregation. But an exclusive focus on her role reflects an oversimplification of the chain of events and seriously underestimates the nature of leadership. Leadership is infinitely more complex than the efforts of any one individual; rather, it is the impact of efforts to influence the actions of leaders and followers opposed to and supportive of the same or related changes. This perspective on leadership requires attention to a network of actors and the sea of other changes in which a leader's influence efforts take place. Four analytical frames help us to attend to this network of influence rather than to a specific leader: Kurt Lewin's field theory; Gunnar Myrdal's principle of cumulative effect; Stephen Jay Gould and Niles Eldredge's theory of punctuated equilibrium; and Margaret Wheatley's work on systems.

Kurt Lewin, Field Theory

Kurt Lewin's field theory espouses that effective change requires understanding "the totality of coexisting facts which are conceived as mutually interdependent" (Lewin, 1951, p. 240). Lewin, a psychologist with training in physics and mathematics, concerned himself with individual and group behavior, including change. He contributed "action research" to the field of problem-centered scholarship. Problem solving, just like effective change, requires placing a problem within a system or field with as many relevant and interdependent elements as possible. Within this field each individual also becomes a dynamic field with interdependent parts, including "life spaces" of family, work, church, and other groups. People take positive and negative influences from their experiences that shape their identity and help explain their behavior. Lewin advocated assembling all the relevant, mutually independent factors to explain social phenomena such as leadership and change. For example, Johns may or may not have been aware that before she met school superintendent McIlwaine, he had tangled with her uncle Vernon Johns over Black students' access to county school bus transportation and with Oliver Hill over Black teachers' pay a dozen years before. Nonetheless, McIlwaine remained aware of those experiences, and they undoubtedly influenced his assessment of Barbara Johns's efforts to lead and his judgment about the nature of the student strike. Because of their influence on McIlwaine, these prior conflicts became part of the field of the controversy. Their hidden nature suggests the difficulties of gathering and assessing all the facts relevant to an event.

Gunnar Myrdal, the Principle of Cumulative Effect

Gunnar Myrdal and his colleagues completed their epic study, *An American Dilemma: The Negro Problem and Modern Democracy*, before the appearance of Lewin's field theory. They offered a theoretical framework for the condition of African Americans very much like Lewin and extrapolated it to a method of social research (Myrdal, 1944, p. 1066). Myrdal's study begins with the notion of a system in stable equilibrium and rejects it as inadequate to provide a "dynamic analysis of the process of change in social relations" (Myrdal, 1944, p. 1065). The static equilibrium of a system is merely a starting point of the balance of opposing forces. In the simplest of systems, with only two opposing elements, a change in one brings about a change in the other, which in turn brings on more change. The changes may be subtle enough to appear stable but only because of the constant state of adjustment. Any system is far more complex with many interrelated elements; even the simplest system with two opposing elements becomes complex when we examine the composites of each element.

Myrdal proposed a principle of cumulation to explain change within a system of dynamic social causation. Change accumulates as one change brings on another change, and the elements of a system and their composites or subsystems represent a second form of cumulation. The principle states, assuming an initial static state of balanced forces:

Any change in any one of [its] factors, independent of the way in which it is brought about, will, by the aggregate weight of the cumulative effects running back and forth between them all, start the whole system moving in one direction or the other as the case may be, with a speed depending upon the original push and the functions of causal interrelation within the system. (Myrdal, 1944, p. 1067)

Myrdal elaborated that the final effects of the cumulative process may be out of proportion to the magnitude of the original push. More to the point of our case, although the initial push may be withdrawn—the school strike ended—"the process of change will continue without a new balance in sight" (Myrdal, 1944, p. 1066). This happens largely because the system in which any change occurs is far more complicated than it appears. Every element of the system interrelates with every other element, and every element has its peculiarities and irregularities (Myrdal, 1944, p. 1068).

Myrdal concluded in terms central to our concern about causality: "This conception of a great number of interdependent factors, mutually cumulative in their effects, disposes of the idea that there is one predominant factor, a 'basic factor'" (Myrdal, 1944, p. 1069). This includes leadership.

Indeed, the notion of leadership may be a construct of our attempts to understand causality within a system of change. This radically alters the enduring debate: Does change create leaders or do leaders create change? The cumulative principle would suggest that the actions of leaders may influence others to take action that in turn influences others in a continuing chain—thus the answer to the question is neither and both. Change does not create leaders, nor do leaders create change; *and* change creates leaders and leaders create change. Observers apply the construct of leadership to people's actions—actions that are intended to influence the actions of other people—within a system of change. The construct of leadership may be used retroactively to suggest causality. The accuracy of that assessment depends upon the boundaries of the system; the broader the boundaries, the less likely any set of actions has a primary causal relationship to systemic change. Leadership is more easily applied to actions in a system of static equilibrium and a circumscribed set of cumulative factors.

Both Myrdal and Lewin borrowed heavily from quantum mechanics in particular for concepts of field and the steady state of disequilibrium. Both men emulated physics in their hope that human behavior and systems of change, however complicated, could be expressed mathematically.

Stephen J. Gould and Niles Eldredge, Punctuated Equilibrium

Concepts of equilibrium and change also feature prominently in the work of scientists Stephen Gould and Niles Eldredge (1972). Their theory of punctuated equilibrium explains major changes in nature after long periods of stasis that cause divergence or branching of a new animal or plant species (Gould, 1991). Real change occurs if this divergence establishes a trend wherein the new species succeeds more frequently than the previous one.

Like field and systems theories, social scientists extrapolated the concept of punctuated equilibrium to explain changes in social systems that occur after long periods of incremental change punctuated by brief periods of major change (Schlager, 1999). This phenomenon helps to explain how Johns and the other student leaders could launch a successful trend of mass resistance to racial inequality after decades of incremental change facilitated by previous generations stretching back to the era of slavery. Brief periods of punctuated equilibrium, such as the creation of a community of free Blacks in 1810 (Ely, 2004), established a trend of sustained resistance to an unjust racial system in Prince Edward County and other Black communities, even in the face of retribution from White power holders.

Margaret Wheatley, the New Science and Leadership

Margaret Wheatley's work (1992) permits us to bridge the concepts of punctuated equilibrium in paleobiology and the physics of quantum mechanics to leadership in a manner that builds upon the field theory of Lewin and the cumulative principle of Myrdal. Wheatley explains that physics had introduced field theory to explain gravity, electromagnetism, and relativity. The common element of fields in each of these is that they are "unseen structures, occupying space and becoming known to us through their effects." The space of fields and, we may add, their time, is not empty but "a cornucopia of invisible but powerful effective structure" (Wheatley, 1992, p. 49). Both Lewin and Myrdal also suggested that to understand human behavior and social change we need to recognize that time and space are not empty and begin to fill in their invisible but effective structure.

Wheatley also explains the relevance of field theory in the life sciences in a manner analogous to Myrdal's principle of cumulation. Morphogenic fields develop through the accumulated behaviors of a species' members. Successive members find it easier to acquire a skill, such as bicycle riding, in a setting where many others have accumulated it. Contrary to Newtonian concepts of causation, it is the energy of the receiver that takes up the form of a morphogenic field (Wheatley, 1992, p. 51). In leadership terms, the efficacy of leaders comes from shaping a field in which others, by their own actions, may participate in the energy and forms of the field. Barbara Johns certainly did this for students, their parents, and many others. But she was also within the fields that others—including Rev. Griffin, Superintendent McIlwaine, Principal Jones and teacher Inez Davenport, and the other teachers at Moton High School—had shaped.

Wheatley elaborates on the consequence of this conception of field for leadership:

> The idea that leaders have vision, set goals and then marshal their own energy and that of others to achieve these goals is a Newtonian view of change focused on a prime mover and a mechanistic concept of change. Although partially true—some elements of old science still hold in the new science— this focus overlooks the complex fields of cumulative interactions across time and space in which all of this takes place. We might conceive of change as a destination sought through the leader as engine—a linear and railroad track analog. This would ignore the fact that even railroads function within fields— including elements from appropriations to weather—that influence when and

where trains arrive or if they run at all. Better, Wheatley argues, to think about organizational culture and the deliberate and intentional formation of fields that reinforce the values and goals of an organization and fill its spaces and history with coherent messages. (Wheatley, 1992, pp. 52–57)

Of course, this view is limited to those fields within an organization—such as the Moton High School PTA—and does not take into account the field in which these organizations interact with other actors with opposing values and goals— such as the Prince Edward County School Board.

Dynamic Systems of Interdependent Parts, Change, and Causality

Wheatley's work invites us to view the field of leadership as a dynamic system in which change is a constant. Myrdal describes it as rolling equilibrium and alerts social scientists that they have to study:

processes of systems actually rolling in the one direction or the other, systems which are constantly subjected to all sorts of pushes from outside through all the variables, and which are moving because of the cumulative effect of all these pushes and the interaction between the variables. (Myrdal, 1944, p. 1067)

Peter Vaill describes this system as "permanent white water" (1996, p. 2) and "chaotic change" (1989) but attributes these conditions to recent changes rather than newly discovered enduring attributes of systems as Wheatley does.

Regardless of these important differences, many leadership scholars acknowledge that in the context of a dynamic, interdependent system, leaders play a far different role than the one often ascribed to them. For example, Adam Yarmolinsky takes issue with James MacGregor Burns about leaders initiating change. Yarmolinsky (2007) points out that leaders join a system in the midst of change and simply do their best to mediate and direct change in a shifting environment. Ronald Heifetz similarly, if implicitly, acknowledges that leaders, especially those without authority, modulate the distress within dynamic systems (Heifetz, 1994, p. 207).

Likewise many leadership scholars acknowledge the complexity of such systems of fields and recognize that these fields undergo constant change. Vaill writes of organizations as universes with galaxies of knowledge and information (Vaill, 1989, p. xii). Heifetz (Heifetz & Linsky, 2002) and Vaill also place importance on the personal attributes of the leader, thus opening up a whole other dimension that can affect and further complicate the fields of organization and change, much as Lewin predicted.

The organizational and personal complexities of this constant change were fully evident in the Prince Edward County case. For example, the series of events that played such a pivotal role in the Supreme Court's unanimous decision on this case were at least as complicated as the events comprising the racial history of Prince Edward County. To offer only one example, the death of Chief Justice Vinson made possible a strong majority opinion in *Brown v. Board of Education.* Earl Warren, who assumed the role of chief justice, was determined to have a unanimous decision. His determination was no doubt influenced by the guilt he felt for the role he had played in the internment of West Coast Japanese Americans when he was governor of California during the Second World War. *Brown v. Board of Education* gave him the opportunity to repent his own transgressions and to end those of the nation (Kluger, 1975, pp. 661–662).

Warren began his penance before *Brown*. In 1946 a federal district court declared the segregation of Mexican-American school children in California unconstitutional in *Mendez v. Westminster*. The case anticipated the issues of *Brown*, although the grounds of segregation were national origin rather than race. After the federal circuit court upheld the lower court, Governor Warren lobbied the legislature in 1947 to pass bills that ended legal segregation for all groups in California. Even a scholar as conscientious as Richard Kluger overlooked how influential this experience would prove to be for Warren. The California case, like the *Brown* case, was a complex field that developed its own twists and ironies. Gonzalo Mendez, the lead plaintiff in the case, was able to pursue his grievance because of the income he derived farming land that he had leased from the Munemitsus after the Japanese-American family had been "relocated" to an internment camp. Warren's most egregious public policy indirectly provided him the opportunity to pursue one of his most progressive official acts (Teachers Domain, n.d.; Ruiz, 2001).

Wheatley offers another element of fields that Lewin and Myrdal did not foresee, namely, the manifestation of the entire system in each of its parts. Fractals best express this property of systems of dynamic change. Zoom in on any part of a chaotic system and one finds recurring patterns. Every part of a field of change may manifest the transformative change of the entire field, but a focus on a minute part of the field may obscure the perception of the pattern that comes from examining subsets in relation to large sets. The pattern of the entire system may be found in each of its elements, but without some sense of the whole, the pattern may go unrecognized. Needless to say, without a sense of that pattern the nature of each part of the system may be misunderstood. When considering each part of the system of change in the Prince Edward County case, for example, elements of other systems of change are readily apparent. The school strike had precursors in other forms of resistance within the slave and freed-Black community of the county and in the repressive measures of the White community. The fullest meaning of those preceding resistance acts and the school strike emerges from the pattern they share with each other. An exclusive focus on one or the other or on any other factor apart from its relationship to the system of change limits its meaning and our perception of the recurring pattern among them.

The principle of uncertainty, which Wheatley mentions and which makes up part of the new science, provides particularly rich insight into causality. Physicist Werner Heisenberg helped to usher in the new science of quantum mechanics. Heisenberg resolved many of the controversies of quantum mechanics by explaining that one cannot know the position and momentum of a subatomic particle at the same time. The more one knows about its position, the less one knows about its momentum and vice versa. The properties of the observed depend upon the instruments used to observe them. The leadership of Barbara Johns depends then upon what other factors we take into account in the system of change in racial segregation. When considering the Moton High School strike factor, her leadership plays a preeminent role. At the level of federal decisions for school desegregation, her leadership fades into a fractal subsystem of a larger system. Moreover, a fair evaluation of Johns's leadership depends upon examining this system of change from her perspective. Her leadership would be less prominent if we examined the system through the efforts and actions of Rev. Griffin, Oliver Hill, or Superintendent McIlwaine. In terms of the uncertainty principle, the more we focus on the leadership of Johns, the less discernible other leadership becomes.

This has profound implications for causality. If our certainty about one actor comes at the cost of uncertainty regarding other parts of a dynamic system, how can we be sure that the actions of one influenced the intended change? Although the case is quite clear that Johns's leadership spurred the student strike, we might also consider the other factors that influenced people's action and argue that Johns's exhortations would not have had any effect had it not been for the interaction with other elements of the system—the lack of success and frustration of the Moton High School PTA; the World War II service of Rev. Griffin, Principal Jones, and Johns's father; the support of the initial small band of student strike leaders; and so on. This uncertainty seems to demand that we examine every inexhaustible subset to the greatest microscopic level of scrutiny and then relate them. In truth, we could never examine every relevant fact and interrelated event in sufficient detail to explain with certainty what caused what. According to Heisenbert, "In the sharp formulation of the law of causality—'if we know the present exactly, we can calculate the future'—it is not the conclusion that is wrong but the premise" (American Institute of Physics & David Cassidy, 2005). The academic implications of these matters are that we can understand the leadership of this case only by the patterns that we look for and, once we find them, we may be surprised to learn that constituent elements of the case may vary from what we would expect. In this case, for example, it is possible that some White residents of the county want integration more than some African American residents. The practical implications are that such micro-variations do not affect our understanding of the leadership of Johns and others. However, our understanding will be insufficient without incorporating enough elements of the system into our analysis to make clear the patterns of behaviors and the probability of the interrelatedness. This is precisely the caution that authors such as Wheatley and Vaill offer: a focus on leaders and their actions distorts our understanding of leadership in systems of change.

Mindfulness

Underlying this investigation into the theories and observations of Lewin, Myrdal, Gould and Eldredge, and Wheatley is the common emphasis on mindfulness—a central tenet of Buddhism. In order to understand and practice leadership, it is necessary to engage in critical reflection on the acts of leaders, the context in which those acts take place and their likely consequences. The tenets of this critical reflection include conceptualizing acts within a field of interactive and interrelated parts rather than in a straight line from acts to results. In this manner both leaders and those who study leadership are more likely to anticipate unintended and unwanted consequences.

Our perception of these consequences increases with our knowledge of the boundaries of the system of change or field in which someone attempts to lead.

In the *I Ching,* Chinese scholars posit a universe composed of a single unifying element with two complementary and opposing parts—a *yin* and a *yang.* The complexity of the universe is contained in its basic element and in all the derivative elements that flow from the original *Tao.* These elements combine in systems of equilibrium based on complementarity and in a dynamic flow of energy, *Feng Shui,* founded on their oppositional characteristics (Couto & Fu, 2004). The premises of this realm—fields of energy, change and stability, complementarity and opposition—provided Neils Bohr and other pioneering physicists a metaphysical context for discovering quantum mechanics and expanding scientific thought beyond theories of Newton and even Einstein. Physicist Werner Heisenberg and his colleague Erwin Schroedinger found their inspiration in the metaphysics of Hinduism. These systems of thought provide a very different metaphor for causality than the mechanics of a machine, to which Scottish philosopher David Hume subscribed. Instead causality is rooted in dynamic, interactive systems of interrelated parts that resemble and differ from each other (Capra, 1982, pp. 79–89).

Lest it appear that we have strayed too far from causality, change, and leadership, let us not forget the numerous references, albeit cursory and oblique, to Lao-Tsu, Taoism, and Confucius in leadership scholarship. Peter Vaill deals somewhat more substantially with Taoism, after first confessing to the elusiveness of its elliptical thinking. Vaill dwells on the concept of *wu-wei,* or nonaction, and its place in leadership. *Wu-wei* was evident in the Johns case when the teachers and principal left the assembly hall at the students' request during the organization of the strike. Vaill also hints at the significance of examining this and other epistemological and ontological systems for the understanding of change. He envisions the possibility of organizations benefiting from the Eastern realization that the meaning of organizational capabilities, including leadership and change, "can emerge only through the most careful and continuous contemplation" (Vaill, 1989, p. 190).

Social Tensions

In our conversations about the links of causality and mindfulness to actions that result in change, Fredric Jablin suggested that the impetus for change might emerge from social tensions. This idea resonated as a meaningful way to understand the dynamic and socially constructed nature of change in human systems.

Social tensions arise among groups from conflicts about identity, resources, power, and ethics. These tensions are embedded in interactions within and between groups as they form and continually reform the structures and systems that comprise society. Table 1.1 identifies several social factors and ensuing tensions that underlie change. In the Johns case, conflict arising from these tensions created pervasive conditions for change in Prince Edward County.

Identity and Meaning

Individuals and groups create meaning in society by naming, defining, and assigning value to themselves and others in their environment. Social tensions

TABLE 1.1   Social Tensions

Factors	Social Tensions
Identity and meaning	Assigning identity—Asserting identity Rendering insignificant—Establishing value
Resource availability and distribution	Restricted resources—Accessible resources Individual resources—Collective resources
Power	Disenfranchised power—Authorized power
Ethics	Inequitable actions/conditions— Equitable actions/conditions

concerning meaning commonly develop as strains between assigned identity (naming) and asserted identity (self-claimed) and upon rendering identities insignificant (worthless). When one group assigns a name and lower social worth to another group, the resulting tensions can evolve or erupt into social change. Rosenblum and Travis (2003) assert, "Because naming may involve a redefinition of self, an assertion of power, and a rejection of others' ability to impose an identity, social change movements often lay claim to a new name, and opponents may express opposition by continuing to use the old name" (p. 6).

In 1951 Whites identified African American citizens of Prince Edward County as "coloreds" in the most polite terms and as dehumanizing epithets in the worst terms. There was no doubt that African Americans were deemed inferior and unequal, while White citizens were valued highly and deemed superior. These name and value distinctions shaped disparities in other aspects of society including the rights of Blacks to resources, power, and ethical treatment.

Resource Availability and Distribution

Tensions concerning resources emerge from the availability and distribution of goods, services, wealth, property, and other benefits or needs that groups in society value or require. Accessibility and restriction of resources are more often determined by social mores (the haves and have-nots) than natural abundance or limitations. Tensions for change emerge from struggles over who has the right to possess resources—the individual, the collective, or some combination of both.

U.S. citizens established the right to universal public education as a valued collective resource long before Barbara Rose Johns entered Moton High School. In 1951 resources for educating Black children in Prince Edward County were sorely lacking, even under the separate-but-equal standards of *Plessy v. Ferguson*. Moton High School's PTA, principal, and community members continuously appealed to the all-White school board to upgrade buildings and supplies only to be placated or summarily ignored. Even when funds for buildings and supplies were available, White school board members had no intention of supporting equal public education and facilities for African American children.

Power

Participants in the change process create, leverage, or challenge power constructs to bring about major change. In our session at Mount Hope, members of the Gold Team agreed that "power is not fundamentally a thing that individuals possess in some greater or lesser quantity but is more than anything an aspect of social relationships" (Couto, Faier, Hicks, & Hickman, 2002, p. 3). The capacity to impact social relations is affected by a group's attainment of or restriction from various forms of social power and the group's ability to use power to influence others. Tensions develop among groups that have attained various forms of power (authorized or legitimate, reward, coercive, expert, informational, or referent [French & Raven, 1959]) and groups that are restricted, disenfranchised, or negatively impacted by the exercise of these forms of power.

The exercise of legitimate power contributes to stability and organization in social interactions; however, misuse or exploitation of power bases results in inequality and loss of rights or freedoms for selected groups. In 1896 with the landmark case *Plessy v. Ferguson*, White Southerners succeeded in reversing and suppressing any gains African Americans had made in terms of civil rights and human dignity. The U.S. Supreme Court used its power in this case to establish a legal basis for separate-but-equal conditions for Blacks and Whites in the South. The result of this decision gave tacit permission to White power holders to create separate but decidedly unequal conditions for Black citizens.

Ethics

Joanne Ciulla (2004, p. 4) maintains that ethics is "the heart of leadership"; likewise, inequity, inequality, and excessive self-interest are at the heart of social tensions and conflict. Ethics in social interactions compel members of society to take into account the impact of their actions on others and consider what "ought to be" done in situations with other human beings. Al Gini explains that "ethics, then, tries to find a way to protect one person's individual rights and needs against and alongside the rights and needs of others" (Gini, 2004, p. 29). Social tensions emerge when groups experience or perceive inequitable treatment at the hands of power holders and dominant groups.

Inequities in the treatment of Black and White citizens in the Jim Crow South were intentional and inhumane. In 1939 the Prince Edward County School Board built its first public high school for African American students with no cafeteria, auditorium, locker rooms, infirmary, or gymnasium—features that were standard in White schools in the county. Moton High School was built to hold 180 students, but in 1947 it served more than 360 students.

The county school board responded by building temporary facilities made of wood and covered with tar paper behind the school. These "shacks," as they were called by local citizens, leaked when it rained and were poorly heated. Barbara Johns and other Moton High students were well aware of the superior quality of facilities and equipment at the White high school. These inequities coupled with long-term neglect and disregard by school board officials increased frustration and tensions among students.

From an ethical perspective, change in its most humane and enlightened form intentionally uplifts the human conditions of some without harming the welfare of others, while change in its most detrimental form fosters the aims of egocentric or amoral individuals and groups at the expense or demise of others. Leadership studies research examines both elevating and harmful forms of change. Scholars James MacGregor Burns (1978, 2003) and Bernard Bass (1985; Bass & Avolio, 1994) examine the uplifting effect of transforming and transformational leadership, just as scholars Jean Lipman-Blumen (2005), Barbara Kellerman (2004), and others research the causes and consequences of toxic or bad leadership.

Illustrations of both harmful and elevating forms of change permeate the story of Barbara Rose Johns and school desegregation in Prince Edward County. Leadership by Southern Whites created and sustained social arrangements that legitimated their own amoral needs and wants by denying the civil rights and well-being of Black citizens. In contrast, strike organizers at Moton High School used their moral agency to advocate for improved educational conditions for Black students without harming the rights of White citizens.

Conditions for Change: Climate, Timing, and Threshold Points

Though social tensions underlie change, tensions alone do not initiate change. The elements in Table 1.2, climate, timing, and threshold points, are essential

TABLE 1.2 Conditions for Change

Factors	Conditions		
	From:		**To:**
Climate	Passive	→	Threatening
Timing	Premature	→	Opportune
Threshold points	Lacking	→	Prevalent

factors in prompting change. Climate encompasses the totality of environmental cues, feelings and experiences of groups in social contexts. Conditions for change emerge over time as social climates affecting the well-being of specific groups become more threatening or uncertain.

Threatening conditions were present in the situation surrounding events in Prince Edward County. Moton High School's PTA, principal, and community members advocated for improved resources and facilities for their children on a continuous basis. In the existing separate and unequal environment it was evident that postponements and rejections of their requests were not isolated incidents. As a result, each obstacle contributed to the Black community's cumulative experience of discrimination and mistreatment.

Timing is also a central factor in change. Cumulative acts that when taken together are larger than any singular or specific moment in history, create opportune openings where concerted action is capable of sparking change—a punctuation in social equilibrium. The previous actions of many African Americans to defy segregation—including the actions of Johns's uncle, Rev. Vernon Johns, that resulted in better school bus services for African American children in the county in 1939—paved the way for Moton High School students to stage a sustainable strike. The actions of Vernon Johns formed part of a complex web of change leading to desegregation.

The concept of thresholds provides further insight into conditions that trigger change. Mark Granovetter (1978) describes threshold as "that point where the perceived benefits to an individual of doing the thing in question . . . exceed the perceived costs" (p. 1422). By extending the idea of threshold to groups, we conclude that significant social change is set in motion when a group collectively reaches a threshold point.

It is conceivable that thresholds are also points where courage transcends fear. Legalized racism and accepted acts of violence toward African Americans reinforced fear and uncertainty in people who dared to assert their objections to an unethical structure. At the same time these acts served to build cumulative experience, conviction, and collective courage.

There were several major threshold points in the Moton High School case. One threshold point occurred when Barbara Johns recruited a small group of trusted friends to meet secretly and plan a student strike in the foreseeable event that efforts by the school principal and PTA would not result in a decision to build a new high school. When the school board failed to announce plans for a new school, Johns's strike group put their plan into action.

The group arranged for the school principal to be away from campus, then notified each classroom that there would be a brief assembly in the auditorium. Johns and her compatriots then called on the 450 students gathered at the assembly to unite in collective purpose and stage an orderly strike on the school grounds. On April 23, 1951, Johns and the entire student body marched out of Moton High School determined to change the abysmal conditions in their school.

Another crucial threshold point occurred on the fourth day of the strike. NAACP lawyer Spottswood Robinson asked students to bring their parents to a meeting where he would determine whether they supported their children's willingness to proceed with a lawsuit to end segregation in public schools. Rev. Francis Griffin held the mass meeting at his church and urged Black solidarity in the fight to end segregation. Barbara Johns spoke passionately on behalf of the students. The desegregation plan received a rousing endorsement from the majority of those present, though there were some dissenters. At the close of the meeting, Rev. Griffin summarized the sentiments of the group: "Anyone who would not back these children after they stepped out on a limb is not a man" (Kluger, 1975, p. 478).

Leadership as Intended Change

This detailed account permits us to address questions of change and causality. In what way did Barbara Rose Johns provide leadership to end school desegregation? Did her actions pass the litmus test that James MacGregor Burns set for leadership—"the achievement of purpose in the form of real and intended social change" (Burns, 1978, p. 251)? Clearly, there is a succession of related events from the school strike to *Brown v. Board of Education*. There is also, clearly, a succession of related events, albeit less direct, from the school strike to the campaign of massive resistance. Figure 1.1 outlines some of the sequential relationships of events and actors from the school strike to *Brown v. Board of Education*. It includes subsequent events such as massive resistance on both the state and county level and occurrences on both the national and local level in the civil rights movement.

If Johns was a leader in school desegregation because her actions tied into the Supreme Court's *Brown v. Board of Education* ruling, was she also a leader in the campaign of massive resistance for the same reason? Did her leadership cause the closing of the schools in Prince Edward County as well as their eventual reopening and integration? Clearly she intended improved school facilities and not school closings. Was she then only responsible for the changes she intended? If so this might suggest a very low ethical standard, namely, that leaders are responsible only for their intended outcomes and not for the consequences of their actions. As a leader did she bear any responsibility for the poverty that Griffin was reduced to or for Lancaster's loss of his job as Negro county farm agent?

Perhaps we can absolve Johns of these negative outcomes to the extent that we cannot hold her responsible for the expected and unexpected actions that others took in reaction to her leadership. Max Weber, however, made acceptance of the intended and unintended outcomes of our efforts to influence public events a mark of the calling to political leadership. Johns was in a system of change and, according to Weber, it would be irresponsible for her not to acknowledge the interdependence of contending factors in these fields. Johns and the school board had their own separate but interdependent systems of power. Each bears responsibility in the dual sense of causality and moral accountability for their system's actions, actions which they intended to influence. But, again citing Weber, responsibility in the sense of moral accountability also requires that we use judgment to anticipate negative reactions and outcomes and attempt to avoid them. An ethic of responsibility requires that we pursue values with proportionality (Weber, 1946, pp. 115–116). Weber helps us understand that Johns and the school board operated in separate but interrelated dynamic fields. Johns can only be held responsible for the negative outcomes of massive resistance and school desegregation in Prince Edward County if those outcomes can be traced to her intentions or to an excess in her actions. Clearly, they cannot.

Just as clearly we have identified a sobering caveat of leadership. Burns's litmus test of the achievement of real and intended social change comes with Weber's measured melancholic observation: "The final [and intermediate] result of political action often, no, even regularly, stands in completely inadequate and often even paradoxical relation to its original meaning" (Weber, 1946, p. 117).

Questions remain about the role of intended change in Johns's leadership. Initially she did not intend to desegregate the schools but only to improve the facilities of Moton High School. She supported and championed the NAACP's shift to desegregation as a means to gain improved facilities. Do we test her leadership by the achievement of desegregation or the improvement of facilities? The state immediately took steps to improve facilities as a means to avoid desegregation, but by that time the NAACP's position had hardened to the point of preferring closed schools to improved ones. In this sense, the NAACP bears more responsibility than Johns for the lost educational opportunities from 1959 to 1964.

FIGURE 1.1 The Leadership of Barbara Rose Johns

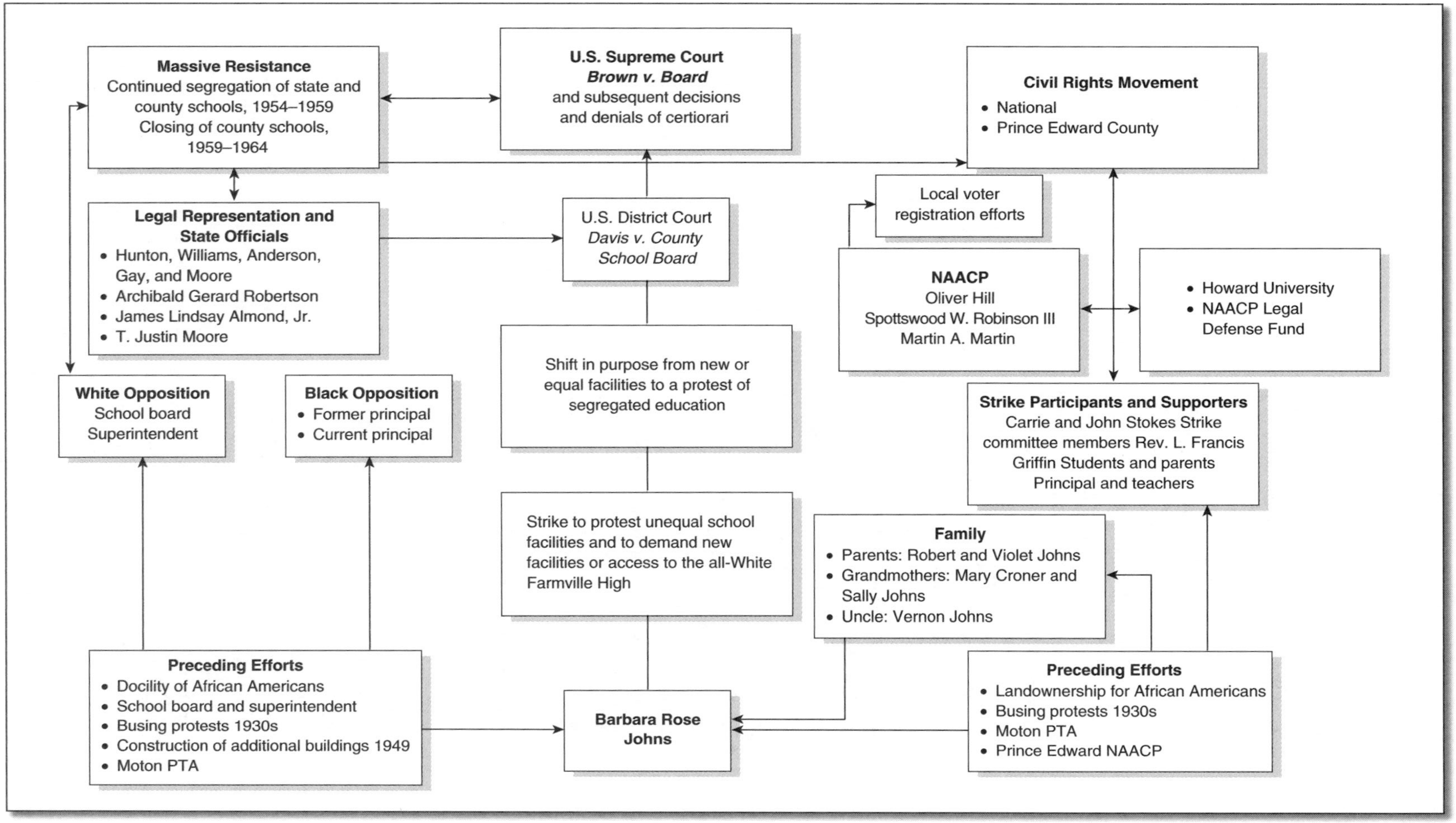

Civil Rights Movement
- National
- Prince Edward County

- Howard University
- NAACP Legal Defense Fund

Local voter registration efforts

NAACP
Oliver Hill
Spottswood W. Robinson III
Martin A. Martin

Strike Participants and Supporters
Carrie and John Stokes Strike committee members Rev. L. Francis Griffin Students and parents Principal and teachers

Family
- Parents: Robert and Violet Johns
- Grandmothers: Mary Croner and Sally Johns
- Uncle: Vernon Johns

Preceding Efforts
- Landownership for African Americans
- Busing protests 1930s
- Moton PTA
- Prince Edward NAACP

U.S. Supreme Court
Brown v. Board
and subsequent decisions and denials of certiorari

U.S. District Court
Davis v. County School Board

Shift in purpose from new or equal facilities to a protest of segregated education

Strike to protest unequal school facilities and to demand new facilities or access to the all-White Farmville High

Barbara Rose Johns

Massive Resistance
Continued segregation of state and county schools, 1954–1959
Closing of county schools, 1959–1964

Legal Representation and State Officials
- Hunton, Williams, Anderson, Gay, and Moore
- Archibald Gerard Robertson
- James Lindsay Almond, Jr.
- T. Justin Moore

Black Opposition
- Former principal
- Current principal

White Opposition
School board
Superintendent

Preceding Efforts
- Docility of African Americans
- School board and superintendent
- Busing protests 1930s
- Construction of additional buildings 1949
- Moton PTA

Just as the overall *Brown* decision had some unintended consequences (Sullivan, 2004), Johns's actions brought about some changes she intended and some she did not. While her initial goal was one of equalization, the NAACP viewed equalization as a very limited form of change because racial subordination could and often did continue even after students of all races obtained equal facilities. When the county ultimately desegregated its public schools, Johns achieved her intended purpose—equal facilities for Black and White students—albeit in an unforeseen, unintended way. In this sense did equalization and desegregation symbolize a deeper form of change: the recognition of the value and intelligence of all the county's students and the end of all forms of racial discrimination within the school system? How do Johns's leadership and the NAACP's leadership rate against these intended outcomes? The difference the efforts of Johns and the NAACP made in improved educational opportunities, processes, and outcomes provides the best measure of their effectiveness.

Although she played a part in the formative stages of the lawsuit, Johns did not play a part in subsequent events in the county after her parents, fearing for her safety, sent her to live with her uncle Vernon in Montgomery, Alabama, shortly after the student strike. Johns married on New Year's Eve 1953 and subsequently moved to Philadelphia, far removed from the consequences of the strike and its ensuing controversy. Did her leadership stop after she launched the strike or did it continue because of the consequences of her initial action? Regardless of intention then, did her role as leader end when she no longer influenced events in the present? Or did her leadership remain to influence later events, again regardless of her intentions? Can we distinguish her role as leader from her leadership—the former being the actions that she took to influence the actions of others, and the latter being the consequences of those actions? If we are to accept the time and space of a field as relevant to the actions of influence within it, then Johns's leadership remains a factor in the field of civil rights movement in Prince Edward County and beyond.

Leadership as the Cause of Change

Johns did not operate in a leadership vacuum; rather, she interacted with other leaders in this narrative of change. It is instructive to examine the influences on each of the other leaders involved in the Prince Edward County case: the Howard University Law School education of Oliver Hill and Spottswood Robinson; the conflict that Superintendent McIlwaine had with Vernon Johns over transportation for African American children 12 years prior to meeting his niece; the impact that fighting a war of liberation in a segregated army in World War II had on Rev. Griffin, Principal Jones, and Barbara Johns's father as well as the effect of the subsequent desegregation of the armed forces by President Truman in 1948. This examination suggests that a set of interdependent actors each with their own set of influences comprised a system of change in the Prince Edward County case, a system limited only by our ability to ferret out all of its conditions. In this type of immense and interactive system, Johns's actions might be considered analogous to a butterfly flapping its wings in the Amazon basin, thereby setting off a string of events that ultimately causes rain in Des Moines, Iowa. Or Johns's actions might have had much more of a direct impact, causing us to analyze the specific circumstances of the case, such as the conversations in the Johns's family store; Inez Davenport's reasons for encouraging Johns to take a lead in improving the school facility; and Principal Jones's determination to run a democratic school and support student-led initiatives, a determination that extended to his momentous decision to leave the assembly hall at Johns's request at a time when he could have squelched the strike before it got started.

Events did not unfold in a straight line from Johns to the U.S. Supreme Court. Johns dealt directly with students, students' parents, other residents in the county and the Richmond office of the NAACP. She aligned herself with the elected student leaders of Moton High School who should possibly also be considered leaders in the school desegregation effort. Johns received advice and assistance first from Inez Davenport and Rev. Griffin and later from the NAACP. Did the boundaries of her leadership diminish when the NAACP entered or did they broaden under the influence of all the people who interacted with her? If it was the latter, should we then examine the influences on those people who influenced Barbara Rose Johns—not only those mentioned in this account but also her family members and the community of property-owning African American farmers served by her family store?

Some of these influences were small and personal—a spoken word. Some were momentous and public—the inability of the Moton PTA to make progress. Some influences were specific to that time and place, while others had historical roots, which although long forgotten, were compelling nonetheless. For example, historically large numbers of free Blacks lived in Prince Edward County during a time of legalized slavery. In the years preceding the desegregation case, an economically independent group of African American farmers and landowners had grown and flourished in Prince Edward County, of whom Vernon Johns was just one example, albeit the most dramatic. In time Johns's efforts in the Prince Edward County school desegregation case may fade from the collective memory just as memories of some of these earlier historical events had faded by 1951.

Burns's litmus test of leadership as the achievement of real and intended change sets a high standard. Clearly Johns achieved her purpose of conducting a school strike and, as a consequence, she influenced the actions of others. It is relatively easy, as we have seen, to detail the action that leaders take to influence others. It is much more difficult to judge the influence of those actions on other leaders. Whereas leading is replete with intentions, leadership concerns the assessment of the consequences of leaders' actions. And how do we deal with and assess the changes that ensued because of a leader's action? Joseph Rost's critique of Burns only compounds the problem. His definition of leadership as "an influence relationship among leaders and followers who intend real changes that reflect their mutual purposes" (Rost, 1991, p. 103) obfuscates the possibility that some influence relationships may make real changes, although unintended, and may stimulate some to act for contrary purposes. In order to move beyond the dilemma of unintended changes and contrary purposes, we may have to distinguish between leading and leadership.

Leading is an attempt to influence others in the present moment. The story of the strike offers numerous examples of efforts to lead, including the students' letter to the NAACP lawyers, the massive resistance tactics employed by some of Virginia's politicians and newspaper editors, and Earl Warren's determination to win a unanimous opinion in the U.S. Supreme Court. We can define these attempts at leading as *leadership* only after assessing their full impact. Even then, what is and is not leadership depends upon what is and is not included in the system of change.

By limiting the influence relationship to leaders and followers and insisting on intention, Rost and many, many others confuse the nature of leadership. The actions of a person may influence a leader to take action even though it was not intended. Barbara Johns's paternal uncle and grandmother both instilled a great deal of confidence in her and served as role models of resistance to racial subordination in personal and public matters. Their actions would not be considered leadership in an ordinary interpretation of Rost's definition, but an extraordinary interpretation—which focuses on influence relationships primarily—would incorporate their actions into the leadership that brought about school desegregation. Although they did not directly affect the change effort in the way that Rev. Griffin and the NAACP lawyers did, Johns's uncle and grandmother nurtured Johns's self-esteem, making it possible for her to assert herself in the school desegregation case. The omission of significant influential relationships is but the first shortcoming in any theory of change that limits its focus to leaders and followers.

The second shortcoming of Rost's conception of leadership is that it tends to concentrate on the efforts of one set of leaders and followers. In truth and in practice, leaders—those who take action to influence others—set off reactions in other leaders for conflicting purposes. Obviously, Johns's plans for the school strike had severe critics who took action to prevent the strike and desegregation. There were African American leaders opposed to the strike and efforts to integrate who vied with Johns for influence in the African American community. Principal Jones, for example, wrote a letter to parents asking them to send their children back to school. In sum, a system of change does not have only one set of leaders and followers; rather, it has many interdependent and interactive sets of leaders and followers.

These two factors of change, namely, myriad influences and many sets of leaders and followers, came into play most dramatically on the morning of April 23 when Principal Jones left the assembly at the request of Johns and the other strike leaders. He could have refused to leave and ordered the students to return to their classrooms, protesting that their strike plans would only harm his own change efforts. Certainly his boss, the superintendent of schools, thought this is exactly what he should have done. And had he done so, it is very unlikely that events in Prince Edward County would have unfolded as they did. Here was a leader, a person in authority, who did not use his influence to coerce compliance.

Several factors might have influenced his action: he might have withdrawn his opposition because he tacitly supported the students' actions; he might have been making a concession to Inez Davenport, Johns's favorite teacher and Jones's fiancée, who had encouraged Johns to take some action to address the poor facilities; he might have wanted to show support for the orderly and democratic manner in which the students conducted themselves regardless of whether he agreed with their plans. He sought to instill initiative and organization in his students and may have been reluctant to squelch their efforts for this reason. Richard Kluger describes Jones as a man trapped between his convictions as a Black leader and his obligations to his White employees (Kluger, 1975, p. 469). His convictions won out at the moment he was asked to leave. The assembly was itself the result of his influential encouragement of student initiative and his own example of striving to acquire better resources for the school. Ironically, Jones was a leader in terms of the influence he had on an action he could not ultimately support. His leadership, his influence on the school strike, came from his decision not to use his authority, or to act by inaction.

When we examine change through one particular leader, we can see how seemingly unrelated events become a network of influence because of their effect on that one person. When we analyze a change event from the perspective of different leaders, we must add and subtract elements of influence and think about how the consequence of the events affected different leaders differently. For example, if we choose to examine the whole system of change in Prince Edward County through T. Justin Moore, lead attorney for the school board, we would have to consider very different influences and consequences than we would if we were considering the same system of change from the perspective of Johns or Jones.

Leadership as Action for Change

Action to bring about change entails more than a single leader or initiator, as the Prince Edward County school desegregation case illustrates. Individuals can achieve a common purpose only when they join together in an act of generativity—forming a group to accomplish goals that an individual could not achieve alone (Forsyth, 1999, p. 67). During our Mount Hope discussions, the concept of generativity was especially important in the Gold Team's conceptions of leadership. The scholars at Mount Hope grappled with the question: What processes or conditions characterize the emergence, maintenance, and transformation of leadership and followership? The Gold Team responded, "Leadership is a creative and generative act—literally bringing new realities into being through collaboration with others" (Couto et al., 2002, p. 2).

Members of the Moton High School student body assumed active roles as leaders or followers in an effort to attain their common goal. Robert Kelley (1995) explains that leadership and followership are *equal* but different roles often played by the same people at different times. Individuals who assume leadership roles have the desire and willingness to lead as well as a clear vision and interpersonal, communication, and organizational skills and abilities. Effective followers (or participants) form the other equally important component of the equation and are distinguished by their capacity for self-management, strong commitment, and courage. Individuals involved in leading change are willing to bring their respective abilities to the change effort in whatever roles they choose or accept.

Leaders and participants achieve momentum or movement through their coordinated actions (co-acting) for change. Paradoxically, individuals who assume leadership roles rely on their imagination—an invisible thought process—before attempting to implement a plan of action. Groups seeking change must be able to imagine or envision alternative social arrangements and define problems or issues in new ways (Couto et al., 2002, p. 2). A pivotal role of leaders in the change process involves communicating imagined futures and creating new meanings that inspire action. During our discussions at Mount Hope, the Gold Team proposed the following:

Leading change frequently entails competing narratives about the necessity, sufficiency, and possibility of change. Narratives fulfill various purposes; they motivate, define group identity, make limits, provide the building blocks for imagination and creativity, teach lessons, and legitimate or undermine forms of power, authority, and coercion. One way in which humans convey these social constructions of knowledge is through storytelling, a uniquely social discourse of human life.

Telling a story offers an account of reality that seeks either to affirm or contest an existing meaning, which expresses the nature and origins of a particular set of social relations that can be economic, political, and/or cultural dimensions. The need for change results in contested or negotiated interpretations, definitions, and values. (Couto et al., 2002, p. 2)

Barbara Rose Johns and the group of student leaders envisioned a high school for Black students that provided them with facilities and resources to receive the quality education to which they were entitled. They developed a plan for Moton High School students to challenge an existing power structure and gain parity with White schools in Virginia. The climate, timing, and threshold points converged to form a prime opportunity for movement—a point of punctuated equilibrium (Gould & Eldredge, 1972) where significant and sustained change became possible for Black children. The strike committee put their plan into action by calling together the entire student body, communicating a collective vision for change, and proposing a strike plan. The strike plan gave form, meaning, and power to a common purpose that seemed attainable through collective action by the students. Certainly this cadre of leaders met the criteria for the role of leaders described by Kelley (1995): they had the desire and willingness to lead as well as a clear vision and interpersonal communication and organizational skills.

The role of the student body represented an equally important component of this equation. A successful strike was fully dependent on the willingness of the students to assume roles as effective participants or followers. These roles would require an equally strong commitment to the goal and plan of action, a capacity for self-discipline and self-management, and tremendous courage in the face of danger. No one knew what would actually happen once the strike committee revealed its plan and put it into action. The risks of punishment, expulsion, violence and other repercussions loomed ominously. What the students did know was that the conditions in their school were totally unacceptable. They had waited long enough and were determined to remain steadfast until their situation changed.

The school principal, teachers, parents, and community members comprise a second group of effective participants or followers in the school desegregation case. The decision of the principal and teachers to leave the auditorium when asked by student leaders required commitment to the students' common purpose (or at least commitment not to interfere), self-control to refrain from using their positional power, and courage in the face of imminent sanctions from the school board. The parents and community members exhibited a similar commitment and a willingness to embrace the actions of their children. They, too, refrained from using positional authority to stop the strike and exhibited exceptional courage despite inevitable repercussions from White power holders.

The Prince Edward County school desegregation case also illustrates Kelley's (1995) assertion that the same people often play different roles of leadership and followership at different times. The school principal, teachers, parents, and community activists functioned in leadership roles and advocated tirelessly for better conditions in Black schools. Yet on April 23, 1951, the adult leaders assumed roles as followers and let the students take on leadership roles.

Conclusion

This discussion of leadership, change, and causality grounded in the leadership of Barbara Rose Johns and the Moton student body offers an opportunity to provide several generalizations about leadership across contexts. Figure 1.2 summarizes the analytical factors discussed throughout this chapter. These factors will likely take distinct forms and occur at varying stages or degrees based on contextual elements at macro and micro levels. Our challenge as a community of leadership scholars, educators, practitioners, and students is to identify the broadest range of contributing factors, understand their impact, generate new factors that contribute to the leadership of change in human systems, and use them ethically.

Barbara Rose Johns and the Moton High School students proceeded with intention, purpose, and collective action to gain facilities and conditions equal to their White counterparts. Yet they had no idea when they met with attorneys Oliver Hill and Spottswood Robinson that their actions would ultimately lead to the overthrow of legally segregated schools in the United States. The student strikers achieved more than separate but equal schools; they achieved legal desegregation of schools throughout the country. Major unintended consequences also accompanied this major change— the closure of Prince Edward County schools, job losses, and the unanticipated relocation of many teachers, families, and students, including Barbara Rose Johns.

How can leadership groups in any context anticipate and prepare for the intended and unintended consequences of their actions and thus be responsible in Weber's sense of intention and proportion? In truth, there is no absolute way to foresee and plan for the various outcomes that change may bring. However, the Native American wisdom of the Iroquois advises us to consider the impact of the decisions we make today on the seventh generation of humans (Lyons, 1992).

Peter Schwartz advocates a process of scenario development that helps decision-makers take a long view in a world of uncertainty (1996, p. 3). He contends that scenarios are not predictions but mechanisms to help people learn. Scenario building involves more than guessing. It requires a process that uses factual information and indicators of early trends to project alternative futures. The process entails eight sequential factors:

1. Identifying a central issue or question

2. Listing key factors in the micro-environment that may directly affect the central question

3. Identifying forces in the macro-environment that may affect the central issue

4. Assigning rank and weight to the micro- and macro-environmental factors based on their impact on the original issue or question

FIGURE 1.2   Analytical and Contextual Elements

ANALYTICAL ELEMENTS Precursors to Change	CONTEXTUAL ELEMENTS Historical Social Cultural Organizational Community Political Societal		

Causality
• Systems and field theory
  (interdependency, coexisting facts)
  ○ Subsystems
  ○ Patterns—fractals
• Dynamic social causation (cumulation)
• Invisible (unseen) structure (time,
  space, energy, uncertainty)
	Causality		

Mindfulness • Critical reflection • Seeing total context • Consequences or costs	Mindfulness		
Change			
Social Tensions • Identity and meaning • Resource availability and distribution • Power • Ethics	Social Tensions		
Conditions for Change • Climate • Timing • Threshold points	Conditions for Change		
Leadership			
Leadership as Intended Change • Intentional and predictable • Unpredictable and unintentional	Leadership as Intended Change		
Leadership as the Cause of Change • Interdependent actors and influences • Direct influences and indirect influences	Leadership as the Cause of Change		

Leadership as Action for Change
• Purpose
• Coactors—Leaders and participants
• Momentum or movement
  ○ Imagination and generativity
  ○ Communication and meaning-making
  ○ Coaction
	Leadership as Action for Change		

Assessment of Outcomes • Intended consequences • Unintended consequences • Impact on future events and change	Assessment of Outcomes		

5. Identifying the forces that are most significant and most uncertain, clustering and plotting each force along an axis from uncertainty to certainty or the reverse, and choosing the two most significant axes to form a grid with four distinct quadrants

6. Amplifying details of each quadrant to form four different plots (or scenarios)

7. Considering the implications of each scenario

8. Taking action based on early indicators of movement toward or away from a desirable scenario (Schwartz, 1996, pp. 241–247)

A final factor, "acting with feedback" (Harman, 1998, pp. 193–194), fosters ongoing learning and flexibility as leaders and participants move toward a desired common goal. Although scenario building is a method used most often in business or organizational settings, it provides a useful means for developing informed action in other settings, including community, social, and political environments.

We offer several concluding observations for further reflection based on our use of four analytical factors—field theory, cumulative effect, punctuated equilibrium, and systems thinking—to examine the Prince Edward County school desegregation case. We hope these analytical factors and the observations they provide are useful across contexts.

- We can assess leadership only after some change has occurred. We can observe leaders acting to influence outcomes in the present.
- The nature of leadership in any change effort corresponds to the historical and social context in which we place it and the leader(s) through which we examine a network of change.
- The less we consider historical and cultural context, the fewer influential events and factors we take into account.
- The interaction of a leader's effort with the efforts of other leaders and participants shapes the outcome and hence the significance and nature of leadership.
- Every change effort takes place within a system of change that provides opposition and modification of other leadership.
- The more credit a particular leader is given for change, the less we recognize the impact of systems in which events take place and the contributions of co-actors to the outcome.

Our Mount Hope colleagues asked members of the Gold Team how we could ever know or conclude anything or sustain order and stability if we believe that reality, including leadership and change, is socially constructed. If we extrapolate lessons from the natural sciences to social systems, we conclude that the "long view" provides perspective on human capability to imagine and change social systems. While social construction of human systems can result in restricted or inequitable systems of power, privilege, and access, our hope for social relationships is in leadership that helps people imagine and effect humane futures for themselves and the seventh generation. In the words of the Gold Team, "Imagination enables self-reflection and social criticism, as well as socialization, and thus makes possible a form of leadership that proposes alternative social arrangements and new forms of legitimate human needs and wants" (Couto et al., 2002, p. 2).

Note

1. The framework and concepts for this chapter emerged over various sessions with scholars in the General Theory of Leadership (GTOL) project. We also incorporated considerable portions of the Gold Team's concept paper, written by Richard Couto, Elizabeth Faier, Douglas Hicks, and Gill Hickman during the GTOL project.

References

American Institute of Physics, & David Cassidy. (2005). *Heisenberg—Quantum mechanics, implications of uncertainty, 1925–1927.* Retrieved July 14, 2005, from http://www.aip.org/history/heisenberg/p08c.htm

Bass, B. M. (1985). *Leadership and performance beyond expectations.* New York: Free Press.

Bass, B. M., & Avolio, B. J. (1994). *Improving organizational effectiveness through transformational leadership.* Thousand Oaks, CA: Sage.

Brown v. Board of Education, 344 U.S. 1 (1952).

Burns, J. M. (1978). *Leadership.* New York: Harper Torchbooks.

Burns, J. M. (2003). *Transforming leadership: A new pursuit of happiness.* New York: Atlantic Monthly Press.

Capra, F. (1982). *The turning point: Science, society, and the rising culture.* New York: Bantam Books.

Ciulla, J. B. (Ed.). (2004). *Ethics, the heart of leadership* (2nd ed.). Westport, CT: Praeger.

Couto, R. A., Faier, E. A., Hicks, D. A., & Hickman, G. R. (2002). *The Integrating Leadership Project: Gold Team report.* Unpublished manuscript.

Couto, R. A., & Fu, C. (2004, June). *The authentic leadership of the sacred texts.* Paper presented at the Summit on Authentic Leadership, Lincoln, NE.

Davis v. County School Board, 103 F.Supp. 337, 340 (E.D. Va. 1952).

Ely, M. P. (2004). *Israel on the Appomattox: A Southern experiment in Black freedom from the 1790s through the Civil War.* New York: Knopf.

Forsyth, D. R. (1999). *Group dynamics.* Belmont, CA: Wadsworth.

French, J. R. P., Jr., & Raven, B. (1959). The bases of social power. In D. Cartwright (Ed.), *Studies in social power* (pp. 150–167). Ann Arbor, MI: Institute for Social Research.

Gini, A. (2004). Moral leadership and business ethics. In J. B. Cuilla (Ed.), Ethics, the heart of leadership (2nd ed., pp. 25–43). Westport, CT: Praeger.

Gould, S. J. (1991). Opus 200. *Natural History, 100*(8), 12–18. Retrieved March 14, 2005, from http://stephenjaygould.org/library.html

Gould, S. J., & Eldredge, N. (1972). Punctuated equilibria: An alternative to phyletic gradualism. In T. J. M. Schopf (Ed.), *Models in paleobiology* (pp. 82–115). San Francisco: Freeman, Cooper. Retrieved March 14, 2005, from http://www.blackwellpublishing.com/ridley/classictexts/eldredge.asp

Granovetter, M. (1978). Threshold models of collective behavior. *American Journal of Sociology, 83*(1), 1420–1443.

Harman, W. W. (1998). *Global mind change: The promise of the 21st century* (2nd ed.). New York: Warner Books.

Heifetz, R. A. (1994). *Leadership without easy answers.* Cambridge, MA: Belknap Press.

Heifetz, R. A., & Linsky, M. (2002). *Leadership on the line: Staying alive through the dangers of leading.* Cambridge, MA: Harvard Business School Press.

Hume, D. (1748). *Of the idea of necessary connexion, Part I and Part II.* Retrieved March 10, 2005, from www.bartleby.com/37/3/

Kellerman, B. (2004). *Bad leadership: What it is, how it happens, why it matters.* Cambridge, MA: Harvard Business School Press.

Kelley, R. (1995). In praise of followers. In J. T. Wren (Ed.), The leader's companion: Insight on leadership through the ages (pp. 193–204). New York: Free Press.

Kluger, R. (1975). *Simple justice: The history of Brown v. Board of Education and black America's struggle for equality.* New York: Knopf.

Lewin, K. (1951). *Field theory in social science: Selected theoretical papers.* New York: Harper.

Lipman-Blumen, J. (2005). *The allure of toxic leaders: Why we follow destructive bosses and corrupt politicians—And how we can survive them.* Oxford, UK: Oxford University Press.

Lyons, O. (1992, December). *The year of the indigenous peoples (1993).* Speech given to the United Nations delegates. Retrieved July 13, 2005, from http://www.ratical.org/many_worlds/6Nations/OLatUNin92.html

Myrdal, G., with R. Sterner & A. Kose. (1944). *An American dilemma: The Negro problem and modern democracy.* New York: Harper & Row.

Plessy v. Ferguson, 163 U.S. 537 (1896).

Rosenblum, K. E., & Travis, T. M. C. (2003). *The meaning of difference: American constructions of race, sex and gender, social class, and sexual orientation* (3rd ed.). New York: McGraw-Hill.

Rost, J. C. (1991). *Leadership for the twenty-first century.* Westport, CT: Praeger.

Ruiz, V. L. (2001). *South by southwest: Mexican Americans and segregated Schooling, 1900–1950.* Retrieved August 18, 2005, from http://www.oah.org/pubs/magazine/deseg/ruiz.html

Schlager, E. (1999). A comparison of frameworks, theories, and models of policy processes. In P. A. Sabatier (Ed.), Theories of the policy process: Theoretical lenses on public policy (pp. 233–257). Boulder, CO: Westview Press.

Schwartz, P. (1996). *The art of the long view: Planning for the future in an uncertain world.* New York: Doubleday.

Smith, R. C. (1996). *They closed their schools: Prince Edward County, Virginia, 1951–1964.* Farmville, VA: Council of Women. (Original work published 1965)

Sullivan, K. M. (2004). What happened to "Brown"? *New York Review of Books, 51*(14), 47–52.

Teacher's Domain. (n.d.). *Mendez v. Westminster: Desegregating California's schools.* Retrieved August 18, 2005, from http://www.teachersdomain.org/6-8/soc/ush/civil/mendez/

Vaill, P. B. (1989). *Managing as a performing art: New ideas for a world of chaotic change.* San Francisco: Jossey-Bass.

Vaill, P. B. (1996). *Learning as a way of being: Strategies for survival in a world of permanent white water.* San Francisco: Jossey-Bass.

Weber, M. (1946). Politics as a vocation. In H. Gerth & C. W. Mills (Eds. & Trans.), *From Max Weber: Essays in sociology* (pp. 77–128). New York: Oxford University Press.

Wheatley, M. J. (1992). *Leadership and the new science: Learning about organization from an orderly universe.* San Francisco: Berrett-Koehler.

Yarmolinsky, A. (2007). The challenge of change in leadership. In R. A. Couto (Ed.), Reflections on leadership (pp. 45–56). Lanham, MD: University Press of America.

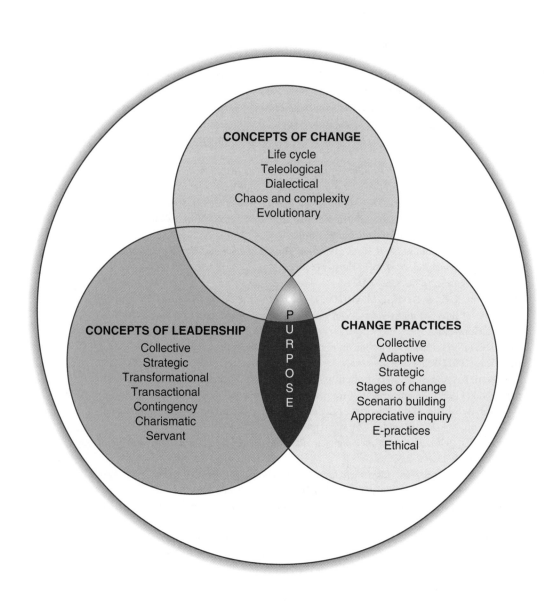

CONCEPTS OF CHANGE
Life cycle
Teleological
Dialectical
Chaos and complexity
Evolutionary

CONCEPTS OF LEADERSHIP
Collective
Strategic
Transformational
Transactional
Contingency
Charismatic
Servant

PURPOSE

CHANGE PRACTICES
Collective
Adaptive
Strategic
Stages of change
Scenario building
Appreciative inquiry
E-practices
Ethical

PART II

Leading Change in Organizational Contexts

Introduction

The next three chapters examine concepts and practices of leading organizational change. Chapter 2 examines concepts of organizational change, Chapter 3 considers concepts and theories of leadership that fit the context, and Chapter 4 looks at applicable change practices. Chapter 4 also includes five applications and reflections from various types of organizations—business, religious, government, education, and nonprofit/nongovernmental—to provide an opportunity to apply the concepts and practices discussed in Chapters 2–4 to actual situations.

The Environment of Organizational Change

Organizations clearly function today in a world where environmental factors, such as new markets in new venues, new technologies and information systems, international competitors and partnerships, changes in family structures and lifestyles, cultural and ethnic pluralism, decline and revitalization in urban environments, and environmental sustainability, compel entities to change. These elements link people and organizations locally and internationally in an environment of turbulence, unpredictability, and constant change. Which primary factors or indicators in the environment are important to organizational well-being and survival? What are the indicators? How do organizations succeed in this environment?

The now familiar idea of a turbulent environment has become commonplace in the vernacular of organizational leaders and members. Commonplace, however, does not mean that organizations can easily navigate turbulent environments. Researchers Emery and Trist (1973) described a turbulent environment as having "dynamic processes arising from the field [environment] itself which create significant variances for the component systems" (p. 52). They used an example from the ecosystem to illustrate this phenomenon:

> Fairly simple examples of this may be seen in fishing and lumbering where competitive strategies, based on an assumption that the environment is static, may, by over-fishing and over-cutting, set off disastrous dynamic processes in the fish and plant populations with the consequent destruction of all the competing social systems. . . . It is not difficult to see that even more complex dynamic processes are triggered off in human populations. (pp. 52–53)

Turbulent environments are not necessarily problematic or negative. Implications for leaders and members of organizations suggest that their ability to adapt, develop capacity (resources and competencies), and form valuable interdependent relationships will increase their prospects for sustainability in this context. As a result, organizations that adapt successfully and find new opportunities see their environment as more dynamic than turbulent (McCann & Selsky, 1984, p. 461).

Emery identified another context beyond the turbulent environment and shaped by forces totally beyond management, which he called a "vortical environment" (McCann & Selsky, 1984, p. 460). Several scholars (Baburoglu, 1988; Bogner & Barr, 2000; McCann & Selsky, 1984; Zohar & Morgan, 1996) continue to define and expand the idea of vortical environment by suggesting that organizations may face hyperturbulence, defined as "the condition in which environmental demands finally exceed the collective adaptive capacities of members sharing an environment" (McCann & Selsky, 1984, p. 460). Within this environment, companies may face hypercompetition where rapid changes in technology, regulations, ease of entry and exit by rival firms, and ambiguous consumer demands create competence-destroying change, making it difficult to gain any long-term advantages (Bogner & Barr, 2000, p. 212).

Turbulent and hyperturbulent environments present intensely challenging contexts for organizational change. Leaders and members must strive to make sense of these contexts to guide effective change in their organizations. Bogner and Barr (2000) identified three crucial activities in the literature on sensemaking in organizations—developing cognitive diversity, implementing rapid decision making, and taking experimental actions (p. 217). They refer to these activities collectively as adaptive sensemaking. The first activity, developing cognitive diversity, brings together individuals or teams with differing viewpoints, frameworks, or backgrounds to make decisions while they concurrently develop a base of shared understanding. The second activity, implementing rapid decision making, entails relying on real-time information, environmental cues, and prompt feedback to make decisions concerning the organization. Finally, taking experimental actions involves learning about unknowns or the unknowable ex ante (unknowable in advance of the event) in an environment by testing the waters—taking action, assessing the outcomes or consequences, and using the information to make future decisions.

Bogner and Barr's (2000) research suggests leaders and members who use adaptive sensemaking must focus on the process or "hows" of succeeding in hypercompetitive environments rather than focus on the "whats" (p. 224). The indicators of and responses to turbulent and hypercompetitive environments require more research, theory building, and data about praxis. Still, scholars and practitioners acknowledge that the nature and complexity of the environment in this era greatly influence organizational change.

Purpose of Organizational Change

Leading change often occurs when organizations anticipate, respond to, or adapt to challenges and opportunities in their internal or external environment. The purpose of change in an organization is to bring about a difference in form, quality, or state of the organization (Van de Ven & Poole, 1995, p. 512) so that the organization survives and achieves its mission and goals. Leaders and members strive to generate major improvements in some aspect of the organization, such as its structure, services or products, strategic focus, branding or market image, client/customer service, interaction with competitors, decision-making authority or power sharing, and so on.

Leaders and members of organizations can raise several guiding questions as they encounter and prepare for the ongoing process of change and development: Which primary factors or indicators in the environment are important to our well-being and survival? What are the indicators? How do we proceed in this environment? What kind of organizational change do we want or need, or, in many cases, what kind of change are we confronting currently? What type of leadership do we want or need to accomplish change? Which practices do we employ to implement change? These guiding questions structure the connections in Table II.1 among theories and ideal types of change, concepts of leadership, and viable change practices in the three chapters of Part II. Several assumptions underlie these connections.

1. Complexity, rather than reductive or linear thinking and processes, is a reality in many 21st century organizations, and it influences almost all aspects of leading change.

2. The dynamic and turbulent external environment of organizations is a primary contributor to complexity and the change processes that accompany it.

3. The complexity generated by dynamic environments requires organizational members to opt for compilations or combinations of theories and ideal types of change, concepts of leadership, and change practices, rather than any single approach to leading change in organizations. These compilations of concepts and practices can and often do function interdependently in the change process.

4. Concepts and practices of leading change apply to multiple participants (leaders and followers) in various roles and at different levels in and outside the organization.

5. Change processes are fluid and occur over time and space with multiple actors under various environmental circumstances.

6. The connections among concepts and practices of leading change in Table II.1 do not preclude other possible combinations and linkages.

TABLE II.1   Connecting Components of Organizational Change

What kind of organizational change do we need/want? or What kind of change are we confronting currently? (Chapter 2)	What type of leadership do we need/want to accomplish change? (Chapter 3)	Which practices do we employ to implement change? (Chapter 4)
Life cycle *Sample theories:* • Stage theories of development or innovation in organizations Change innately programmed into the organization Example: a pharmaceutical company's stages in the development and approval process for a new drug	Transactional Path-goal (contingency theory) Servant Invisible Team Leader-member exchange (LMX)	Organizational learning Stages of praxis (for maturity and revitalization cycles) Ethics and change
Teleological *Sample theories:* • Systems theory/systems dynamics • Strategic theory Change enacted purposely by members of the organization Example: a product or service innovation in an organization's area of strength or capacity—Apple's creation of the iPod	Transformational Charismatic Path-goal (contingency theory) Task-relations-and-change (contingency theory) Strategic Collective/collaborative leadership Leader-member exchange (LMX)	Stages of praxis Strategic planning and goal setting Collective/collaborative practices • Adaptive practices • Organizational learning • Institutionalized leadership • Empowerment/shared power Ethics and change
Dialectical *Sample theories:* • Conflict/conflict resolution theories • Chaos/complexity theories Change generated by conflict and synthesis Examples: mergers and acquisitions involving different organizational cultures—fire and police services or Eastern companies and Western workers or private sector management of public sector employees and services	Charismatic Transformational Collective/collaborative leadership Strategic Leader-member exchange (LMX)	Collective/collaborative: • Adaptive practices • Organizational learning • Institutionalized leadership • Empowerment/shared power • Complex adaptive systems • Ethics and change

What kind of organizational change do we need/want? or What kind of change are we confronting currently? (Chapter 2)	What type of leadership do we need/want to accomplish change? (Chapter 3)	Which practices do we employ to implement change? (Chapter 4)
Chaos/complexity (an emerging theory; Poole & Van de Ven, 2004) *Sample theories:* • Chaos/complexity theories • Self-organizing systems Change and problem solving occur by searching for emerging themes or patterns in systems and forming self-organizing teams and structures around these themes or patterns Examples: the Orpheus Chamber Orchestra, some evangelical churches or ministries, many community groups and organizations	Collective/collaborative leadership	Adaptive practices: • Organizational learning • Institutionalized leadership • Empowerment/shared power Ethics and change
Evolutionary *Sample theory:* • Organizational ecology Change generated through organizational learning, imitation, and adaptation over long time periods or deviation after long periods of stasis Examples: the progression from agrarian and craft work to industrialization and work in bureaucracies or the transition from bureaucracies to information technology and project or teamwork structures	Transactional Servant Path-goal (contingency theory) Leader-member exchange (LMX) Adaptive	Stages of praxis Adaptive practices: • Organizational learning Ethics and change

NOTE: Ideal types are adapted from Van de Ven and Poole (1995).

The chapter begins with a vignette depicting change in an actual company. Throughout the three chapters in Part II, segments of the vignette provide examples of certain concepts and practices of leadership and change.

Change Vignette

Technology Solutions Turns Disaster Into Dividends

Technology Solutions, Incorporated,[1] began as a private Internet-technology staffing and consulting firm in 1990. The company currently has two divisions—consulting services and products. Consulting services assists clients with software development and provides short- or long-term staffing for positions such as project managers, business analysts, database developers, and network engineers, among others. The centerpiece of Technology Solutions' products division is its special-education management software designed to help educators manage the broad array of data collection and dissemination associated with the special-education process. The company has received several prestigious awards for its innovative products and services and its work in the community.

Clients of Technology Solutions range from large Fortune 100 companies to small start-up businesses. The business model varies with each client. Technology Solutions employees must be responsive and adapt to the situation at hand. Because most employees are so flexible, they are innovative and generally receptive to change; they are not limited in their range of clients or how they do business. People can cross lines and roles without hesitation. This flexibility helps in accomplishing projects and tasks while creating a motivating and innovative workplace. Each day company members can be called to perform a new job.

Technology Solutions' president and founder is a quintessential high-tech entrepreneur—talented, energetic, innovative, and exuberant. He enjoys and inspires the work in a nontraditional office setting characterized by a pool table, disco ball, and a ready supply of doughnuts. It is difficult to imagine now that only a few years ago Technology Solutions suffered a financial setback and companywide layoffs. Prior to the setback, business was booming and company members valued their numerous perks and their fun and upbeat work environment. Technology Solutions' revenue jumped 52% in one year alone. However, this exponential growth came to an abrupt halt when the market shifted. The sharp economic downturn hit the high-tech sector particularly hard. The formerly very prosperous company had to switch to survivor mode if it were going to succeed.

The president of Technology Solutions explained that his job as leader is to initiate change even when things are going well: "We must build the foundation for the next level of growth. Change goes against the grain in the way a lot of people think, but that is the way it is." People often do not think change is necessary when actually it is imperative. For example, many employees found the shift to a staffing-based market difficult to accept. The company president reported that Technology Solutions went through significant organizational change when he discovered that purchase orders from clients increasingly requested consulting or technology staffing at the clients' worksites rather than project-based work performed at Technology Solutions' headquarters. "My employees felt I was throwing away our profits," he said regarding the initial reaction to the changes he implemented. Ultimately, however, his intuition proved correct: The project division closed due to lack of demand, and the company survived on its staffing division.

Change in the market economy led to a shift in the company's direction, decisions, and practices. Technology Solutions had to revamp its work environment, structure, and staffing as a result of change in the economy. The company reversed its work assignments so that more employees worked at sites out in the field and fewer employees worked at the company headquarters.

Technology Solutions shifted its off-site to on-site staffing ratio from 20:80 to 80:20. In addition, the company formed new business groups to go after sections of the market it had not previously targeted and hired employees who could offer expertise in those targeted areas. The company shut down divisions that were not growing and expanded prosperous divisions to take advantage of new opportunities. The shift in emphasis to consulting and workforce outsourcing forced Technology Solutions into five separate rounds of layoffs. The company had to transform itself in a short period of time.

The market shift led to a rough transition for members of the company. The president found it difficult to communicate with the 80% of employees who worked off site. Originally, the company was characterized by a very flat organizational structure, according to company employees, but during the economic downturn, the company assumed a more hierarchical structure. For a while employees experienced difficulty dealing with the uncertainty in the office as they watched friends and coworkers being laid off. Everyone felt as if they were walking on eggshells as the company's environment changed and the economy fell. Morale suffered. A rumor mill about changes contributed to stress in the office. Several employees commented that it was difficult not being involved in the decision making regarding the company's direction and structure. Some said they frankly did not think Technology Solutions was particularly adept at embracing change.

Long-term members of the company thought the organization's fundamental values and the relationship between leaders and employees changed. In the past, everyone had shared in the company's decision making. However, as Technology Solutions encountered a financial downturn and survival became a major goal, decision making about the company's direction became more centralized. The company president hired new management staff, including a chief operating officer. The change led several employees to conclude that leaders were not upholding the company's stated core values, which included a commitment to quality products, service, and employees; building strong relationships with clients, employees, and the larger community; developing and enhancing knowledge; fostering a sense of personal responsibility; and modeling fiscal responsibility. Some employees said that even though the core values were communicated to everyone, the company did not abide by them during hard times.

Despite the president's efforts to maintain a flexible and fun environment, Technology Solutions developed a different culture with more hierarchy, fewer in-house projects, more layoffs, and an increase in other cost-cutting measures, such as the elimination of the employees' beloved "Doughnut Wednesday" and the suspension of the company's community volunteer program. Some employees who had been with the company for several years became disgruntled with the changing environment. They sensed a barrier between upper managers and employees that had not existed previously.

With the challenges of organizational restructuring, the president worked to maintain an environment that embraced change by encouraging employees to learn and pursue knowledge. Continuous learning is extremely important in the technology industry because knowledge in this field advances quickly. Employees and the company share responsibility for getting employees the training and latest information necessary to stay current in their field. "Like dental hygiene where you have to keep your teeth brushed every day, in 'learning hygiene' you have to keep your mind brushed," the president said.

(Continued)

(Continued)

Technology Solutions encourages employees to embrace change through empowerment. Employees have the freedom to be creative and develop the newest and most innovative ideas possible, even if that means they sometimes make mistakes. There is no micromanaging.

Company employees receive considerable satisfaction from the work itself. When a problem arises, the project manager often solicits four possible solutions from employees. Recognition and positive reinforcement encourage employees to contribute their best efforts to each project. The role of leaders and managers in the organization is to help employees discover themselves and learn to relate to one another authentically. Managers practice this approach by listening to employees and implementing a "no secrets" policy.

Employees think that the nature of the information technology business, rather than any cajoling from managers, forces them to be innovative. They are all aware that if they do not know of or understand the latest technology available, the business will not survive. One senior manager's comments about continuous change echoed those made by employees: Change is inevitable and constant in an organization based on computer technology. Managers encourage employees to be creative and think outside the box, which fosters continual innovation.

Employees also mentioned that many company practices stimulate them to take action, including the free sharing of ideas, the open-door policy among all company members, and the discussions during company meetings. One manager said that the leader's job is easier at Technology Solutions than at many other firms because employees are hard working, motivated, and team oriented. "No one in the organization is stove piped . . . [each person is] able to cross over depending on the task," another manager commented.

The company promotes learning and continuous self-development in its employees. Company members often take the time to share ideas with each other in hopes that this process will spark new thoughts. Employees said that they always feel comfortable seeking guidance from any member of the organization, including the president. Individuals throughout Technology Solutions provide this type of inspiration regardless of their title or position. Many employees commented on the importance of being creative and having access to the newest and most innovative ideas possible.

Not everyone adapts well to change in structure and purpose, even in environments that welcome technological change. The president said that roughly two thirds of his company accepts change, but the other third does not. As an example, the third involved in the shutdown might say that because the company closed the division where they worked and had knowledge and expertise, they now had to acquire new knowledge and expertise, which made them feel uncomfortable. These employees resist change, in contrast to the two thirds of employees in the growing sector who might welcome change. The newer employees and managers tend to embrace the company's change in structure and purpose, according to one company executive. The challenge at this point seems to be getting the rest of the organization aligned in this mindset and creating a transforming environment for all members of the company.

Clearly, these changes created tension and distress. Previously, the company was smaller and everyone was involved in decision making. As the company grew larger, employees were not as involved in every business decision. Employees lamented the fact that they did not have a choice regarding the changes that occurred; they simply had to adapt to the changes and move on. The company was recreated and reconstructed during the 12-month period following the economic downturn in the fall of 2001. As a result, change became an inevitable part of company members' lives.

Organizational change helped Technology Solutions remain viable through uneven economic conditions punctuated by significant gains and losses. Modifications, such as changing management and the decision-making process, cutting costs, closing a division, and restructuring the ratios of employees on site and off site, helped to move the organization forward so that it could embrace new opportunities and challenges. Few members of Technology Solutions felt the impact of these changes more profoundly than the company's founder and president.

Note

1. Although the company's name has been changed, the situation described in this vignette actually occurred. Members of the Senior Seminar class at the Jepson School of Leadership Studies, University of Richmond, collected the relevant data and developed this case. The researchers included Jon Blute, Dorothy Donaby-Juntunen, Erika Fiest, Eric Hines, Lori Kinast, Kate Materna, Gregory Mullen, Sarah Nickerson, Erin Powers, Jennifer Roberts, Timothy Sullivan, and William Wright.

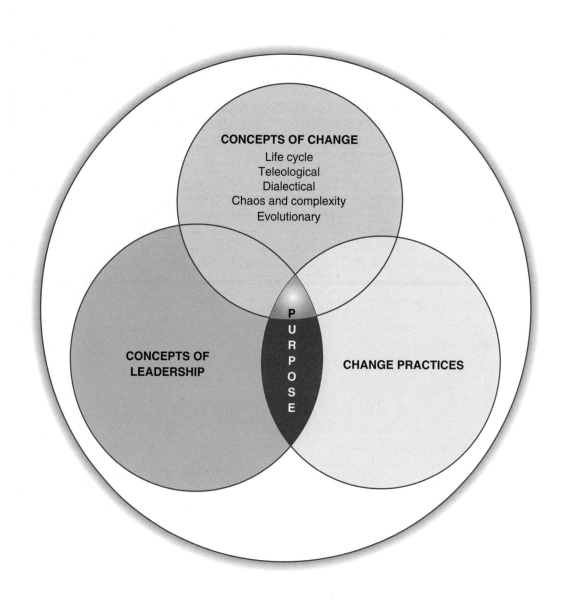

CHAPTER 2

Concepts of Organizational Change

What Kind of Organizational Change Do We Want or Need?

Technology Solutions faced many of the challenges that companies, nonprofit organizations, and government agencies confront in dynamic environments. Their first priority in the change process was survival. It was apparent to senior managers, based on the change in requests from clients, that the company had to respond to the shifting economic and workforce needs. The purpose of change at Technology Solutions was to adjust the company's focus to emphasize consulting services and workforce staffing at the client's worksite and develop new opportunities in the company's areas of capacity and strength. This shift in focus required change and innovation in the company's services and products, which in turn required change in its structure, decision-making process, in-house and off-site staffing ratio, expertise of company members, and number of employees in each company division.

The story of Technology Solutions provides valuable insight into concepts of organizational change. Van de Ven and Poole (1995) explained how and why organizations change by grouping nearly 20 different process theories from multiple disciplines into four schools of thought (also called motors or ideal types)—life cycle, teleological, dialectical, and evolutionary. Researchers show that organizations actually draw from various combinations or compilations of these theories and ideal types instead of relying on a single type.

Van de Ven and Poole (1995) begin their explanation of change motors or types by defining several key terms: (1) change, an empirical observation of difference in form, quality, or state over time in an organizational entity; (2) development, a change process from initiation or onset of the entity to its end; and (3) process theory, an explanation of how and why an organizational entity changes and develops (p. 512).

Life-Cycle Theory

Table 2.1 uses Van de Ven and Poole's four schools of thought or ideal types to illustrate the drivers, units, or levels of analysis, processes, and modes of organizational change. The first ideal type, life-cycle theory, embodies a biological or human development metaphor of stages and organic growth. Like a living organism, some organizations or groups within organizations go through a predetermined cycle of start-up (birth), growth (adolescence), maturity (adulthood), and decline (death) or revitalization (recovery). Organizations involved in life-cycle change "often explain development in terms of institutional rules or programs that require developmental activities to progress in a prescribed sequence" (Van de Ven & Poole, 1995, p. 515).

Life-cycle theory is an inherent component of certain organizations, such as pharmaceutical companies in which the developmental process involves a sequence of proposals, clinical trials, and regulatory reviews before receiving approval from the Food and Drug Administration (FDA) to bring a new drug to market. Other examples include nonprofit or government agencies that receive a large part of their funding from government grants and appropriations or private foundations. Compliance with the grant or appropriation cycle literally determines life or death for these organizations. If the agencies receive their grants, they are revitalized and live to experience the cycle again; if not, they decline or cease to exist.

Van de Ven and Poole (1995) identified the process and pace of change in the life-cycle ideal type as first-order, continuous, or incremental change (p. 524). This mode characterizes change as predictable, gradual, or slightly varied from the past (see Table 2.1). Most types of life-cycle change result in low uncertainty for members of the organization and competence-enhancing change, which is improvement in existing designs and capabilities (Abernathy & Clark, 1985, p. 6).

Life-cycle change has limited applicability to the Technology Solutions case, except for the company's relative age and stage of development. At the time of its major change, the company was in a growth or adolescent phase of organizational development. Its relative stage of growth may have positioned Technology Solutions to survive a radical turnaround in its goals and structure, whereas a more mature organization may have encountered even more resistance to change.

Teleological Theory

The second ideal type, teleological theory, provides a useful perspective for examining much of the change at Technology Solutions. This school of thought, derived from the philosophical doctrine of teleology, suggests that change or movement occurs through the use of purpose and goals to guide the organization toward a desired objective. Van de Ven and Poole (1995) affirmed that the theory works when like-minded individuals or groups act together as a single entity:

> It is assumed that the entity is purposeful and adaptive; by itself or in interaction with others, the entity constructs an envisioned end state, takes action to reach it, and monitors the progress. Thus, proponents of this theory view development as a repetitive sequence of goal formulation, implementation, evaluation, and modification of goals based on what was learned or intended by the entity. (p. 516)

TABLE 2.1 Organizational Change: Drivers, Units of Analysis, Processes, and Modes

Drivers of Change, Motors, or Ideal Types	Unit or Level of Analysis	Process of Change	Mode and Pace of Change

Life cycle
 	
Sample theories:
 	
• Stage theories of development or innovation
 	
Change innately programmed into the organization
 	
Example: a pharmaceutical company's stages in the development and approval process for a new drug
	Within one organization or group	Metaphor: organic growth
		
		Movement through stages of change: start-up > growth > maturity > death/decline or revitalization
		
		Intellectual heritage: biology, human development
			• First-order change:
			  ○ Prescribed/ predictable mode
			  ○ Patterned on existing framework
			  ○ Low uncertainty
			• Continuous change (based on past or current framework)
			• Incremental change (slow, gradual change)

Teleological
 	
Sample theories:
 	
• Systems theory/systems dynamics
• Strategic theory
 	
Change enacted purposely by members of organization
 	
Example: a product or service innovation in an organization's area of strength or capacity—Apple's creation of the iPod
	Within one organization or group	Metaphor: purposeful cooperation (internal)
		
		Emergent sequence of change: goal setting > implementation > evaluation > modification > setting of new goals
		
		Intellectual heritage: teleology (philosophy)
			• Second-order change:
			  ○ Creative or innovative mode (new purpose, goal, capabilities, or products/services)
			  ○ Unpredictable
			  ○ High uncertainty
			• Discontinuous change (break from past framework)
			• Radical change (novel or unprecedented)

Dialectical
 	
Sample theories:
 	
• Conflict/conflict resolution theories
 	
Change generated by conflict and synthesis
 	
Examples: mergers and acquisitions involving different organizational cultures—fire and police services or Eastern companies and Western workers or private sector management of public sector employees and services
	Between two or more organizations or groups	Metaphor: opposition, conflict
		
		Intellectual heritage: Hegelian philosophy, Marxist theory, conflict theory
			• Second-order change:
			  ○ Creative or innovative mode (new purpose, goal, capabilities, or products/ services)
			  ○ Unpredictable
			  ○ High uncertainty
			• Discontinuous change (break from past framework)
			• Radical change (novel or unprecedented)

(Continued)

TABLE 2.1 (Continued)

Drivers of Change, Motors, or Ideal Types	Unit or Level of Analysis	Process of Change	Mode and Pace of Change
Chaos/complexity (an emerging theory; Poole & Van de Ven, 2004) *Sample theories:* • Chaos/complexity theories • Self-organizing systems Change and problem solving occur by searching for emerging themes or patterns in systems and forming self-organizing teams and structures around these themes or patterns Example: the Orpheus Chamber Orchestra, some evangelical churches or ministries, many community groups or organizations	Within one organization or group and between organizations or groups	Metaphor: self-organizing or "autogenesis" Intellectual heritage: complex systems theory, chaos theory (from physics, chemistry, biology, mathematics)	• Second-order change: ○ Creative or innovative mode (new purpose, goal, capabilities, or products/services) ○ Unpredictable ○ High uncertainty • Discontinuous change (break from past framework) • Radical change (novel or unprecedented)
Evolutionary *Sample theory:* • Organizational ecology Change generated by organizational learning and imitation over long periods of time Example: The progression from agrarian and craft work to industrialization and work in bureaucracies or the development from bureaucracies to information technology and project or teamwork structures	Across multiple organizations or groups	Metaphor: competitive survival Intellectual heritage: natural selection through growth and decline (Darwin); learning and imitation (Lamarck); gradual change with periodic interruption that produces new species (Gould & Eldredge, 1972)	• First-order change: ○ Prescribed/ predictable mode ○ Patterned on existing framework ○ Low uncertainty • Continuous change (based on past or current framework) • Incremental change (slow, gradual change)

NOTE: Ideal types are adapted from Van de Ven and Poole (1995).

The teleological ideal type is the foundation for many theories and models of change:

- *Social construction* (Berger & Luckmann, 1966)—individuals and society develop shared meaning (shared beliefs and conceptions) of what reality is and embed this shared meaning in the institutions and structures of society; as a result, social reality is said to be socially constructed.

- *Decision making* (March & Simon, 1958)—organizational members develop certain goals and objectives by employing four major processes—problem solving, persuasion, bargaining, or politics.
- *Equifinality* (Katz & Kahn, 1966)—this concept, which is within systems theory (described separately), suggests there are several equally effective ways to reach a goal.
- *Adaptive learning* (Heifetz, 1994; March & Olsen, 1976; Schön, 1971; Senge, 1990)—organizational members work to improve their actions and resulting organizational outcomes using a learning cycle that entails assessing individual beliefs that lead to individual actions, which in turn lead to organizational action and a response from the environment that can induce improved individual beliefs.
- *Functionalism* (Merton, 1968)—this method of analyzing social and cultural units is used to determine how well these units work together and adapt to support and sustain society as a whole.
- *Strategic change* (Chakravarthy & Lorange, 1991)—This concept is described separately in this section. (Van de Ven & Poole, 1995, p. 516)

From the founding of Technology Solutions, senior managers developed objectives (goal setting) for the organization—serving clients through delivery of technology-based projects—and took appropriate action to carry out their goals (implementation). When profits began to shrink after a major boom, senior managers assessed the trends in purchase orders from clients to identify changes in their clients' needs (evaluation). These findings led to significant change in their original objectives (setting new goals) and vital innovations in the company's products and services. Creativity and change are built into organizations such as Technology Solutions, where members have the ability to generate any goals they deem appropriate. As a result, Van de Ven and Poole (1995) use the metaphor of purposeful cooperation among internal constituents to symbolize the teleological ideal type (p. 514).

The process and pace of change in the teleological ideal type can be described as second order (a break with the past), discontinuous, or radical (Van de Ven & Poole, 1995, pp. 523–524). These modes describe change that is innovative, frame breaking, unpredictable, or revolutionary (Table 2.1). The new goals of senior managers at Technology Solutions—workforce outsourcing and new market and product development—led to innovation and a radical departure from the past.

This second-order change resulted in high levels of uncertainty, unpredictability, and competence-destroying challenges—development or innovation that disrupts or destroys existing designs and capabilities to create new ones (Abernathy & Clark, 1985, p. 6) for employees when senior managers shut down declining divisions and enlarged profitable ones. Many employees became more insecure as they experienced layoffs, cutbacks, vanishing perks, and a loss of work in their areas of competence.

Systems Theory

Even though the level or unit of analysis in teleological change is one organization or entity (vs. two or more), the external environment greatly influences organizational change and decisions by participants in the process. Systems theory or system dynamics helps participants in teleological change see the vast array of causes and effects that make up a situation in contrast to seeing problems in disjointed, linear, or simplistic ways (Yukl, 2006, p. 203).

Jay Forrester (1961), credited with the founding of system dynamics, posited that problems (organizational, social, or political) have multiple sources that require a more complex understanding of the dynamic interrelationships of events within and between organizational units, functions, or levels and interrelationships between the organization and its environment. He cautioned that situations may only worsen if change leaders attempt to solve a problem in one area without considering the broader cause-and-effect relationships or consequences (intended and unintended) within the whole system (Forrester, 1995, pp. 11–12). For instance, it would have been an inadequate response by senior managers at Technology Solutions to blame the problem of plummeting profits solely on the methods or assertiveness of their marketing and sales staff without taking into account factors such as a changing economy, shifting client needs, the company's internal capabilities and structure, and the company's need to differentiate its products and services from others. These and other factors are wholly interdependent.

The structure of change in systems theory is usually depicted in a flow diagram, similar to Figure 2.1, consisting of four facets—input, throughput, output, and feedback:

> Input describes the conditions at any given moment in time. Throughput describes the actions that take place, based on the apparent input. Output describes the future results of those actions. Finally, feedback returns information to the system about its performance. By this means, the system regulates itself. (Harter & Phillips, 2004, p. 1516)

FIGURE 2.1   Systems Theory

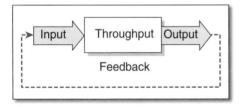

In the case of Technology Solutions, assessment by senior managers of the changing economy, shifting client needs, declining business, and plummeting profits (input) led them to change the company's capabilities, internal structure, method and location of service delivery, and product development (throughput). These changes resulted in an increase in clients, improved profits, new products, a decrease in internal staff, and the recruitment of experts for off-site staffing (output). An evaluation of performance based on the company's actions allowed senior managers to determine their successes and identify new challenges (feedback).

Strategic Change

Participants involved in teleological change depend on information from the external environment about new occurrences, opportunities, and threats to create strategic change. Strategic change focuses on actions to achieve a competitively superior fit between the organization and its environment based on the organization's vision, mission, values, and purpose (Daft & Lane, 2002, p. 487). Balaji Chakravarthy (1997) contended that in a turbulent environment where the behavior of competitors and other aspects of the environment are unpredictable, strategic change depends on an organization's ability to sustain flexibility, create distinctive competencies, and become a repeat innovator (p. 80). Chakravarthy stated the following criteria are needed to create and support this kind of flexibility:

> A firm needs to rely more on its front-line entrepreneurs who are close to the business pulse and can sense the flow of innovation. Constraining them with top-down strategic intent can be counterproductive, but their innovative ideas need to be channeled within a guiding philosophy—a broad vision of the opportunities that the firm seeks to participate in. (pp. 80–81)

Environmental factors often play a role in the decision by some organizations to pursue a cooperative or collaborative change strategy with competitors or companies from a different business sector. These cooperative arrangements, known as interorganizational relationships (IORs), take various forms, including partnerships, strategic alliances, joint ventures, and research consortia, among others (Ring & Van de Ven, 1994, p. 90). Much like cooperative conflict resolution (Forsyth, 2006, pp. 438–439), cooperative change involves the development of superordinate goals by two or more competitive or diverse organizations that represent the common interest of all parties. The common interests these parties focus on may include goals such as cocreating a new product or service, obtaining a broader clientele, or gaining new or scarce resources. IORs involve multiple actors who interact during an indefinite or specified span of time in a joint effort to mediate or respond to an uncertain environment. Parties enter these relationships based on their perceptions of trust, efficiency, and equity or fair dealing with each other and may codify their arrangement in a formal agreement (Ring & Van de Ven, 1994, p. 94).

Cooperative or collaborative change has it drawbacks. As McCann and Selsky (1984) pointed out, this approach can be too expensive or too threatening based on the amount and variety of resources to be managed, may not prevail over historical antagonisms between parties or substantive differences in values and goals, and may overwhelm the capacity of organizational partners to accept and make sense of increasing amounts of information and interdependencies (p. 463).

Cooperative change may seem counterintuitive in a highly competitive context; however, numerous companies, such as Microsoft and Nortell, use this approach to codevelop new products, such as communications software. Many nonprofit organizations join together in a cooperative change effort for fundraising and other common purposes pertaining to nonprofit functions.

Chaos and Complexity: Emergent Theories

Chaos theory and its offshoot, complexity theory, encompass characteristics of systems theory and certain characteristics of dialectical theory; however, chaos and complexity theories may represent a new and distinct generation of thought. These theories maintain that "relationships in complex systems, like organizations, are nonlinear, made up of interconnections and branching choices that produce unintended consequences and render the universe unpredictable" (Tetenbaum, 1998, p. 21). Rather than looking for concrete, linear, and nonconflicting answers to complex situations, chaos theory contends that problem solving and change occur by searching for emerging themes or patterns in a system and forming self-organizing structures around these themes or patterns.

Chaos theory embraces conflicting views and approaches by using both/and rather than either/or perspectives. Tetenbaum (1998) found that some organizations, such as Visa, Motorola, and Sony's PlayStation unit, have created chaordic organizational cultures to provide the resilience and flexibility needed to handle continual and unforeseen change. These organizational cultures foster knowledge and information sharing, innovation and creativity, teamwork and project orientation, diversity, and strong core values (pp. 27–29).

Complexity theory assumes "that some events, given our knowledge and technology, are unknowable until they occur, and may indeed be unknowable in advance" (Eve, Horsfall, & Lee, as cited in Schneider & Somers, 2006, p. 354). This theory encompasses three interrelated elements not found in general systems theory—nonlinear dynamics, in which structures are characterized by high states of energy exchange with the environment and extreme instability; chaos theory, in which an attraction or magnetism forms a discernable pattern over time called a "strange attractor" (Wheatley, 1992, pp. 122–125); and adaptation and evolution, in which an ability to modify or change is evidenced through a process of self-organization and interdependence among individuals or subunits (Schneider & Somers, 2006, pp. 354–355).

Within complexity theory, the concept of complex adaptive system (CAS) may provide the best organizational capacity to adapt and change in unknown or unknowable settings. An organization that develops a CAS can function as a "poised" system that has the capability to position itself on the edge of chaos (Schneider & Somers, 2006, p. 355). CASs become poised through adaptive buffering, emergence, self-similarity, and self-organization.

Adaptive buffering allows organizations optimal flexibility—the right amount of experimentation and energy exchange with the environment; whereas too much flexibility results in disruption or instability, too little results in rigidity. Emergence is the spontaneous bottom-up interaction among organizational actors and units that generates cooperation and facilitates order in the midst of change. Self-similarity means all units and subunits (departments, teams, geographic divisions, etc.) share a vital component of the organization as a whole (similar to fractals in nature). One way to create self-similarity is to build organizational identity, a form of social identity that reflects beliefs members hold in common about characteristics of the company or agency. When this identity resides in the heads and hearts of the organization's members, individuals or teams can remain flexible and open to change while maintaining a sense of continuity (Schneider & Somers, 2006, pp. 357–358).

The dialectical ideal type may provide an intellectual foundation for some tenets of chaos and complexity theory. Dialectical change brings about ideas, knowledge, and technology that differ from current and opposing conceptions and yields an outcome (synthesis) that is often "unknowable in advance." To this end, chaos theory can be revolutionary and frame breaking, though some scholars argue the theory is primarily evolutionary (Schneider & Somers, 2006, p. 354). Because the outcome or synthesis of dialectical change sets the stage for new challenges to the system, this synthesis may become a new strange attractor for the next seeds of change.

Van de Ven and Poole (2004) did not include chaos and complexity theories as ideal types or motors in their 1995 change typology; however, they acknowledge in a later publication that these theories comprise one of several trends in organizational change research and "have great potential to provide rigorous models for critical aspects of change including emergence, interlevel relationships, critical incidents, and unintended consequences" (p. xv).

Dialectical Theory

The third ideal type, dialectical theory, begins with "the Hegelian assumption that the organizational entity exists in a pluralistic world of colliding events, forces, or contradictory values that compete with each other for domination and control" (Van de Ven & Poole, 1995, p. 517). These conflicts may be internal (conflicting goals), external (conflicting organizations), or both. According to dialectical theory, change occurs when people responsible for existing organizational values, goals, or modes of operation (thesis) → encounter opposition from people whose opposing perspectives gain adequate power to challenge the status quo (antithesis) → resulting in the creation of a novel set of values, goals, or modes of operation (synthesis) that departs from both the current perspective and the opposing one.

The changes at Technology Solutions contained elements of dialectical theory. For example, senior managers built a thriving business by serving clients through the development and delivery of in-house technology-based projects at the company's headquarters (thesis) until business declined sharply due to changes in the economy and changes in requests from clients (antithesis). These external challenges resulted in a radical change in services and staffing at Technology Solutions along with a change in the mode and location of service delivery. Challenges to the company's status quo also caused senior managers to expand their mission and capacity by exploring new markets and developing innovative business products, such as special-education management software, to expand the company's mission and capabilities (synthesis). This new synthesis set the stage for other challenges to Technology Solutions' status quo, which will likely set the process in motion again.

Dialectical and teleological ideal types embody several of the same modes of frame-breaking organizational change, including second-order, discontinuous, and radical change (Van de Ven & Poole, 1995, pp. 523–524). Like the teleological school of thought, the dialectical embodies high levels of uncertainty, unpredictability, and competence-destroying change. The dialectical ideal type differs from the teleological in that change arises from conflict rather than constructed plans, the outcome or synthesis results in a change that was not purposely developed and guided, and typically the process and outcome are more chaotic in character than they are when constructed by organizational members.

Evolutionary Theory

The third ideal type, evolutionary theory, focuses on organizational ecology involving cumulative change over time in organizational entities across communities, industries, or society at large. Van de Ven and Poole (1995) used this biological metaphor to explain the three components of an evolutionary ideal type—variation, selection, and retention. Variation creates new forms of organizations through random chance; selection of organizations occurs through competition for scarce resources, resulting in the environment selecting the best entity; and retention perpetuates and maintains certain organizational forms and practices (p. 518).

Evolutionary change can be generated through natural selection, organizational learning, imitation, and adaptation over long time periods or deviation after long periods of stasis. Darwinists contend that change occurs as organizations inherit traits through intergenerational processes of natural selection (survival of the fittest), such as differential birth and death rates. In contrast, the Lamarckian view, which maintains that organizations change by developing or adopting new traits through learning and imitation within a generation, seems more applicable and relevant to contemporary organizations (Van de Ven & Poole, 1995, p. 519). Evolutionary theorists who support Gould and Eldredge's (1972) concept of punctuated equilibrium explain that major change in organizations occurs when a deviation or discrepancy in organizational traits happens after long periods of gradual change. Real change takes place if this deviation establishes a trend wherein the new organizational traits succeed more frequently than the previous ones—such as the change in work and structure from the industrial to the information era.

The evolutionary ideal type, like the life-cycle ideal type, characterizes change as predictable, gradual, or slightly varied from the past. They share several modes of organizational change, including first-order, continuous, or incremental change, which result in low uncertainty and competence enhancement for members of the organization (Van de Ven & Poole, 1995, pp. 522–523). The evolutionary ideal type differs from life cycle in that it focuses on competition among organizations in an environment where resources are limited for each entity's survival. For example, competition from Japanese automobile makers, whose employees build high-quality cars by working in teams, forced U.S. automobile makers to change from individual to team approaches to compete for the same customers.

Conclusion

Van de Ven and Poole's (1995) framework organizes process theories of change from multiple disciplines that help explain how and why change unfolds in organizations. Using four drivers of change or ideal types—life-cycle, teleological, dialectical, and evolutionary—they provide a coherent structure that incorporates concepts such as first-order and second-order change, continuous and discontinuous change, and incremental and radical change. Added to this framework, the chapter examines chaos/complexity theory, systems theory, and strategic change. Collectively, these concepts help organizational members understand the kind of change they want, need, or are experiencing so that their actions help facilitate the change they desire.

References

Abernathy, W. J., & Clark, K. B. (1985). Innovation: Mapping the winds of creative destruction. *Research Policy, 14*(1), 3–22.

Baburoglu, O. N. (1988). The vortical environment: The fifth in the Emery-Trist levels of organizational environments. *Human Relations, 41*(3), 181–210.

Berger, P. L., & Luckmann, T. (1966). *The social construction of reality: A treatise in the sociology of knowledge.* Garden City, NY: Doubleday.

Bogner, W. C., & Barr, P. S. (2000). Making sense in hypercompetitive environments: A cognitive explanation for the persistence of high velocity competition. *Organization Science, 11*(2), 212–226.

Chakravarthy, B. (1997). A new strategy framework for coping with turbulence. *Sloan Management Review, 38,* 69–82.

Chakravarthy, B. S., & Lorange, P. (1991). *Managing the strategy process: A framework for a multibusiness firm.* Englewood Cliffs, NJ: Prentice Hall.

Daft, R. L., & Lane, P. G. (2002). *The leadership experience* (2nd ed.). Fort Worth, TX: Harcourt College.

Emery, F. E., & Trist, E. L. (1973). *Towards a social ecology: Contextual appreciation of the future in the present.* London: Plenum Press.

Forrester, J. W. (1961). *Industrial dynamics.* Cambridge, MA: M.I.T. Press.

Forrester, J. W. (1995, November). The beginning of system dynamics. *McKinsey Quarterly,* 4–16.

Forsyth, D. R. (2006). *Group dynamics* (4th ed.). Belmont, CA: Thomson/Wadsworth.

Gould, S. J., & Eldredge, N. (1972). Punctuated equilibria: An alternative to phyletic. In T. J. Schopf (Ed.), *Models in paleobiology* (pp. 82–115). San Francisco: Freeman, Cooper.

Harter, N., & Phillips, J. (2004). Systems theory. In G. R. Goethals, G. J. Sorenson, & J. M. Burns (Eds.), *Encyclopedia of leadership* (pp. 1515–1520). Thousand Oaks, CA: Sage.

Heifetz, R. A. (1994). *Leadership without easy answers.* Cambridge, MA: Belknap Press.

Katz, D., & Kahn, R. L. (1966). *The social psychology of organizations.* New York: Wiley.

March, J. G., & Olsen, J. P. (1976). *Ambiguity and choice in organizations.* Bergen, Norway: Universitetsforlaget.

March, J. G., & Simon, H. A. (1958). *Organizations.* New York: Wiley.

McCann, J. E., & Selsky, J. (1984). Hyperturbulence and the emergence of type 5 environments. *The Academy of Management Review, 9,* 460–470.

Merton, R. K. (1968). *Social theory and social structure.* New York: Free Press.

Poole, M. S., & Van de Ven, A. H. (2004). *Handbook of organizational change and innovation.* Oxford, UK: Oxford University Press.

Ring, P. S., & Van de Ven, A. H. (1994). *Academy of Management Review: Developmental processes of cooperative interorganizational relationships.* Briarcliff Manor, NY: Academy of Management.

Schneider, M., & Somers, M. (2006). Organizations as complex adaptive systems: Implications of complexity theory for leadership research. *Leadership Quarterly, 17,* 351–365.

Schön, D. A. (1971). *Beyond the stable state.* New York: W. W. Norton.

Senge, P. M. (1990). *The fifth discipline: The art and practice of the learning organization.* New York: Doubleday/Currency.

Tetenbaum, T. J. (1998). Shifting paradigms: From Newton to chaos. *Organizational Dynamics, 26*(4), 21–32.

Van de Ven, A. H., & Poole, M. S. (1995). Explaining development and change in organizations. *Academy of Management Review, 20,* 510–540.

Wheatley, M. J. (1992). *Leadership and the new science: Learning about organization from an orderly universe.* San Francisco: Berrett-Koehler.

Yukl, G. A. (2006). *Leadership in organizations* (6th ed.). Upper Saddle River, NJ: Pearson/Prentice Hall.

Zohar, A., & Morgan, G. (1996). Refining our understanding of hypercompetition and hyperturbulence. *Organization Science, 7,* 460–464.

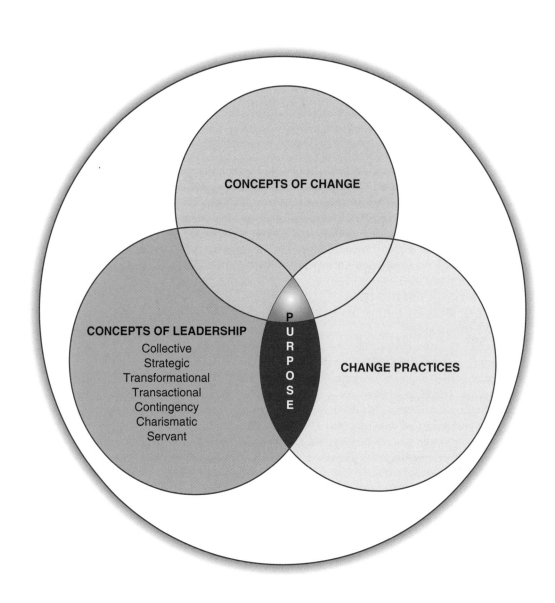

CHAPTER 3

Concepts of Leadership in Organizational Change

What Type of Leadership Do We Want or Need to Accomplish Change?

Complex organizational settings make it difficult to create a framework for leading change that links only one leadership concept to one theory of change. Organizational members in complex settings will need to use a compilation of leadership concepts and theories to adapt and change the organization in accordance with their environment. As a result, the more pertinent question may be, what compilation of leadership concepts do we need to bring about the type of change we want? The leadership theories and concepts in this section represent potential components of an overall leadership approach to bring about organizational change and encompass multiple levels of analysis, ranging from interaction between the organization and its external environment to project teams.

Collective/Collaborative Leadership

Reliance on the collective or collaborative capabilities of organizational members and teams provides a logical means for leading change in turbulent or dynamic environments. Still, leader-focused theories and authority structures, combined with a shortage of models and experience, make it difficult to benefit fully from the collective capabilities of groups or organizational members in a Western context. Effective use of collective capabilities relies on adaptive work, cultural proficiency, organizational learning, and a willingness to experiment.

Allen and colleagues (1998) pointed out that this form of leadership has been given different names: collective, collaborative, shared, participatory, cooperative, democratic, fluid, inclusive, roving, distributed, relational, and postheroic (p. 46).

Although there is no consensus on the name, the underlying premise of leadership in complex organizations is that "answers are to be found in community" in group-centered organizations where "everyone can learn continually" (Allen et al., 1998, p. 47). *Collective* or *collaborative leadership* in this text refers to leadership that uses the talents and resources of all members, not simply a single leader or executive team, to bring about change or generate creative and adaptive solutions in 21st century environments. As a result, followers are being transformed into partners, coleaders, lifelong learners, and collaborators, and adaptive leaders are undertaking new roles as creators and sustainers of contexts that allow people to lead themselves (Allen et al., 1998; Chaleff, 1995; Kouzes & Posner, 2002; Manz & Sims, 1993).

Tapscott and Williams (2006) indicated that companies have entered a new era of collaboration and innovation they call Wikinomics. Like the Internet encyclopedia Wikipedia, collaboration in this new era invites the broadest possible participation from individuals inside and outside an organization. The authors describe Wikinomics as "deep changes in the structure and modus operandi of the corporation and our economy, based on new competitive principles such as openness, peering, sharing, and acting globally" (Tapscott & Williams, 2006, p. 3). The concept of openness in this context goes beyond traditional ideas of access, flexibility, or engagement to porous boundaries that allow numerous external and internal participants to engage in innovation, research and development, problem solving, and the creation of new products and services. Peering describes a process that takes place when mass collaboration occurs among large numbers of people and corporations or other organizations to drive innovation, growth, and development. Sharing entails creating value for the organization by providing access to some (but not all) of its intellectual property, computing power, scientific knowledge, and other resources. This process allows organizations to expand markets and create new opportunities. Finally, acting globally means organizations work, innovate, and design across physical and geographical boundaries, tapping into a global talent pool and creating an ecosystem for designing, producing, and delivering products or services worldwide.

Overall, Tapscott and Williams (2006) predicted a new era of collaboration, described as follows:

> We will harness human skill, ingenuity, and intelligence more efficiently and effectively than anything we have witnessed previously. Sounds like a tall order. But the collective knowledge, capability, and resources embodied within broad horizontal networks of participants can be mobilized to accomplish much more than one firm acting alone. . . . the ability to integrate the talents of dispersed individuals and organizations is becoming *the* defining competency for managers and firms. And in the years to come, this new mode of peer production will displace traditional corporation hierarchies as the key engine of wealth creation in the economy. (p. 18, italics in original)

Though Tapscott and Williams described this new form of collaboration in a business context, all forms of organizations—nonprofit, government, and virtual—are a part of the collaborative phenomenon.

Shared Leadership

Shared leadership is "a dynamic, interactive influence process among individuals in groups in which the objective is to lead one another to the achievement of group or organizational goals or both" (Pearce & Conger, 2003, p. 1). The process involves peer or lateral influence and can involve upward or downward hierarchical influence. It differs from traditional leadership in that shared leadership is broadly distributed among a set of individuals where the influence process involves more than downward influence on members of the organization.

Robert Kelley (1988, 1992) emphasized that both leaders and followers engage in leadership. Their work is interdependent, fosters the same leadership ends, and engages participants in the change process as coleaders. Kelley (1988) indicated that leadership and followership are "equal but different" roles (p. 146). Roles structure behavior and determine the "part" that members take in groups or organizations (Forsyth, 2006, pp. 11–12). Even so, these roles are not fixed because members can move in and out of different roles within or between various groups. Kelley (1998) described the roles in leadership as follows:

Effective followership—"People who are effective in the follower role have the vision to see both the forest and the trees, the social capacity to work well with others, the strength of character to flourish without heroic status, the moral and psychological balance to pursue personal and corporate [i.e., organizational] goals at no cost to either, and, above all, the desire to participate in a team effort for the accomplishment of some greater common purpose."

Effective leadership—"People who are effective in the leader role have the vision to set corporate [i.e., organizational] goals and strategies, the interpersonal skills to achieve consensus, the verbal capacity to communicate enthusiasm to large and diverse groups of individuals, the organizational talent to coordinate disparate efforts, and above all, the desire to lead. (p. 147)

Kelley (1988) described effective followers as "well-balanced and responsible adults who can succeed without strong leadership, adding:

[They are critical thinkers who] carry out their duties and assignments with energy and assertiveness . . . manage themselves well . . . [sustain commitment] to the organization and to a purpose, principle, or person outside themselves . . . build their competence and focus their efforts for maximum impact . . . [and] are courageous, honest, and credible. (pp. 143–144)

Schneider and Somers (2006) described a similar leadership role they identify as tags: "As tags are associated with action and outcomes, not necessarily with individuals or positions, one might co-function as leader, sharing the role in tandem" (p. 356). Tags exercise considerable influence, which moves others to action through their facilitation of cooperation, interaction, and resonance among agents involved in change or adaptation processes.

Because many leadership theories and concepts mainly focus on "the leader," it is difficult at times for members of organizations to visualize and develop roles for followership that maximize their contributions to leading change. The importance of both exemplary leadership and followership is most visible in project teams, described later in this chapter. Roles in project teams are relatively fluid and often allow the same person to serve as team leader and team member at different points in time. Kelley (1988) emphasized that preparation for effective followership in organizations requires the same conscious and deliberate efforts as preparation for effective leadership. He urged members of organizations to develop training programs and other opportunities to develop capabilities in both functions.

The assumption described earlier—that concepts and practices of leading change can apply to multiple participants (leaders and followers), in various roles, and at different levels inside and outside the organization—stems from concepts of leadership and followership roles in Kelley (1988, 1992) and later work by Schneider and Somers (2006) on the concept of a complex adaptive system. Accordingly, these different but equal roles apply to each type of change—life-cycle, teleological, dialectical (including chaos and complexity theory), and evolutionary change.

Adaptive Leadership

The term *adaptive leadership* is appearing with more frequency in literature on organizational change, particularly in relation to chaos and complexity theory. Scholars began to infer the components and processes of adaptive leadership as they described the requirements for organizational adaptability in response to turbulent environments. On the basis of these descriptions, it is probable that adaptive leadership generates and sustains a context where people develop and use their capacity to pursue new opportunities, meet unknown conditions or threats, and solve problems that emerge from a complex, dynamic environment. This form of leadership may require the adaptive behaviors shown in Figure 3.1, among others: setting the context, encouraging organizational members to function as tags, establishing ethical standards, engaging in adaptive work, developing cultural competency, and creating adaptive capability.

Setting the context entails creating an organizational climate or context for change and designing the learning experiences for participants in the process (Schneider & Somers, 2006, p. 356; Wheatley, 1992). Such climates should encourage organizational members to function as tags. Like Kelley's (1988) description of effective or exemplary followers, tags lead with or without authority, often in a temporary capacity, to influence people and the processes of meaning making, cooperation, and action taking (Schneider & Somers, 2006, p. 356).

One of the most important functions of formal and informal leadership involves establishing ethical standards of behavior for all organizational activities, including change. Al Gini (2004) indicated that as a communal exercise ethics is the attempt to work out the rights and obligations one has and shares with others (p. 28). Ethics requires people involved in organizational leadership and change to take into account the impact of their actions on others. The guiding question for setting ethical standards and making ethical decisions is, what ought to be done in regard to the others we work with and serve? (Gini, 2004, p. 40). Ethics is about the assessment and evaluation of *values*, defined as ideas and beliefs that influence and direct people's choices and actions. Values can form the centering mechanism and moral compass for organizations in dynamic environments.

FIGURE 3.1   Adaptive Leadership

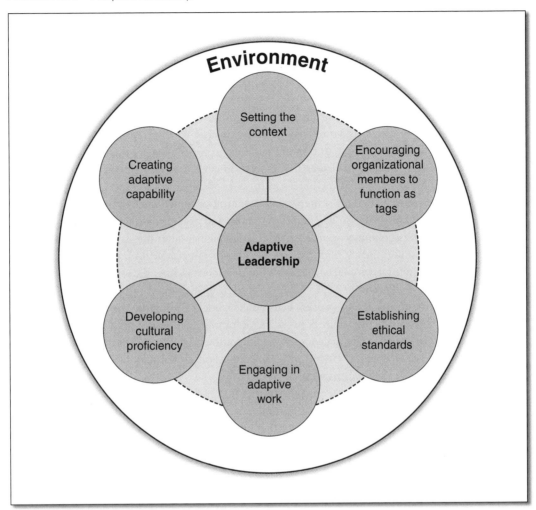

Application of ethical standards and values in the process of leading change requires organizational members to engage in adaptive work. Ronald Heifetz (1994) described adaptive work as "the learning required to address conflicts in the values people hold, or to diminish the gap between the values people stand for and the reality they face" (p. 22). The role of leadership in adaptive work is to orchestrate the conflict among competing value perspectives and hold people to the hard work of solving these problems together (p. 23).

Often, competing value perspectives originate from cultural differences among members and other stakeholders of the organization. Organizations where stakeholders bring a variety of differences—culture, age, gender, geographical origins, race, physical and sensory abilities, ethnicity, learning styles, class, language, occupations, affiliations (political, religious, and social), preferences, educational background, and others—provide expanded opportunities for their members to imagine new possibilities, do things differently, and develop more innovative and adaptive responses in dynamic and turbulent environments (Glover, Rainwater,

Jones, & Friedman, 2002). A major function of adaptive leadership is to develop organizational contexts that intentionally attract, learn from, explore, struggle with, and experiment with different ideas, perspectives, and cultures embedded in diverse environments. Heifetz's (1994) concept of adaptive work, combined with a shared commitment among diverse members to advance the organization's well-being, can enhance the capacity of organizational members to lead change in a complex adaptive system.

Adaptive leadership in diverse environments requires organizational members to develop cultural proficiency, defined as a change in perspective or "way of being" that enables people to respond to an environment shaped by diversity and allows them to deal with issues that emerge in such environments (Lindsey, Robins, & Terrell, 2003, p. 5). Acquiring cultural proficiency is a component of continuous learning that changes the way an organization functions by institutionalizing cultural knowledge in its policies, practices, and organizational culture. This adaptive work is no longer seen as external or supplemental to the "real" work of the organization (Lindsey et al., 2003, p. 117) but as imperative for its thriving.

Cultural proficiency also includes understanding the organization's culture. Glover, Rainwater et al. (2002) warned against dismantling an organization's culture in the change process before fully understanding the meaning, content, and function that the culture provides. Culturally proficient individuals in leader roles who demonstrate their understanding of the organization's culture and respect for the people who cherish it increase the likelihood that members will respond positively to adaptive changes.

Creating adaptive capacity means that members of the organization are prepared to create and recreate fundamentally new structures and assume the new behaviors and responsibilities that accompany them (Glover, Friedman, & Jones, 2002, p. 21). Decisions about these and other substantive forms of change depend on the capability of organizational members to monitor the external environment—an ongoing process of scanning and interpreting events along with collecting and analyzing information about opportunities, threats, and trends that may affect the organization. Adaptive capacity requires people in direct contact with customers and other stakeholders of the organization to engage in monitoring and disseminating information about the external environment (Yukl & Lepsinger, 2004, p. 100). An organization's adaptive capacity can be constrained by limiting external monitoring solely to individuals in senior leadership roles.

The Technology Solutions case presented in the Introduction to Part II illustrated several elements of adaptive leadership. The company president created an organizational climate and culture that embraced change by encouraging employees to learn and pursue knowledge, stay current in their field, be creative and develop the most innovative ideas possible, solve problems together, and share information. Employees said that the nature of the information-technology business forced them to be creative and use innovative thinking. However, change at Technology Solutions may have focused somewhat narrowly on technological innovation and creativity, while leaving adaptive leadership of the overall company to the traditional realm of senior leadership.

Adaptive leadership requires increasingly more reliance on the collective or collaborative capabilities of organizational members to engage in monitoring the external environment, broadly disseminating information, and generating new structures, behaviors, services, and products. The use of collective capabilities in the Technology Solutions case was not explicit with regard to external monitoring and other organization-level functions. Even so, comments from employees about the degree of autonomy in their work and about their innovation, collaboration, and mutual problem solving are strong indicators of the potential for greater collective involvement at the organization level.

Tao Leadership

The concepts of collective or collaborative leadership are not new. In the *Tao of Leadership,* Heider and Dao de Jing (1985) drew on the ancient wisdom of Lao Tzu's teachings from the *Tao Te Ching* (Lao Tsu, Feng, & English, 1972), or the *Book of the Way and Virtue* (there are a number of ways to translate the title), to provide insight for leading in a collective manner. Three examples from his writings illustrate the leader and group roles in collective work, the mindset and introspection that facilitate collective work, and the leadership processes that promote collective work.

In the first example from the chapter "Beyond Techniques," Lao Tzu described the interconnectedness of leader and group roles:

> The group members need the leader for guidance and facilitation. The leader needs people to work with, people to serve. If both do not recognize the mutual need to love and respect one another, each misses the point. They miss the creativity of the student-teacher polarity. They do not see how things happen. (Heider, 1985, p. 53)

In the second example, Lao Tzu focused on the mind-set and introspection that facilitate collective work. He posed several compelling questions in his teachings on unbiased leadership to guide the work of individuals in leader roles:

> Can you mediate emotional issues without taking sides or picking favorites?
>
> Can you breathe freely and remain relaxed even in the presence of passionate fears and desires?
>
> Are your own conflicts clarified? Is your own house clean?
>
> Can you be gentle with all factions and lead the group without dominating?
>
> Can you remain open and receptive, no matter what issues arise?
>
> Can you know what is emerging, yet keep your peace while others discover for themselves?
>
> Learn to lead in a nourishing manner.
>
> Learn to lead without being possessive.
>
> Learn to be helpful without taking the credit.
>
> Learn to lead without coercion.
>
> You can do this if you remain unbiased, clear, and down-to-earth. (Heider, 1985, p. 19)

In the third example from the chapter "Being a Midwife," Lao Tzu explained the leadership processes that support collective work:

> The wise leader does not intervene unnecessarily. The leader's presence is felt, but often the group runs itself. . . . Imagine that you are a midwife; you are assisting at someone else's birth. Do good without show or fuss. Facilitate what is happening rather than what you think ought to be happening. If you must take the lead, lead so that the mother is helped, yet still free and in charge. When the baby is born, the mother will rightly say: "We did it ourselves!" (Heider, 1985, p. 33)

Current leadership structures, such as self-directed work teams, team leadership, and leader as coach, mentor, or trainer, use collective capacity to enhance the organization and its members. The following story of Johnsonville Sausage Company provides a prime example of how an Eastern-oriented, collective leadership philosophy translates in a Western business environment.

Ralph Stayer, former chief executive officer (CEO) of Johnsonville Foods, became dissatisfied with the traditional hierarchical leadership model that he established at Johnsonville Sausage Company, even though the company was successful by all standard business indicators (Belasco & Stayer, 1993; Peters & Video Publishing House, 1988). Stayer discovered that Johnsonville could not become the exemplary organization he envisioned because his form of leadership did not allow company members to use their intellect, talents, and abilities fully. Instead, employees waited for him, the leader, to tell them what to do and when to do it. After engaging in mindful questioning and introspection (similar to Lao Tzu's unbiased leadership), Stayer realized that he, not his employees, was the problem. He began to restructure the company using a leadership philosophy that mirrored Lao Tzu's teachings in "Being a Midwife." Stayer's new thinking changed the leader-member roles and distribution of power in the company as follows:

- Leaders transfer ownership for work to those who execute the work.
- Leaders create the environment for ownership where each person wants to be responsible.
- Leaders coach the development of personal capabilities.
- Leaders learn fast themselves and encourage others also to learn quickly. (Belasco & Stayer, 1993, p. 19)

Stayer brought in instructors to teach team members the functions previously performed by middle managers and changed the role of middle manager from boss to coach, mentor, and teacher. In a company of sausage workers, not technology specialists, he restructured the organization into self-directed work teams that made their own decisions; hired, evaluated, and fired their own team members; set their team's schedules; managed their own budget; and rotated team leader and team member roles. Like Lao Tzu's analogy in "Being a Midwife," members of Johnsonville could truly say, "We did it ourselves."

Anyone in the company could propose new ideas or business ventures. In his video *The Leadership Alliance*, Peters (Peters & Video Publishing House, 1988) told the story of how Ralph Stayer's administrative assistant came to him with a business startup idea for a Johnsonville sausage catalog business. Stayer replied, "Fine with me," and the administrative assistant started a successful new business for the company.

Johnsonville Sausage Company became a learning organization with incentive and reward structures tied to learning. This was no easy transition. One former middle manager, now coach, commented, "We thought Ralph was losing it" (Peters & Video Publishing Company, 1988). Over time, members of the organization, including Stayer, continued to learn and use collective or collaborative leadership to develop their capabilities and the innovative and adaptive capacity of Johnsonville. The company remains a successful and thriving business.

Ubuntu **Leadership**

The philosophy of ubuntu leadership comes from traditional African concepts of leadership and life as a collective function. *Ubuntu* means "a person can only be a person through others" (Mikgoro, 1998). It exists only in the interaction between people in groups and functions to sustain humanity and dignity. Ubuntu embodies the belief that an individual's most effective behavior occurs when he or she is working toward the common good of the group. The indigenous concept of ubuntu is being restored and infused into education, law, business, nonprofit organizations, and government in South Africa.

In organizations, leaders and members must integrate ubuntu into their processes, structure, policies, and practices to benefit from this philosophy. Organizational change occurs through interactive forums, collective value creation and clarification, self-accountability for decisions and actions consistent with group values, accountability to each other, and community problem solving (Boon, 1996, pp. 88–124).

According to Boon (1996), critical organizational discussions take place in interactive forums where members of all departments, sections, or teams work collectively to create the values that will govern the organization. The forums occur regularly and serve to build trust and meaningful relationships among participants. Members identify and develop consensus on the core values and work to narrow the gray areas in a manner similar to adaptive work. Participants consider the openness, interaction, and integrity of the process as important as the outcome.

The group's value consensus provides a basis for members to exercise self-accountability and accountability to each other. Members of the organization also handle serious matters, such as a lack of accountability or a values conflict, as a community rather than through a single leader. If it is impossible or impractical to hold an interactive forum, individuals can choose to have a group of elected elders act on their behalf to resolve the problem (Boon, 1996, pp. 117–118). Elders must examine each situation in relation to core values. They are accountable to their colleagues and can take any action they deem appropriate. Ultimately, the use of ubuntu in organizations results in a collective process of leadership and change that holds all members of the group responsible and accountable.

Invisible Leadership

Sorenson and Hickman's (2002) concept of invisible leadership proposes a collective form of leadership that can spur teleological, dialectical, and chaos/complexity forms of change and may be useful in the startup, growth (adolescence), or revitalization phases of life-cycle change. Invisible leadership "occurs when individuals, without regard for recognition or visibility, are motivated to take action by a passionate commitment to achieve a common purpose that is greater than the [group] members' individual self-interest and, in certain cases, even greater than the group's overall self-interest" (Hickman, 2004, p. 751). Sorenson and Hickman used the term *charisma of purpose* to refer to the dedication to a powerful purpose as the motivating force for people to take action and even give up personal needs or safety.

The researchers identify several interconnected components of invisible leadership:

- A compelling common purpose that draws people who have deep commitment to its intent. (This purpose does not appear magically but forms as the result of a cumulative set of events or ideas.)
- Individuals who are driven by their passionate commitment and ownership of the purpose and a willingness to take the necessary action to achieve it.
- An opportunity (event) or resource (human or intellectual capital) that makes collective action toward the purpose possible.
- The self-agency to act on behalf of the common purpose even in the face of sacrifice or fear.
- A readiness to use individual strengths in leader or follower roles with or without visible recognition.
- The willingness to rise above self-interest, when necessary, for the sake of the group's common purpose. (Hickman, 2004, p. 751)

Sorenson and Hickman (2002) cited the example of the Orpheus Chamber Orchestra as one illustration of invisible leadership at work in an organizational setting. The Orpheus Chamber Orchestra is a conductorless ensemble founded on the belief that musicians can create extraordinary music when an orchestra uses the full talents and creativity of every member (Seifter, Orpheus Chamber Orchestra, & Economy, 2001). Instead of a traditional conductor, the musicians use a democratic leadership process in which leader and follower roles are fluid and rotating, permitting members of the ensemble to share equally in the group's leadership. All the while, the group's leadership remains invisible to the public. The driving force of the orchestra is its common purpose:

> Above all, Orpheus Chamber Orchestra is marked by our passionate dedication to our mission. That passion drives every musical and business decision that we make. Our organization's mission isn't imposed from above, but is determined—and constantly refined—by the members themselves. (Seifter & Economy, 2001, p. 16)

Team and E-Leadership

Contemporary organizations accomplish a great deal of their work, including leading change, in teams, a phenomenon known as team leadership. Forsyth (2006) indicated that teams have several basic qualities:

- *Interaction*: Teams create, organize, and sustain group behavior. Teams focus primarily on task-oriented activity, because they are based in workplaces, and their members are paid to address work-related concerns. Teams also promote relationship-sustaining interactions.
- *Interdependence*: Team members' interactions are cooperative and coordinated. Members work together, combining their individual inputs in a deliberate way.
- *Structure*: Teams are structured groups. Group norms, members' specific roles in the group, and communication patterns are often explicitly stated.
- *Goals*: Teams are goal oriented. Teammates' interdependence is based on the coordination of actions in pursuit of a common goal
- *Cohesiveness*: Teams are typically cohesive, particularly in the sense that their members are united in their efforts to pursue a common goal. (pp. 160–161)

Organizations have discovered that the collective or collaborative capabilities of teams typically result in more creative and productive outcomes than individual work. In fact, team effectiveness depends on the ability of team members to develop strong collaborative abilities (Hill, 2007, p. 220). The widespread use of teams in organizations is changing the concept and authority structures of leadership from leader-centered to group-centered processes (Yukl, 2006, p. 342). Like the Johnsonville Sausage Company, organizations that embrace group-centered leadership in teams transform the role of leader to consultant, teacher, coach, and facilitator because task, decision-making, control, and other functions are shared in the group. Group-centered leadership is not the model used in all cases. There are a number of reasons why some organizations and teams use a leader-centered rather than team-centered approach: The leader resists sharing control, lacks trust and confidence in the capabilities of group members, lacks adequate interpersonal skills to deal with emotional or relational issues among team members, fears appearing weak or incompetent, or encounters obstacles and constraints, including temporary teams with short timeframes, traditional rituals or procedures, and legal requirements in charters and bylaws (Yukl, 2006, pp. 342–343).

Teams lead change as part of an organizational initiative or a team-generated initiative, or both, in alignment with organizational vision, mission, and values. In complex organizational settings, leading change in teams requires that organizations consistently develop adaptive capacity (as described earlier) throughout all their teams so that they can act individually and collectively to meet the challenges and opportunities of a dynamic external environment.

An underlying assumption of most mid- to late 20th leadership theories is that leadership and change will occur in face-to-face (FTF) situations. In reality, organizational members use technology to varying degrees in their leadership interactions, a phenomenon known as e-leadership. Avolio and Kahai (2003) pointed out that "e-leadership takes place in a context where work is mediated by information technology," and, as a result, leader-follower communication and information collection and dissemination take place through this medium (p. 326). *E-leadership* is defined as "a social influence process mediated by AIT [advanced information technology] to produce a change in attitudes, feelings, thinking, behavior, and/or performance with individuals, groups, and/or organizations" (Avolio, Kahai, & Dodge, 2000, p. 617).

Much of the research on e-leadership focuses on virtual teams. Virtual teams are geographically dispersed, often across time zones or countries, and may bring together members with diverse expertise, capabilities, and cultural backgrounds from one or more organizations or sections to work toward a common goal. Virtual or e-leadership facilitates collaborative work that generally would not be feasible or cost effective without information technology. Does leadership by means of information technology create a new form or concept of leadership? The answer is possibly.

A small body of emerging research seems to indicate that e-leadership, by necessity, relies on the collective capabilities of team members to varying degrees and requires team members to be reasonably self-directed. Avolio and Kahai (2003) provided insights from various contributors to a special issue of *Organizational Dynamics* about the impact of a virtual medium and context on leadership. Several factors suggested by the contributors point to the possibility that e-leadership may have components that are unique to virtual versus FTF concepts of leadership:

- Virtual team leadership is expressed through the interplay of team members and technology and is not under the control of any one person.
- E-leadership requires virtual team leaders and members to project some level of "telepresence." This means that they must use the technology to convey a sense of themselves and a sense of "being there" to members of the team. At the same time, certain technology often removes the influence that identifiable characteristics, such as age, ethnicity or race, physical appearance and abilities, and gender, may have on leaders and members.
- If "information is power," then e-leadership alters the power dynamics in the leader-follower or leader-team member relationship. E-leadership alters the patterns of how information is acquired, stored, interpreted, and disseminated, which broadens access to information and changes what people know, how people are influenced and by whom, and how decisions are made in organizations.
- There are certain leader behaviors that are likely to enhance a virtual team's ability to function together: virtual collaborative skills, virtual socialization skills, and virtual communication.
- The software employed by virtual groups, such as groupware (software that helps members of groups or teams in different locations to work collectively), can potentially take on roles in teams, including leadership roles. (Avolio & Kahai, 2003, pp. 327, 332–336)

Stace, Holtham, and Courtney (2001) reported similar findings in their preliminary field research on e-change and concluded, "It is unarguable that the technologies of the E-revolution have led to a greater democratization of the workplace" (p. 412). They acknowledge that multichannel corporations (called bricks and clicks companies because they conduct business using physical and electronic sites or channels) are more likely to use directive-change processes mixed with some consultative processes (p. 412). The researchers predict that over time, multichannel corporations will move increasingly toward consultative-change processes due to the expectations, education, and skills of younger generation workers, who look for involvement as a precondition of organizational membership. They view the e-revolution as a movement that "appears to be pushing the boundaries of change *upward* to more collaborative and consultative approaches and *outward* to more transformative modes of change" (p. 414).

Prospects for Collective or Collaborative Leadership

The emergent concepts of collective or collaborative leadership require considerably more theory building, research, and insight from praxis. Adaptive leadership may help organizations learn and benefit from the embedded conflict in dialectical change and complexity that challenge previous ways of thinking, interacting, and organizing. The development of adaptive, invisible, team, and virtual leadership concepts and of modified forms of Tao and Ubuntu leadership holds considerable promise for advancing chaos, complexity, dialectical, and teleological change.

An increasing number of research studies provide insight into collective leadership as an organization-wide phenomenon. For example, Denis, Lamothe, and Langley (2001) drew on a study of five public health-care organizations in Canada to develop a process model of collective leadership. Their study examined strategic leadership (to be described later in this chapter) as a collective process of "executive leadership teams," rather than leadership by a single CEO. They wanted to discover how collective leadership operates to achieve deliberate change in situations where leadership roles are shared, objectives are divergent, and power is diffuse (p. 809). The researchers identified six components concerning collective leadership and change:

1. Major substantive change in pluralistic organizations is more likely to be established under unified collective leadership in which each member of a "leadership constellation" plays a distinct role and all members work together harmoniously. . . . A team assembling a variety of skills, expertise, and sources of influence and legitimacy [can achieve the type of substantive change that is not feasible for a single leader].

2. Unified collective leadership is necessary but is always fragile in a context of diffuse power and multiple objectives, where leaders rule at least partly by the consent of the led. . . . A [leadership] constellation [can] be shattered by internal rivalry . . . , dislocation from its organizational base . . . , or [lack of ability to adapt] to the needs of the environment.

3. Change in pluralistic organizations tends to occur in a cyclical manner in which opposing pressures are reconciled sequentially rather than simultaneously.

4. The effect of leaders' actions on their political positions drives cycles of change. [Leaders must consider the effect of two competing forces on their political positions—promoting the aspirations of their organization and its stakeholders (credibility enhancing) and offering concessions that support the leadership constellation and satisfy their stakeholders, while refraining from offering too many concessions (credibility draining).]

5. Despite the presence of opposing forces, four factors can contribute in different ways to the stabilization of change in a pluralistic setting: slack [sufficient resources]; social embeddedness [leaders' involvement in interconnected social networks where they have implicit knowledge of how things are done]; creative opportunism [the ability to create win-win situations for organizations in the constellation]; and time [for the change to occur], inattention [from other organizational members for a while], and [protection of the leaders'] formal position.

6. Increased pluralism [intensifies] the need for counterbalancing sources of stability, such as slack, social embeddedness, creative opportunism, and time, inattention, and formal position. . . . [In several organizations in the study,] extreme pluralism add[ed] to the difficulty of forming unified leadership constellations because no group [could] unite all sources of power, expertise, and legitimacy and still remain grounded in its own organizational base. (pp. 833–834)

Subsequent studies can build on the findings of this research to examine collective leadership as a phenomenon of the whole organization. Denis et al. (2001) acknowledged that their study focused more narrowly on leadership elites, "albeit *collective* elites"; however, they see great potential for broadening the research and practice of collective leadership to include people and processes at all levels of the organization (p. 835). In the meantime, their study provides a viable connection between organization-wide collective leadership and strategic leadership.

Strategic Leadership

Theoretical literature on strategic leadership primarily emerged from studying the roles of executive leaders and senior management teams in highly competitive and turbulent environments (Hunt, 2004, p. 40). Strategic leadership adapts and changes the patterns, aims, behaviors, and capabilities of an organization as a whole so that it thrives in an increasingly turbulent and competitive environment (Boal, 2004, pp. 1498–1499). Strategic leaders are "responsible for knowing the organization's environment, considering what it might be like in 5 or 10 years, and setting a direction for the future that everyone can believe in" (Daft & Lane, 2005, p. 510).

Strategic leadership seems most compatible with teleological and dialectical change. Participants involved in teleological change create their own goals (social construction) and reach consensus internally; however, this process often incorporates strategic analysis and goal setting due to the context of 21st century environments. In the Technology Solutions case, for example, the company president and senior managers employed strategic leadership while initiating purposeful change in direction, goals, and product innovation (teleological change). They assessed the company's strengths and weaknesses in relation to changes in the highly competitive external environment and then implemented new initiatives and strategies. The adaptive capacity of Technology Solutions was clearly challenged by changing the company's focus from in-house consulting to workforce outsourcing, forming business groups for newly targeted markets, hiring employees with expertise in new market areas, and laying off employees without capabilities in the new areas. This change in strategic direction, though difficult, allowed the company to survive rather than meet impending demise.

Strategic leadership can advance dialectical change through actions such as direct challenge to competitors through new-product innovation (e.g., Apple vs. IBM), elimination or absorption of competitors (buying or taking over other companies), or collaboration with other organizations in joint ventures. Effective use of strategic leadership during dialectical change requires that participants develop resilience, flexibility, and multiple strategies to handle outcomes (synthesis) from conflicting goals and perspectives in the external environment.

The concept of strategic leadership has gained rapid acceptance among organizational leaders and provides an engaging area of research for leadership scholars. Hunt (2004) suggested a need for more research on underlying explanatory factors in strategic leadership and more emphasis on several promising new research thrusts, including absorptive capacity—the ability to learn by recognizing, assimilating, and applying new information; adaptive capacity—strategic flexibility and the ability to change in highly competitive and erratic conditions; and managerial wisdom—the ability to perceive variation in the environment, understand social actors and their relationships, and take the right action at a critical moment (pp. 40–41).

Transformational Leadership

Transformational leadership motivates others to do more than they originally intended or thought possible (Bass & Riggio, 2006, p. 4). Leaders motivate followers "by (1) making them more aware of the importance of task outcomes; (2) inducing them to transcend their own self-interest for the sake of the organization or team; (3) activating their higher-order needs" (Yukl, 2006, p. 262). Transformational leadership components, commonly known as the four I's, inspire participants to achieve high performance levels:

- *Idealize Influence (II)*—Followers see leaders as role models they admire, respect, and trust, and, consequently, want to emulate the leader's high standards and ethical behavior;
- *Inspirational Motivation (IM)*—Leaders involve followers in envisioning an attractive future state or compelling vision; they provide meaningful, challenging work and communicate clear expectations that encourage followers' commitment to the shared vision and goals (charisma);
- *Intellectual Stimulation (IS)*—Leaders stimulate followers to be innovative and creative by questioning assumptions, reframing problems, and approaching old situations in new ways; and
- *Individualized Consideration (IC)*—Leaders provide special attention, support, and encouragement to foster growth and achievement of followers through individualized mentoring and coaching. (Bass & Riggio, 2006, pp. 6–7)

Transformational leadership is well suited for teleological and dialectical change because it stimulates the creativity, innovation, and critical thinking of followers (IS) and inspires commitment to a compelling common vision. An essential goal of transformational leadership is to encourage growth and achievement in followers (IC), often with the intent of developing followers into transformational leaders. The development component (IC) of transformational leadership increases the capabilities of followers to meet the turbulent and competitive conditions that accompany dialectical and teleological change.

Transformational leadership permeated the work environment at Technology Solutions. The charismatic president was an admired and respected role model, full of energy and inspiration and able to engage company members in fun, intellectual stimulation and meaningful work. Individual coaching and mentoring were fundamental practices throughout the company. The company president was essentially able to sustain transformational leadership during and after the economic downturn that triggered both teleological and dialectical change. Still, a third of the company members felt betrayed and alienated by the consecutive layoffs and change in vision, direction, and employee competencies to save the company.

Did the company president exhibit authentic transformational leadership during the difficult times in the company? Were there leadership concepts, decision-making processes, and actions that would have changed or reduced the alienation and feelings of betrayal among some company members? Did the company president maximize use of the collective intellect of a creative, innovative, and highly educated employee group in the decision-making and change processes (discussed further in a later section on empowerment)?

Bass and Riggio (2006) cited research conducted by Nystrom and Starbuck that found in crisis situations, such as the one Technology Solutions faced, transformational leaders convert crises into challenges by questioning assumptions, identifying opportunities, and focusing on new ways of thinking and doing things (p. 77):

> It is important for the leaders themselves to believe they face a challenging problem rather than a crisis. They are more open to ideas and suggestions from their subordinates. More effective decisions are reached as a consequence. . . . [T]hose managers who thought they were in a challenging situation were most likely to explore and incorporate subordinates' views into their own. They were most likely to integrate their subordinates' opposing opinions into their own decisions, and they indicated most often the desire to hear more arguments. (pp. 78–79)

Irving Janis's (1982) well-known study of groupthink (when groups avoid or censor pertinent ideas and information in decision making to preserve group cohesiveness) substantiates the importance of the intellectual stimulation (IS) component of transformational leadership in decision making. He examined inherent problems in cases where groupthink led to inadequate or disastrous decisions. To improve the quality of decisions, Janis advised groups to use effective decision-making techniques by generating alternative scenarios and assessing their pros and cons, limiting premature seeking of concurrence, and correcting misperceptions and biases (Forsyth, 2006, pp. 364–366).

The Technology Solutions case does not provide details concerning how the president presented the company's situation or handled decision making with organizational members, but the case raises the kinds of questions and issues that can help organizational leaders and members choose a course of action and examine possible consequences for internal and external stakeholders.

Charismatic Leadership

Charisma is an integral factor in leadership theory—most essentially in transformational leadership theory. Charisma is the inspirational motivation (IM) component of transformation leadership theory (Bass, 1985; Bass & Avolio, 1994; Bass & Riggio, 2006). Additionally, scholars study charismatic leadership as a distinct theory of leadership. They attribute charismatic leadership to individuals who, by the power of their person, have profound and extraordinary effects on their followers (Bass, 1985; Conger & Kanungo, 1988; House, 1977; Howell, 1990; Weber, 1947). It usually reflects perceptions by followers that the leader is endowed with exceptional qualities (Yukl, 2006, p. 252). Several characteristics distinguish charismatic leaders: "their vision and values, rhetorical skills, ability to build a particular kind of image in the hearts and minds of their followers, and personalized style of leadership" (Hughes, Ginnett, & Curphy, 2006, p. 412).

Critics of transformational and charismatic leadership warn against the potential dark side of these theories wherein leaders become manipulative, self-serving, or authoritarian to exploit followers and fail to entrust followers with genuine power (empowerment). In response to these criticisms, Bass and Riggio (2006) distinguished between authentic and inauthentic transformational leadership. Authentic transformational leadership is morally uplifting and stimulates colleagues and followers to view their work from new perspectives; embrace the mission and vision of the team and organization; develop the ability and potential of others; and motivate individuals to look beyond their own interests to concerns that benefit the group. In contrast, inauthentic, or unethical, leadership is exploitative, self-concerned, self-aggrandizing, and power oriented (pp. 12–14).

Charismatic leadership can activate teleological and dialectical change in organizations, especially in crisis conditions or turbulent environments. During teleological and dialectical change, the leader's charisma engenders respect, trust, and admiration from followers; inspires commitment to the organization's vision and goals; develops followers' capabilities; and encourages high levels of performance.

Servant Leadership

Servant leadership provides ongoing resources, support, and encouragement to individuals engaged in the change process. Robert Greenleaf (2002), a renowned AT&T executive, management consultant, and lecturer, believed that service to followers was the primary responsibility of leaders. Service includes nurturing, defending, and empowering followers by listening to them, learning about their needs and aspirations, and being willing to share in their pain and frustrations

(Yukl, 2006, p. 420). Greenleaf (2002) provided certain criteria for successful servant leadership as follows:

> The best test . . . is this: Do those served grow as persons? Do they, *while being served*, become healthier, wiser, freer, more autonomous, more likely themselves to become servants? *And*, what is the effect on the least privileged in society? Will they benefit or at least not be further deprived? (p. 27)

Greenleaf (2002) insisted that businesses and other institutions that establish a servant-leadership ethic of "people building" rather than "people using" ultimately thrive as organizations and benefit society. Accordingly, servant leadership can apply to organizations with inherent life-cycle stages where individuals or teams need sustained resources and support to meet the challenges of an external approval process. The people-building focus of servant leadership may help organizations prevent the decline or extinction stages of life-cycle change. It can also support participants as they modify their organization's traits, structure, or functions in keeping with evolutionary change and development in organizational structure or behavior.

Transactional Leadership

Transactional leadership "occurs when one person takes the initiative in making contact with others for the purpose of an exchange of valued things" (Burns, 1978, p. 19). Leadership occurs through a social exchange process. James MacGregor Burns pointed out that the substance of this exchange may be economic, political, or psychological in nature and each participant is aware of the power resources and attitudes of the other.

Transactional leaders use either contingent rewards (CR) or management-by-exception (MBE) to encourage higher levels of performance from followers, according to the full-range-of-leadership model (Avolio, 1999, pp. 40–41, 49). The full-range-of-leadership model expands the gamut of leadership styles by adding the two components of transactional leadership (CR and MBE) and laissez-faire (LF), or inactive leadership, behaviors to the four components of transformational leadership (detailed in a later section in this chapter). CR consists of positive exchanges where followers anticipate rewards, such as performance bonuses, more autonomy over their work, a promotion, favor with senior managers, or teleworking privileges. Regarded as less effective than managing through the use of contingent rewards, MBE is a corrective transaction wherein leaders, regardless of whether they have been passive observers or active monitors of their followers' activities, step in and take corrective action when they discover that their followers have made mistakes. LF leadership is a passive style that demonstrates a lack of involvement or transaction with followers. Research findings indicate that LF is the most ineffective form of leadership, though it can apply in situations where the leader has no stake or reason to be involved with matters between followers (Bass & Riggio, 2006, p. 208). Avolio (1999) explained that in the full-range-of-leadership model, leaders exhibit each style to some degree, but leaders with more optimal profiles seldom use LF leadership (pp. 38–39).

Transactional leadership supports life-cycle and evolutionary change when individuals or teams can readily see what they will gain in exchange for their meaningful participation or performance in the change process. It can provide incentives during life-cycle change, especially in the startup, growth, or revitalization stages. Transactional leadership is more effective generally in relatively stable or incrementally changing environments that accompany life-cycle and evolutionary change, rather than in unstable or turbulent environments (Bass & Riggio, 2006, pp. 87–89). Burns (1978) contended that this form of leadership is effective when each person in the exchange is treated with respect as a person and gains his or her desired outcome (p. 19). Burns warned that the outcome of this reciprocal transaction will not bind leaders and followers together in the long-term pursuit of a higher purpose (p. 20), specifically, because there is no strong commitment to a moral purpose.

Contingency Theories of Leadership

Contingency Theory

Contingency theory "maintains that leadership effectiveness is maximized when leaders correctly make their behaviors *contingent* on certain situational and follower characteristics" (Hughes et al., 2006, p. 361). According to Fred Fiedler (1964), contingency theory maintains that effective leadership is a good fit among three variables: the leader and followers—leader-member relations; the task—degree of task structure; and the power inherent in the position—leader position power (pp. 158–161). Although there are several prominent contingency theories that may be applicable to leading change, this section of the chapter focuses on two that seem most relevant—path-goal theory and task-relations-and-change theory.

Path-Goal Theory

The aim of leadership in path-goal theory (Evans, 1973; House & Mitchell, 1975; Vroom, 1964) is to influence the satisfaction, motivation, and performance of participants. Similar to transactional leadership, there is the promise of valued rewards (the goal) for followers who achieve the desired performance or objective. Path-goal theory adds a factor to transactional leadership given that leaders help followers find the best way (the path) to attain an objective. The theory identifies four leader behaviors for various situations:

- *Supportive leadership:* Giving consideration to the needs of participants, displaying concern for their welfare, and creating a friendly climate in the work unit. Situation: When the task is stressful, boring, tedious, or dangerous.
- *Directive leadership:* Letting participants know what they are expected to do, giving specific guidance, asking participants to follow rules and procedures, and scheduling and coordinating the work. Situation: When the task is unstructured, participants are inexperienced, and there is little formalization of rules and procedures to guide the work.

- *Participative leadership:* Consulting with participants and taking their opinions and suggestions into account. Situation: When the task is unstructured, this behavior increases role clarity.
- *Achievement-oriented leadership:* Setting challenging goals, seeking performance improvements, emphasizing excellence in performance, and showing confidence that participants will attain high standards. Situation: When the task is unstructured (i.e., complex and non-repetitive), this behavior increases self-confidence and expectation of successfully accomplishing task. (Hughes et al., 2006, pp. 378–385)

Contingency theories imply that there is one type of leadership for each situation, yet the complexity of change in contemporary organizations requires that leaders use several behaviors, often at the same time. In this environmental context, it makes sense to use the leadership behaviors in path-goal theory in an adaptable manner. Path-goal leadership may facilitate life-cycle change as participants strive to meet certain prescribed objectives (e.g., in the Food and Drug Administration approval process); teleological change as participants increase organizational viability through purposely enacted goals (e.g., Technology Solutions' new direction); and evolutionary change as participants adopt prevailing organizational and business structures or processes (e.g., moving from individual work to teamwork). Given the influx of knowledge workers and the use of teams in contemporary work settings, adaptive uses of path-goal leadership make joint endeavors between leaders and participants and participant-driven processes viable for life-cycle, teleological, and evolutionary change.

Task-Relations-and-Change Theory

The task-relations-and-change model is a three-factor taxonomy of leadership effectiveness that adds change behaviors to the traditional contingency theories. The framework provides greater adaptability of leader behaviors in complex situations and departs from the "one behavior for each situation" or mutually exclusive contingency approaches. Yukl, Gordon, and Taber (2002) used a half century of theories and research on leadership effectiveness and incorporated specific change-oriented behaviors to develop a questionnaire. Their survey results identified three meta-categories of interrelated behaviors: task behaviors—short-term planning, clarifying responsibilities and performance objectives, monitoring operations and performance; relations behaviors—supporting, developing, recognizing, consulting, and empowering; and change behaviors—external monitoring, envisioning change, encouraging innovative thinking, and taking personal risks to implement change (Yukl, Gordon, & Taber, 2002, p. 18).

Yukl et al. (2002) incorporated definitions of change behaviors, along with well-established descriptions of task and relationship behaviors:

Envisioning change: presenting an appealing description of desirable outcomes that can be achieved by the unit, describing a proposed change with great enthusiasm and conviction.

Taking risks for change: taking personal risks and making sacrifices to encourage and promote desirable change in the organization.

Encouraging innovative thinking: challenging people to question their assumptions about the work and consider better ways to do it.

External monitoring: analyzing information about events, trends, and changes in the external environment to identify threats and opportunities for the organizational unit. (p. 25)

The inclusion of change behaviors in this taxonomy facilitates connections between concepts of change and concepts of leadership. Like path-goal theory, task-relations-and-change theory may advance life-cycle, teleological, and evolutionary change. Its change component, unlike that in path-goal theory, introduces essential leadership behaviors for dealing with forces in an organization's external environment. For instance, leaders and members in the Technology Solutions case implemented intentional (teleological) change primarily in response to real threats and opportunities in the company's external environment. The president and other participants exhibited the change behaviors described in task-relations-and-change leadership to meet changing client demands, create new products and services, and stabilize the business.

Task-relations-and-change leadership can also help participants in dialectical change build adaptive capacity using leadership behaviors such as risk taking, innovative thinking, and external monitoring. These leadership behaviors may be especially useful for responding to the antithesis and synthesis components of dialectical change. While task-relations-and-change leadership addresses change behaviors, few leadership theories address explicitly the conflict elements of dialectical change.

Conclusion

The leadership component of change is a collective process in which no single form or concept of leadership will accomplish the change organizational members wish to achieve. Instead, a compilation of leadership concepts that guide action will better position organizations to deal with both external and internal requirements of change. Change that requires interaction between the organization and its external environment may require strategic, transactional, and charismatic leadership, whereas internal leadership may entail adaptive, ubuntu, team, and invisible leadership. Multiple combinations are possible in most change processes. The need for an ensemble of leadership approaches means that organizations must prepare and rely on people throughout the company, agency, or nongovernmental organization to assume leadership in the change process.

References

Allen, K. E., Bordas, J., Hickman, G. R., Matusak, L. R., Sorenson, G. J., & Whitmire, K. J. (1998). Leadership in the 21st century. In B. Kellerman (Ed.), *Rethinking leadership: Kellogg leadership studies project 1994–1997* (pp. 41–62). College Park, MD: James MacGregor Burns Academy of Leadership.

Avolio, B. J. (1999). *Full leadership development: Building the vital forces in organizations.* Thousand Oaks, CA: Sage.

Avolio, B. J., & Kahai, S. S. (2003). Adding the "e" to leadership: How it may impact your leadership. *Organizational Dynamics, 31,* 325–338.

Avolio, B. J., Kahai, S. S., & Dodge, G. E. (2000). E-leadership: Implications for theory, research, and practice. *Leadership Quarterly, 11,* 615–668.

Bass, B. M. (1985). *Leadership and performance beyond expectations.* New York: Free Press.

Bass, B. M., & Avolio, B. J. (1994). *Improving organizational effectiveness through transformational leadership.* Thousand Oaks: Sage.

Bass, B. M., & Riggio, R. E. (2006). *Transformational leadership* (2nd ed.). Mahwah, NJ: Lawrence Erlbaum.

Belasco, J. A., & Stayer, R. C. (1993). *Flight of the buffalo: Soaring to excellence, learning to let employees lead.* New York: Warner Books.

Boal, K. B. (2004). Strategic leadership. In G. R. Goethals, J. M. Burns, & G. J. Sorenson (Eds.), *Encyclopedia of leadership* (pp. 1497–1504). Thousand Oaks: Sage.

Boon, M. (1996). *The African way: The power of interactive leadership.* Cape Town, Africa: Zebra Press.

Burns, J. M. (1978). *Leadership.* New York: Harper & Row.

Chaleff, I. (1995). *The courageous follower: Standing up to and for our leaders.* San Francisco: Berrett-Koehler.

Conger, J. A., & Kanungo, R. N. (1988). *Charismatic leadership: The elusive factor in organizational effectiveness.* San Francisco: Jossey-Bass.

Daft, R. L., & Lane, P. G. (2005). *The leadership experience* (3rd ed.). Mason, OH: Thomson/South-Western.

Denis, J., Lamothe, L., & Langley, A. (2001). The dynamics of collective leadership and strategic change in pluralistic organizations. *Academy of Management Journal, 44,* 809–837.

Evans, M. G. (1973). *Extensions to a path-goal theory of motivation.* Toronto: University of Toronto.

Fiedler, F. E. (1964). A contingency model of leadership effectiveness. In L. Berkowitz (Ed.), *Advances in experimental social psychology* (pp. 149–190). New York: Academic Press.

Forsyth, D. R. (2006). *Group dynamics* (4th ed.). Belmont, CA: Thomson/Wadsworth.

Gini, A. (2004). Moral leadership and business ethics. In J. B. Ciulla (Ed.), *Ethics: The heart of leadership* (2nd ed., pp. 25–43). Westport, CT: Praeger.

Glover, J., Friedman, H., & Jones, G. (2002). Adaptive leadership: When change is not enough (Part 1). *Organization Development Journal, 20*(2), 18–38.

Glover, J., Rainwater, K., Jones, G., & Friedman, H. (2002). Adaptive leadership (Part 2): Four principles for being adaptive. *Organization Development Journal, 20*(4), 18.

Greenleaf, R. K. (2002). *Servant leadership: A journey into the nature of legitimate power and greatness.* New York: Paulist Press.

Heider, J. L., & Dao de Jing. (1985). *The Tao of leadership : Lao Tzu's* Tao Te Ching *adapted for a new age.* Atlanta, GA: Humanics New Age.

Heifetz, R. A. (1994). *Leadership without easy answers.* Cambridge, MA: Belknap Press.

Hickman, G. (2004). Invisible leadership. In G. R. Goethals, J. M. Burns, & G. J. Sorenson (Eds.), *Encyclopedia of leadership* (pp. 750–754). Thousand Oaks, CA: Sage.

Hill, S. E. K. (2007). Team leadership. In P. G. Northouse (Ed.), *Leadership: Theory and practice* (4th ed., pp. 207–236). Thousand Oaks, CA: Sage.

House, R. J. (1977). *A 1976 theory of charismatic leadership.* Toronto: Faculty of Management Studies, University of Toronto.

House, R. J., & Mitchell, T. R. (1975). *Path-goal theory of leadership.* Seattle: University of Washington.

Howell, J. M. (1990). *Charismatic leadership: A 1990 theory and seven empirical tests.* London: University of Western Ontario.

Hughes, R. L., Ginnett, R. C., & Curphy, G. J. (2006). *Leadership: Enhancing the lessons of experience* (5th ed.). Boston: McGraw-Hill/Irwin.

Hunt, J. G. (2004). What is leadership? In J. Antonakis, A. T. Cianciolo, R. J. Sternberg (Eds.), *The nature of leadership* (pp. 19–47). Thousand Oaks, CA: Sage.

Janis, I. (1982). *Groupthink* (2nd ed.). Boston: Houghton Mifflin.

Kelley, R. E. (1988). In praise of followers. *Harvard Business Review, 66*(6), 142–148.

Kelley, R. E. (1992). *The power of followership: How to create leaders people want to follow, and followers who lead themselves.* New York: Doubleday/Currency.

Kouzes, J. M., & Posner, B. Z. (2002). *The leadership challenge* (3rd ed.). San Francisco: Jossey-Bass.

Lao Tsu, Feng, G., & English, J. (1972). *Tao te Ching.* New York: Vintage Books.

Lindsey, R. B., Robins, K. N., & Terrell, R. D. (2003). *Cultural proficiency: A manual for school leaders* (2nd ed.). Thousand Oaks, CA: Corwin.

Manz, C. C., & Sims, H. P. (1993*). Business without bosses: How self-managing teams are building high-performing companies.* New York: Wiley.

Mikgoro, J. Y. (1998). *Ubuntu and the law in South Africa.* Retrieved February 9, 2009, from http://epf.ecoport.org/appendix3.html

Pearce, C. L., & Conger, J. A. (2003). All those years ago: The historical underpinnings of shared leadership. In C. L. Pearce & J. A. Conger (Eds.), *Shared leadership: Reframing the hows and whys of leadership* (pp. 1–18). Thousand Oaks, CA: Sage.

Peters, T. J., & Video Publishing House (Directors). (1988). *The leadership alliance* [Video]. Des Plaines, IL: Video Publishing House.

Schneider, M., & Somers, M. (2006). Organizations as complex adaptive systems: Implications of complexity theory for leadership research. *Leadership Quarterly, 17,* 351–365.

Seifter, H., Orpheus Chamber Orchestra, & Economy, P. (2001). *Leadership ensemble: Lessons in collaborative management from the world's only conductorless orchestra.* New York: Henry Holt.

Sorenson, G. J., & Hickman, G. R. (2002). Invisible leadership: Acting on behalf of a common purpose. In C. Cherrey & L. Matusak (Eds.), *Building leadership bridges* (pp. 7–24). College Park, MD: James MacGregor Burns Academy of Leadership.

Stace, D., Holtham, C., & Courtney, N. (2001). E-change: Charting a path towards sustainable e-strategies. *Strategic Change, 10*(7), 403–418.

Tapscott, D., & Williams, A. D. (2006). *Wikinomics: How mass collaboration changes everything.* New York: Portfolio.

Vroom, V. H. (1964). *Work and motivation.* New York: Wiley.

Weber, M. (1947). *The theory of social and economic organization.* New York: Oxford University Press.

Wheatley, M. J. (1992). *Leadership and the new science: Learning about organization from an orderly universe.* San Francisco: Berrett-Koehler.

Yukl, G. A. (2006). *Leadership in organizations* (6th ed.). Upper Saddle River, NJ: Prentice Hall.

Yukl, G., Gordon, A., & Taber, T. (2002). A hierarchical taxonomy of leadership behavior: Integrating a half century of behavior research. *Journal of Leadership and Organizational Studies, 9*(1), 15–32.

Yukl, G. A., & Lepsinger, R. (2004). *Flexible leadership: Creating value by balancing multiple challenges and choices.* San Francisco: Jossey-Bass.

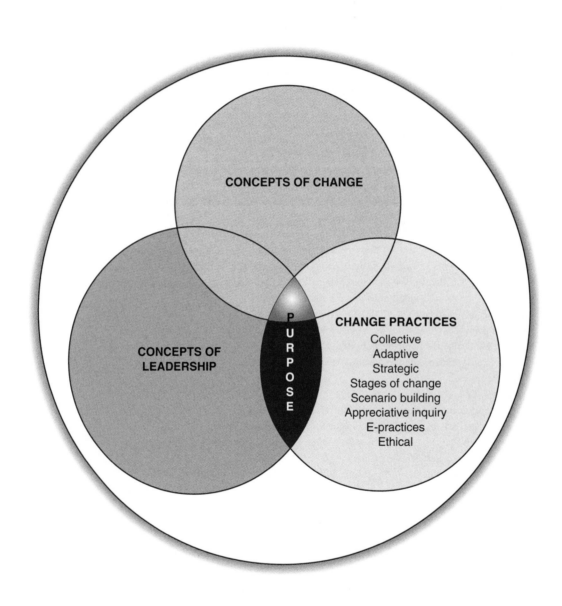

CHAPTER 4

Organizational Change Practices

Which Practices Do We Employ to Implement Change?

The focus of considerable scholarship on leading change stems from studies of change practices in organizations. Researchers strive to determine which practices generate the most effective processes and outcomes. This section highlights several categories of practice—collective or collaborative approaches, strategic planning and goal setting, stages of praxis, and ethical practices—and links them to concepts of organizational change and leadership. Additionally, several practices including environmental scanning (periodic or continuous), scenario planning, and scenario building help to address several questions raised earlier in the chapter about the environment. Which primary factors or indicators in the environment are important to organizational well-being and survival? What are the indicators? How do organizational leaders and members proceed in this environment?

Collective/Collaborative Approaches

The literature on organizational leadership and change includes a small and diffuse body of research on collective or collaborative change approaches. Included in this category are institutionalized-leadership and change practices, organizational learning, and empowerment or shared power. These practices are interrelated and mutually reinforcing, as indicated in Figure 4.1. They function to support teleological, dialectical, and chaos/complexity change in conjunction with collective concepts of leadership.

FIGURE 4.1   Collective/Collaborative Practices

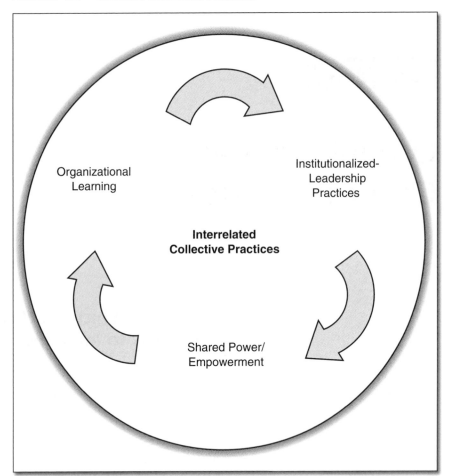

Institutionalized-Leadership and Change Practices

O'Toole (2001) and his colleagues surveyed more than 3,000 leaders at various organizational levels in 10 large companies in Asia, Europe, and North America. They also interviewed 20–40 of the individuals who completed the survey from each company. O'Toole discovered that companies with the highest collective leadership capacity used systems that used institutionalized-leadership and change practices throughout their organizations. "We found that there is something palpably different about a company that emphasizes building enabling systems versus one that depends on a single personality at the top" (O'Toole, 2001, p. 168). Similar to Kelley's (1988) description of effective or exemplary followers, O'Toole (2001) made the following discovery:

> [People throughout these companies] act more like owners and entrepreneurs than employees. . . . Take the initiative to solve problems. . . . Willingly accept

accountability for meeting commitments and [living organizational values].... Share a common philosophy and language of leadership.... [and] create, maintain, and adhere to systems and procedures designed to measure and reward . . . distributed leadership behaviors. (pp. 160–161)

Two major institutional practices when used together contributed to long-term success: coherence and agility. Coherence encompasses the common behaviors that are found throughout an organization and that are directed toward achieving the organization's goals, and agility represents the organization's institutionalized ability to detect and cope with changes in the external environment, especially when the changes are hard to predict (O'Toole, 2001, p. 167). O'Toole found that the successful companies focused on building human capacity collectively rather than relying on a small number of individuals to lead and change the organization.

O'Toole (2001) measured each organization's effectiveness using 12 leadership systems:

- *Vision and strategy:* Extent to which corporate strategy is reflected in goals and behaviors at all levels.
- *Goal setting and planning:* Extent to which challenging goals are used to drive performance.
- *Capital allocation:* Extent to which capital allocation decisions are objective and systematic.
- *Group measurement:* Extent to which actual performance is measured against established goals.
- *Risk management:* Extent to which the company measures and mitigates risk.
- *Recruiting:* Extent to which the company taps the best talent available.
- *Professional development:* Extent to which employees are challenged and developed.
- *Performance appraisal:* Extent to which individual appraisals are used to improve performance.
- *Compensation:* Extent to which financial incentives are used to drive desired behaviors.
- *Organizational structure:* Extent to which decision-making authority is delegated to lower levels.
- *Communications:* Extent to which management communicates the big picture.
- *Knowledge transfer:* Extent to which necessary information is gathered, organized, and disseminated. (p. 165)

The highest-performing companies intentionally selected specific systems to emphasize and did not attempt to focus on all of the systems. To develop collective capacity throughout the organization, leaders and members had to ensure that their professional development, performance appraisal, and compensation systems foster coherent practices. These practices ensure alignment among systems so that a compensation system for project teams, for example, includes rewards for collaborative teamwork and does not unintentionally perpetuate competitive individual performance.

Organizational Learning

Organizational learning is a process that adapts the organization and its members to change in the external environment by encouraging experimentation and innovation, continually renewing structures and practices, and using performance data to assess and further develop the organization (London & Maurer, 2004, p. 244). The Technology Solutions case in Chapter 2 shows the company's emphasis on learning and continuous self-development in its employees through sharing ideas to spark new thoughts, seeking guidance from any member of the organization, and providing access to the newest and most innovative ideas possible.

Donald Schön (1971) was one of the early scholars to recognize the need for organizational learning as a process to foster change collectively. He made the following contention:

> [Organizational participants] must become able not only to transform our institutions, in response to changing situations and requirements; we must invent and develop institutions which are "learning systems," that is to say, systems capable of bringing about their own continuous transformations. (p. 30)

Since Schön's initial work, organizational-learning systems have become an integral component of the change literature. Senge (1990) popularized organizational learning as a generative process that enhances the capacity of organizational participants to create. He stated that five essential elements must develop as an ensemble to create a fundamental learning organization:

- Personal mastery—continually clarifying and deepening personal vision, focusing energies, developing patience, and seeing reality objectively;
- Mental models—changing ingrained assumptions, generalizations, pictures and images of how the world works;
- Shared vision—unearthing shared "pictures of the future" that foster genuine commitment;
- Team learning—aligning and developing the capacity of a team to create the results its members truly desire; and
- Systems thinking—integrating all the elements by fusing them into a coherent body of theory and practice. (pp. 6–10)

Several theories and concepts of leadership incorporate learning as a part of organizational development and change. Transformational, adaptive, and task-relations-and-change leadership encourage organizational learning by similar means, including challenging people to question assumptions; take risks; be innovative and creative; reframe problems and cultivate new approaches; analyze information about events, trends, and changes in the external environment; and then pursue new opportunities, meet unknown conditions or threats, and solve problems.

According to Berson, Nemanich, Waldman, Galvin, and Keller (2006), the literature on organizational learning implies that leadership can influence learning among organizational members and foster a learning culture. Individuals in leadership roles need to develop three essential organizational characteristics to facilitate a learning culture: participation—involvement of organizational members in processes such as decision making, learning, inquiry, challenge, and the creation of greater autonomy; openness—receptiveness to diverse ideas, tolerance, and free flow of information; and psychological safety—freedom to take risks, trust, and support (pp. 580–581).

Shared Power or Empowerment

Movement toward shared power or empowerment is a logical course of action as organizations place greater reliance on the collective or collaborative capabilities of their members to innovate and respond in turbulent or dynamic environments. Shared power or empowerment entails two components: delegating or distributing leadership, authority, responsibility, and decision-making power, formally vested in senior executives, to individuals and teams throughout the organization, and equipping organization members with the resources, knowledge, and skills necessary to make good decisions (Hughes, Ginnett, & Curphy, 2006, p. 537).

Like the example of empowerment at Johnsonville Sausage Company, discussed in Chapter 3, senior executives must examine themselves to determine whether they are willing and ready to share power with employees as coleaders or partners in the process of leading change. Inauthentic attempts at empowerment can be more detrimental to organizational members than maintaining the status quo. Hughes et al. (2006) indicated that "empowered employees have latitude to make decisions, are comfortable making these decisions, believe what they do is important, and are seen as influential members of their team" (p. 539). The authors further described the following best practices for empowerment:

- having leaders in the organization decide whether the organization really wants or needs empowerment;
- creating a clear vision, goals, and accountabilities;
- developing others (through coaching, forging a partnership, developing knowledge and skills, promoting persistence, and transferring skills);
- delegating decision making to followers;
- leading by example; and
- making empowerment systemic—a strategic business practice that is reinforced in selection, performance appraisal, rewards, training, organizational structure, and so on. (pp. 539–542)

Strategic Planning

Executive leaders initiate strategic planning as a part of their overall design to adapt, change, and position the organization to thrive in a highly competitive and turbulent environment. Strategic planning generally originates from the top and involves members at various levels of the organization in certain components of the process. In business settings, companies use strategic planning to establish and sustain competitive advantage in their industry. Nonprofit and government agencies also use strategic planning to provide intentional direction to their organizations and adapt to external changes that affect their services and stakeholders.

Primary components of strategic planning include creating or updating the vision and mission, conducting an environmental scan, setting strategic direction using goals and strategies, and implementing and updating the plan. A vision, much like a compass, points an organization toward its desired end goal, or "true north." It is a realistic, credible, and appealing future for the organization that sets a clear direction; defines a more successful and desirable future; fits the organization's history, culture, and values; and reflects the aspirations and expectations of major stakeholders (Miller & Dess, 1996; Nanus, 1992; Yukl, 2006). A good vision links the present to the future, energizes people and garners commitment, gives meaning to work, and establishes a standard of excellence (Daft & Lane, 2005, p. 516). A mission is the tangible form of the vision that identifies the organization's purpose or reason for existing and identifies its uniqueness or distinctiveness (Miller & Dess, 1996, p. 9).

The vision and mission serve as a base or foundation for planning the organization's future (teleological change), whereas the strategic component involves specific positioning of the organization for competitive advantage or effective service delivery on the basis of factors outside the organization. Relying on multiple sources and multiple disciplines or inputs, leaders and members use environmental scanning to gather information about trends in the external environment:

- Stakeholder analysis—an assessment of the expectations, wants, and needs of all parties that have an interest or stake in the organization, including leaders, team members, managers, employees, customers/clients, recipients of services, and investors/shareholders, among others;
- Competitors' activities—knowledge of competitors' products, services, and methodologies through benchmarking and other information-gathering approaches;
- Demographic changes—changes in the age, ethnic composition, growth, or decline of the population;
- Social and lifestyle changes—women in the workforce, health and fitness awareness, erosion of educational standards, spread of addictive drugs, concern for the environment;
- Technological changes—advances in and use of all forms of technology;
- Economic changes—stock market indices, budget deficits, consumer-spending patterns, inflation rates, interest rates, trade deficits, unemployment rates;
- Legislative/regulatory and political changes—changes in crime laws, environmental protection laws, deregulation, antitrust enforcement, laws protecting human rights and employment; and
- Global changes—economic alliances, changes in consumer tastes and preferences, economic development, international markets, and poverty and disease rates. (Dess, Lumpkin, & Eisner, 2008, pp. 19, 44–50, 380)

The executive leadership team uses information from the environmental scan to determine the organization's opportunities and threats along with its strengths and weaknesses. On the basis of this analysis, the team identifies core competencies (capabilities that combine expertise and application skills) in the organization, evaluates whether there is a need for a major change in strategy, and identifies promising strategies along with possible outcomes of each strategy (Yukl, 2006, pp. 378–380). Frequently, a broad cadre of managers and members are invited to participate in the strategy formulation process. Strategies represent desired states of affairs that the organization wants to reach or end points toward which organizational efforts are directed (Daft & Lane, 2005, p. 526). They are the indicators of the organization's progress toward its vision, mission, and strategic direction.

Clearly, strategic leadership uses strategic-planning processes to bring about strategic change in organizations. Strategic planning is also compatible with teleological and dialectical change. As stated earlier, teleological change is constructed internally by leaders and members of the organization, yet this form of change cannot be fully effective without considering the kind of information that the environmental-scanning component of strategic planning highlights. Dialectical change can also benefit from the environmental-scanning component of strategic planning, even though strategic positioning may or may not be feasible in dialectical change.

Strategic planning is often a lengthy process in many organizations. With the increasing pace and unique patterns of change in society, organizations will need continuous scanning and highly participative processes with a broader base of members (beyond executive levels) to determine appropriate action in the short term while planning for the long term. The strategic-planning process may assume a different structure or different characteristics in a less-predictable and less-controlled environment of continuous change, experimentation, and learning. Some communication scholars and practitioners suggest that planning strategically may mean engaging in scenario planning—exploring possible outcomes of what could happen in the future and planning for those possibilities (Ströh & Jaatinen, 2001, p. 162). Scenario planning, similar to Peter Schwartz's (see Chapter 1) concept of scenario building, uses information from continuous-scanning processes to develop and plan for probable scenarios, while keeping plans flexible and adjustable.

Stages of Praxis

Kurt Lewin (1951) provided some of the earliest research on stages of praxis in organizational change. His force-field model identified three fundamental stages of change: unfreezing—the stage where organizational participants recognize that their old methods are no longer useful, often due to crises, threats, or new opportunities; changing—the phase where people seek new ways of doing things and choose new approaches; and refreezing—the stage in which leaders and participants implement the new approaches and establish them in the organizational culture (Yukl, 2006, p. 286). Lewin's earlier work provided a foundation for subsequent models (Kanter, 1983b; Kanter, Stein, & Jick, 1992; Kotter, 1996; Nadler, Shaw, & Walton, 1995) that expanded the stages, methods, and practices of organizational change. Figure 4.2 compares Lewin's three-stage model to a much later eight-stage model developed by John Kotter (1996). Kotter's model provides a fitting structure for examining praxis shared by other familiar models.

FIGURE 4.2   Stages of Praxis

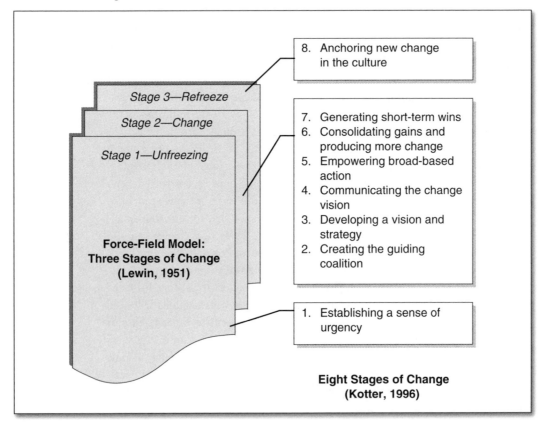

The Unfreezing Stage

The purpose of unfreezing old ways of doing things (Lewin, 1951), establishing a sense of urgency (Kanter et al., 1992; Kotter, 1996), or initiating a galvanizing event (an action or situation that requires a change response) (Kanter, 1983a, p. 22) is to draw attention to the critical need for organizational change. This sense of urgency or galvanizing event may stem from a current or impending crisis. Yet it is just as likely to come from the organization's inability to adapt—that is, the ability of its members to see and take action to address the gap between the current organization and its need to modify or change its culture, structure, behaviors, and responsibilities. According to Kotter (1996), this stage involves identifying and discussing crises, potential crises, or major opportunities that may galvanize or inspire change (p. 21). Crises include economic threats, like the situation at Technology Solutions; competitive threats; changing markets; shifting demographics; or other changes in the external or internal environment. A galvanizing event may present a crisis or entail a new opportunity, such as launching new products; developing new markets, innovations, or services; and interacting with stakeholders in new ways, such as engaging in community volunteering or environmental sustainability programs.

Both crises and opportunities can create fresh or revitalized momentum in an organization, especially when these crises or opportunities are acknowledged as authentic by members of the organization. Many people fear change and resist change efforts even in situations where a crisis or beneficial innovation is justified. There are multiple reasons why members of organizations resist change:

1. Lack of trust—distrust of the people who propose the change;

2. Belief that change is unnecessary—satisfaction with the status quo and no clear evidence of serious problems with the current way of doing things;

3. Belief that the change is not feasible—a view that the change is unlikely to succeed, too difficult, or likely to fail like some previous efforts;

4. Economic threats—fear that the change may benefit the organization but result in personal loss of income, benefits, or job security;

5. Relative high costs—concern that the cost of change may be higher than the benefits due to loss of resources already invested in the current approach or loss of performance as employees learn the new procedures and debug the new system;

6. Fear of personal failure—organizational members' reluctance to abandon known skills or expertise and their insecurity about mastering new ways of doing things;

7. Loss of status and power—fear of shifts in power for individuals or subunits that may result in loss of status in the organization;

8. Threat to values and ideals—resistance to change that appears incompatible with personal values or strongly held values embedded in the organization's culture; and

9. Resentment of interference—opposition of individuals to perceived control, manipulation, or forced change by others in situations where they have no choice or voice in the change. (Yukl, 2006, pp. 285–286)

Despite these fears, various organizations have implemented successful change processes by using the stages approach with effective forms of leadership and change.

The Changing Phase

Lewin (1951) referred to the next stage simply as the changing phase; later scholars (Kanter et al., 1992; Kotter, 1996; Nadler et al., 1995) defined several additional stages in the changing phase. Specifically, Kotter delineated six stages—creating the guiding coalition, developing a vision and strategy, communicating the change vision, empowering broad-based action, generating short-term wins, and consolidating gains and producing more change (p. 21).

Creating the guiding coalition involves putting together a group with enough power to lead the change and getting the group to work together as a team. This group could comprise the tags, described earlier as members of the organization who lead with or without authority, often in a temporary capacity, to influence people and the processes of meaning making, cooperation, and action taking. They have the kind of influence that moves others to action through their facilitation of cooperation, interaction, and resonance among individuals involved in change or adaptive processes.

Developing a vision and strategy relates to the processes described in strategic planning or creating an image of a realistic, credible, and appealing future for the organization that energizes people, inspires commitment, gives meaning to work, and establishes a standard of excellence. The guiding coalition then develops a strategy to achieve the vision.

Communicating change[1] requires that change leaders use every vehicle possible to communicate constantly the new vision and strategies to organizational members and model the behavior expected of employees. In four case studies of planned change, the researcher concluded that "creating [and communicating] vision, maintaining buy-in to mission, sense-making and feedback, establishing legitimacy, and communicating goal achievement" are essential elements for maintaining commitment to organizational change (Lewis, 2000, p. 151).

Ströh and Jaatinen (2001) suggested that single incidents of change, such as a crisis, require different approaches to communication than do continuous changes (p. 159). They caution that technical communication channels, such as newsletters, electronic and face-to-face updates, or annual reports, are good but not sufficient in organizations where continuous change is a way of life. Effective communication channels need to be consciously embedded and facilitated in the continuous change process through dialogue, relationship building, diversity of ideas, and participative decision making for change (p. 159).

The use of dialogue, discourse, or conversation is a prominent theme in the literature on communicating change (Ford & Ford, 1995; Heracleous & Barrett, 2001; Jabri, 2004; Kellett, 1999). Kellett (1999) pointed out that creating collaborative learning through dialogue is one approach to generating continuous and intentional change in organizations (p. 211). Creating dialogic conversations is an intentional process with fundamental characteristics and guidelines:

- Dialogue provides a "container" for collective thinking with dedicated time to allow the process to emerge;
- The purpose of dialogue is to create thoughtful exchange, generate mutual understanding, make assumptions explicit, and take action with regard to the issues people care about and need to discuss;
- The spirit of inquiry is essential to dialogue and involves focusing on connections, embracing diverse perspectives, and allowing shared understanding to transform us;
- The process of reflective questioning relies on our ability to listen, value others, and address deep issues; and
- A dialogue is a practical approach for developing a meaningful vision or mission statement, understanding what needs to change and how the change aligns with other factors in the organization, and understanding and negotiating conflicts expressed in the dialogue process. (Kellett, 1999, p. 212)

Another key communication role in continuous change involves building relationships within and across the organization and building transorganizational relationships to develop networks and achieve creativity, innovation, mutual problem
solving, and shared meaning. Given this emphasis on relationships between entities, one researcher remarked, "Relationships are all there is to reality and nothing
exists independent of its relationships with the environment" (McDaniel, 1997, p. 24).

Dialogue that encourages diversity of ideas is critical for continuous change in
organizations. Yet diversity brings both conflict and cooperation, "marked by the
struggle of multiple voices to be heard" (Kellett, 1999, p. 213). Dialectic communication is a process through which change occurs:

> In a change process, if there is an effective negotiation or resolution of core
> dialectics between the stakeholders, it is likely to be a collaborative change that
> is marked by a respect for difference. If, as Baxter and Montgomery say,
> "Relational well-being is marked by the capacity to achieve 'both/and' status"
> (p. 6), then "healthy" organizational change will be marked by talking through
> dialectics, or at least the respect for differences as they figure into change deci-
> sions. (p. 213)

Communication in continuous change environments is highly participatory by
necessity. Organizations must facilitate dialogue within and across groups to generate and sustain a free flow of information, diversity of ideas, high levels of cooperation, and substantive involvement in decision making.

Empowering broad-based action requires getting rid of obstacles, changing systems or structures that undermine the change vision, and encouraging risk taking
and nontraditional ideas, activities, and actions (Kotter, 1996, p. 21). Earlier in the
chapter, empowerment was described as delegating or distributing leadership,
authority, responsibility, and decision-making power and equipping organizational
members with the resources, knowledge, and skills necessary to make good decisions. Empowerment can facilitate broad-based action in the change process when
leaders and members fully endorse and incorporate it in their organizational values, culture, and practices. Organizational systems can be configured to reinforce
empowerment in selection, performance appraisal, rewards, and training processes
along with communication and work structures.

Generating short-term wins involves making change visible by recognizing,
rewarding, and celebrating achievements along the way. This includes setting and
achieving short-term goals that support the change initiative; recognizing and
rewarding people who made the wins possible; demonstrating or showcasing completed projects and new products or services; publicizing new ventures, partnerships, or collaborative work arrangements; and recognizing monthly, quarterly, or
annual accomplishments. Kotter (1996) identified three characteristics of a good
short-term win—it's visible and large numbers of people can see it for themselves,
it's unambiguous, and it's clearly related to the change effort (pp. 121–122). He
pointed out that one possible drawback to acknowledging and celebrating short-
term wins is the tendency of some people to lose momentum and motivation for

completing the larger change. As a result, recognition of intermediate successes needs to be balanced with a realistic perspective that much more remains to be done. Clear or visible gauges of the work ahead are as important as indicators of successes to date.

Consolidating gains and producing more change occur when the guiding coalition, tags, and participants in change throughout the organization learn from and use the gains at each juncture to develop expertise and experience for producing more change. Because complex organizations function through inter-dependencies—people work in cross-functional and project teams across the organization and between organizations—change in one part of the system pro-duces a kaleidoscope effect by changing all or most parts of the system. In other words, change in interconnected systems produces more change. This is a good outcome for the achievement and sustainability of the larger change, but it can be frustrating in the short run.

According to Kotter (1996), cumulative gains along the way provide increased credibility to change all systems, structures, and policies that no longer fit the trans-formation vision. Actions in this stage include hiring, promoting, and developing people who can implement the change vision and reinvigorating the process with new projects, themes, and change agents (pp. 21, 143).

Refreezing or Anchoring New Approaches in the Culture

This phase represents the last stage of change, as defined by Lewin or Kotter, respectively. Both Lewin and Kotter recognized this stage as the fitting time and place to establish or anchor new approaches and behaviors in the organizational culture (shared assumptions, beliefs, values, language, etc.). Many scholars (Deal & Kennedy, 2000; Kotter, 1996; Schein, 1992) acknowledge that culture is the most difficult element to change in an organization, and it is much more challenging to alter culture in mature organizations. Schein (1992) offered several primary and secondary ways to influence cultural change. Each of these factors reinforces the connection between new behaviors and organizational success:

- Primary ways to influence culture
  - *Attention*—the amount of attention leaders focus on certain issues or factors in the organization;
  - *Reactions to crises*—the values and assumptions expressed by leaders during crises;
  - *Role modeling*—the messages about values and expectations leaders communicate through their actions or through deliberate modeling such as coaching and teaching;
  - *Allocation of rewards*—the criteria used in the organization to allocate rewards; and
  - *Criteria for selection and dismissal*—values expressed through criteria for recruiting, selecting, promoting, and dismissing members of the organization.

- Secondary ways to influence culture

    ○ *Design of systems and procedures*—placing an emphasis on the new app-roaches or change in budgets, planning processes, reports, training programs, performance reviews, and so on;

    ○ *Design of organizational structure*—designing an organizational structure that facilitates the philosophy, working relationships or interdependencies, and flexibility needed to implement change and adapt to the environment;

    ○ *Rites and rituals of the organization*—the ritualization of certain types of behaviors can serve as a powerful reinforcer of leaders' assumptions;

    ○ *Design of facilities*—designing facilities that reflect the change in approach or philosophy such as open layouts; open access to conference rooms, dining facilities, and workout spaces; or similar offices for all members of the organization;

    ○ *Stories, legends, and myths*—transmitting stories about actual events, people, or actions that exemplify the philosophy, values, and approaches that are important for change in the culture; and

    ○ *Formal statements*—conveying the new or modified philosophy, values, and approaches in organizational publications and other appropriate venues. (Schein, 1992, pp. 230–252; Yukl, 2006, pp. 290–293)

A final factor in refreezing or anchoring new change in the culture is developing a means to ensure ongoing leadership development. If change is dependent only on individuals currently serving in formal (chief executive officer) and informal (tags) leadership roles, then change processes will likely end when these individuals leave. This statement may seem obvious; however, lack of adequate leadership develop-ment has been the downfall of many promising attempts to generate organizational change. Individual and team leadership development along with O'Toole's (2001) concept of institutionalizing leadership in the people and systems of organizations provide the greatest potential for initiating, developing, and benefiting from change.

The practices identified in the stages-of-praxis category most often apply to tele-ological (intentional and constructed change) and strategic change. These stages can also facilitate evolutionary change when organizations need to adopt new structures, organizational types, or traits. They can apply to the maturity and revi-talization phases of life-cycle change, especially as organizations face inertia or potential demise. Organizations in the maturity phase of life-cycle change have the hardest time embracing new opportunities or structures due to their entrenched organizational culture and history of success. Communicating a change strategy or vision among organizational members can foster dialectical change.

Different phases can require different forms of leadership. For example, charis-matic leadership frequently succeeds in generating a sense of urgency by inspiring a motivating vision or purpose in the hearts and minds of organizational members. In the case of invisible leadership, however, the purpose itself may be the motivat-ing factor (charisma of purpose) that drives organizational members to work toward a goal. Strategic leadership can help organizational participants shape the vision and strategies that will focus the change effort, and transactional and task-relations-and-change leadership may empower broad-based action to implement changes in behavior, work structures, or processes and generate short-term wins. Transformational leadership can operate during most stages of praxis; it may be particularly effective during the stage of consolidating gains and producing more change during the last phase involving anchoring new approaches in the culture. Coleadership or exemplary followership functions throughout the stages of praxis in a team effort to accomplish the common purpose of the change.

Scenario Building

Schwartz (1996) advocated an eight-step process of scenario building (also discussed in Chapter 1) that helps leaders and members take a long view in a world of uncertainty (p. 3). He contended that scenarios are not predictions but mechanisms to help people learn. Scenario building involves more than guessing. It requires a process that uses factual information and indicators of early trends to project alternative futures. The eighth factor, which corresponds with Willis Harman's (1998) concept of "acting with feedback" (pp. 193–194), fosters ongoing learning and flexibility as leaders and participants move toward a desired common goal. Although scenario building is a method used most often in business or organizational settings, it provides a useful means for developing informed action in other settings, including nonprofit and government agencies.

Scenario building is especially useful for teleological change and strategic leadership due to its planned, constructed approach. However, it may also be relevant to dialectical change, including chaos and complexity theory and collective or collaborative forms of leadership, because it helps organizations prepare for multiple possibilities and identify early indicators in uncertain environments. In virtual or multichannel organizations, scenario building is highly compatible with e-leadership, which uses technology such as groupware to brainstorm and generate multiple responses simultaneously.

Appreciative Inquiry

Appreciative inquiry (AI) is an organizational change practice developed by Cooperrider and Srivastva (1987). It focuses on aspects of the organizations that are working well—the positive history and stories, best organization members, and the relationships that contribute to advancement—rather than on negatives, such as distrust, resistance, and barriers to positive possibilities. AI begins with and retains the "positive principle"—hope, excitement, caring, esprit de corps, urgent purpose, joy in creating something meaningful together—to sustain momentum throughout the process (Fitzgerald, Murrell, & Miller, 2003, p. 6). The process has five essential phases:

1. Choose the positive as the focus for inquiry.

2. Inquire into stories of life-giving forces.

3. Locate themes that appear in the stories and select topics for further inquiry.

4. Create shared images for a preferred future.

5. Find innovative ways to create that future. (Seo, Putnam, & Bartunek, 2004, p. 95)

AI uses a social constructionist approach to organizational change, a teleological model that focuses on the human ability to construct new realities for the organization through an intended process of change. Cooperrider and Srivastva's (1987) AI model departs from previous change approaches because it fully supports the idea that "organizational members have the capacity to create their own future," it rejects interventionist approaches that focus on problem-solving with a heavy emphasis on positivist methods, and it employs less linear methods, such as "stories, narratives, dreams, and visions that stimulate human imagination and meaning systems" (Seo et al., 2004, p. 96).

AI has received positive attention and considerable use by practitioners. Yet there has been little academic research conducted on this method. Future researchers need to raise and examine several methodological and organizational questions regarding AI: Do the methodologies and philosophy used in AI omit significant factors from the change process? For example, does the "positive only" approach of appreciative inquiry resolve underlying problems, conflicts, and mistakes in the organization or does it inadvertently mask or ignore them? Can positivist methodologies (survey research, experiments, etc.) in combination with AI methodologies (dialogues, interviewing, imagining) add or reveal vital information for organizational change that would not be apparent or available using AI methodologies alone? How does AI compare to other theories of change and organizational development? What are the comparative outcomes of AI in relation to other organizational change approaches over time?

E-Practices

Leading change in virtual teams requires some of the same practices as those used by face-to-face (FTF) teams, as well as some different practices. In a study of effective practices in virtual teams, Lurey and Raisinghani (2001) found that these teams, like their FTF counterparts, must have a shared purpose, their members must rely on each other to perform the work, and team leaders must facilitate positive group processes, generate team-based reward systems, and select the most appropriate team members for projects or change initiatives (p. 532). Virtual teams need additional factors to be effective:

- added connectivity among team members through more structured or formal processes including clearly developed and designated roles for team members and very explicit team goals; and
- more attention to communication issues that enhance personal contact and connection among team members such as facilitating face-to-face interaction when possible and identifying and using the most appropriate technology for the people and project. (p. 532)

Respondents in Lurey and Raisinghani's (2001) study used daily e-mail, personal telephone calls, and voice mail most frequently. Other means of communication, including group-telephone and online-computer conferencing, FTF interaction, groupware, shared databases, and videoconferencing, received less frequent use. The researchers suggested that the availability and use of videoconferencing may be effective in bringing together geographically dispersed team members.

To enhance successful e-practices, Zigurs (2003) made the following recommendations for virtual team leaders:

- provide training on participation in virtual teams;
- use team-building exercises in face-to-face processes, when possible;
- provide for both task and relational roles;
- establish standards for communication of contextual cues with each message;
- use process-structuring tools but build in adaptability for individual needs;
- use frequent communication and feedback to nurture emergent leadership and self-leadership that moves the team forward;
- put special and continuous emphasis on relational development; and
- anticipate unintended consequences and debrief the team's responses and approaches to these events. (p. 348)

Virtual organizations and multichannel corporations need the capacity to innovate, change, and respond quickly to meet the needs of customers or service recipients in a round-the-clock Internet environment. Change in virtual organizations and virtual divisions of multichannel organizations entails practices that are information rich and highly collaborative. Stace, Holtham, and Courtney (2001) suggested that these organizations base their design on principles of self-management, collaborative behavioral protocols, shared strategic intent, and equitable sharing of returns (p. 417). They advised that organizations base their e-practices on time spent in productive interchange, trust developed between people, and territory, defined as psychological space and a stake in outcomes (p. 417).

On the basis of current information, e-practices seem to apply to teleological (planned, constructed) and dialectical change, including chaos and complexity theory, in multichannel and virtual organizations. They align with virtual leadership, or e-leadership, and may be fitting for other collective forms of leadership, such as adaptive, team, and invisible. Research on effective virtual or e-practices is still developing. E-change may ultimately constitute a new form of change with its own characteristics and processes.

Ethical Practices

Ethics require leaders and followers in organizations to take into account the impact of their actions in relation to others. Ethics are principles of right conduct or a system of moral values. The guiding question for ethical decisions and practices in leading change is, what ought to be done in regard to coworkers and customers (Gini, 2004, p. 28)? Gini (2004) pointed out that "ethics is primarily a communal, collective enterprise" (p. 28), which makes ethical practices especially relevant in this era of collective and collaborative approaches to leading organizational change, including adaptive, ubuntu, Tao, invisible, team, and virtual leadership.

Critical issues for ethical practices in leading change consist of authenticity, trust, and reciprocal care, among others. Authenticity entails honesty—with one's self and others, between and among organizational leaders and members, and between organizational members and other partners, collaborators, and stakeholders. Authenticity is critically important in the practice of empowerment or shared power, which is a fundamental component of collective or collaborative leadership and change. Ciulla (2004) maintained that "the obvious difference between authentic and bogus empowerment rests on the honesty of the relationship between leaders and followers" (p. 76). She warned that it is not adequate for members of an organization to "feel" empowered; they must "be" empowered to make decisions, take action, and be accountable for their efforts on behalf of the organization (p. 76).

Leaders in positions of authority have a choice to share power with members of the organization or not, but bogus empowerment is both inauthentic and ineffective in the long run. Leaders must weigh the risk in each direction. If organizational leaders choose empowerment or shared power, they need to develop the training, resources, systems, and practices that support it. Most of all, senior leaders must have enough self-knowledge and introspection to know whether they are truly capable of sharing power or whether they fear that most organizational members are unable to handle shared power appropriately, and, therefore, members' mistakes will reflect negatively on leaders. If leaders decide not to empower members, they need to develop substantial capacity within the senior executive team to lead change in a dynamic environment. They must assess the potential impact on their competitive position or service delivery in relation to similar organizations with and without shared power among their members.

Authenticity is a significant factor in developing a sense of urgency or establishing a galvanizing event in the stages-of-praxis approach. Organizational members will likely become indifferent and highly suspect of any change effort when executive leaders attempt to revitalize an organization by "creating" a scare tactic to generate a sense of urgency. Instead, organizational leaders and members must build an honest, compelling case for revitalization on the basis of information, involvement, and commitment.

Openness, or transparency, is included here under the rubric of authenticity. Openness reinforces authenticity and trust by making processes, decisions, and information open and available to members of the organization. In the Technology Solutions case, members indicated that the company's transparency practices—a "no secrets" policy, free sharing of ideas, the open-door policy among all company members, and the discussions during company meetings—contribute to an open and innovative environment. Team members at Johnsonville Sausage performed budgeting and finance, hiring and firing, scheduling, and quality control. Processes, decisions, and information in the organization were transparent, enabling members to take appropriate actions. Members were fully aware of the company's financial status and competitive position in the market, and they knew whether cost cutting, layoffs, or downsizing were necessary for the company to thrive.

Earlier in this book, I cited Tapscott and Williams (2006), who discussed the idea that openness, or the new-era transparency, goes beyond disclosure of information to internal members of the organization. It includes a vast array of external collaborators. As a result, senior leaders need to decide whether they can honestly practice openness in the organization. If they decide to implement openness in the organization's innovations, processes, decisions, and information, then they need to develop systems and practices that support transparency along with procedures that protect some (but not all) confidential and proprietary information. If leaders decide not to practice full transparency, they still need to develop an organizational culture of trust where members experience authenticity and integrity in leader-member relationships. They also will need to evaluate the potential impact on their competitive position or service delivery of maintaining a highly proprietary and confidential organization.

Trust is the foundation of a relationship between and among leaders and members of an organization. Robert Solomon (2004) contended, "*Trust* characterizes an entire network of emotions and emotional attitudes, both between individuals and within groups and by way of a psychodynamic profile of entire societies" (p. 95). He characterized trust as a social role, a reciprocal relationship, a dynamic decision that makes leadership possible, something to be given that transforms a relationship at its most basic level (pp. 95–99). Honesty builds trust so that members have confidence in a leader's word that the need for change is authentic, that power is indeed shared, and that the member has true agency to effect change in the organization, while leaders have confidence that members can lead themselves, build competence, use their shared power to advance the change initiative, and sustain commitment to the organization's purpose.

Reciprocal care develops from a relationship of trust where "every person matters and each person's welfare and dignity is the concern of us all" (Allen et al., 1998, p. 57). Leading change in a collective or collaborative context creates greater interdependence and mutual responsibility between organizational leaders and members. The leader-follower relationship shifts from a traditional dynamic, where leaders assume responsibility for members, to a shared dynamic, where leaders and members assume responsibility for each other. This relationship involves reciprocal care for the rights, treatment, diversity, and well-being of leaders and members.

Leaders and members in organizations with ethical practices establish a "healthy moral environment," where ethical behavior and expectations are explicitly stated and conscientiously practiced and where ethical practices are not inadvertently undermined by contradictory messages in the organizations' environments (Ciulla, 1995, p. 494). The ethical practices of authenticity, trust, transparency, and reciprocal care apply to leadership and change concepts in this chapter and are necessary for collective or collaborative approaches. They provide the essential underpinning for the communal, collective enterprise of ethics in the process of leading change.

Conclusion

Although there is no one approach or formula to choosing the most appropriate practices for leading change, leaders and members of companies, nonprofit organizations, and government agencies can use the guiding questions in each of the chapters on organizational change to assess and select their options. Organizational members can inspire and generate change that allows their organizations to flourish in the midst of a turbulent environment when they consider and select mutually reinforcing forms of leadership, change, and practice. Table 2.1 in the introduction provides examples of connecting components of organizational change—concepts of change, concepts of leadership, and change practices. Intentional consideration of all three components of change is more than an analytical tool, though it definitely serves that purpose. It is a means of preparing people and their organizations for new ventures into the unknown, fueled by human innovation and advanced technologies.

Note

1. I am deeply indebted to my late colleague Fredric M. Jablin for his help in identifying articles and sources for the discussion on communication in this section.

References

Allen, K. E., Bordas, J., Hickman, G. R., Matusak, L. R., Sorenson, G. J., & Whitmire, K. J. (1998). Leadership in the 21st century. In B. Kellerman (Ed.), *Rethinking leadership: Kellogg leadership studies project 1994–1997* (pp. 41–62). College Park, MD: James MacGregor Burns Academy of Leadership.

Berson, Y., Nemanich, L. A., Waldman, D. A., Galvin, B. M., & Keller, R. T. (2006). Leadership and organizational learning: A multiple levels perspective. *Leadership Quarterly, 17,* 577–594.

Ciulla, J. B. (1995). Messages from the environment: The influence of policies and practices on employee responsibility. In J. T. Wren (Ed.), *The leader's companion: Insights on leadership through the ages* (pp. 492–499). New York: Free Press.

Ciulla, J. B. (2004). *Ethics, the heart of leadership* (2nd ed.). Westport, CT: Praeger.

Cooperrider, D. L., & Srivastva, S. (1987). Appreciative inquiry in organizational life. In R. W. Woodman & W. A. Pasmore (Eds.), *Research in organizational change and development* (Vol. 1, pp. 129–169). Greenwich, CT: JAI Press.

Daft, R. L., & Lane, P. G. (2005). *The leadership experience* (3rd ed.). Mason, OH: Thomson/South-Western.

Deal, T. E., & Kennedy, A. A. (2000). *Corporate cultures: The rites and rituals of corporate life.* Cambridge, MA: Perseus Books.

Dess, G. G., Lumpkin, G. T., & Eisner, A. B. (2008). *Strategic management: Creating competitive advantages* (4th ed.). New York: McGraw-Hill/Irwin.

Fitzgerald, S. P., Murrell, K. L., & Miller, M. G. (2003). Appreciative inquiry: Accentuating the positive. *Business Strategy Review, 14*(1), 5–7.

Ford, J. D., & Ford, L. W. (1995). The role of conversations in producing intentional change in organizations. *Academy of Management Review, 20*(3), 541–570.

Gini, A. (2004). Moral leadership and business ethics. In J. B. Ciulla (Ed.), *Ethics, the heart of leadership* (2nd., pp. 25–43). Westport, CT: Praeger.

Harman, W. W. (1998). *Global mind change: The promise of the 21st century.* San Francisco: Berrett-Koehler.

Heracleous, L., & Barrett, M. (2001). Organizational change as discourse: Communicative actions and deep structures in the context of information technology implementation. *Academy of Management Journal, 44,* 755–778.

Hughes, R. L., Ginnett, R. C., & Curphy, G. J. (2006). *Leadership: Enhancing the lessons of experience* (5th ed.). Boston: McGraw-Hill.

Jabri, M. (2004). Team feedback based on dialogue: Implications for change management. *Journal of Management Development, 23*(2), 141–151.

Kanter, R. M. (1983a). *The change masters: Innovations for productivity in the American corporation.* New York: Simon & Schuster.

Kanter, R. M. (1983b). Change masters and the intricate architecture of corporate culture change. *Management Review, 72*(10), 18–28.

Kanter, R. M. S., Stein, B. A., & Jick, T. (1992). *The challenge of organizational change: How companies experience it and leaders guide it.* New York: Free Press.

Kellett, P. M. (1999). Dialogue and dialectics in managing organizational change: The case of a mission-based transformation. *Southern Communication Journal, 64*(3), 211–213.

Kelley, R. E. (1988). In praise of followers. *Harvard Business Review, 66*(6), 142–148.

Kotter, J. P. (1996). *Leading change.* Boston: Harvard Business School Press.

Lewin, K. (1951). *Field theory in social science: Selected theoretical papers.* New York: Harper.

Lewis, L. K. (2000). Communicating change: Four cases of quality programs. *Journal of Business Communication, 37*(2), 128–155.

London, M., & Maurer, T. J. (2004). Leadership development: A diagnostic model for continuous learning in dynamic organizations. In J. Antonakis, A. T. Cianciolo, & R. J. Sternberg (Eds.), *The nature of leadership* (pp. 222–245). Thousand Oaks, CA: Sage.

Lurey, J. S., & Raisinghani, M. S. (2001). An empirical study of best practices in virtual teams *Information and Management, 38,* 523–544.

McDaniel, R. R. J. (1997). Strategic leadership: A view from quantum and chaos theories. *Health Care Management Review, 22*(1), 21–37.

Miller, A., & Dess, G. G. (1996). *Strategic management* (2nd ed.). New York: McGraw-Hill.

Nadler, D.. Shaw, R. B., & Walton, A. E. (1995). *Discontinuous change: Leading organizational transformation.* San Francisco: Jossey-Bass.

Nanus, B. (1992). *Visionary leadership : Creating a compelling sense of direction for your organization.* San Francisco: Jossey-Bass.

O'Toole, J. (2001). When leadership is an organizational trait. In W. Bennis, G. M. Spreitzer, & T. G. Cummings (Eds.), *The future of leadership: Today's top leadership thinkers speak to tomorrow's leaders* (pp. 158–174). San Francisco: Jossey-Bass.

Schein, E. (1992). *Organizational culture and leadership* (2nd ed.). San Francisco: Jossey-Bass.

Schön, D. A. (1971). *Beyond the stable state.* New York: Random House.

Schwartz, P. (1996). *The art of the long view: Paths to strategic insight for yourself and your company.* New York: Currency Doubleday.

Senge, P. M. (1990). *The fifth discipline : The art and practice of the learning organization.* New York: Doubleday/Currency.

Seo, M., Putnam, L., & Bartunek, J. (2004). Dualities and tensions of planned organizational change. In M. S. Poole & A. H. Van de Ven (Eds.), *Handbook of organizational change and innovation* (pp. 73–107). New York: Oxford University Press.

Solomon, R. (2004). Ethical leadership, emotions, and trust: Beyond "charisma." In J. B. Ciulla (Ed.), *Ethics, the heart of leadership* (2nd ed., pp. 83–102). Westport, CT: Praeger.

Stace, D., Holtham, C., & Courtney, N. (2001). E-change: Charting a path towards sustainable e-strategies. *Strategic Change, 10,* 403–418.

Ströh, U., & Jaatinen, M. (2001). New approaches to communication management for transformation and change in organisations. *Journal of Communication Management, 6*(2), 148–165.

Tapscott, D., & Williams, A. D. (2006). *Wikinomics: How mass collaboration changes everything.* New York: Portfolio.

Yukl, G. A. (2006). *Leadership in organizations* (6th ed.). Upper Saddle River, NJ: Prentice-Hall.

Zigurs, I. (2003). Leadership in virtual teams: Oxymoron or opportunity? *Organizational Dynamics, 31,* 339–359.

Applications and Reflections

The applications and reflections section provides an opportunity to relate the concepts and practices of leading change in Chapters 2–4 to several real-life situations. These situations illustrate the challenges of leading change in various types of organizations, including business, religious, government, education, and nonprofit/nongovernmental organizations.

Application 1   BUSINESS

The New Rules

by Betsy Morris

Even now, nearly five years after his retirement from General Electric, Jack Welch commands the spotlight. He is still power-lunching, still making the gossip columns, still the charismatic embodiment of the star CEO. His books are automatic bestsellers. More than any other single figure, he stands as a model not just for the can-do American executive but for a way of doing business that revived the U.S. corporation in the 1980s and dominated the world's economic landscape for a quarter-century. Just try to find an executive who hasn't been influenced by his teachings. What came to be known as Jack's Rules are by now the business equivalent of holy writ, bedrock wisdom that has been open to interpretation, perhaps, but not dispute.

But the time has come: Corporate America needs a new playbook. The challenge facing U.S. business leaders is greater than ever before, yet they have less control than ever—and less job security. The volatility of the markets is so unpredictable, the pressure from hedge funds and private-equity investors so relentless, the competition from China and India so intense, that the edicts of the past are starting to feel out of date. In executive suites across the country, a dramatic rethinking is underway about fundamental assumptions that defined Welch and his era. Is an emphasis on market share really the prime directive? Is a company's near-term stock price—and the quarterly earnings per share that drive it—really the best measure of a CEO's success? In what ways is managing a company to measure of a CEO's success? In what ways is managing a company to please Wall Street bad for competitiveness in the long run?

Jack Welch, needless to say, is having none of it. When *Fortune* caught up with him recently, he was as confident and outspoken as ever. "I'm perfectly prepared to change," says Welch (who co-writes a column in *Business Week* with his wife, Suzy). "Change is great." But, he asserts, he sees no reason to back away from the principles by which he and other star CEOs like Roberto Goizueta of Coca-Cola managed. If applied correctly, Welch contends, his rules can work forever.

Sorry, Jack, but we don't buy it. The practices that brought Welch, Goizueta, and others such success were developed to battle problems specific to a time and place in history. And they worked. No one questions today that bloated bureaucracy can kill a business. No one forgets the shareholder—far from it. Yet those threats have receded. And they have been replaced by new ones. The risk we now face is applying old solutions to new problems.

(Continued)

(Continued)

Early on, Welch argued that lagging businesses—those not No. 1 or No. 2 in their markets—should be fixed, sold, or closed. In a 1981 speech titled "Growing Fast in a Slow-Growth Economy," he announced that GE would no longer tolerate low-margin and low-growth units. GE, he told analysts at the Pierre Hotel in New York, "will be the locomotive pulling the GNP, not the caboose following it." As much as any other single event, Welch's words marked the dawn of the shareholder-value movement. And GE eventually became its star. No question who was Welch's boss. His report card: the stock price. His goal: consistent earnings growth.

As his ruthlessly efficient strategy wrenched GE into high performance, the company's stock took off. Soon virtually everything Welch said became gospel—often to the extreme. When Welch embraced Six Sigma, the program began to proliferate all over corporate America. He talked about being the leanest and meanest and lowest-cost, and corporate America got out its ax. Welch advocated ranking your players and weeding out your weakest, and HR departments turned Darwinian. As time went on, the mantra of shareholder value took on a life of its own. Cheered on by academics, consulting firms and investors, more and more companies tried to defy history (and their own reality) to sustain growth and dazzle Wall Street as Welch was doing. Accounting tricks, acquisition mania, outright thievery—executives went overboard. "It became all about 'real men make their numbers,'" says one CEO. "What were we thinking?"

This, says Harvard Business School's Rakesh Khurana, is the legacy of the Old Rules. Managing to create shareholder value became managed earnings became managing quarter to quarter to please the Street. "That meant a disinvestment in the future," says Khurana, author of *Searching for a Corporate Savior.* "It was a dramatic reversal of everything that made capitalism strong and the envy of the rest of the world: the willingness of a CEO to forgo dividends and make an investment that wouldn't be realized until one or two CEOs down the road." Now, he believes, "we're at a hinge point of American capitalism."

There is another model. In breathtakingly short order, the rock star of business is no longer the guy atop the Fortune 500 (today Rex Tillerson at ExxonMobil), but the very guy those Fortune 500 types used to love to ridicule: Steve Jobs at Apple. The biggest feat of the decade is not making the elephant dance, as Lou Gerstner famously did at IBM, but inventing the iPod and transforming an industry. Dell spectacularly upended Compaq and Hewlett-Packard, yet few big companies paid close enough attention to see that new technologies and business models were negating the power of economies of scale in myriad ways. Nobody has proved that more than Google.

Yet in the corridors of corporate power, the old rules continue to cast an outsized shadow. Many CEOs are following a playbook that has, at best, been distorted by time. "How do you think about building shareholder value when a lot of people are really just going to hold the share for the moment?" says Jim Collins, a former Stanford Business School professor and the author of *Good to Great* and *Built to Last.* "The idea of maximizing shareholder value is a strange idea when [many shareholders] are really share flippers. That's a real change. That does make the notion of building a great company more difficult."

That doesn't mean everything about Welch's era is wrong. Indeed, we named him "manager of the century" in 1999. Were he at GE today, he might well be in the forefront of the current wave of rethinking, as his successor, Jeffrey Immelt, surely is. Still, in the way of all good analogies, we must begin by tearing down the old so that we can really open ourselves to something different. In that spirit, then, here are seven old rules whose shortcomings have become apparent and seven replacements that point toward a new model for success. Some of the old rules are inspired directly by Welch's teachings; others are not. You may not agree with all of our conclusions (Welch certainly didn't—see "Welch Fires Back"). We welcome the debate. What's most important is to get the discussion started.

Old rule: Big dogs own the street.

New rule: Agile is best; being big can bite you.

Until the very end of the last century, big meant good in the business world. B-schools taught the benefits of economies of scale. The greater your revenue, the more you could spread fixed costs across units sold. With size came dominance—of airwaves, store shelves, supply chains, distribution channels. Until the mid-1990s, a company's market value usually tracked its revenue.

Then strange things started to happen. Microsoft's market cap passed IBM's in 1993, even though Bill Gates' $3 billion in revenue was one-twenty-second that of IBM. Scale didn't insulate GM from near-catastrophic decline. The big dogs seemed to hit a wall. (The median Fortune 500 company is now three times the size it was in 1980, in real terms, and thus much harder to manage.) Citigroup, built through acquisitions by Sandy Weill to deliver consistent earnings, suddenly found the market focused on whatever bad news emerged in Citi's far-flung units instead of on the smoothness of its overall performance. Big Pharma used to be prized for its unmatched R&D spending; now it is the smaller biotech firms that generate the cutting-edge drugs—and drugmakers Merck, Bristol-Myers, and Eli Lilly all have smaller market caps than biotech Genentech, despite significantly higher revenue and profits.

Technological advances and changing business models have diminished the importance of scale, as outsourcing, partnering, and other alliances with specialty firms (with their own economies of scale) have made it possible to convert fixed costs into variable ones. Dell, it turned out, was not an anomaly, it was just the beginning—a pioneer at all this, keeping its costs down by outsourcing disk drives, memory chips, monitors, and more, freeing itself to focus on (and clean up in) direct selling and just-in-time assembly.

Old rule: Be no. 1 or no. 2 in your market.

New rule: Find a niche, create something new.

Nobody wants to be a laggard, of course, and there is much to be said for being the market leader. Nike, Wal-Mart and Exxon certainly don't wish they were anything else. But more and more, market domination is no safety net. Disney's stranglehold on animated films meant nothing once Pixar's digital innovation hit the scene. AOL's established user base couldn't slow down Google.

Look at Coca-Cola, whose still-strong No. 1 position in cola turned out to be not an insurance policy but proof of what consulting firm McKinsey calls the "incumbent's curse." Coke's archrivalry with Pepsi was always about market share—capturing it or defending it by tenths of a percentage point in grocery stores, restaurants, and faraway lands. Coke executives defined their industry as "share of stomach"—that is, the total ounces of liquid

(Continued)

(Continued)

an average person consumes in a day and what percentage of it can be filled with Coke. CEO Roberto Goizueta told Jack Welch in a conversation in *Fortune* a decade ago that the soft drink industry wouldn't run out of growth until "that faucet in your kitchen sink is used for what God intended"—dispensing Coke from the tap.

But eventually Coke's monomaniacal focus backfired. When bottled waters like Evian and Poland Spring began to gain traction, Coke didn't pay sufficient attention. Its board vetoed management's proposal to buy Gatorade in 2000 (sending the sports drink into the arms of Pepsi). Such niche products were viewed as low-volume distractions. Yet last year, in a turnabout that would have been inconceivable a decade ago, soda sales fell, and water, sports drinks, and energy drinks all soared. The jaw dropper: Energy drinks—which boast a profit margin of 85%, according to Bernstein Research—are now expected to outearn every other category of soft drink within three years.

Not everyone missed the opportunity. Out in Corona, California, tiny Hansen Natural Corp. didn't care about being No. 1 or No. 2. CEO Rodney Sacks was instead noticing how consumers were migrating from carbonated soft drinks to juices, iced teas, and "functional drinks." So in the 1990s he began moving Hansen beyond its base as a maker of natural sodas (Mandarin Lime, Orange Mango) toward vitamin and energy drinks. Never mind that the energy-drink market was tiny then. "We look for niches and see how they grow," he says. Since launching an energy drink called Monster four years ago (deftly packaged in a dramatic-looking 16-ounce can adorned with a clawmark), Hansen's sales have quadrupled to $348 million, vaulting its shares to $79 from a split-adjusted $2.

Coke has gotten religion. CEO Neville Isdell's team is pushing an array of new drinks, including a half dozen of its own energy entries that have earned the company a significant stake in the U.S. market. "We believe there is value in those niches," Isdell told *Fortune* this spring. "It will not drive the volume number, but volume is something we've often chased to the detriment of the long-term business."

Starbucks, on the other hand, is a drink-seller that has avoided the incumbent's trap. "We've never said we wanted to be No. 1 or No. 2," says CEO Jim Donald. Starbucks isn't a brand per se; it's more an identity that's morphed from a product (a latte) to a place to get wireless, to a place with music to meet friends. "If we said we wanted to be the No. 1 coffee company, that's what would be on our mind," Donald says. Instead, the company has kept moving, evolving, trying new things. "It doesn't matter where you end up," says Donald. "It matters that you're the company of choice."

Old rule: Shareholders rule.

New rule: The customer is king.

Whenever you ask a CEO about the importance of customers, you hear the requisite platitudes. But in fact, customers have often lost out in the relentless push to maximize shareholder value (as represented by the stock price) and to maximize it immediately. One Bain & Co. study found a huge gap between the perceptions of executives—80% of whom think they are doing an excellent job of serving customers—and the perceptions of customers themselves: Only 8% of them agree. Every four years, according to Bain, the average company loses more than half its customers. Aggressive pricing (on hotel phone bills, rental-car gas charges, and credit card fees, to name a few examples) has increased as the profit pressure on companies has mounted, says Bain's Fred Reichheld. Abusing customers this way, says Reichheld, "destroys the future of a business." He believes that such behavior—and not scandals like Enron and Tyco—is why fewer than half of all Americans have a favorable opinion of business today.

This is shareholder-value theory taken to the extreme: the tail wagging the dog. One CEO, who asked not to be named, describes the pressures this way: Businesses became disconnected from their fundamentals, producing "perceived value" instead of real value, because that's what the stock market rewards. When investor-driven capitalism took over from managerial-driven capitalism, as Harvard's Khurana puts it, CEOs began managing the company by earnings per share instead of focusing on details like new products, service calls, customer-satisfaction scores—all those things that are supposed to produce the earnings per share.

Yet some renegades thumbed their noses at Wall Street and truly kept the consumer experience front and center. Think Apple, which has from inception been predicated on dreaming up what customers want before they know it. Or look at Genentech, whose employees are greeted each day by billboards of the cancer patients who take its drugs, to remind everyone of the importance of their work. At GE, CEO Immelt has instigated what he calls "dreaming sessions" to brainstorm with key customers. He also requires all businesses to be judged using a metric called Net Promoter Score, developed by Reichheld and his colleagues at Bain, that measures how likely a customer is to have you back. "When everything is focused on delivering for customers, that makes employees proud," Reichheld says. "They become the powerful engine."

Old rule: Be lean and mean.

New rule: Look out, not in.

In 1995 Jack Welch "went nuts," as he later put it, over Six Sigma, a set of methods for improving quality—plus a powerful way to reduce costs—that had been developed by Motorola in the 1980s. At GE's annual managers' meeting in Boca Raton the following January, he told his troops that embracing Six Sigma would be the company's most ambitious undertaking ever. GE's "best and the brightest" were redeployed to put the methods into action. And it worked. Welch would later write that Six Sigma helped drive operating margins to 18.9% in 2000 from 14.8% four years earlier.

No wonder that after Welch adopted Six Sigma (to which he devotes a chapter of his book Winning), more than a quarter of the Fortune 200 followed suit. Yet not all firms were able to find the same magic. In fact, of 58 large companies that have announced Six Sigma programs, 91% have trailed the S&P 500 since, according to an analysis by Charles Holland of consulting firm Qualpro (which espouses a competing quality-improvement process).

One of the chief problems of Six Sigma, say Holland and other critics, is that it is narrowly designed to fix an existing process, allowing little room for new ideas or an entirely different approach. All that talent—all those best and brightest—were devoted to, say, driving defects down to 3.4 per million and not on coming up with new products or disruptive technologies. Innovation is "a meta-stable entity," says Vishva Dixit, vice president for

(Continued)

(Continued)

research of Genentech, who oversees 800 scientists at a company that has created some of the most revolutionary anticancer drugs on the market. "Nothing will kill it faster than trying to manage it, predict it, and put it on a timeline."

An inward-looking culture can leave firms vulnerable in a business world that is changing at a breakneck pace—whether it's Craigslist stealing classified ads from local newspapers or VoIP threatening to make phone calls virtually free. "The availability of information and the opening of key markets is exploding," says Clay Christensen, a Harvard Business School professor and the author of *The Innovator's Dilemma*, "and now you put a few million Chinese and Indian engineers to the test of disrupting us too." No business can afford to focus its energies on its own navel in that environment. "Getting outside is everything," says GE's Immelt (who still deploys Six Sigma). From the day he took over as CEO, he says, he knew the company would need to be "much more forward-facing in the future than we ever were in the past." He explains: "It's not about change. It's about sudden and abrupt and uncontrollable change. If you're not externally focused in this world, you can really lose your edge."

Old rule: Rank your players; go with the A's.

New rule: Hire passionate people.

At GE under Welch, employees were ranked as A, B, or C players, and the bottom group was relentlessly culled. "We're an A-plus company," Welch told his executives in 1997, according to Robert Slater's book, *Jack Welch and the GE Way*. "We want only A players. Don't spend time trying to get C's to be B's. Move them out early."

Pretty soon places as diverse as Charles Schwab and Ford began ranking employees. But as with Six Sigma, the practice became overdone. Welch's "vitality curve," in the hands of less deft managers, became the "dead man's curve," or "rank and yank." Everybody, it seemed, was expendable. There was a price to pay. According to a Rutgers and University of Connecticut poll in 2002, 58% of workers believed most top executives put their own self-interest ahead of the company's, while only 33% trusted that their bosses have the firm's best interests at heart. "All of a sudden, when big companies had to change and respond to the marketplace and move quickly, they found out they couldn't, because they didn't have people engaged and aligned around the corporate mission," says Xerox CEO Anne Mulcahy. "Then being big is a disadvantage. If you're not nimble, there's no advantage to size. It's like a rock."

While studying companies trying to transform themselves, Christopher Bartlett of Harvard Business School and a colleague found the major obstacle was inefficient use of increasingly disenfranchised employees. "People don't come to work to be No. 1 or No. 2 or to get a 20% net return on assets," Bartlett says. "They want a sense of purpose. They come to work to get meaning from their lives."

Steve Jobs has emphasized that Apple hires only people who are passionate about what they do (something that, to be fair, Welch also talked about). At Genentech, CEO Art Levinson says he actually screens out job applicants who ask too many questions about titles and options, because he wants only people who are driven to make drugs that help patients fight cancer. GE still ranks employees, but Immelt has also added a new system of rating— red, yellow, or green—on five leadership traits (including creativity and external focus).

Employees are rated against themselves, not one another. Immelt doesn't talk about jettisoning the bottom 10%. He talks about building a team. "When you're 18 years old, you say, 'The iPod is neat,'" Immelt explains, "but people don't dream about making a gas turbine. If we can recruit the best 22-year-olds, we can double and triple in size. If not, then we're already way too big. You've got to be pragmatic about what turns people on."

Old rule: Hire a charismatic CEO.

New rule: Hire a courageous CEO.

As big shareholders began to throw their weight around in the 1980s, boards sacked their CEOs and named dazzling replacements. And the celebrity CEO was born. The stars of that era were a varied crew: Jacques Nasser, Lou Gerstner, George Fisher, Michael Armstrong, Jack Welch, Ken Lay, Al Dunlap, Sandy Weill, Carly Fiorina. Some got more credit than they deserved, others more blame. A voracious business press helped burnish (or break) reputations. The bull market fueled the myth that a truly superior CEO could hit earnings targets quarter after quarter and propel the stock price unrelentingly higher.

But the tactics used by this generation of leaders—squeezing costs, deftly managing financial and accounting decisions, using acquisitions to grow—did not always provide long-term solutions. (A McKinsey study of 157 companies that bulked up through acquisition in the 1990s found that only 12% grew significantly faster than their peers, and only seven firms generated returns that were above industry-average.) Today many of those methods have fallen out of favor. Tellingly, one top management tool du jour is the stock buyback, which can buoy share prices and pacify investors—but also indicates that the CEO has no better ideas for deploying capital.

If the celebrity CEO needed a spotlight, then today's leaders need internal fortitude. Of 940 executives surveyed by Boston Consulting Group last year, 90% said organic growth was "essential" to their success. But less than half were happy with the return on their R&D spending. And therein lies the rub: Organic growth is not a quick fix.

Real growth requires placing big bets that probably won't pay off until far into the future—and today's impatient culture offers little incentive. What practically killed Xerox was its leaders' resistance to making the technological leap from analog copying to digital, which was almost guaranteed (as most such changes are) to cut margins. By the time they were finally forced to, their business was in free fall. The company was eventually charged with improperly accelerating revenues and overstating earnings. (It settled without admitting wrongdoing and paid a $10 million fine.)

"You have to change when you're at the top of your game in terms of profit," says Mulcahy, who cleaned up the mess, made the changes to digital and color, and is now trying to jump-start revenue. "It's hard to do. Your business looks its best. Your margins are at their best. All that makes your job easier. Then you're like, 'Oh, shit, here we go again.' You've got to jump into that risk pool, and once again you're in this mode of 'You know, this could fail.'"

Never before has a CEO more needed to take risks, but rarely has Wall Street been less receptive. A recent Booz Allen study found that a CEO is vulnerable to ouster if his stock price has lagged behind the S&P 500 by an average of 2% since he took the top job. Cisco Systems CEO John Chambers says he knows a number of colleagues who are planning to

(Continued)

(Continued)

step down because of the difficulty of balancing the short-term pressures of the Street with what's in the long-term best interest of the company.

But standing tall is precisely what all those corner-office pros get paid the big bucks for, isn't it? "You have to have the courage of your convictions," says Chambers. Immelt agrees that you must be willing to spend time "in the wilderness with no love." And directors need some courage too: to resist pressure to judge a CEO by the company's stock price today and get back to harder measures like return on invested capital. Hark back again to that seminal Jack Welch speech in 1981. It hardly took the world by storm—in fact, Welch has talked about how little it seemed to impress analysts that day, barely moving the stock. But leadership is not about following the rules of the past. It is about standing up for what you believe is best, regardless of the consequences.

Old rule: Admire my might.

New rule: Admire my soul.

Today bravado is dangerous. Soft-drink companies became bad guys when they were slow to leave the school lunchroom. Nike got smacked by sweatshop allegations. Try surfing wakeupwalmart.com to see how powerful a critical community of Internet activists can be. That old notion that has served Goldman Sachs so well is creeping back into vogue: It's okay to be greedy as long as it's "long-term greedy." Says Isdell at Coke: "I do not [agree with] Milton Friedman—that the role of the corporation is solely to make money. Our legitimization in society is a very important part of what we do."

Having a "soul" as a corporation is more than contributing to causes or being transparent about executive compensation or adhering to environmental regulation (though it is certainly all of those things). It is defining a company's vision in a sustainable, long-term way—and to hell with what the hedge funds or other pay-me-now investors say. CEOs must get better at courting long-term investors—explaining their strategies, saying exactly what they intend to do, avoiding the temptation to sugarcoat. "There is so much pressure to hit your numbers," says Genentech's Levinson. "I've been very clear with Wall Street since 1995 that if we see an opportunity to make better drugs and more money down the road at a short-term cost, we will do that every time. And you need to know that's the kind of company we are."

That's easier to do, of course, when you're a glamorous, fast-growing little biotech. So it raises the question: Does the rest of corporate America have the moral fiber to defy the present, when needed, and focus on the future? And do shareholders have patience enough to support them? In other words, are they willing to be long-term greedy—or are they just greedy?

Welch Fires Back

Neutron Jack Defends His Turf

by Betsy Morris

Jack Welch was about to head to a television studio for what he calls "the best job I've ever had"—on-air analyst for the Boston Red Sox pre-game cable show—when we caught up with him. As usual, he had no shortage of opinions.

- On the power of size. It's great to be big. Being big doesn't mean you have to be slow. It doesn't mean you have to have tons of layers. It doesn't mean you can't have highly entrepreneurial people. . . . You can get fat. Monopolies are often guilty of not moving. If GE had stayed pat and we didn't grow in financial services and we stayed No. 1 in light bulbs, we'd have been in deep yogurt. But that doesn't mean you don't want to be big and strong.
- On leadership. You want to be No. 1. There's nothing wrong with that. You don't want to be a loser. Nos. 3, 4, and 5 don't have the same flexibility. You don't have the same level of resources. You can't do R&D at the same level. I agree being No. 1 in a static environment is not by itself sufficient. No. 4 might have smarter management that uses money more wisely. What you do with the resources that come from being a leader— that's what determines your future.
- On keeping lean. I was all for de-layering and flattening organizations. Today I'd flatten them even more. Some companies are still too hierarchical. Some are right out of Bethlehem Steel.
- On exploiting niches. It's not inconsistent at all with wanting to be No. 1, No. 2. In a big company you'd better be out exploring new niches. Today's niches, tomorrow's big things. Those aren't inconsistent.
- On customers. When has there ever been a divergence between shareholders and customers? No one is out saying, "Let's screw this customer today, and if we do, our share price might go up 20 cents." They're just not doing it.
- On looking outward. GE in the 1990s was all about looking outward. We traveled to other companies constantly to bring back best practices. It is one of the great ways to multiply the intellect in your organization.
- On ranking employees. That was very controversial. Weed out the weakest. The Red Sox and the Mets are playing tonight. Guess what? They're not putting on the field guys in the minors. It's all about fielding the best team. It's been portrayed as a cruel system. It isn't. The cruel system is the one that doesn't tell anybody where they stand.

SOURCE: From "Welch fires back: Neutron Jack defends his turf"; "The New Rules," by B. Morris, 2006, *Fortune, 154*(2), pp. 70–72, 74, 78, 80, 84, 87. Copyright 2006 Time Inc. All rights reserved. Reprinted with permission.

REFLECTION

- Which leadership and change concepts best fit each of the new rules?

- What concepts and practices can businesses use to counter an "inward-looking culture"?

- Christopher Bartlett and Steve Jobs emphasize purpose and passion in employees' work. What can companies do to inspire authentic purpose and passion?

- Considering concepts and practices of leading change in this chapter, what argument would CEOs use to convince their board of directors and stockholders of the importance of "balancing the short-term pressures of [Wall Street] with what's in the long-term interest of the company"?

Application 2 RELIGIOUS ORGANIZATION

Wanted: Excited Christians: Declining Congregations Are Either Being Pruned for Growth, or Burned for Their Failure to Grow

By Carol Ann Keys

> *I know all the things you do, and that you have a reputation for being alive—but you are dead. Wake up! Strengthen what little remains, for even what is left is almost dead. I find that your actions do not meet the requirements of my God. Go back to what you heard and believed at first; hold to it firmly. Repent and turn to me again. If you don't wake up, I will come to you suddenly, as unexpected as a thief.*

—Revelation 3:1–3

Once upon a time, in a land not so far away, there was a little church of The Presbyterian Church in Canada. This church had a long and proud history in its land, and the people of this church believed that God would bless them for their faithfulness forever. Every Sunday the little congregation gathered to worship its Lord in a dignified and orderly manner. But the years went by and slowly the congregation began to fall asleep, and attendance at the little church started to fall quietly away.

First the younger people left and later the Sunday school shut down. The younger generation was bored and disinterested in what the little church had to offer. The message of the good news of Jesus Christ was not being presented to them in a manner which ignited their interest or held their attention. The culture in the land was changing at a pace unprecedented in its history, but the little congregation insisted that the Lord must be worshipped in the same way. The young people said "Okay," and they registered their kids in Sunday morning hockey or went Sunday shopping or slept in.

The people told themselves, "Young people aren't interested in religion, there is nothing we can do." And so one by one the people of the little church grew older and began to die, and soon even the mighty Presbyterian Church Women folded. "What are we to do?" said the session members to each other. "There aren't enough people here to pay our expenses. How will we be able to continue to worship the Lord?"

Two of the elders of the little church joined with their minister to form a committee of session, which grew to include three more people from the congregation. They were charged with finding a solution to this problem. Faithful servants of the Lord, they worked tirelessly to find the clues they needed, and after many months of searching they reported back. "We have sought a vision from God," they said, "and this is what He told us: We need to open the doors of our little church to everyone in the land. We need to meet the people at the level of their culture and at their point of greatest need, and then we need to deliver the good news of Jesus Christ to them in a way they will enjoy and understand. We need to reach out to everyone in this land, young and old, rich and poor, and be the example of Jesus Christ in word and deed. We need to show our land that this little church has a purpose, and a mission, and that we are ready, able and willing to act on it. We need to explain to everyone in the land who we are, and why we are here, and tell them and show them who their neighbour is—because they no longer know. The people of this land have forgotten about the Lord."

The session was uneasy. They liked their little church the way it was. They liked the people they had. Most of all they liked the way they worshipped. The committee tried to show the people of the church they had nothing to fear. The minister gave them scriptural assurance that change has been the call of God to his people throughout all time. The committee told stories of other Presbyterian churches that had successfully made the transition from old to new worship styles resulting in phenomenal growth. They asked the people of the little church to read a contemporary translation of the Bible in order to add value and insight to their understanding of the Lord's purposes for his church. They challenged the little church to better discipleship.

Hopefully, they rationalized, this would help the congregation at the little church understand that "reformed and reforming" has been the cry of the Presbyterian Church since its Reformation inception. Most of all, however, the committee longed to show the little church how wonderful the new music of the Christian church could be. They had seen for themselves how younger people in growing Presbyterian churches had positively responded to changes in worship music and worship style—music which did not include the use of an organ. "What," they asked their people, "would you be willing to give up to bring Jesus Christ back to the people of this land?"

The people of the little church listened to the committee but they didn't like what they heard. It was a John:1 kind of thing; the people saw the light, but they preferred the darkness. The committee knew that unless the little church could grasp and truly understand its biblical reason for existence (and then embrace what it has been commanded to do) then there was little reason for them to continue as a congregation in the church of Jesus Christ. The little church did not have new people coming to it because new people were never truly wanted or even invited. There wasn't any sincere thought put into the fact that younger people, who were so desperately needed in this little church, did not understand or enjoy the traditional worship practices. Especially the organ. What were they willing to give up? Nothing. The people of the little church just didn't see it as their issue. As far as they were concerned, the little church was open for business and everyone was welcome to join them in a service of traditional worship on any Sunday morning at 10:30—just like the sign on the front lawn said.

The committee of session was disbanded and the minister sent on her way. The two elders and their families left the little church because God had given them a glorious opportunity to see the possibilities available to any church. An exciting church, they had learned, does not need be an oxymoron. To be an exciting church you simply need to have excited Christians. The little church had been far from either.

Today the congregation at the sleepy little church continues to worship in a land not so far away. Their finances are faltering and they are without a minister. There appears to be no particular anxiety about death at this little church. It is accepted, and so far as God allows these things to be seen, there will not be a fairy tale ending. Their light is very dim, and they will sleep away their existence until they breathe no longer.

Carol Ann Keys has lived this story.

SOURCE: From "Wanted: Excited Christians," by C. A. Keys, 2007, *Presbyterian Record*, *26*(2), pp. 26–27. This article was first published in the *Presbyterian Record*, March 2007. Reprinted with permission.

REFLECTION

Many congregations, regardless of denomination, face these circumstances. According to the life-cycle theory, this church is facing imminent decline or death. Yet most congregations in similar situations do not want to see their churches close.

- What concepts and practices of leading change can congregations use to revitalize or recover and prevent the continuing decline described by Carol Keys?

- Use the guiding questions throughout the chapter (and summarized in the conclusion) to develop a change proposal for churches in this situation.

Application 3   GOVERNMENT

Virtual Networks: An Opportunity for Government

By Frank DiGiammarino and Lena Trudeau

Meeting the Changing Needs of Citizens

The interactive Web is forcing some of government's time-worn institutions to rethink their relationship with their most important client: the public. A good illustration of this kind of reckoning can be found in our municipal library systems, which—in the age of Amazon.com and Barnes and Noble megastores—are under increasing pressure to stay relevant and engaged with the communities they serve.

"The younger generation today is wired differently than people in my generation," said sixty-nine-year-old Harry Courtright, explaining to the *New York Times* last summer why the fifteen-branch library system he oversees in Arizona's Maricopa County jettisoned the once sacred Dewey decimal system of classifying books in favor of one designed for the majority of users, who come to browse without a particular title in mind.

Courtright and his colleagues are facing fundamental questions of identity. What is a library in the twenty-first century? How does the role of librarian change in light of customer reviews and other peer-to-peer networking opportunities that online bookstores routinely provide? Will the one-third of Americans who count themselves among Generation Y ultimately expect public libraries to work more like Netflix? Will we eventually be a society of on-demand books?

The implications for government, which delivers a wide range of services to an ever more sophisticated public, are immense. Libraries provide just one example of the opportunity virtual networks offer public-sector leaders—faced with expanding mandates, increasingly constrained budgets, and unwieldy organizational structures—to rethink their service delivery model.

Emergence of the Virtual Network

The paradigms that define our current understanding of organizations can be traced back to the 1930s and early public administration scholars like Luther Gulick, who claimed that organizations should departmentalize work by purpose, process, clientele, or place and should not combine dissimilar activities in single agencies. Gulick argued that although most work contains all four elements, systems must organize around only one of these core principles, to the exclusion of the other three. Today's government institutions reflect this thinking, with agencies that provide services and information often managed in vertical silos.

Virtual networks, in contrast, place a premium on breaking down these silos and connecting various audiences across (and within) them for better delivery to the citizen. The "wiki" platform for virtual collaboration takes its name from the Hawaiian word for "fast" and features built-in functionality that allows quick content analysis—users can see the labels that have been applied to content, how content has been edited and reviewed, and the relationships that have formed between various pieces of data. This allows for nearly limitless access and searchability that is shifting the structure of thought from the hierarchical and vertical to the diffuse and horizontal. Particularly in light of Generation Y's increasing role in the federal workforce, government leaders have the responsibility to understand the nature of this evolution and embrace virtual networks as a way to be more efficient while remaining relevant.

"While the government is still buying Rolodexes, the younger generations have 600 friends on Facebook and 250 professional colleagues on LinkedIn," said Steve Ressler, 27, a cofounder of Young Government Leaders, a professional organization of more than 1,000 younger federal employees from more than thirty departments and agencies. "It's very important for us to see Web 2.0 technologies in the workplace. We are used to working horizontal, are not afraid of authority, and want our ideas heard."

Technology and Leadership

The cause of deploying Web 2.0 in government continues to gain committed champions, and the mounting success stories can be attributed more to leadership than technology. In April 2006, the Office of the Director of National Intelligence (ODNI) created the classified "Intellipedia" wiki site to allow 16 intelligence agencies to quickly and collaboratively share classified information. Without compromising security, the goal was to transcend traditional silos and gain the agility required to combat loosely connected networks of terrorists and similarly diffuse but urgent threats. The site allows frontline agents to post information on any aspect of intelligence along with other agencies in the intelligence community.

This powerful collaborative tool has been put to practical use on several occasions, including the 2006 crash of a small plane into a New York City high-rise. Within two hours, Intellipedia garnered more than eighty updates, enough to determine with confidence that the crash was not a terrorist act. Intellipedia has also been useful in providing up-to-date, peer-driven intelligence on North Korean missile tests, bomb-making by Iraqi insurgents, and instability in Nigeria. In testimony presented to Congress on September 10, 2007—6 years after the terrorist attacks of September 11—Director of National Intelligence Admiral Michael McConnell lauded Intellipedia for enabling "experts from different disciplines to pool their knowledge, form virtual teams, and quickly make complete intelligence assessments. . . . The solution does not require special networks or equipment but has dramatically changed our capability to share information in a timely manner."

"It's not complicated technology; it's not expensive," says Assistant Secretary of Homeland Security for the Transportation Security Administration (TSA) Kip Hawley. "The biggest challenge, the biggest learning, is that somebody has to make the decision to just

(Continued)

(Continued)

go ahead and do it." In addition to TSA's classified involvement with Intellipedia, Hawley has overseen the launch of a new blog for the traveling public and an internal IdeaFactory, where TSA's 43,000 frontline transportation security officers can confer collectively on job-related issues and ideas. The site empowers employees to share ideas on how to improve the organization across multiple lines; these ideas are available for every employee to see and evaluate. Employees vote for the ideas they like and offer constructive criticism. Within a week of its launch, TSA employees had submitted more than 150 ideas, offered more than 650 comments, and voted on ideas more than 800 times.

The Collaboration Project

Hawley recently discussed these initiatives at the first meeting of The Collaboration Project (see box), the National Academy of Public Administration's newly launched leadership forum that uses research, best practices, and other resources to help apply the benefits of Web 2.0 and collaborative technology in government.

The Collaboration Project

The National Academy is taking the lead on Web 2.0 in government by launching The Collaboration Project—an independent leadership forum to jump-start the cause of collaborative technology to drive innovation and change in government. Designed for leaders looking to overcome the technical, organizational, and cultural barriers involved, the project convenes members in person and through a virtual collaboration space to share best practices, case studies, white papers, and leadership tools for implementation.

"This is a big idea that's being introduced to a somewhat alien culture," said National Academy president and chief executive officer Jenna L. Dorn, "but we are convinced that collaborative technology has the potential to transform government in America, to tap into the expertise of people outside the hierarchy of any single agency or department, to make government more transparent, and to open the door to a broader array of experts focused on solving a particular problem or to citizens who want to contribute to making government work better."

The Collaboration Project kicked off operations with its first in-person meeting in February, drawing a diverse group of key decision makers, including congressional staff, chief information officers (CIOs), chief technology officers, chief financial officers, and other senior leaders from more than a dozen federal agencies, including the Environmental Protection Agency (EPA), Coast Guard, Government Accountability Office, Small Business Administration, and Departments of Homeland Security, Transportation, and Defense.

TSAs Kip Hawley inspired meeting participants with his presentation on the successful Web 2.0 advances at his agency. "It's self-policing," Hawley told the audience, explaining how the various parties collaborate in responsible and inventive ways without the need for excessive oversight by forum monitors. "We've found that the lighter the touch on editing, the better the quality of ideas and the quality of the discussion."

SOURCE: From "Virtual Networks: An Opportunity for Government," by F. DiGiammarino and L. Trudeau, 2008, Public Manager, 37(1), pp. 5–11. Reprinted with permission.

REFLECTION

- What factors in today's environment challenge Luther Gulick's ideas about how government should function?

- Which concepts and practices of leading change contributed to the changes in public agencies described by DiGiammarino and Trudeau?

- What other change or opportunities could virtual networks offer internal and external stakeholders?

Application 4   EDUCATION

Revolution From the Faculty Lounge: The Emergence of Teacher-Led Schools and Cooperatives

By Joe Williams

Progressivism in Wisconsin

In Wisconsin, the home of legendary progressive crusader "Fighting Bob" LaFollette, the concept of teacher cooperatives has been taking a slightly different turn. In Milwaukee, a city where charter schooling and even private school vouchers have been part of the landscape of education for several years, teachers have also begun taking to the idea of running small schools that they feel will better meet the needs of their students.

Unlike the teachers who work for the EdVisions cooperative, teachers at Milwaukee's teacher cooperative schools remain employees of the Milwaukee Public Schools and dues-paying members of the Milwaukee Teachers' Education Association (MTEA), but they provide their services to district-sponsored charter schools as an autonomous team. (All the cooperative schools are district-sponsored charters, rather than independent charters, because this arrangement allows the teachers to continue to participate in the state's teacher retirement system.) They don't own their practice in an economic sense, but they are allowed by both the district and their union to own what happens within their autonomous school communities. The teachers select their colleagues, decide on the work assignments, determine the expenditures, and—most importantly, they say—shape the learning program.

"The teachers in these cooperatives literally 'own' what happens in their schools, which creates a climate where accountability and flexibility go hand-in-hand," observes Milwaukee Superintendent William Andrekopoulos. Unionized teachers in Milwaukee have already formed 11 professional partnerships that run charter schools under the state's laws that allow for worker cooperatives. Wisconsin's cooperatives are organized under Chapter 185 of the state's statutes and are tax exempt nonprofit organizations. All full-time teachers at the school site are automatically considered members of the cooperative, and all have the same rights and privileges.

The I.D.E.A.L. Charter School opened in the fall of 2001 as the first teacher cooperative in Milwaukee. The partners collectively hold the charter, although, because of a quirk in the state's charter school law, only one teacher signs it. The teachers continue as district employees and are paid the contract rate, but they can decide how many teachers of what type the school

(Continued)

(Continued)

needs, and so they can reallocate expenditures. There is a memorandum of understanding with the MTEA, the bargaining agent for the district's teachers, that waives certain provisions of the master contract. The union has been cooperative, the board of education is happy, and the teachers are protected but still have full control of "professional issues."

Any teacher in the district may apply for a vacant teaching position at any cooperative, but the existing team has the right to interview all the candidates and to select the teachers that the district will then assign to the school. The current agreement allows these interviews up until an established deadline, after which teachers must fill the vacancies using traditional seniority rights—a practice that some members of the cooperatives hope to eliminate in the future since teacher selection is crucial to the team building that allows cooperatives to thrive.

What Happens in These Co-ops?

While the hallways and classrooms of cooperative schools don't always look entirely different from what you would find in a typical school, it is the regular partner meetings that stand out as unconventional. Unlike the often-inflexible, compliance-based cultures that exist in traditional schools—where the principal implements district-wide edicts and there is little room to make meaningful adjustments based on the particular needs of individual schools—partner meetings under the professional partnership model demonstrate what is possible when teachers have a say over what happens in schools.

"All the teachers are at the table," says Avalon's Whalen, who now works as a consultant for EdVisions, helping other teams of teachers around the nation to form cooperatives. At Avalon, about 12 weeks before the doors first opened to students, the teachers got together and simply divided up the lengthy list of tasks that needed to be completed. The concept of "professionalism," Whalen says, ends up meaning something different when you have complete ownership of the work experience. It often means that teachers willingly participate in cafeteria duty, bathroom duty, and hallway duty, for example, because a professional team has determined that resources would be better spent on instruction than on school aides. It isn't that the aides wouldn't be nice to have, Whalen notes, but such costs can be converted into hiring additional teachers, which keeps class sizes lower and keeps the focus on student instruction.

Sometimes the decisions confronting the teacher/owners of a school aren't particularly interesting to much of the outside world, but they illustrate the kinds of everyday issues that can't be easily solved by large, bureaucratic school systems. Signs are also beginning to emerge that teachers will use this new level of flexibility to better understand and respond to the academic needs of their students.

At the Milwaukee Learning Laboratory and Institute, for example, which opened in the fall of 2005, the partnership's teachers determined in the first few months that their students needed to hone their organization, research, and study skills. The students were so weak in these areas that it limited their learning in other subject areas, such as science. For some students, an inability to work on their own was making their lessons irrelevant.

The teachers decided to alter the student schedules midstream to provide an ad hoc course in study skills. They created the time for this unplanned instruction by dropping science class for one marking period. Once the students at the small school were brought up to speed on their research and study skills, the partnership changed the schedules again, so that all students doubled up on science for the final marking period. Thus the students made up for the lost classes and, because they had a better grip on handling homework and research, made better use of their science time than they would have otherwise. "We could never have done that in a large high school that wasn't run by the teachers," said David Coyle, the lead teacher under the partnership arrangement.

Teachers who are members of these cooperatives spend a great deal of time honing the decision-making process, since that is the professional cornerstone on which the school culture is built. "We've had to struggle at times with the question of whether or not we make decisions by consensus or by majority rule," Avalon's Whalen says. "The vast majority of decisions end up being made by consensus, but the tough ones end up being by majority rule."

Conceptually, since the EdVisions and Milwaukee teacher co-op schools are public "schools of choice," there is a connection between the decisions the teachers make about their offerings and the desires of students in the marketplace. If students don't want to attend these schools, they cease to exist.

There are also some built-in levers that ensure the quality of the team members. Teachers who don't cut it in the partnerships, based on evaluations by a cooperative peer-review system, are allowed to return to the traditional employment pool of the district with their seniority intact. The same applies to teachers who decide on their own that the partnership model just isn't a good fit.

One of the Milwaukee teacher cooperatives, Advanced Language and Academic Studies (ALAS), was started by a group of teachers who had grown frustrated working in the perennially troubled South Division High School, a school serving primarily Latinos on Milwaukee's South Side. "We were frustrated with the fact that no one would take responsibility for what was happening," said Linda Peters, the lead teacher at ALAS. In some ways, it was remarkable that the rebellious South Division teachers found one another at all. But, in addition to a burning desire actually to do something to help their students, they had one thing in common: they all avoided the large high school's teachers lounge like the plague. "It was like a den of negativity," one South Division refugee remarked.

At ALAS, there is no room for negativity, teachers say. As soon as a problem is identified, it becomes the professional team's collective responsibility to solve it. There is no need to establish study commissions or run decisions through myriad layers of district-level bureaucracy. Identify a problem, decide collectively on a solution, and implement it. The model is about streamlined school operations. The hours are long, and the hats the teacher/owners wear are many. The partners meet regularly to tackle problems as they arise, and, because there is no principal, they can't leave until someone has taken charge of whatever situation the staff collectively deems worthy of an intervention.

Teachers say the most important change they sought from their teacher union contract was the ability to choose like-minded colleagues who share their vision of education. If anything, teachers say they would like even more flexibility on this issue for the sake of preserving school culture. "We're really hard on ourselves. The pressure comes from within," says Kevin Kuschel, who was driven to join the co-op, in part, by his belief that bilingual students were more capable of taking Advanced Placement courses in subjects like history than South Division seemed to believe. "This is our baby, and we want the baby to be successful," Kuschel continues.

Even students see the difference in terms of staff cohesion when teacher partners work as a team. "The students understand the staff is a unit. There is no playing one teacher off against another," Roxanne Mayeur, a teacher at Milwaukee's Community High School, told

(Continued)

(Continued)

the *Milwaukee Journal Sentinel.* "We don't think administrators are useless or a negative thing, [but] it is important that this movement be about teachers having more of a voice."[1]

Mark Van Ryzin, a doctoral candidate at the University of Minnesota who has studied the teacher partnerships in both Milwaukee and Minnesota, says that virtually anything is possible. "With these professional partnerships, teachers can not only make more of the day-to-day decisions but can also undertake whole-school reform and redesign" if they believe that's what's necessary to contribute to student learning. "If the teachers, as a group, are more comfortable in a traditional classroom-based school, that is what they create. If the teachers are reformers at heart, they can incorporate any sort of pedagogical or technological innovation and create a very different kind of school," Van Ryzin points out. "The ultimate authority lies with them."

Lead Teachers, Not Principals

Generally, there are no principals at these teacher-led schools, so that the teacher voice will drive every decision regarding the education to be delivered. Instead of a principal, most professional partnerships of teachers operate with a single teacher who is designated as the "lead teacher." These individuals are responsible for running partner meetings and other events and for dealing with the state or district bureaucracies when that's necessary.

Yet, even when the school community is sensitive to the need to share responsibilities, many foundations and government agencies that work with the schools rely upon traditional norms and require the signature of the school principal on forms. Teachers said this can be a tricky hurdle, organizationally, because it means one person ends up getting a lot of additional responsibility dumped into his or her lap. In Wisconsin, for example, the wording of the state's charter school law contributes to the piling-on for lead teachers because it states that charters may be granted only to sole individuals, not teams of teachers, so one teacher's name automatically ends up on the charter contract. Several lead teachers interviewed in Milwaukee expressed hints of frustration that they end up doing the work of principals without the pay bump that serving as a principal usually provides.

Teachers in partnership schools also point out that some forms of decision making are more fun—professionally speaking—than others. Everyone "wants to make a decision about the budget, but no one wants to call a snow day," says Avalon's Whalen. She suggests that there are some tasks—usually far removed from instruction—that teachers still want someone else to deal with.

Many outsiders are quick to point out that ultimately someone must be in charge of handling the day-to-day administrative duties. But supporters of the partnerships say the fact that the "partnership" is responsible for the school doesn't mean that there's "nobody in charge." Rather, it means that the partnership—rather than a district central office— decides who's in charge and in charge of what. Some partnerships, for example, might opt to hire an administrator to support the work of the teachers; others may decide to contract out for administrative services, either because they prefer to have more time with students or because they prefer not to have administrative work.

One thing that becomes clear at all of these teacher-run schools is that the workload for teachers is considerably heavier than under traditional arrangements. Some observers worry that this will work against bringing these teacher-run schools to scale. Simply put, they say, these types of school ownership arrangements aren't for everyone, and teachers must decide for themselves whether the professional satisfaction they gain is worth the cost in additional time and responsibility. "One of the things I worry about is whether or not we can get enough people to keep buying into this approach," Whalen says. "You can't hire the teacher who thinks that teaching is a nine-month job. It really is a full-time commitment."

Note

1. Sarah Carr, "Where Teachers Rule: A School with No Principal?" *Milwaukee Journal Sentinel*, July 18, 2005.

SOURCE: From "Revolution From the Faculty Lounge: The Emergence of Teacher-Led Schools and Cooperatives," by Joe Williams, 2007, *Phi Delta Kappan*, *89*(3), pp. 210–216. Reprinted with permission.

REFLECTION

- What forms of collective leadership do teacher-led schools illustrate?
- What strengths and weaknesses do these forms of leadership present for public schools?
- How can teacher cooperatives align their concepts of change and leadership with change practices to take advantage of their strengths and decrease weaknesses?
- Who are the stakeholders in teacher-led schools? How do these schools benefit or create problems for each group of stakeholders?

Application 5 | NONPROFIT

Adult Literacy Center

The mission of the Adult Literacy Center (ALC) is to help adults develop basic reading and communication skills through one-on-one tutoring so that they can fulfill their goals and their roles as citizens, workers, and family members. For adults with limited literacy skills, voting, reading a newspaper, or even ordering food at a restaurant is a difficult task. Illiteracy is commonly correlated with higher school dropout, unemployment, and crime rates and increased poverty. Even more problematic, illiteracy has intergenerational consequences—children of adults with limited literacy are more likely to have limited literacy skills.

The need for adult literacy education in Montclair Township was first identified by the Edgemont Group of Montclair Township with the founding of the Adult Literacy Center's predecessor, Reading to Succeed Project (RSP) in 1987. The RSP was formed in response to the ever increasing problem of adult literacy found throughout the township. It is estimated that 52%, or 94 million, Americans read below the sixth-grade level, a number growing at a rate of 2 million per year. The Literacy at Work study estimated the economic impact and business losses attributable to basic skill deficiencies run into the hundreds of millions of dollars. The Adult Literacy Center's role as a nonprofit literacy program in reversing this trend

(Continued)

(Continued)

is accomplished through the dedicated work of a small, full-time staff that helps integrate and connect tutors and students in one-on-one relationships to improve basic reading skills.

The Adult Literacy Center served 320 students in 2007, a sizable number given the current levels of staffing, funding, and space, but this number is only a fraction of the township's 100,000 adults in need. The staff consists of four full-time employees, including the executive director, office manager, education resource coordinator, and trainer/volunteer coordinator; the seven part-time employees, who work between 4 and 20 hours per week; and the volunteer tutors, whose number totals approximately 100.

Jane Atwater, the executive director, has been at ALC for 3 years; however, she has become increasingly frustrated in her position, and rumors are circulating among staff members that she plans to leave. A large part of her frustration stems from the board of directors. Turnover on the board has been very high, and only one fourth of the members are continuing in their position. The continuing members provide little stability because they are consumed with arguing about which of them will become president. Board and subcommittee meetings are sporadic and lack substance. Board members do not fully understand their roles and have not played a vital role in fundraising, friend raising, or policy setting policy and direction for the executive director. Their attempt to develop a strategic plan resulted in a document without a clear vision or strategic direction and with only a few goals.

Jane spends most of her time developing and submitting grant applications to keep the center running. Even though the ALC filmed a moving documentary with testimony from graduates about the success of the program, the center lost its grant funding from the township due to inadequate documentation and assessment of student progress. They had little or no data (such as pre- and posttests) to support their case for continued funding.

Students speak in glowing terms about the program and their supportive tutors. However, among the full-time staff, many personnel problems are brewing—in-fighting, claims of favoritism, and employee turnover. Allegations of favoritism stem from board member interference in hiring decisions—that is, board members using their influence to hire certain part-time staff or volunteers into full-time positions. As a result, there is ongoing resentment and limited teamwork among the staff.

The executive director is at her wits' end. She has solicited the help of a nonprofit institute at a nearby university to help turn this situation around.

SOURCE: This application is based on the research of members of the Leading Change class: Sean Baran, Sam Beese, Marlene Bennett, Kristen Berlacher, Lauren Bifulco, Rachel Brushett, Drake Bushnell, Liz Friend, Whitney McComis, Meagan Powell, Luke Purcell, Lindsey Reid, David Roberts, Killian Tormey, and Will Vanthunen.

REFLECTION

- How should Jane Atwater and the nonprofit institute begin the change process in this situation?

- Considering the various stakeholders, what concepts and practices of leading change should they consider?

PART III

Leading Community and Organizational Change

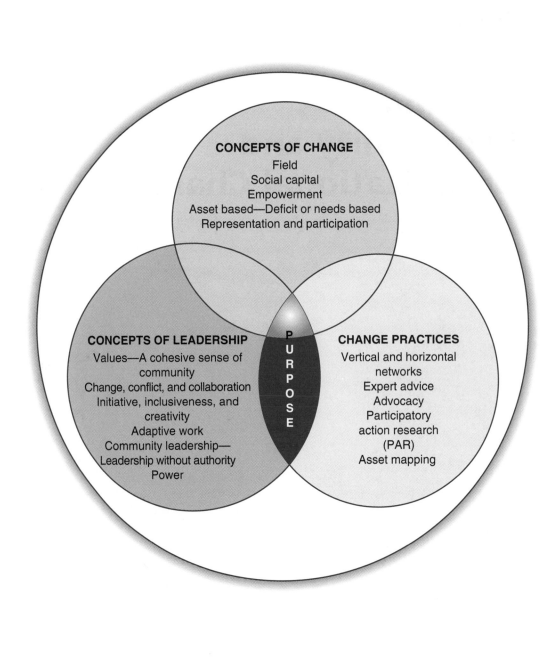

CONCEPTS OF CHANGE
Field
Social capital
Empowerment
Asset based—Deficit or needs based
Representation and participation

CONCEPTS OF LEADERSHIP
Values—A cohesive sense of
community
Change, conflict, and collaboration
Initiative, inclusiveness, and
creativity
Adaptive work
Community leadership—
Leadership without authority
Power

PURPOSE

CHANGE PRACTICES
Vertical and horizontal
networks
Expert advice
Advocacy
Participatory
action research
(PAR)
Asset mapping

CHAPTER 5

Community Change Context

Richard A. Couto, Sarah Hippensteel Hall, and Marti Goetz

Introduction

Change within the community context permits the introduction of new elements into the theoretical concepts of leadership and offers a different perspective on leadership for change, such as power and empowerment. This perspective pays attention to the nature of representation and participation in change efforts. Social capital, implied in all efforts at change, is particularly relevant in the community context. Field, a concept of change discussed at some length in Chapter 7 in its application to the political context, plays an important role in the community context as well.

Community change, not unlike change in other contexts, requires information. In the community change context, change agents turn to their own resources to conduct participatory action research (PAR). This is one small manifestation of an asset-based approach, which concentrates on the resources a group has, as opposed to a deficit-based approach, which concentrates on the resources a group lacks. Advocacy plays a role in community change not seen in other change contexts.

Purpose of Community Change

At the overlay of theoretical concepts of leadership, theoretical concepts of change, and change practices resides the purpose of community leadership for change: the vitality of a democratic civil society. Citizen leadership and voluntary associations and advocacy groups form one leg of the three-legged stool of civil society. These citizen groups hold government agencies accountable for the enforcement of regulations and prod them to action. Citizen groups also play a role in guaranteeing that businesses are mindful of the health of their workers and neighbors and of the environmental quality of the surrounding area.

Without citizen leadership and the values of community that it brings to the decision-making process, choices all too frequently reflect the expeditious consideration of business and political interests.

Change Vignette

Citizens for the Responsible Destruction of Chemical Weapons

The *Dayton Daily News* headline read, "A Victory for All the Little Guys" (McCarty, 2003), and the "little guys" of Jefferson Township were celebrating. The Army had announced a stop-work order on a contract it had awarded to a local waste-treatment company, Perma-Fix. Thus, an industrial hazardous chemical, VX hydrolysate, would not be transported into the community for treatment and discharged into the county's wastewater-treatment facility. Mary Johnson, a celebrating member of the grassroots organization Citizens for the Responsible Destruction of Chemical Weapons (CRDCW) happily invoked the David and Goliath parallel: "It just goes to show you what a community of different people can do when it comes together" (DeBrosse, 2003a).

The case of the CRDCW invites examination of Johnson's pride in community leadership for change. Some generic aspects of change leadership can certainly be found in the community context, but some unique aspects of change leadership reside there as well. For example, whereas values may be common to the theoretical concepts of leadership in all contexts, leadership in the community context generally emerges when a threat to a group with some cohesive identity surfaces. In an effort to thwart this threat and preserve community, community leadership conducts adaptive work that differs from that conducted by leadership in all other contexts in its lack of formal authority of position. Thus, the adaptive work of community leadership most closely resembles leadership without authority (Heifetz, 1994; Heifetz, 2007). Likewise, although empowerment applies to leadership in all contexts, in the community context lies empowerment's most genuine form—self-empowerment—that which entails full participation and direct representation of community members in decision making. This type of empowerment leads to examination of a much-neglected area of study about leadership and change—power (Csaszar, 2005; Hughes, Wheeler, & Eyben, 2005; Rowlands, 1997).

Following the 1997 U.S. ratification of the international Chemical Weapons Convention treaty and the passage of several U.S. laws, the U.S. Army became responsible for destroying its chemical weapons stockpile. VX, a nerve agent so deadly that less than 0.001 of an ounce of the thick, oily liquid can kill if it comes into contact with the skin or is inhaled, was one of those slated for neutralization. Following the terrorist attacks of September 11, 2001, the army expedited the neutralization of its VX stockpile, which had been stored in sturdy steel containers at the Newport (Indiana) Chemical Depot. The use of sodium hydroxide in neutralizing VX created a highly corrosive by-product, VX hydrolysate. The army had very limited experience in treating and disposing of VX hydrolysate (National Research Council, 1998).

On January 9, 2003, the army awarded a subcontract to Perma-Fix Environmental Services for the treatment and disposal of its VX hydrolysate by-product. Perma-Fix, a national environmental services company, provides waste-management and industrial waste–management services to hospitals, research laboratories, nuclear plants, and other institutions and agencies, including the U.S. Departments of Energy and Defense, at its nine major waste-treatment facilities across the country. The subcontract called for Perma-Fix to treat about 300,000 gallons of VX hydrolysate— about 80 truckloads—at its plant in the Drexel neighborhood of Jefferson Township in Montgomery County, Ohio. The township is a mix of urban neighborhoods and rural farmland. The urban area, Drexel, abuts Dayton and has about 30% of the township's almost 7,000 residents. Thirty-five percent of Drexel's population is African American, and 33% of its families have incomes below the poverty level, according to the 2000 U.S. Census Report. Shipments were scheduled to come almost 200 miles from the Newport Chemical Weapons Depot to Drexel beginning in October 2003.

Community Residents Become Alarmed. The army's plans alarmed some local residents, who had successfully opposed proposals for landfills in their area beginning in the late 1980s. They had stayed together as an informal group, Land Lovers against Neighborhood Dumps (LLAND), without directors, officers, or a tax-exempt status. A telephone tree kept them informed and organized.

In August 2002, LLAND concluded its protest of another proposed landfill just as rumors began to circulate that Perma-Fix was looking into an army contract to dispose of a hazardous material. No one had ever heard of VX hydrolysate, so Laura Rench, a founder of LLAND, began researching it. Rench grew up in Jefferson Township and owned and managed a local Christmas tree farm there.

She called Perma-Fix and asked the company to confirm or dispel the rumors about the plan to treat VX hydrolysate in a Drexel waste-management facility. When Perma-Fix didn't give her an answer, she spoke to the Jefferson Township trustees. The three trustees were aware of Perma-Fix's discussions with the army, assured Rench that the proposal was a good one that would bring jobs to the area, and told her about the scheduled public meeting mentioned in the contract (L. Rench, personal communication, September 2, 2005).

Rench's conversations with the residents of the Drexel area offered cause for alarm. Residents had been very unhappy since Perma-Fix moved to their area in 1986. The *Dayton Daily News* had reported neighborhood complaints and employee accidents several times. Most recently, in October of 1999, a near-fatal accident occurred when a worker inhaled toxic fumes while cleaning the inside of a tanker truck (Mong, 1999a). That same month the newspaper reported that residents in the area were complaining of "foul-smelling, headache-producing air," which they believed was coming from the Perma-Fix plant (Mong, 1999b, p. 1).

While gathering this information, Rench met Drexel resident Michelle Cooper. News of the VX hydrolysate contract renewed Cooper's long-time concerns with Perma-Fix. The two women joined forces and began going door to door in the neighborhood. They shared the little information they had with residents but encountered many people who were reluctant to talk with them. People seemed fearful about standing up to the U.S. Army at a time when the nation was preparing to invade Iraq to neutralize its alleged stock of weapons of mass destruction, including, ironically, VX. This initial reluctance of Drexel neighbors to talk or take action frustrated Rench and Cooper, who felt a sense of urgency because there was very little time to organize and they had not even completed their research on VX hydrolysate. Meanwhile, the U.S. Army had already awarded the contract to Perma-Fix and wanted the neutralization process to begin in 10 months.

(Continued)

(Continued)

Alarm Becomes Action. To reach and recruit more residents, Rench and Cooper called a meeting at a local elementary school for January 17, 2003. A LLAND member suggested to Rench that she should contact Jane Forrest Redfern, who had helped LLAND on a landfill fight in the area in her role as executive director of Ohio Citizen Action (OCA). Founded in 1975, OCA, the state's largest environmental organization with 100,000 dues-paying members, had successfully helped many Ohio communities deal with environmental issues, including hazardous-waste concerns, groundwater protection, and new landfill locations. It followed a community-organizing model first laid out by the father of community organizing, Saul Alinsky (1971). Redfern had worked for several decades in the Dayton area on environmental protection issues and had a history of significant local accomplishments in reducing risks to the Miami Valley's drinking water supply. One person who had worked with Redfern described her as being "as comfortable in a room full of developers as she is in a room full of environmentalists. She helps people find their voice, which is one of the purest forms of effective leadership" (Dempsey, 2003).

Rench invited Redfern to this first meeting and shared the information she had gathered and the community's concerns. Rench also told Redfern that she needed to "charge the group up" (L. Rench, personal communication, September 2, 2005). Redfern agreed to help and got excited about the issue and what the community could do to protect itself from the threat of VX hydrolysate. Using the LLAND telephone tree, Rench informed people of the meeting.

At the same time Rench was recruiting Redfern, Willa Bronston, an African American resident of Drexel, independently began her opposition to the Perma-Fix VX hydrolysate disposal plan. She first heard about the plan on the local evening news and immediately called a township trustee to see what could be done to stop the plan. Nothing, she was told. Bronston heard about the meeting LLAND was organizing and decided to attend (W. Bronston, personal communication, September 8, 2005).

The night of the meeting, Redfern, with relatively little knowledge of the VX hydrolysate issue, used her experience to shape the agenda. She knew the meeting had to address two questions: What do residents want for their community? When will residents know they have won? Such meetings, she had learned, often generate four responses to these questions: a short-term solution, a long-term solution, a call for government action, and a desire for reliable information from someone residents can trust to be accountable. Redfern asked the dozen or so people in the room to introduce themselves and then conducted an inventory of what people knew about the issue. During the course of the meeting, as Redfern expected, those attending provided clear answers to two of the four questions:

- They wanted the U.S. Army to keep the treated nerve agent by-product in Newport and not send it to Drexel for secondary treatment.
- They wanted Perma-Fix to be a good neighbor and abide by environmental regulations and not pollute the nearby neighborhoods or the environment.
- They wanted public officials, government agencies, and companies to be accountable for their actions and inactions.
- They wanted the truth. (W. Bronston, personal communication, September 8, 2005; J. Redfern, personal communication, September 6, 2005; L. Rench, personal communication, September 2, 2005)

Redfern asked LLAND members to take inventory of their resources, including the skills and knowledge available within their own ranks and the skills and knowledge they would need to obtain outside the group (J. Redfern, personal communication, September 6, 2005). This inventory helped the group identify and assess their allies, those whose support they needed, those likely to oppose them, and those neutral about the issue.

Redfern explained the issues at stake and what it would take for the community to stop Perma-Fix from bringing the VX hydrolysate to the neighborhood. Drawing on her experience, she assured them they could prevail against Perma-Fix and the U.S. Army. Encouraged by the accomplishments of so much in just a few hours, LLAND members left the meeting buoyed by newfound confidence. They began to conduct further library and Internet research to determine the accuracy of their information and to identify any gaps in information.

On January 23, 2003, the U.S. Army and Perma-Fix held a daytime public-information session, set up like an open house with display booths, at the Board of Education building. Bronston called her lifelong friend Mary Johnson and two other neighbors and asked them to attend the meeting. They observed right away that few people were in attendance and began to worry that the low turnout might be interpreted as tacit community support of the project. When Bronston and her friends asked the U.S. Army and Perma-Fix representatives about the experiences at other treatment locations for VX hydrolysate, they learned that the process was experimental. They left with the same concerns they had brought to the meeting—concerns about risks to the residents living near the Perma-Fix facility, especially given that the Drexel neighborhood didn't have a fire department nearby to respond to emergencies.

Even though they had met Redfern and Rench, Bronston and Johnson did not interact much with the LLAND group, and they did their own research. Johnson, a retired nurse, wanted to understand the basic science of nerve gas and what happens to it during disposal. Bronston and Johnson canvassed their neighborhood, knocking on hundreds of doors, talking to people about what they knew, and asking for help. But they found, as Rench had, that most people expressed a reluctance to be involved.

They created a presentation to give to township trustees, county commissioners, and officials in the fire department, the wastewater-treatment plant, the environmental agency, and other agencies. At the Montgomery County Commission meeting on February 4, 2003, they did their best to present all their findings, concerns, and questions within the 3-minute timeframe allotted to each of them. When the commissioners asked the two women what they wanted them to do, Bronston and Johnson responded that they would like the commissioners to take a moral stand. The commissioners declined to do so, leaving Bronston and Johnson very disappointed (W. Bronston, personal communication, September 8, 2005; M. Johnson, personal communication, September 8, 2005).

Several LLAND members also attended the commission meeting. Afterwards, they spoke with Bronston and Johnson about working together. Up to this point, two separate teams had been doing the same research and coming to the same conclusions. Bronston and her friends met with LLAND members several times and eventually decided to join forces to form Citizens for the Responsible Destruction of Chemical Weapons (CRDCW).

Mobilizing Resources. CRDCW moved into action and divided responsibilities. Bronston and Johnson were asked to visit every jurisdiction in the Greater Dayton area, ask for residents'

(Continued)

(Continued)

support, and encourage communities to pass resolutions against the VX hydrolysate disposal plan. Bronston and Johnson met with residents of cities, towns, and villages; members of churches, the NAACP, and the Urban League; officials of regional government agencies; and many other individuals. Having learned from their experience with the Montgomery County commissioners, they drafted a resolution that the officials could use as a template to pass a resolution against the plan. Then when officials asked what Bronston and Johnson wanted them to do, the women handed them the draft resolution and asked them to support it (W. Bronston, personal communication, September 8, 2005; M. Johnson, personal communication, September 8, 2005).

In the meantime, Rench, Redfern, and other members of the original LLAND group conducted research and enlisted Ellis Jacobs of the Legal Aid Society of Dayton in their cause. They knew Legal Aid was a nonprofit organization that provided civil legal assistance to poor families and individuals in the Greater Dayton area, including communities such as Drexel. Jacobs immediately went to work trying to find ways that the army contract could be rescinded or cancelled. He quickly learned that the VX hydrolysate disposal plan at Drexel didn't contain an environmental impact statement (EIS). All federal agencies, including the U.S. Army, are required by the National Environmental Policy Act to conduct a study on the consequence of any action on the environment. Jacobs sent a letter to the U.S. Army stating that no EIS was on file for the proposed disposal process slated for the Perma-Fix facility. The army responded that it had filed a "generic off-site disposal facility" EIS and a Final Finding of No Significant Impact (FONSI) on the area, land, ecological resources, water, socioeconomic resources, or people "living near the site." Both of these documents had been filed before the selection of the Drexel site. Jacobs pointed out the obvious, namely, that the EIS and FONSI could not be applied to Drexel without first conducting a study of the impact on Drexel specifically (E. Jacobs, personal communication, September 2, 2005).

Jacobs also discovered that the U.S. Army had a clause in its proposed contract with Perma-Fix of Dayton that required "public acceptance" of the plan before Perma-Fix could begin treating shipments of VX hydrolysate and then discharging it into Montgomery County's wastewater-treatment system. At the request of Jacobs and the CRDCW, U.S. Representative Mike Turner asked the army to define public acceptance (J. Redfern, September 6, 2005). In his response, Assistant Secretary of the Army Claude M. Bolton Jr. explained to Jacobs that approval of the Ohio EPA, with its public involvement process, satisfied the army's public acceptance requirement. The Ohio EPA, on the other hand, told Jacobs that it had no authority in the matter, and even if it did public involvement did not mean public acceptance; approval of a permit did not require the latter (E. Jacobs, personal communication, September 2, 2005). Legally, the army was obligated to demonstrate public acceptance of the project, however tortuous the logic of setting criteria might be. Bronston and Johnson's work proved invaluable in suggesting a lack of public acceptance. They obtained resolutions opposing the VX hydrolysate disposal plan from 37 entities, including 20 different jurisdictions!

CRDCW members took other steps to display the lack of public acceptance. They scheduled an accountability session on April 10, 2003, at the local high school to bring all parties together in one place and to show that the community was active and organized. They compiled a list of local, state, and federal public officials and agency representatives, making sure to include the Montgomery County commissioners, and U.S. Army and Perma-Fix representatives. The CRDCW sent an invitation explaining the purpose of the meeting and stating that invitees would find their name and affiliation on a designated chair at the front of the room. The CRDCW also informed the media of the session. Thus, members of the audience and the media could easily ascertain which agencies had failed to send a representative by looking at the clearly labeled empty chairs. The CRDCW asked each agency to give a 5-minute presentation about what their agency was doing about the issue. More than 200 people attended. Redfern recalled an army representative claiming that the meeting "was the most well-organized session they had ever attended" (J. Redfern, personal communication, September 6, 2005).

Redfern also taught CRDCW members to work with the media in a way that generated a lot of negative publicity about the issue. CRDCW members learned how to issue press releases, contact the assignment editor, and follow up once a press release was issued. Redfern suggested a goal of some kind of media exposure about the VX hydrolysate disposal plan and the problems at the Perma-Fix facility no less than once every 10 days. CRDCW far exceeded this goal. The *Dayton Daily News* ran nearly 70 articles about VX hydrolysate or the Perma-Fix facility from the time Redfern was invited to help the CRDCW in January 2003 to the battle's conclusion in October 2003—an average of one story every 4 days.

Media events and coverage helped get the word out about the issue and build community opposition to the VX hydrolysate disposal plan. Eventually, the CRDCW framed its fight in a national context, explaining that the Drexel community health effects resulting from such a disposal plan would have ramifications across the country. At about the same time, the U.S. Army began to make decisions about the best places to neutralize their chemical stockpiles given Homeland Security concerns. The army decided temporarily that keeping the VX hydrolysate in Newport was a better idea than risking additional Homeland Security issues by transporting it the long distance to Drexel on public transportation routes.

CRDCW raised residents' awareness of environmental issues. For example, Redfern began educating the neighbors near the Perma-Fix facility about the firm's history of environmental problems, such as the release of noxious fumes that caused burning eyes, nausea, and headaches. One resident said, "Often, particularly in the morning, it smells so awful that I get dizzy and sick to my stomach" (E. Jacobs, personal communication, September 2, 2005). The problem was particularly evident in the evenings and on weekends, whether because it was worse at those times or simply more noticeable given that more people were at home during those times.

Redfern taught neighborhood residents to record their daily observations. They were given odor and incident logs and asked to record any air-related issues, including the date and time and a description of what occurred. Redfern urged residents to call the Regional Air Pollution Control Agency (RAPCA) each time they noticed a strong odor or suspected a violation. RAPCA's mission is to protect the citizens of the Miami Valley from the adverse health and welfare impacts of air pollution. RAPCA has the initial responsibility for maintaining air quality in Montgomery County through enforcement of federal, state, and local air-pollution regulations and implementation of the state's industrial-permit system. RAPCA began to receive an average of two complaints a week from residents in the area.

Redfern also instructed community members in how to conduct a survey of health incidents that occurred around the Perma-Fix facility, which she then submitted to the Agency for Toxic Substances and Disease Registry (ATSDR). The ATSDR, an agency of the U.S. Department of Health and Human Services, has a mission to serve the public by using the best science, taking

(Continued)

(Continued)

responsive public health actions, and providing trusted health information to prevent harmful exposures and disease related to toxic substances.

Seeking Public Action and Local Support. RAPCA records, which Jacobs required the agency to make public, showed the agency found 150 "instances of emissions" attributable to biological reactors from 2001 to 2003. These emissions produced strong odors and caused many people to suffer from burning eyes. Jacobs also learned that in January 2002 RAPCA had notified officials at Perma-Fix and the Ohio Environmental Protection Agency that Perma-Fix was in violation of federal clean air laws. Since then, RAPCA and the Ohio EPA had been awaiting a ruling from the U.S. EPA that would confirm a violation before following up on this finding. In the meantime, residents, frustrated with RAPCA's inaction, started calling the local Ohio EPA office to complain. The Ohio EPA referred them back to RAPCA. Residents came to realize that unless they demanded action, discussions of the VX hydrolysate issue would simply continue unabated in a bureaucratic stalemate, much like discussion of the 2002 federal clean air violation.

Jacobs sent a letter to RAPCA and the Ohio EPA director pressing one or the other agency to act. Jacobs explained to the *Dayton Daily News*, "We're saying we don't care. Somebody needs to pick up the ball on this, and it's a big ball" (DeBrosse, 2003c; E. Jacobs, personal communication, September 2, 2005). As Drexel neighbors collected more complaints about air emissions, they became more upset that no one was addressing their complaints (J. Redfern, personal communication, September 6, 2005). Finally, after months of receiving surveys and logs from neighbors, RAPCA stated in a letter dated June 12, 2003, that it would start daily surveillance of the Perma-Fix facility's air emissions (E. Jacobs, personal communication, September 2, 2005).

CRDCW members not only undertook a broad media campaign, they also undertook a deep media campaign on a local level. They posted fliers all over the affected communities, including in grocery stores and churches. Members stood on local street corners gathering signatures on petitions and telling people about the issue at the same time.

Most of these efforts proved effective in raising awareness and recruiting people to oppose the VX hydrolysate disposal plan, but one of them backfired. CRDCW encouraged people to sign preprinted postcards it created and then mail the cards to the program manager of the U.S. Army, Office for Chemical Demilitarization, who oversaw the neutralization issue. The postcard read, "As a resident of the Miami Valley, I strongly oppose transporting partially treated VX Nerve Agent (VX hydrolysate) to the Miami Valley for further treatment and disposal into our sewers and waterways" (J. Redfern, personal communication, September 6, 2005). Hundreds of people signed these cards, added their names and addresses, and mailed them. The army's policy of sending an acknowledgment letter for every letter received meant that everyone who filled in their name and address received a letter from the U.S. Army that stated, "The Army is also doing its best to support Homeland Security Initiatives by eliminating a potential terrorist target as expediently as possible" (E. Jacobs, personal communication, September 2, 2005). At a time when the army was at war and terrorist threats ranged from orange to red, these letters raised questions about CRDCW's credibility among some local residents (L. Rench, personal communication, September 2, 2005).

During this time, the U.S. Army was recruiting members for their community advisory panel and implementing their plan for outreach activities and public involvement. But only one community representative actually joined the panel. The panel held three meetings—March 18, April 2, and May 29—to "educate the community" and answer questions about the VX hydrolysate disposal plan. Representatives from the CRDCW attended each of the three meetings. They asked the panel prepared questions and, after receiving answers, they stood up, sang a gospel song, and left.

In addition to these public forums, in May 2003 Jacobs signaled that a local resident and the NAACP were prepared to go to federal court to sue the U.S. EPA, the Ohio EPA, and Perma-Fix of Dayton for violation of Executive Order 12898, Federal Actions to Address Environmental Justice in Minority Populations and Low-Income Populations. Jacobs explained that the U.S. Army was in violation of the law by its action to move a hazardous program from the Newport Chemical Depot to the Drexel neighborhood in Jefferson Township:

> The U.S. Army is clearly violating the Executive Order on Environmental Justice by moving the second phase of treatment from a rural location that is 97 percent white and where treatment will take place at least 2.6 miles from residences to a densely-populated urban location where the treatment will take place directly across the street from residences in an area that is more than 33 percent people of color and where no less than 33 percent of the households are below the poverty level. (E. Jacobs, personal communication, September 2, 2005)

Jacobs pointed out that the army acknowledged there would be hazardous air emissions from handling and processing VX hydrolysate and dangers from transportation and processing accidents and fires. Yet the army had not made any effort to measure the effects on the environment, the surrounding neighborhood, and the health of individuals stemming from the specific process to be used at Perma-Fix. After further research, the Legal Aid Society of Dayton filed suit in August 2003 against the U.S. Army and its program manager for chemical demilitarization on behalf of CRDCW and several local residents.

Despite all of this, Montgomery County commissioners still refused to speak out against the VX hydrolysate disposal plan or become directly involved in any way. The CRDCW insisted that they get involved because the commissioners had control over the county wastewater-treatment plant, which would have to handle the discharge from the Perma-Fix-treated VX hydrolysate.

When the commissioners finally acted, they hired an outside consultant to determine how the discharge would affect the county's wastewater-treatment process; the commission was responsible for the quality of discharge that left the county wastewater-treatment facility and flowed into the river, regardless of where the waste came from before it entered their plant. In response to the consultant's report, on October 8, 2003, the Montgomery County Sanitary Engineer's Office refused to issue a permit for the Perma-Fix facility to discharge treated waste products from neutralized VX hydrolysate into the county's wastewater system. It cited "the considerable number of unanswered questions, incomplete, missing or inadequate data, apparent treatment process deficiencies and the risks—health and ecological—involved" (DeBrosse, 2003b, p. A1).

On October 11, 2003, U.S. Representative Mike Turner called Redfern to officially announce that the U.S. Army was withdrawing its contract from the Perma-Fix facility in Dayton. The CRDCW drafted a press release and arranged for a press conference with Representative Turner. The U.S. Army did not state the exact reason it had withdrawn the contract. Regardless, the CRDCW—the little guys—had won!

Concepts of Change

So how does a relatively powerless and underrepresented group of people organize to effectively protect their community against the threat of an environmental hazard? What is the recipe that brings individuals together around a local issue and helps them succeed in their fight? The answers entail familiar aspects of theoretical concepts of leadership—values, adaptive work, leadership without authority, and the common and distinguishing elements of leadership. These concepts may apply a bit differently in the community context. The primary value and nature of adaptive work in this and other community change contexts, for example, are the defense of a community against a threat. The community context also best illustrates leadership without authority or at least without positional authority.

As is often the case, an expansive field of actors and events surrounded what appeared to be a local change effort. CRDCW faced the threat of global terrorism, specifically the fear of a terrorist attack that would release deadly VX somewhere in the United States. The U.S. war in Iraq played a minor part in the case, given its association with the war on terror in general and its initial, ironic mission to destroy Saddam Hussein's weapons of mass destruction, including VX. National and international disarmament efforts started the VX hydrolysate problem by requiring the neutralization of VX. The corporate structure of Perma-Fix and its safety-practice history involving local, state, and federal environmental agencies, factored into the case. The county engineer, commissioners, and a consultant from Northwestern University all played a part in assessing the quality of the wastewater resulting from the VX hydrolysate treatment.

Some actors and groups in this case clearly had local roots. The work LLAND had done in opposing landfills in the area had a cumulative effect on the local citizenry. No one could have foretold how LLAND's work years earlier would influence the efforts of CRDCW. Similarly, Ohio Citizen Action and the Legal Aid Society of Dayton did not have previous ties to CRDCW. Nevertheless, both organizations offered relevant skills and resources in support of CRDCW efforts.

Racism played a major role in this case as well. The history of racism in the United States led to legislation designed to prevent the perpetration of further injustices against minorities by prohibiting the disposal of toxic wastes in minority communities (United States Environmental Protection Agency, 1998). This legislation gave CRDCW a strong legal footing for combating the proposed VX hydrolysate treatment plant in the Drexel community.

Social Capital

Looking at the VX hydrolysate case through the lens of social capital also proves instructive. Sociologist James Coleman first developed the concept of social capital as an analog to other forms of capital—financial, physical, and human—in organizational and for-profit contexts. He used it to refer to the bonds among people who are the human capital of an organization. Political scientist Robert Putnam (1995, 2000; Putnam, Leonardi, & Raffaella, 1993) took this concept and considerably expanded it to include social networks among people in community contexts. These community social networks stemmed from membership in groups ranging from labor organizations to bird-watching clubs. The cultural norms of trust and cooperation developed in these community settings spilled over, in Putnam's estimation, into business and political contexts. Putnam later researched membership in various associations and groups in the United States and found a decline in social capital; more people were bowling alone, in a manner of speaking, than in leagues. Putnam's social capital thesis may come into play in the VX hydrolysate disposal case to explain how LLAND and other associations provided experience in group action that permitted Bronston, Cooper, Johnson, and Rench to collaborate quickly. His thesis falls short in explaining why residents of Drexel and Jefferson Township—one better off than the other—both had the social capital to collaborate. If poverty is associated with a deficit of social capital, then the low-income neighborhoods should have remained inactive.

The lens of citizen leadership provides another look at social capital, especially when citizen leaders are considered social capital entrepreneurs. Citizen leadership suggests that social capital is not so much a characteristic of a group or an individual as it is an investment in people as members of a community. This investment includes not only developing the moral resources of trust, cooperation, and association but also fostering the social goods and services that permit people to sustain themselves in a community marked by a reasonable degree of well-being. Most often, public policy in the United States invests social capital—education, health care, income floors, and so on—based on membership in the workforce. The more lucrative your work, the more social capital you have; the more social capital invested in you, the better your employment opportunities. Citizen leaders become social capital entrepreneurs by investing in people regardless of their place in the labor force and sometimes precisely because they are not part of the labor force—the elderly and very young, disabled, unskilled, and unemployed—and thus are likely to be bypassed by other forms of social capital investment.

In the VX hydrolysate disposal case, the concept of social capital entrepreneurship counted the environment as a social good. The risks associated with the disposal of VX hydrolysate fell to Drexel because the neighborhood had a dearth of social capital investment. More precisely, Drexel was put at risk of social capital disinvestment by the proposed disposal plan that almost certainly would have resulted in the degradation of the neighborhood's environment, thereby denying residents the ability to sustain themselves in a community of well-being. The relation of environmental risks and social capital as investment in people as workforce members implicitly resides in the environmental justice policies of the EPA. The pattern of locating the most toxic wastes in communities with the least income and lowest rates of employment underscores the neglect of social goods among people not considered valuable to the workforce. Although legislation exists that was intended to redress this type of inequity, it might never have been acknowledged without the citizen leadership, or social capital entrepreneurship, of CRDCW. CRDCW invested the moral resources necessary to guarantee that the social good of environmental quality not be further eroded in a low-income, high-unemployment area.

Empowerment

Empowerment is a specific moral resource best expressed in leadership change efforts at the community level. Discussions of empowerment often confuse it with the delegation of power and sometimes with the mere appearance of change in the forms and expressions of power. Genuine empowerment, by contrast, involves new and improved forms of representation and participation in decision making. Social advocacy pioneer Sherry R. Arnstein (1969) assembled a ladder of participation ranging from citizen control at one end to manipulation at the other, with varying degrees of effective and ineffective participation in between. These levels of participation are in turn marked by varying degrees of influence and power. A ladder of participation and representation appears in Figure 5.1. The three top rungs of participation entail degrees of power, and the next three entail degrees of recognition that imply some power. The last two rungs, therapy and manipulation, are forms of control by those in authority and nonparticipation by those served by programs. Accompanying these forms of participation are forms of representation that range from direct participation, as exemplified by the participation of CRDCW members in their own meetings as well as the panel meetings organized by the U.S. Army and Perma-Fix, to indirect participation, as exemplified by the citizens selected by the U.S. Army and Perma-Fix to represent residents of the area. The degree of direct representation and full participation in the accountability session offered an even clearer distinction: CRDCW practiced citizen control by organizing the accountability session and then setting the rules, including representation and participation of authorities, and CRDCW practiced consultation and informing during the panel sessions that were governed by rules established by individuals in positions of authority.

The Facets and Forms of Power

Empowerment, as measured by representation and participation, brings us face to face with power, a much-neglected element of leadership, according to James MacGregor Burns (2007, pp. v–vi). Political sociologist John Gaventa's (1980) early work brought the three dimensions of power to the fore in a synthesis and analytical

FIGURE 5.1 A Ladder of Citizen Participation

Citizen control Delegated power Partnership	Degrees of citizen power	↑ Full participation
Placation Consultation Informing	Degrees of tokenism	Partial participation
Therapy Manipulation	Degrees of nonparticipation	↓ Disfranchisement

framework of the history of a coal-mining region of central Appalachia. In his book, Gaventa dealt exclusively with one form of power—*power over* others—and resistance to it. Gaventa explained then and more recently that *power over* others has three dimensions:

- *Visible*—when those in authority use sanctions or coercion to accomplish their ends, often expressing the futility of resistance by saying things like "You can't fight the Army!"
- *Hidden*—when those in authority do not have to make their power visible by using sanctions and coercion because the people's mere knowledge of the authorities' capability to use sanctions and coercion is enough to deter opposition. Such was the case when Perma-Fix and the U.S. Army used a generic environmental-impact statement rather than one specific to the Drexel community.
- *Invisible*—when groups in and out of power hold to the same set of beliefs about what is right and just. Even though these beliefs support great inequality, they are not viewed as unjust but as part of a natural order that social conditions manifest. The hesitancy to confront the U.S. Army at a time when it was mobilizing to conduct a war on terrorism draws on values to which almost all Americans are thoroughly socialized. (Gaventa, 1980, 2005)

Empowerment increases the visibility of power: People move from the "commonsense" acceptance of a decision, such as the location of a VX hydrolysate–processing plant at Drexel, to the realization that there are winners and losers hidden in any arrangement. When people challenge the arrangement, their power becomes visible. Redfern played a key role in this process of power analysis, or what Paulo Freire (1993), a Brazilian adult educator, calls conscientization.

But a complete analysis of empowerment must not only consider the *power over* but also the *power to*, defined as the sense of power that individuals or group members must possess if they are to bring about change. In the VX hydrolysate case, this sense of power began with Redfern's explanation of what needed to be done and her confidence that the group could succeed with hard work. The power within and the power with go hand in hand with the *power to*. Empowered group members come to understand the power they have as part of the group (the power with) and the power group members have within themselves (the *power within*). Using this power entails serious internal conflict because people who have come to accept hidden forms of power—the invisible dimension of *power over*—must now challenge their "commonsense" views. This brings them to unfamiliar and uncertain territory that may be somewhat intimidating. For example, CRDCW experienced a setback in its mobilization efforts when residents who had registered their opposition to VX hydrolysate reprocessing in Drexel received letters from the U.S. Army invoking homeland security. These letters fed residents' doubts about their *power to* challenge an authority such as the U.S. Army about certain decisions it makes.

A true sense of empowerment does not take the form of *power over* other group members but is much more aligned with a sense of *power to* bring about change by developing a sense of *power within* one's self and then seeking to direct that power in collaboration with others. Ultimately, community change leadership, much more than change leadership in other contexts, emphasizes power as a resource a group may mobilize to conduct its adaptive work.

Gaventa (2005) offered a "Rubik's power cube" analogy. The cube contains the four forms of power—over, to, with, and within (Csaszar, 2004; Hughes et al., 2005; Rowlands, 1997). Each form has three dimensions—visible, hidden, or invisible. Gaventa added different levels for power and participation—global, national, and local. Clearly, CRDCW participated and exercised power primarily, but not exclusively, at the local level. When CRDCW members asked a congressional representative to clarify the nature of public approval of U.S. Army plans for disposal of hazardous wastes and their by-products, what had been a local issue took on national implications. The CRDCW also played a small part in the global effort to deal with weapons of mass destruction.

Gaventa (2005) suggested that power and participation occur in different spaces—closed, invited, and claimed or created. CRDCW encouraged the participation of residents at its meetings, thereby creating spaces for people to discover the *power within* them to work with others to accomplish change. CRDCW members claimed space by singing in panel meetings where they were expected only to listen and ask questions. Clearly, they did not participate in the space where the army made its final decision to cancel the contract with Perma-Fix. But their organized resistance to the plan represented a new space for both them and the army.

Power over continues as long as people focus only on the closed or invited spaces dictated by those in positions of authority and power. Empowerment comes with a sense of the *power within* groups without authority to create space for participation and decision making. Again, the accountability meeting and the panel meetings demonstrated the power of the "powerless" party to create a space in which all parties are invited to participate.

This discussion of power underscores the relational dimension of leadership and change. Power with has a synergistic quality. It has roots in the *power within* and the *power to*. It undermines the authority of those who rely on *power over*. It spills over into new forms of representation and participation in decision making, all of which promote genuine forms of empowerment. This implies that the forms and amounts of power are not fixed but created and cocreated. Thus, *power within* is the self-discovery of capacity for action and *power to* is the exercise of that sense of agency. Done in conjunction with others—namely, power with—these two forms of power create a synergy of vitality and transformation at the personal, local, national, and global levels of Gaventa's Rubik's cube.

Concepts of Leadership

Values—A Cohesive Sense of Community

The values of community—some sense of connectedness to a place, a group of people, or a common problem or an issue—lie at the center of theoretical concepts of leadership. Although a sense of community may often be present among a group of people, something needs to trigger it so that people mobilize resources. Most often this trigger takes the form of a clear threat to the community, such as the environmental threat described in the case study in this chapter.

Jefferson Township gradually became more cohesive as more residents learned of the VX hydrolysate problem. People called on friends to accompany them to meetings. A telephone tree created to combat a previous environmental threat to the community still connected people to each other years after the initial impetus to assemble it had passed. Residents made new community connections based on a sense of place and a common threat. Black and White residents collaborated.

Residents mobilized group resources to do the adaptive work necessary to deal with a threat to group values and welfare (Heifetz, 1994, 2007). They compiled and organized the information they already had and then charged certain group members with researching and disseminating additional information. They did so without the benefit of any official authority stemming from organizational or political position. Whatever authority residents had came from their position within the CRDCW, an organization they had started. Their adaptive work resembles a very high degree of leadership without authority and, thus, what Heifetz (2007) termed the "most useful analytical unit of leadership" (p. 34).

Citizen Leadership—Leadership Without Authority

We may extrapolate on this case study further by referring to citizen leadership (Couto, 1995). Citizen leadership facilitates organized action among people traditionally underrepresented in official decision-making processes. It takes as its premise the dignity and worth of each individual, regardless of race, age, gender, income, or any other demographic factor. Unlike leaders in other contexts, citizen leaders most often do not choose to lead and reluctantly leave private lives for public roles. Most often, their first action is to approach public officials, such as the Jefferson Township trustees, to do something about a particular problem. Often the lack of information and action from those in formal positions of authority creates a realization that citizens will have to do the adaptive work themselves. In a law of inverse proportion, citizen leaders come to trust themselves more as they come to trust public and corporate authorities less. The adaptive work of citizen leaders occurs in response to a clear, simple question: Will our children have the chance to live in dignity and health in their community?

Adaptive Work

The adaptive work of community leadership offers the means to redress the conditions that undermine and understate the human dignity of community members. Thus, community leadership supports civil society. In so doing, it has to overcome a lot, including the beliefs of many community residents that they do not count and that the values of others always outweigh their own values. In the case study detailed in this chapter, for example, many residents initially cited the futility of fighting the U.S. Army.

Change, Conflict, and Collaboration

The three constants of leadership—change, conflict, and collaboration—were evident in this case study as well. CRDCW members conflicted with Perma-Fix officials, U.S. Army representatives, and political officials at the local and county levels. They collaborated with each other, with Ohio Citizen Action (itself a collaborative network of environmental groups), with the 37 organizations and jurisdictions that supported their resolution, with their congressional representative, and with countless others.

Despite their conflict with some local and county officials, CRDCW members nevertheless participated with them in some events, such as accountability night, and later collaborated with them in opposing the plant. The Montgomery County commissioners didn't take action until CRDCW members brought them into the conflict on their side. CRDCW opposed change, thus challenging the assumption that leadership always initiates change and suggesting that, in some cases at least, it may actually prevent change. Adam Yarmolinsky (2007) suggested that rather than initiating change, leadership mediates change.

Leaders must be mindful of the interrelationship between change, conflict, and collaboration. As a community leader once explained, conflict clarifies values and thus provides a better foundation for possible collaboration (Couto, 2002, pp. 90–91). The experience of another community leader suggests principles of conflict as respectful engagement—seeing conflict as temporary in an enduring collaborative relationship, educating oneself and others to resolve conflict, making a set of humane assumptions about those with whom one is in conflict, and giving credit to others for favorable outcomes (Couto, 2002, pp. 140–141).

Initiative, Inclusiveness, and Creativity

Leadership may have common tasks, but values, initiative, inclusiveness, and creativity differentiate some forms of leadership from others. The case study in this chapter illustrates how a few individuals took the initiative to oppose the VX hydrolysate disposal plan, a little later friends and neighbors joined in their efforts, and eventually various individuals and groups merged into CRDCW in a successful bid to combat the disposal plan. Leadership entails acting on behalf of values, but when or if people choose to act varies greatly and is affected by the amount of information they have and events going on around them.

Creativity was evident in many CRDCW actions. The creative labeling of chairs for the accountability session, for example, clearly identified those who were not participating and created a compelling photo opportunity for journalists. CRDCW also demonstrated creativity with their gospel singing at the panel hearings conducted by the U.S. Army and Perma-Fix. Creativity is more than artistic expression, however; it also involves the type of strategic thinking and problem solving demonstrated in the mobilization of CRDCW resources and the networking with other groups and resources. Finally, creativity enables people to have fun—an important rule for community organizing (Alinsky, 1971, p. 128).

Change Practices

Successful community change efforts generally have four elements:

- A cohesive sense of identity and a sense of imminent threat to it
- Strong local leadership
- Vertical and horizontal networks
- Expert outside advice (Couto, 1999)

The discussion of theoretical concepts examined the first factor. Rench, Cooper, Bronston, and Johnson stand as examples of strong and effective local leadership. This leaves the last two elements of community change leadership to examine.

Vertical and Horizontal Networks

The discussion of social capital and community leadership as social capital entrepreneurship touched on networks. Now we examine networking as an essential element of community change leadership. Initially, community leadership may be at a complete loss about where to start to accomplish the change it seeks. The VX hydrolysate case typified most community change scenarios in that residents turned to one another, to local authorities, and to people within the organization(s) that posed the threat (Perma-Fix and the U.S. Army, in this case). If these networks do not help, community leadership then looks for groups that have made or are making similar change efforts. This horizontal network informs community leaders of lessons learned and mistakes made. Leaders in one community receive empathy and support from leaders in another community, not only in terms of the how-to's of conducting change but also in terms of the personal sacrifices they must make in giving up time with family and friends to pursue a change initiative and the personal conflicts they must face while leading without authority.

Often local community leadership learns of its horizontal network through links to organizations in a vertical network. In the VX hydrolysate case, Ohio Citizen Action assisted local groups across the state. Even before the founding of CRDCW, Redfern explicitly shared with local residents the lessons about the horizontal networks of communities like theirs and how these networks were instrumental in achieving desired change.

The vertical network parallels the levels of participation in Gaventa's (2005) Rubik's cube. To be successful, local community leadership needs the horizontal help of other local groups and resources as well as the vertical help of regional, state, national, and perhaps even international groups. These horizontal and vertical networks are interrelated, one informing the other. A LLAND member, for example, suggested that Rench contact Redfern; Redfern in turn brought with her a horizontal network of local residents with experience in similar change efforts and a vertical network of additional resources.

Expert Advice

These networks provide local community leadership with outside expert advice, another element critical to success at the local level. Redfern proffered outside expert advice when she taught local residents how to handle media relations and other events, such as the accountability session, that make up an organizing campaign. She also understood the nature of community-organizing campaigns and the risks of burnout and intimidation. She often assessed the group to modulate provocation (see, e.g., Heifetz, 1994, pp. 206–231). Her work reflected some basic tenets of Alinsky-style organizing, such as keeping a group focused and working on change within their realm of experience and getting opponents outside their realm of experience (Alinsky, 1971, p. 127).

CRDCW also brought in outside expert Jacobs of the Legal Aid Society of Dayton. He framed the processing of VX hydrolysate in legal terms that addressed the inadequacy of a generic environmental-impact statement and environmental justice. Without the benefit of his legal expertise, local leadership may not have succeeded in their efforts to protect their cohesive community from an imminent threat.

Outside experts within community leadership's vertical networks provide access to decision makers and help frame problems for the latter to redress. Bronston and Johnson, for example, created a horizontal and vertical network of decision makers and groups to influence other decision makers. CRDCW brought these networks to bear on the Montgomery County Commission, which eventually took up the matter of VX hydrolysate process despite considerable reluctance.

Advocacy

The VX hydrolysate case exemplified a best-practices model of community organizing, one that involved listening to residents' concerns, identifying patterns in those concerns, and then pulling people together to create an action plan to address those concerns. It involved power and empowerment and democratic practices of representation and participation in decision making (Szakos & Szakos, 2007, pp. 1–12).

Often organizing is confused with advocacy, another change practice of community leadership. They may be the same if community members organize to advocate for themselves and if they are directly represented and participate fully in their advocacy. Advocacy and organizing differ substantially when one group advocates on behalf of another, thus resulting in indirect representation and, at best, partial participation of group members.

David Cohen (Cohen, De la Vega, & Watson, 2001), founder of the Advocacy Institute, described advocacy in terms of organizing. In doing so, he underscored the role of community leadership in change efforts for social justice:

> Advocacy consists of organized efforts and actions based on the reality of "what is." These organized actions seek to highlight ignored and suppressed critical issues, influence public attitudes, and promote the enactment and implementation of laws and public policies that turn visions of "what should be" in a just, decent society into reality. Human rights—political, economic, and social—provide an overarching framework for these visions. Advocacy organizations

draw their strength from and are accountable to people—their members, constituents, and/or members of affected groups. Advocacy has purposeful results: to enable social justice advocates to gain access and voice in the decision making of relevant institutions; to change the power relationships between these institutions and the people affected by their decisions, thereby changing the institutions themselves; and to effect a clear improvement in people's lives. (p. 8)

However local their issue and efforts might have been, at some level CRDCW members understood they were advocating for an improved condition not only for themselves but also for others like them. This understanding came across in the jubilant victory celebration of "the little guy."

Participatory Action Research

Effective advocacy demands reliable and relevant information. In the VX hydrolysate case, local residents conducted door-to-door surveys to collect residents' opinions and health histories and library and Internet research to collect data on the nature of VX hydrolysate and its hazards. This research provided local residents with the reliable, detailed information they needed to participate fully in public forums. They had an in-depth understanding of the issue, were able to ask probing questions, and could provide new information or documentation about various aspects of the issue to be decided.

People in authority often dismiss this type of crucial research when the people conducting the research lack scholarly credentials. Increasingly, however, action research and its most genuine community-based form, participatory action research, have received attention and credence even from academic researchers (Lincoln & Guba, 2000; Minkler & Wallerstein, 2003), some of whom even extol the value of "local knowledge" (Geertz, 1983). Community-based participatory action research (CBPAR) permits the community to "own" knowledge about itself, places community leaders in a better position to advocate for policies and with the media, and represents the deliberate training of community leaders by bridging cultural and class differences and differences between community organizing and community advocacy. The tenets of CBPAR address the strategic elements of increasing formal and informal leadership roles of groups underrepresented in policy- and decision-making processes.

CBPAR has deep roots that bloom in varied forms: action science, constructivist inquiry, usable knowledge, participatory research, and, very recently, community-based participatory research for health (Minkler & Wallerstein, 2003). According to one definition, action research engages researchers and community leaders "in a collaborative process of critical inquiry into problems of social practice in a learning context" (Argyris, Putnam, & Smith, 1985, p. 236). Action research, a phrase coined by social psychologist Kurt Lewin (1951), displays the following characteristics:

- A change effort that focuses on a particular problem in a social system and seeks to provide assistance to the client system
- Iterative cycles of discourse between professionals and community members to identify a problem, plan, act, and evaluate

- Reeducation to change well-established patterns of thinking and acting
- Challenges to the status quo from a perspective of democratic values
- Contributions to basic knowledge in social science and social action in every-day life (Argyris et al., 1985, pp. 8–9)

Participatory action research involves the participation of the people for whom the knowledge is being produced and holds researchers accountable to them. Participatory action research has the following characteristics, all of which were evident in the work and research of CRDCW:

- The problem under study and the decision to study it have origins in the community or group affected by the problem.
- The goal of the research is action for change based on the information gathered.
- The community or group affected by the problem controls the processes of defining the problem, gathering the information, and subsequently making the decision about the appropriate action to take.
- Members of the community or group are equal in the research process to those conducting the study.
- Everyone is regarded as a researcher and learner.
- Skills are transferred among all participants and information is shared (Couto, 1987).

Figure 5.2 locates the varieties of community-based research along axes of community participation and intended change. It helps to distinguish the applied and fieldwork research of scholars, such as the water-quality expert the Montgomery County Commission brought in from Northwestern University, based on the degree of change sought and the participation of local residents. Empowerment in participatory action research increases when the direct representation and participation of local residents in the research process increase.

Asset-Based Community Change

A group must believe it has the skills and resources to conduct PAR well before embarking on it; arriving at this belief, or decision, is yet another form of the adaptive work of mobilizing resources. In particular, PAR illustrates another change practice of community leadership—asset mapping and development. An asset approach to community leadership (Kretzmann & McKnight, 1993) is exactly opposite to a needs or deficit approach. Robert Putnam, Robert Leonardi, and Raffaella Nanetti suggested the difference in their 1993 study of Italy. They described a prosperous and well-run area in northern Italy as having the asset of social capital and a poor and mismanaged area in southern Italy as having a deficit of social capital. An asset approach permits local residents or members of a community to think about what they can do for themselves. A deficit approach leads them to think about how they can make up for what they lack with an infusion of external resources. An asset approach contributes to genuine empowerment and

FIGURE 5.2   Taxonomy of Community-Based Research Forms by Methods, Community Involvement, and Change

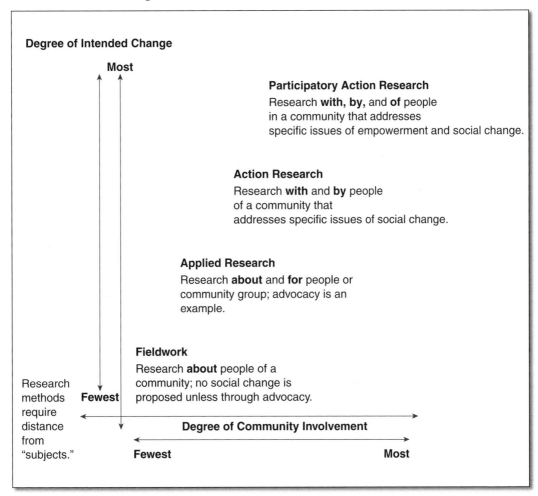

organized self-advocacy. A deficit approach results in others advocating on behalf of a group whose members have only token representation and indirect participation. An asset approach assumes that people are capable of doing their own adaptive work, including mobilizing resources in horizontal and vertical networks. A deficit approach relies on an outside expert or authority figure to do these things for the people. An asset approach permits group members to conduct their own information gathering—with assistance. A deficit approach assumes that others will gather information for and about the group—even if the information gathered is intended for the group's benefit.

CRDCW clearly used an asset approach. Members took inventory of the group's needs and the resources they had to meet those needs. They also identified where to find resources they lacked. CRDCW developed many PAR assets, such as media savvy, political influence, and outside help. Almost all of the outsiders associated with these additional, external resources were accountable to CRDCW.

Conclusion

In the CRDCW case, people worked very hard in community leadership efforts for change. The stress of working so hard for so long against very powerful opponents caused many people to drop out. People had to summon the courage to challenge their own and others' preconceptions about equality and inequality. Unlike many other leadership contexts, the residents of Drexel and Jefferson Township more broadly did not choose to be leaders; rather, they took on leadership roles out of necessity, to combat an imminent threat to their personal and community well-being. After the resolution of the conflict, residents did not continue in or return to positions of authority with all the accompanying perks. Therefore, it was particularly important for the CRDCW members to celebrate and receive recognition for their efforts when they succeeded in thwarting the VX hydrolysate treatment plan for Drexel—hence the headlines about the victory celebration.

The CRDCW experience gave Drexel residents a model of success and the confidence to take on other change efforts. For example, CRDCW wanted to see Perma-Fix clean up its operation and become a better neighbor. Some of the group members worked with RAPCA and Montgomery County to make this happen. Community leadership most often develops in reaction to a threat, however. People are willing to work incredibly hard to hold on to what they value about their community. Once they face down a threat to their community, they often revert to their private roles and the enjoyment of the community they worked so hard to preserve. Moving community leadership from reaction to a threat to action to improve the quality of life in the community is very difficult.

A lot of diverse people came together to fight the VX hydrolysate disposal plan, thereby creating unity within the community. The CRDCW efforts will become part of the collective memory of the community just as the LLAND efforts did, providing social capital to use when another threat to Drexel and Jefferson Township emerges. The community leadership in this case has become part of a horizontal network of success from which lessons may be drawn when other instances requiring community leadership for change arise. It preserves hope in "what a community of different people can do when it comes together" (DeBrosse, 2003a, p. A1).

Application and Reflection

Application

When Community Claims Collide

Ed Long was upset. He had just returned from the Ivanhoe Home Owners Association's (IHOA) specially called meeting. The president explained that the Green Valley Housing Opportunity Program (GVHOP) was planning to build an apartment building in a lot on the edge of Ivanhoe, with the subdivision surrounding the building on three sides. The city's zoning and planning committee had already approved the plans almost a year ago and just notified IHOA of a second meeting to be held in a month. The building would have six apartments with two adults with mental retardation or other developmental disabilities (MRDD) in each.

Ed Long and his neighbors are solidly middle class, and their modest condominiums are their primary asset and the most likely means of financing their children's college education. Long and his neighbors were concerned that the apartment building would change the nature of their community and decrease property values. Ivanhoe is a 15-year-old subdivision with 100 families. A new apartment building with people with special needs would mean a drastic change in the nature of the group of homeowners. The residents' caregivers would come and go at all times, disrupting the informal networks IHOA had established to monitor intruders in the community and in general look after each other. The building would also require developing a wooded lot that served as a green space for the community. Long was further irritated because he felt that the president of IHOA had taken this development lying down.

Over the next several weeks, Long began to organize to stop the housing development at the upcoming zoning and planning committee meeting. He was skilled at organizing from his experience as the president of the local chapter of the Association of State, County, and Municipal Employees Union; Long's experience as an emergency medical technician also helped him. He knew he had to rally the troops, so he began to mobilize IHOA members. Soon the city officials were deluged with phone calls asking for action to stop the development of the proposed apartment building. Long brought members to a meeting of the zoning and planning committee and protested the plan that the committee had approved a year before. Long and his neighbors packed a subsequent city council meeting as well; there was standing room only in the room, and chairs had to be set up in the lobby for the overflow of 100 or so homeowners. These actions brought the approval process to a halt. The city council postponed final approval of the project and tabled its consideration at two consecutive monthly meetings. They hoped that the IHOA and GVHOP would work things out.

The action of the city council was pretty disappointing for Sally Torrisi, the 10-year executive director of the GVHOP. She had been very conscientious to follow all the rules. Federal regulations required that funds be available for the construction of apartments for people with disabilities only if the buildings were located on property zoned for apartments; on property that had access to community services; in cities that needed more affordable housing to qualify for other federal funding; and on property with a seller willing to commit the land for the project for as long as it takes to get approval for the Department of Housing and Urban Development. The Ivanhoe lot met all four criteria.

Torrisi had jumped through other hoops of approval. The site had to meet environmental quality standards to ensure an absence of harmful materials in the soil or water. She had it tested and researched, and it met the requirements. She met with the director of zoning and planning, Bill Norton. The 15-year veteran in this position remembered the parcel of land well. Twelve years ago the lot had been left out of the development of other housing in Ivanhoe. It was zoned for multifamily housing. At her formal presentation to the zoning and planning commission, its members agreed that the community needed more housing for people with disabilities, and this parcel seemed appropriate for that purpose.

(Continued)

(Continued)

This proposed housing was a bold step for GVHOP in several ways. All 48 other units were renovated homes in which no more than four people could live, or they were apartments for two people. This construction would be new, designed, from the beginning, with wheelchair access and other specialized features for 12 people with MRDD. Torrisi hoped that this construction would be a model and more rapidly increase the supply of housing for the 900 persons in the county who needed it.

With the assistance of a real estate attorney with years of experience in affordable housing development across the state, Torrisi took the committee's approval and documentation about the site and gained almost $1,000,000 in funding from HUD, the Federal Home Loan Bank, the county board of MRDD, the state housing finance fund, and a private philanthropy. She called Norton with the good news but learned that he was leaving for another job in the state capital. He also suggested that Torrisi talk with the neighbors. His tone was a bit ominous. Torrisi researched a bit more and found out that the neighbors had a homeowners association that represented the tightly knit community. It functioned officially to monitor compliance with the covenants that all homeowners agreed to when buying property in the Ivanhoe area.

Torrisi tried to reach the IHOA leaders but without success. She met them a year after gaining approval at the second meeting of the zoning and planning committee. Since learning about the apartment development plans, Long had gained notoriety in the IHOA and was selected its new president. In the first meeting with Long before the zoning and planning committee, Torrisi found Long cordial, but with the committee he was vehement in his opposition to the plan and made sure that the committee took note of the large number of residents with him at these ordinarily sparsely attended meetings.

Torrisi was not deterred. She had run into neighbors' opposition in previous projects. Her amiable and accommodating manner generally enables her to approach neighbors in a collaborative manner. Her experience taught her that the quality of GVHOP property maintenance, including professional lawn service, and the friendly manner of MRDD residents won acceptance in the neighborhoods.

In light of the new opposition, the city council delayed action, and Torrisi did her best to accommodate the IHOA's requests for information—reams of paper and myriad documents. She agreed to design alterations at the site that included creating a new street for access to the site and planting trees to block the view of the building.

However, Torrisi drew the line at Ed's request that GVHOP join the IHOA. Doing so would bring the apartment site under the covenant agreement that specified that "any member of the HOA who proposes structural change has to get approval from the Architecture Committee" and give the IHOA a legal right to oppose the apartment development on "structural" grounds. This sounded too much like the back door to zoning out the project and a violation of Fair Housing laws. In addition, the IHOA had a single landscape firm do all the work for the condominiums of the community. Should the GVHOP not employ them, Torrisi imagined, the IHOA would have reasons to nitpick GVHOP for the upkeep of its site.

So Torrisi dug in her heels. The law states that "it is unlawful for local governments to utilize land use and zoning policies to keep persons with disabilities from locating to their area." The law came into being because of discriminatory practices of real estate brokers, financial institutions, and public and private property owners. They frequently used various means, including zoning and covenants, to exclude people based on religion, race, ethnicity, disability, sexual preference, or family makeup. Torrisi was determined that persons with MRDD have the same rights as anyone else to select housing freely in a full and unrestricted market. She was not going to subject GVHOP and its proposed tenants to the IHOA's covenants that could exclude them, despite local zoning laws and federal regulations that permitted them the right to develop the property.

Despite GVHOP's concessions and some ambivalence among a few IHOA members, the two sides could not agree on a mutually acceptable plan. The city council could no longer postpone a decision. They gave the recommendation of the zoning and planning committee to approve the GVHOP proposal and the opposition of the IHOA. They asked a spokesperson for each group to make a short summation of each group's position. Torrisi was asked to go first.

Remarks of Sally Torissi

Members of the Council. My name is Sally Torissi. I am the executive director of the Green Valley Housing Opportunity Program. I would like to put our plan for a six unit apartment building into context; share with you our experience in providing housing for persons with development disabilities; and explain our shared responsibilities to meet federal, state, and local regulations.

I have worked with persons with development disabilities for more than 30 years. During that time, I have seen dramatic changes in practices. Initially, I worked in mental institutions in which persons with mental retardation and developmental disabilities were essentially warehoused. Fortunately, we now recognize the variety of disabilities and the ability for independent or assisted living for many people with disabilities. These are the people whom we serve.

We have provided housing in the community for them and worked with them to become as self-reliant as possible. In that effort of increased self-reliance, GVHOP has pioneered in making people with development disabilities tenants of our housing and not clients of our program. We are accountable to them as their landlord; a dramatic reversal of the former provider-client approach. It has been our goal to take these changes one step further by actually building six apartments, rather than renovating an existing structure, and to do so with accommodating the needs of persons with disabilities in mind.

GVHOP owns 48 properties. We have faced skepticism before, but in every case we have won our neighbors over by the care with which we maintain our properties and the demeanor and personalities of the people who live there. We have worked with the IHOA and accommodated every request that they made except to subject ourselves to their covenants, which might jeopardize the project.

I mentioned our responsibilities because we both have responsibilities in this matter. Federal, state, and local laws regulate and restrict where the housing we propose may be located. GVHOP has complied with every one of these regulations. We have presented our plans to your zoning and planning committee and received their approval to build on this property. We have met the specifications of lenders to gain financing for the proposed building.

Change is difficult, and change in neighborhoods is even more difficult. So there are federal, state, and local laws to make sure that persons with disabilities are not the victims

(Continued)

(Continued)

of continued patterns of prejudice and discrimination. The federal Fair Housing laws protect the rights of minorities against the will of majorities. If every homeowners association has the right to say, "not in my backyard," then we can find no space with access to services for people who are seeking self-reliance, where people with disabilities may live with increased degrees of independence and dignity. Federal and state law sanctions with penalties those who violate the rights of other people to live where they are otherwise legally entitled to live. We do this so that we will not go back to warehousing people in the least desirable locations where no one wants to live.

Look around. There are not large numbers of people with disabilities here to demand their rights. I am not an organizer. I cannot mobilize 100 people with disabilities to demand their rights, nor would I for fear of their encountering the prejudice this housing and the policies that it embodies intend to tear down.

I am an advocate for those people who cannot organize. In this case, I acknowledge that I am somewhat of an irritant to the IHOA but what a pearl of a world this would be if our humanity were expressed in the beauty of our differences. I suggest that it is harmful in the long run to use the instinct of community to separate and protect us from one another rather than creating a global culture of diverse but interwoven communities (Wheatley, 2005, p. 45). I speak for the community of persons with disabilities and I hope you will also. They are depending on me and you to do that. Thank you.

Remarks of Ed Long

Good evening, my name is Ed Long. I have been spokesperson for the Ivanhoe Home Owners Association and recently elected president. I want to thank you for slowing the train that was speeding down the tracks of approval in the wrong direction.

I am an organizer, and I believe that citizens should not be penalized for showing up at this meeting and advocating for themselves, their homes, their families, and their communities. I looked around as Ms. Torrisi suggested. You know what I saw? I saw a consultant and a few board members of GVHOP supporting its proposed plan and a hundred or more residents of this town opposing it.

We are not suggesting a return to the bad old days of institutions and warehousing. In all of IHOA's meetings, there was not one ill word spoken or harsh judgment cast toward people with disabilities. Some of us, including myself, work with them and others of us have family members with disabilities. We are not saying, "Not in my backyard!" We are saying that the federal, state, and local regulations that Ms. Torrisi complied with do not measure a community nor do they preserve it.

The parcel of land in question is surrounded on three sides by the Ivanhoe community. It's like a missing piece of a puzzle. The plans of GVHOP are trying to place a piece that does not fit with the rest of Ivanhoe. That parcel has become part of our community, an asset. We are talking about the integrity of the community. Let me assure you that we would be here in these same numbers if any apartment building were proposed.

Our opposition is not with persons with disabilities but with the "fit" of this building in the heart of Ivanhoe. We are concerned with the additional traffic that such a building would bring into our neighborhood, an addition especially high given the special vehicles and the number of caregivers that persons with disabilities require. We have worked hard over the

15 years since the zoning for this parcel was decided to establish a tightly knit community. Things do change—our community has changed, but the zoning of that parcel did not. It should have to reflect the change around it and to make sure it is integral with Ivanhoe, not the wishes of federal and state officials who have not been here. In that regard, I think it is significant that GVHOP, which has bought the parcel in question, has refused to join the IHOA. Its planned apartment building would be a patch of intrusion to the standards that the rest of us have agreed to.

Yes, of course, people with disabilities have rights, but we are here to assert our rights to a community with integrity. Look around. You won't find people of great wealth in this room. Our homes are our wealth, and our community is our investment in the future of our children. We are not a majority oppressing a minority. It is hard to think of yourself as a majority when you are up against the power of the federal and state government in asserting your right to have a little bit of the American dream and want to hold on to it.

You are our voice in this matter, our elected representatives. Please vote your conscience and do what is right for the people who elected you to represent them. Thank you.

Having heard both sides, the council goes into executive session. Imagine yourself a member of the council. What decision does the city council reach? Why? Illustrate the field of decision making in which you fit as a council member. Who are the other actors and what is their relationship with each other and with the city council? Are there less obvious actors in the field with implications for consequences for your decision, such as other federal agencies, lawyers, and county officials who might take action to enforce Fair Housing laws? How do you define community in this case? What community do you represent and need to speak for? Is there a win-win solution?

REFLECTION

- How does this case parallel the Jefferson Township case?

- Do both communities, IHOA and the persons with MRDD, face threats?

- How does Ed Long exemplify the skills of organizing exemplified in Jefferson Township?

- What is the difference between organizing and advocacy?

- How does GVHOP resemble the U.S. Army and Perma-Fix in the VX hydrolysate case?

- How do Sally Torrisi and Ed Long compare with Jane Forrest Redfern as community change leaders? IHOA with CRDCW? GVHOP with OHA?

- How did Bill Norton's departure affect the decision-making process?

- What is the balance in preserving the homogeneity of a community and increasing its diversity by including people who are absent and perhaps purposefully excluded?

- Which position represents the "real, significant change" that James MacGregor Burns (2007) means when he talks about transforming leadership?

- Who are the "little guys" in this case and what would victory for them mean?

References

Alinsky, S. D. (1971). *Rules for radicals: A practical primer for realistic radicals.* New York: Vintage Books.

Argyris, C., Putnam, R., & Smith, D. M. (1985). *Action science.* San Francisco: Jossey-Bass.

Arnstein, S. R. (1969). A ladder of citizen participation. *Journal of the American Institute of Planners, 35,* 216–224.

Burns, J. M. (2007). Foreword. In R. A. Couto (Ed.), *Reflections on leadership* (pp. v–viii). Lanham, MD: University Press of America.

Cohen, D., De la Vega, R., & Watson, G. (2001). *Advocacy for social justice: A global action and reflection guide.* Bloomfield, CT: Kumarian Press.

Couto, R. A. (1987). Participatory research: Methodology and critique. *Clinical Sociology Review, 5,* 83–90.

Couto, R. A. (1995). Defining a citizen leader. In J. T. Wren (Ed.), *The leader's companion* (pp. 11–17). New York: Free Press.

Couto, R. A. (1999) *Making democracy work better.* Chapel Hill: The University of North Carolina Press.

Couto, R. A. (2002). *To give their gifts: Health, community, and democracy.* Nashville, TN: Vanderbilt University Press.

Csaszar, F. (2005). Understanding the concept of power. In R. Alsop (Ed.), *Power, rights and poverty: Concepts and connections* (pp. 137–146). Washington, DC: World Bank.

DeBrosse, J. (2003a, October 14). Army cancels VX contract. *Dayton Daily News,* p. A1.

DeBrosse, J. (2003b, October 8). County to deny permit for VX plan. *Dayton Daily News,* p. A1.

DeBrosse, J. (2003c, August 6). RAPCA to plant: Fix smell. *Dayton Daily News,* p. B1.

Dempsey, D. (2003, November 14). Redfern leaving Ohio Citizen Action. *Dayton Daily News,* p. B3.

Freire, P. (1993). *Pedagogy of the oppressed* (Rev. ed.). New York: Continuum.

Gaventa, J. (1980). *Power and powerlessness: Quiescence and rebellion in an Appalachian valley.* Urbana: University of Illinois Press.

Gaventa, J. (2005). Reflections on the uses of the "power cube" approach for analyzing the spaces, places and dynamics of civil society participation and engagement. Retrieved February 19, 2007, from www.pso.nl/asp/documentsite.asp?document=807

Geertz, C. (1983). *Local knowledge: Further essays in interpretative anthropology.* New York: Basic Books.

Heifetz, R. A. (1994). *Leadership without easy answers.* Cambridge, MA: Belknap Press.

Heifetz, R. A. (2007). The scholarly/practical challenge of leadership. In R. A. Couto (Ed.), *Reflections on leadership* (pp. 31–44). Lanham, MD: University Press of America.

Hughes, A., Wheeler, J., & Eyben, R. (2005). Rights and power: The challenge for international development agencies. *IDS Bulletin, 36*(1), 63–72.

Kretzmann, J. P., & McKnight, J. (1993). *Building communities from the inside out: A path toward finding and mobilizing a community's assets.* Evanston, IL: Center for Urban Affairs and Policy Research, Northwestern University.

Lewin, K. (1951). *Field theory in social science: Selected theoretical papers.* New York: Harper.

Lincoln, Y. S., & Guba, E. G. (2000). Paradigmatic controversies, contradictions, and emerging confluences. In N. K. Denzin & Y. S. Lincoln (Eds.), *Handbook of qualitative research* (2nd ed., pp. 163–188). Thousand Oaks, CA: Sage.

McCarty, M. (2003, October 15). A victory for all the little guys. *Dayton Daily News,* p. B1.

Minkler, M., & Wallerstein, N. (Eds.). (2003). *Community-based participatory research for health.* San Francisco: Jossey-Bass.

Mong, C. (1999a, October 6). Plant worker rescued from tanker. *Dayton Daily News,* p. 1B.

Mong, C. (1999b, October 7). Strange odors cause stink. *Dayton Daily News,* p. 1 (Neighbor's Section).

National Research Council. (1998). Using supercritical water oxidation to treat hydrolysate from VX neutralization. Washington, DC: National Academy Press. Retrieved June 18, 2007, from http://books.nap.edu/html/hydrolysate/index.html#top

Putnam, R. D. (1995). Tuning in, tuning out: The strange disappearance of social capital in America. *Political Science and Politics, 28,* 664–683.

Putnam, R. D. (2000). *Bowling alone: The collapse and revival of American community.* New York: Simon & Schuster.

Putnam, R. D., Leonardi, R., & Raffaella, N. (1993). *Making democracy work: Civic traditions in modern Italy.* Princeton, NJ: Princeton University Press.

Rowlands, J. (1997). *Questioning empowerment: Working with women in Honduras.* Oxford, UK: Oxfam.

Szakos, K. L., & Szakos, J. (2007). *We make change: Community organizers talk about what they do—And why.* Nashville, TN: Vanderbilt University Press.

United States Environmental Protection Agency. (1998). Final guidance for incorporating environmental justice concerns in EPA's NEPA compliance analyses. Retrieved September 17, 2005, from http://www.epa.gov/compliance/resources/policies/ej/ej_guidance_nepa_epa0498.pdf

Wheatley, M. J. (2005). *Finding our way, leadership for uncertain times.* San Francisco: Berrett-Koehler.

Yarmolinsky, A. (2007). The challenge of change in leadership. In R. A. Couto (Ed.), *Reflections on leadership* (pp. 45–51). Lanham, MD: University Press of America.

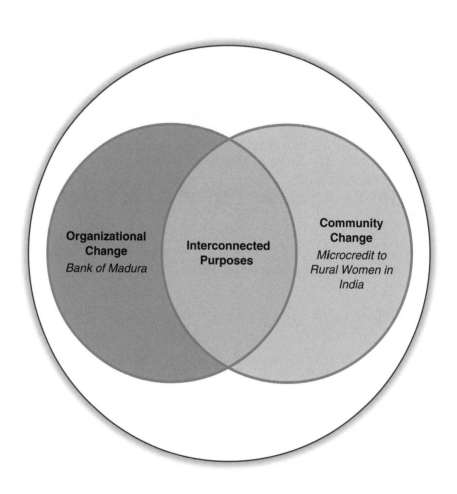

CHAPTER 6

Crossing Organizational and Community Contexts

Introduction

Leading change in one context frequently involves initiating or advocating change in another, especially in today's complex and interconnected society. These connections across contexts commonly produce changes in both settings. This is certainly the case between local government agencies and their constituent communities or nonprofit organizations and the groups and communities they serve. In recent years, however, leading change has become more commonplace between private-sector organizations and the communities in which they do business.

The business model in a growing number of companies incorporates social responsibility through community volunteering, partnering with nonprofit organizations, and grant making, along with traditional modes of philanthropy. Companies with this type of business model stress the connection between a thriving company and a thriving community in their company's vision, mission, core values, and corporate culture. In contrast to previous business models, these companies view their business and social missions as not only compatible but also vitally interconnected. For example, the mission statement for Timberland, maker of outdoor footwear and clothing, illustrates the blending of social action and business aims: "Our mission is to equip people to make a difference in their world. We do this by creating outstanding products and by trying to make a difference in the communities where we live and work" (Timberland Company, 2007). Bank of America Chairman, President, and Chief Executive Officer Kenneth D. Lewis said, "The reason (we are) in business is to help make communities stronger and to help people achieve their dreams. We fulfill this purpose by reaching for higher standards in everything we do—for our customers, our shareholders, our associates and

---

AUTHORS' NOTE: This chapter is dedicated to my late colleague, Dr. K. M. Thiagarajan.

our communities, upon which the future prosperity of our company rests" (Silver City, New Mexico, Chamber of Commerce, 2007; Silverman, 2003).

Companies' active involvement in social responsibility through employee-volunteering programs and partnerships with nonprofit organizations offers hope for a better society by giving person-to-person and employee-to-community contributions of time, expertise, and commitment, thereby establishing a personal connection that is sometimes lacking when companies make only monetary contributions (Hickman, 2006, p. 1). These companies create partnerships and provide volunteers for a variety of community purposes, including education, housing, social services, and health awareness and disease prevention. They also provide vital monetary contributions.

In addition to this model, which represents a changing view of the role of business in society, the blending of business and community missions is also bringing about change in the functioning of both the community and business in some of the most socially active companies.

The vignette in this chapter illustrates this blending of missions and shows how change concepts and practices function across two contexts. The vignette describes efforts of former Bank of Madura Chairman K. M. Thiagarajan and his managers to improve the viability of the bank's rural branches and advance economic development among women in rural Tamil Nadu, India. This vignette is the late Thiagarajan's personal account of these events.

Change Vignette

Microcredit to Rural Women

In 1993, I became the chairman and chief executive of Bank of Madura, a commercial bank in the private sector in India. It was a tradition-bound, moderately profitable, regional bank with low levels of technology and productivity. In response to the economic liberalization initiated by the Indian government at that time and rapid changes in the market, a major restructuring effort was undertaken. Loss-making branches were merged with other branches or closed. New branches were opened across the country in cities with good profit potential. The operations were computerized and automated. New products and services were introduced. Profitability improved substantially.

The chink in the armor was the vast network of rural branches (102 out of a total of 275 branches) located in villages with small populations and low levels of economic activity. The rural branches were started more due to government policies and regulatory pressures than out of commercial considerations. Whereas the policy allowed closure of urban branches, closure of rural branches required various permissions, which were difficult to obtain. Gradually, after obtaining the necessary approvals, some of the branches were merged and the number reduced to seventy-seven. When the option of closure no longer existed, we had to deal with the real issue of how these branches could be revitalized.

At this point I learned about the tremendous work done by the Grameen Bank of Bangladesh, founded by Muhammad Yunus, a pioneer in the field of microcredit. Following his example, in November 1995 we established the Rural Development Division to provide microcredit to poor women in the villages where our branches were located.

In the Indian version of microcredit, which has evolved its own group formation and credit delivery models, self-help groups (SHGs) are the basic unit to which the loan is given. Each SHG is composed of twenty women who voluntarily form the group and choose one another in the knowledge that they have to jointly guarantee the loan. During the first 6 months, they save a small amount each month (they determine the amount, based on their earnings), pool the savings, and deposit these funds in the bank. The monthly deposit is normally in the range of 50 cents to U.S. $1 at the official exchange rate (although in buying power it is worth much more in India, especially in rural areas). They meet twice a month and receive training on how to organize their group meetings, start a bank account, and calculate interest and also learn about women's rights and other general issues. During the second 6 months, besides continuing to save, they begin to lend their savings to group members. The group decides the amount, rate of interest, priority of needs, and other procedures for lending. During this 1 year, the women become quite proficient in handling finance, understanding the implications of cooperating and pooling their savings, and the importance of repayment. They also gain self-confidence, become articulate, and understand the need for joint social action. At the end of the first year, the group becomes eligible to receive credit from the bank, subject to regularity in savings and repayment of internal loans by every group member. Normally, the loan is about U.S. $50 per person, but in the case of Bank of Madura, an individual could receive up to U.S. $200 to undertake small business activities like raising a milk cow, setting up a tailoring shop, or producing food items. Repayment is made every month, and the group collects the amount due and pays the bank. The loan is given without any collateral but is guaranteed by all of the SHG's members. The initial training, peer group pressure to be responsible, and mutual monitoring by the members all help considerably in the repayment rate, which is about 99.5%.

Normally, the self-help groups are formed by NGOs (nonprofits), and banks extend the loans. However, we decided to form the groups ourselves through our branches. This was an unusual move for a commercial bank, and to understand the process, we need to take a look at how banks work in India.

Rural branches are managed or administered by the head of a geographical division, which has many metropolitan, urban, and rural branches. Since the volume of business is very low in rural branches, the division heads do not pay attention to them. The executives and staff in banks, who are better educated and highly paid relative to those in many other segments, do not like to live in villages. Lack of modern amenities, good schools, health care facilities, and entertainment make villages unattractive to them and their families. To illustrate, many government banks have a policy of making the promotion of managers from grade I to grade II contingent on a stint in a rural branch. Such transfers are commonly known as "punishment postings." Most often, staff live in nearby towns and commute to the village. They spend very little time at the branch and do not interact with the villagers, who are poor, uneducated, and socially not their equals.

When the Rural Development Division was started, it became obvious that unless this issue was faced squarely, the division could not take off. As a first step, the management of all the rural branches was brought under the division irrespective of the branch locations. This move made rural branches gain legitimacy and gave a sharp focus to their activities. Next we decided to "attract" people from within the bank who wanted to get involved in rural development work on a voluntary basis instead of compelling people to work in these branches. Although the personnel department was skeptical, people did come forward. Instead of selecting all those who

(Continued)

(Continued)

volunteered, we decided to select people on the basis of their commitment to the project and their willingness to live in the village. The candidates were also told that they should relate to people in the village, especially the women, as equals, without any gender, caste, class, or other biases.

Those who showed any hesitation in the interview were not selected. This move sent strong signals throughout the bank that senior management was committed to the concept of rural development through microcredit. Many individuals who were already in the division opted to stay; however, not all were retained. A thorough review of each person's background was made to ensure that he or she could be part of the new project. Those who were considered unsuitable were transferred out. The personnel policy was also amended to provide automatic transfer to an urban branch to anybody in the Rural Development Division, at any time, who requested this. Within a few months, a team of about 325 highly motivated individuals, from a total of 2,600 employees, was assembled.

The core team of senior executives, headed by the divisional manager, studied various microcredit projects in detail, visited many nonprofits involved in forming SHGs, received training from experts in the field, and met frequently to decide on a strategy. After an intensive 2-day residential workshop without anybody from outside the division, the core team decided to form SHGs themselves without linking with nonprofits. This was a big surprise, but the decision was accepted.

This led to the birth of a "nonprofit" within the for-profit bank. The cost of starting, training, and monitoring SHGs, which is called "capacity building," is an expensive and time-consuming process. This cost is even higher when a bank promotes groups through its own personnel, whose salary levels are much higher than salaries in the nonprofit sector. Besides, the overheads of the bank are also high. This is why banks rely on nonprofits to undertake capacity building and only come in to provide credit.

The decision to directly promote SHGs was based on the reasoning that there would be no additional cost, since the cost of fixed overheads and salaries of individuals in the rural branches was already being incurred. A decision was also made that no increases in staff or overhead costs would be allowed in the Rural Development Division. The capacity of the division to promote SHGs without additional costs was pegged at fifteen hundred SHGs. It was also agreed by the core team of executives in the division that new methodologies to promote SHGs at lower cost would be found when the capacity of 1,500 groups was reached.

The new division was organized around five clusters of branches with a project manager heading each cluster. A training center was started that trained all the staff in the division on promoting, training, and monitoring SHGs. To begin with, the core team decided to go slow: start a few groups and evaluate the process. Since it takes 1 year before a group becomes eligible for a loan, it took time to evaluate the process. Thereafter, groups were started in larger numbers. Initially, the team faced hardships in working in the villages, promoting groups, and training women who were either not very educated or illiterate. These hardships vanished when they saw the difference they were making in the lives of the village women and the hospitality, friendship, and gratitude received from them.

In the year 2001, Bank of Madura merged with ICICI Bank, which is the second-largest financial institution in India. I continued with the bank for 1 year as adviser for the microcredit project before I went on to found the Microcredit Foundation of India in 2002. During the time I was adviser to the project, we selected two hundred women who were members of the SHGs promoted by the bank to start SHGs on their own. These women were well versed in the concept and had demonstrated leadership qualities. They were further trained by the bank personnel before they started forming groups. They were also remunerated for this work, but this cost is considerably lower than the cost of promoting groups by the bank. Now there are 500 village women who are promoting groups under the supervision of bank personnel and linking them with the bank for credit. At last count, there were 8,000 SHGs, with a membership of 160,000 women. When this number and the credit portfolio grow further, the activity has the potential to become profitable.

SOURCE: From "Missionary Leadership: Harnessing the Power of the Mission," by K. M. Thiagarajan, in R. E. Riggio and S. S. Orr (Eds.), *Improving Leadership in Nonprofit Organizations*, pp. 40–43. Copyright © 2004 by R. E. Riggio and S. S. Orr (Eds.). By permission of Wiley & Sons, Inc. Published by Jossey-Bass.

Concepts of Change Across Organizational and Community Contexts

Bank of Madura (now ICICI Bank) and the village women[1] changed each other in ways that were unimaginable at the beginning of their venture. After implementation of the rural development project and establishment of the SHGs, the bank's rural branches came alive and flourished, teeming with village women entrepreneurs with impeccable repayment rates. Bank of Madura turned declining rural branches into thriving entities.

Bank Chairman Thiagarajan and bank managers used a teleological approach to change in both rural banking and community development. The change was intentional and fully planned. Thiagarajan raised the professional standing of rural bank managers from low-status bank employees in "punishment postings" to equal-status managers engaged in banking and social entrepreneurship. The bank managers gained great personal fulfillment from their jobs while serving the communities where they now lived and worked.

In addition to teleological change, the microcredit program was a community change process that included a blend of needs- or deficit-based and assets-based approaches, described in Chapter 3. The bankers used a needs- or deficit-based approach as they identified economic and social challenges in the villages and decided what the rural women needed to develop their communities. The village women were initially suspicious and hesitant to interact with the bank managers. However, the managers persisted by going door to door and talking to one woman at a time. Ultimately, the women began to trust the bankers and listened to their proposal.

At the same time, Thiagarajan and the bank managers identified the community's assets—the village women. They regarded the women as more committed, more responsible, more likely to use the benefits of the microcredit program for their families, and more capable than the village men of providing products or services that the community actually needed. When the first 20 women volunteered to form SHGs, they activated a profusion of social capital in their village and many other communities. The bankers taught the women reading, writing, and the basics of keeping accounts. Subsequently, the women used their knowledge in the SHGs to teach other women all they learned from the bankers. They began to develop authentic empowerment by selecting group leaders called animators, setting up an internal loan program for SHG members, and determining the kinds of business to pursue based on their skills and talents. The bank managers were present essentially to provide support to the SHG's process.

Life began to change for the women as they gained social and financial capital. They were able to hire their husbands and other family members to work in their businesses. They no longer needed to borrow from the money lenders at high-interest rates to cover their children's school fees or emergencies that arose. The bankers and women worked together to tackle other community problems, such as financing low-cost toilet facilities. They even arranged for the women to purchase life insurance so that their families would be protected in the event of their death.

The women claimed rights that accorded them equal status with men. They gained stature and respect in the community. They used their newfound power to meet with village leaders to arrange for drinking water, bus stops in the villages, and the elimination of illicit alcohol. On the domestic front, they no longer had to stay in abusive relationships because they had gained economic independence and the support of other women.

Beyond their teaching and support of the village women, the bank managers also developed social capital through their relationships with each other. They met regularly to exchange ideas and discuss issues, such as how to meet the challenges of working with people from different cultures and with villages with diverse needs, how to streamline or alter bank processes, and how to cope personally with the challenges of living in rural areas.

Concepts of Leadership Across Organizational and Community Contexts

The Bank of Madura vignette illustrates several concepts of leadership across organizational and community contexts. Change, collaboration, and conflict, as described in Chapter 3, were important components of the leadership process. Collective or collaborative leadership was clearly present between the bank chairman and the rural bank managers, between the bank managers and the village women, among the women in the SHGs, and among the rural bank managers. As indicated in Chapter 3, collective or collaborative leadership uses the talents and resources of all members, not just those of a single leader, to bring about change and generate creative and adaptive solutions. Women in the SHGs used leadership without formal authority, described as adaptive work in Chapter 3, to bring about change in their communities, families, and each other.

Thiagarajan used his formal authority to change banking practices toward rural bank managers and create an environment where collaborative leadership could flourish among bankers and between bank managers and village women. He also used transformational leadership to inspire the bank managers to achieve more than they thought possible. He made them fully aware of the significance of the microcredit program for rural women and their communities and induced them to transcend their own self-interest by moving to the villages where the bank's rural branches were located, thereby becoming part of those rural communities. Thiagarajan provided intellectual stimulation by challenging bank managers to use innovative and creative approaches to launch the microcredit program and work with the village women. As a result, the bankers experienced an enriched work life and a sense of personal fulfillment through their involvement with building the social and economic resources in the villages.

Certainly, the bank chairman used transactional leadership by increasing the salaries and status of rural managers to the level of other bank managers in exchange for the participation of competent and committed rural bank managers in the microcredit program. The rural bank managers used transactional leadership in their work with the village women by educating and preparing them to become financially self-sustaining in exchange for their commitment as customers of the rural banks.

The bank chairman demonstrated servant leadership toward the rural bank managers, while the managers became servant leaders to the women in the SHGs. In each case, their work met Greenleaf's test of servant leadership described in Chapter 3: The individuals who were served grew as persons—they become healthier, wiser, freer, more autonomous, more likely themselves to become servants—and the least privileged in society benefited.

Thiagarajan (2004) referred to his leadership and that of the rural bank managers in the microcredit program as *missionary leadership*, which he defined as "the process whereby a leader uses the inherent power of the mission to attract highly committed individuals who want to serve the cause and then enables them to derive satisfaction from such service" (pp. 39–40). He indicated that missionary leadership is based on the "shared desire to serve the mission and is not purely relational" (p. 45). The concept of missionary leadership incorporates many of the ideas in invisible leadership (see Chapter 3), which occurs when individuals, without regard for recognition or visibility, are motivated to take action by a passionate commitment to achieve a common purpose that is greater than the group members' individual self-interest and, in certain cases, even greater than the group's overall self-interest.

The village women in the Bank of Madura vignette provide a prime example of citizen or community leadership. As Couto, Hall, and Goetz indicated in Chapter 5, citizen or community leadership facilitates organized action among people traditionally underrepresented in official decision-making processes and respects the dignity and worth of people regardless of race, age, gender, income, or any other demographic factor (Couto, 1995). Poor women in rural villages of India were notoriously underrepresented and powerless at most levels of government, business, and the community. The story of the women in the initial SHG spread to neighboring villages, and soon these women were helping other women organize their own SHGs, without the assistance of the bank managers. They formed a federation of SHGs to aid and empower other groups to form and taught them about microcredit and social issues such as education, health, and hygiene. They wore uniform saris to show solidarity with each other and used artistic creativity (Chapter 5) through song and dance to share stories of the SHGs.

The change that occurred in the Bank of Madura and rural villages had many elements of transforming leadership, a concept discussed in Chapter 3. James MacGregor Burns (1978) stated that transforming leadership "occurs when one or more persons *engage* with others in such a way that leaders and followers raise one another to higher levels of motivation and morality" (p. 20). Transforming leadership involves individuals in collective purpose linked to social change, with the ultimate objective of elevating the well-being of human existence. Though Burns's definition of transforming leadership originated from the political context, this form of leadership can apply to companies and other organizations that purposely connect their business and social missions to bring about significant change in human conditions.

Burns (1978) did not believe transforming leadership was possible in most organizations because of bureaucracy and economic self-interest. However, the type of leadership exhibited by members of the Bank of Madura and increasingly in some other companies shows that transforming leadership is possible in this context. Transforming leaders and members of organizations shape and define their business mission to encompass collective purpose. They view the viability of their organizations as interconnected with the well-being of people and the environment. The decline of rural branches was an obvious financial concern for the Bank of Madura; at the same time, rural poverty was an equally relevant social concern. Thiagarajan and the bank managers regarded the two situations as fully interrelated.

According to Burns's (1978) definition, leaders and followers who engage in transforming leadership raise one another to higher levels of motivation and morality. Motivation increased steadily among the bankers and village women as they experienced economic success and social change through the microcredit project. Morality, which Burns defines as raising "the level of human conduct and ethical aspiration of both leader and led" (p. 20), increased as the bank managers engaged fully with the women to meet their economic and social needs. The women became leaders and role models in their own village and other communities. Engaged leadership, in the words of Burns, "has a transforming effect on both" the leaders and the led (p. 20). This transforming effect was demonstrated by the bank chairman's subsequent actions. As indicated in the vignette, Thiagarajan was so personally inspired by working with the project that he left the bank to pursue full-time work as founder of the Microcredit Foundation of India.

Change Practices Across Organizational and Community Contexts

Change in the Bank of Madura vignette incorporated most of the adaptive practices identified in Chapter 3—institutionalized-leadership and change practices, organizational learning, and empowerment or shared power. Thiagarajan and the other bank executives used institutionalized-leadership and change practices by establishing a Rural Development Division for rural branches and their managers and raising rural bankers' pay and status to the level of other bankers. They changed the selection process by first recruiting from within the bank volunteers who were committed to rural development and willing to live in the villages and then by evaluating their suitability for the project. They made the bold and creative decision to establish a nonprofit within a for-profit bank and then ran it themselves, rather than working with an external nonprofit SHG. The bankers adapted the microcredit project to the Indian culture by developing their own group formation, credit delivery, and SHG models—a critical step that is often overlooked when establishing microcredit initiatives in different cultures. They facilitated organizational learning by ensuring that managers studied various microcredit projects, visiting nonprofits involved in forming SHGs, and establishing a training center staffed by experts in the field and frequented by all bankers in the division in an effort to gain a better understanding of promoting, training, and monitoring SHGs. All these practices and more institutionalized the leadership of microcredit and rural development in the bank structure.

Thiagarajan and the bank executives empowered the rural bank managers to take risks, innovate, make independent decisions, and provide leadership for the microcredit project. Thiagarajan continued to provide support to the bankers as needed but did not infringe on the leadership of the rural bank managers. The village women ultimately gained the kind of genuine empowerment described in Chapter 5—self-empowerment—that entails full participation and direct representation of community members in decision making, leadership, and change. Using Thiagarajan's example, the bankers provided support as needed to the SHGs, but the animators and other women exercised true leadership in their groups and communities.

The development of social and economic capital in this case involved the use of vertical and horizontal networks (Chapter 5). Vertical networks included the bankers as outside experts who helped frame the problems, taught the women the necessary skills to start SHGs and participate in the microcredit program, and provided access to bank resources. The initial group of 20 village women became a horizontal network for women in other communities who wanted to start SHGs. The Federation of Self-Help Groups formed an even larger and stronger horizontal network with elected representatives from various community SHGs. The self-help groups became so effective that even men in the villages voluntarily formed SHGs.

The Bank of Madura scenario illustrated several ethical practices described in Chapter 4, including respect, authenticity, trust, and reciprocal care. Prior to sending the bankers into the rural villages, Thiagarajan emphasized the importance of respecting the dignity and worth of villagers and treating them as equals, especially the women. Village women had limited voice or power in the community, based on their gender, caste, class, or other factors. The rural bankers under the previous system had exhibited limited respect for villagers, whom they viewed as poor, uneducated, and socially inferior. Attracting women to the microcredit program would prove difficult enough even when they were accorded respect, as the new bankers were to learn. Eventually though, the new bankers' demonstration of respect, authenticity, and sheer persistence gained the women's trust.

Reciprocal care became an essential factor in the growth and success of the SHGs and microcredit program. This form of care was an inherent result of a highly interdependent and collective process. Women within and across communities learned from, loaned money to, and protected each other. These practices allowed the women, their families, the village, and rural bank branches to thrive. Even the bankers engaged in reciprocal care by sharing ideas, solving problems together, and supporting each other.

Conclusion

Change that connects organizational and community contexts is likely to gain momentum in the coming years. Businesses and other organizations are beginning to understand the relationship between their own viability and their efforts to help communities flourish economically and socially. These complex connections require considerable innovation, creativity, adaptive work, and risk taking. Understanding and using concepts and practices of leading change across organizational and community contexts can contribute to advancements in the well-being of society and the environment.

Note

1. Additional information in this chapter concerning Bank of Madura and the self-help groups was obtained from an undistributed independent film titled *Bank of Madura: Microcredit* (2001).

References

Burns, J. M. (1978). *Leadership*. New York: Harper & Row.

Couto, R. A. (1995). Defining a citizen leader. In J. T. Wren (Ed.), *The leader's companion* (pp. 11–17). New York: The Free Press.

Hickman, G. R. (2006). *Organizations of hope: Summary report of the volunteer manager survey*. Unpublished report. Richmond, VA: University of Richmond.

Silver City, New Mexico, Chamber of Commerce. (2007). *Bank of America*. Retrieved August 16, 2007, from http://www.silvercity.org/search_detail.mvc?CID=V33T7MW311

Silverman, G. (2003, September 9). Switch-hitters can't bank on a home run. *FT.com*, p. 1.

Thiagarajan, K. M. (2004). Missionary leadership: Harnessing the power of the mission. In R. E. Riggio & S. S. Orr (Eds.), *Improving leadership in nonprofit organizations* (pp. 39–48). San Francisco: Wiley.

Timberland Company. (2007). *About Timberland*. Retrieved August 16, 2007, from http://www.timberland.com/corp/index.jsp?clickid=topnav_corp_txt

PART IV

Leading Political and Social Change

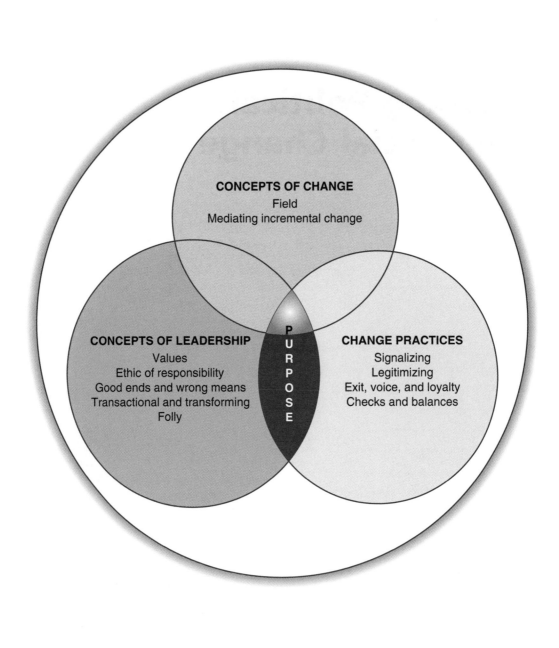

CHAPTER 7

Political Change Context

Richard A. Couto

The terrorist attacks in the United States on 9/11 presented a situation that required new policies and set off a tsunami of political change—a war in Afghanistan, the invasion and occupation of Iraq, and new forms of surveillance on Americans. Another far less noticed policy, extraordinary rendition, authorized the Central Intelligence Agency (CIA) to take non-U.S. citizens to another country for detention and "enhanced interrogation," or what some consider torture. In some cases, the CIA did this without giving any official notice to the person's government or the government from which he was taken. After several years of secrecy and controversy, the administration acknowledged the policy, announced its end and the closure of a set of secret prisons around the world, and declared that all rendered persons had been transferred to the prison at the U.S. Naval Base at Guantanamo Bay, Cuba, and were being held there as "unlawful enemy combatants." The coining of this new legal term and the policies associated with the confinement and treatment of prisoners at Guantanamo represented changes that arose as a result of the events of 9/11 and that were related to extraordinary rendition.

This chapter examines extraordinary rendition as an example of leadership and change in the political context. Although far more dramatic than most other examples of political change, the Bush administration's decision to use extraordinary rendition demonstrates how political change often involves the collision of values. In this case, national security and human rights came into conflict. This case study also provides a canvas on which to portray the elements of the opening figure:

the roles of many political actors, some of them constituted and some not, and illustrations of the processes of leadership in conducting political change. Finally, it deals explicitly with the legitimacy of violence, a factor which distinguishes the political change context from all other change contexts.

Purpose of Political Change

The three spheres of our now familiar figure overlap to create the area of purpose for leadership of political change: "confront situations in which policy must be formulated, promulgated, and executed" (Tucker, 1995, p. 16). The appropriate manner in which to do this has occupied many great minds, such as Confucius and Machiavelli, who gave government authorities outlines for the successful conduct of politics. Values always pervaded this advice; Confucius was concerned that rulers were in harmony with *tao*, and Machiavelli urged rulers to forgo ideological ventures and look to their self-interest, primarily the maintenance of their power.

Conflicting values arise in any conception of a system of political leadership. One set of conflicting values involves social order and individual rights. Plato envisioned a philosopher king as one part of a hierarchy of authority defined not only by stability and order but also by social stratification and inequality. Aristotle, on the other hand, although no radical egalitarian, did assume that legitimate governments—whether composed of one person, a few, or the majority—ruled on behalf of all and gave all sectors of the public (which was less stratified than Plato's republic but still excluded women and slaves) the opportunity to deliberate and to find common ground for action (Mattern, 2006, pp. 391–393).

Even in a democracy with the thumbnail rule of the "greatest good for the greatest number," this tension between order and rights continues. May the rights of the individual impinge on the welfare of the majority? May the majority infringe on the rights of an individual to preserve order? Some of these dilemmas may be resolved by deliberation, as Aristotle hoped, or by the ruler's wisdom, as Confucius hoped. Often, however, they cannot be resolved by deliberation, and political leaders may revert to force to protect one group from another. Leaders may assert individual rights and force the majority to comply with them or may restrict the freedom of individuals and groups for the sake of the majority. Unlike the other contexts discussed in this text, the political context extends power over others to include a monopoly on the legitimate use of force and coercion. Force and coercion may occur in other contexts, but the political context determines what forms of force and coercion may or may not be used.

Thus, political change leadership confronts situations demanding policy decisions that must weigh the tension between competing values, such as order, individual and group rights, and many others. Political change leadership is unique in its authority to use physical coercion, including even violence; however, it enjoys more legitimacy the less it uses coercion.

Change Vignette

Extraordinary Rendition

There was little to suggest that Khaled al-Masri's argument with his wife would lead to front-page stories around the world, unprecedented international legal action, a case before the U.S. Supreme Court, and a national and international debate about U.S. agents' use of torture in interrogations. What happened to him in the 5 months following his angry departure from his home entangled him in an international controversy concerning a network of secret prisons and the United States' use of torture as a weapons in the war on terror.

On New Year's Eve 2003, Masri, hoping to blow off some steam after a fight with his wife, took a bus from the German town of Ulm where he lived to Macedonia for what he thought would be a vacation. At the border, the Macedonian police took him into custody because his name was similar to that of an associate of a 9/11 hijacker and they suspected that his passport was forged. Macedonian authorities informed the CIA's Macedonian station about Masri and his suspicious passport. After several weeks of discussing what to do, the CIA took Masri from his Macedonian jail cell, drugged him, and flew him to an Afghanistan prison. The first night there, he was kicked and beaten and an interrogator warned him, "You are here in a country where no one knows about you, in a country where there is no law. If you die, we will bury you, and no one will know" (Priest, 2005b). Masri had become one of the "ghost detainees" housed in a network of U.S. secret prisons and subject to a U.S. policy of extraordinary rendition.

The CIA Makes a Mistake. After Masri endured a month of severe treatment, which he said included being held in isolation and subjected to interrogations and physical beatings, the CIA determined that his passport was genuine and that he had no connection to terrorists. CIA Director George Tenet apprised National Security Advisor Condoleezza Rice and Deputy Secretary of State Richard Armitage of the mistake: The United States had taken a citizen of another country and detained him in a third country, without notifying either his family or government. Masri and others who experienced extraordinary rendition alleged their interrogations included torture. The U.S. government firmly denied this.

What to do with Masri? Other terrorist suspects swept up by extraordinary rendition were held indefinitely in a network of secret prisons or at the Guantanamo naval base in Cuba as unlawful enemy combatants. This new legal category fell outside the realm of Geneva Conventions guidelines on the treatment of soldiers and civilians during wartime and outside the realm of guidelines established by U.S. treaties and laws, including habeas corpus, on the treatment of individuals charged with a crime.

Masri, however, was no longer a terrorist suspect. How can authorities release someone from a secret prison that is part of a covert operation without making public, or at least compromising, the covert operation? Initially, Tenet suggested a reverse rendition that would include bringing Masri back to Macedonia, releasing him, and denying anything happened. Macedonia had no interest in being part of a reverse rendition, however, and that proposal was quickly rejected. Masri's German citizenship complicated matters. U.S. officials agreed that the German government should hear about these events directly from the U.S. government and not from media reports. It took a month to decide on a course of action. One crucial question was how much to tell the

(Continued)

(Continued)

German government about U.S. actions toward one of its citizens. The CIA preferred minimal disclosure and the State Department full (Priest, 2005b). Eventually, the U.S. ambassador to Germany provided a full accounting, but no apology, to the German interior minister and asked that the German government not disclose its knowledge of the incident, even if Masri went public. The ambassador explained that the U.S. government viewed extraordinary rendition as a covert action essential to waging the war on terrorism and that it needed to remain a state secret.

Shortly after this back-channel informational exchange, Masri reported being visited in his Afghanistan prison cell by someone apparently from the German government. "Sam," the only name the visitor used, explained to Masri "that he was going to be released soon but that he would not receive any documents or papers confirming his ordeal. The Americans would never admit they had taken him prisoner" (Priest, 2005b). Masri was taken from his cell, flown to Albania, transported by van for 6 hours, and released in the mountains at night with directions to the Macedonian-Albanian border. From there he was taken to the Albanian capital and finally flown to Munich. After 5 months of being held and interrogated incommunicado, he was back in Germany (Marty, 2007, pp. 54–62).

Other Remedies for the Mistakes of Extraordinary Rendition. Initially, local German officials doubted Masri's incredible tale of abduction, clandestine travel, detention and torture, and eventual release in the Albanian mountains. Their investigation, however, verified his story. The bus driver confirmed that Macedonian police took Masri from the bus at the border. Test results of Masri's hair samples indicated he suffered from malnutrition during the time he was allegedly in prison. Aviation records showed flights going at the times and to the places alleged in Masri's story. From hotel records, German officials even identified the CIA agents who were most likely to have accompanied Masri on the flight to Afghanistan. The German federal government, however, deferred action and comment on the case to the local prosecutor and court in Munich. Eventually, a Munich court ordered the arrest of 13 U.S. intelligence agents in connection with Masri's abduction and confinement.

Masri's case was only one instance, and not the most extreme, of extraordinary rendition and the alleged use of torture in the war on terrorism. Another example is that of Maher Arar, a Syrian-born Canadian citizen en route from Zurich to Montreal with his wife and child, who was detained at Kennedy Airport in New York in September 2002. Raw and incorrect information provided to U.S. authorities by the Royal Canadian Mounted Police (RCMP) served as the basis for his detention. Arar was rendered to Syria, a nation notorious for its violation of human rights, where for 7 months he was detained in a narrow cell without sunlight, interrogated, and beaten regularly. In another case, the CIA abducted the radical cleric Hassan Mustafa Osama Nasr near his mosque in Milan, Italy, on February 17, 2003. Also known as Abu Omar, he came to Italy in 1997 as a political refugee seeking asylum from the government of his native Egypt; he had participated in a group plotting the Egyptian government's overthrow. Yet in 2003 the CIA took him from Italy to Egypt where he was imprisoned, interrogated, tortured, and finally placed under house arrest.

Other governments determined these actions to be criminal, as they would in the Masri case. A Canadian commission found that the charges of terrorist connections against Arar were baseless and that the RCMP had erred in its policies and exaggerated Arar's danger. Eventually the Canadian government apologized to Arar and compensated him with $11.5 million. The U.S. government did neither. It cited additional secret information it had about Arar and kept him on the U.S. watch list, consequently prohibiting him from entering the United States or traveling over U.S. airspace. The Canadian commission complained that the lack of cooperation from the United States hindered its investigation (Arar Commission, 2006; Mayer, 2005).

In Nasr's case, Italian investigators and judges sought extradition of 26 CIA officials to return to Italy for trial on charges of abducting the cleric. The prosecution of the case created fissures within the Italian government. At the time of his abduction, Italian counterterrorism police had Nasr under surveillance and were developing their own case against him. The CIA abduction foiled that investigation. Then the CIA deliberately misled Italian officials into thinking that Nasr had fled to the Balkans when they actually had him in its custody in Egypt. Milan prosecutors subsequently made the unprecedented move of taking U.S. government officials to court in connection with counterterrorism actions. The Italian national government placed a modest obstacle in the Milan court's path by denying Nasr a visa to travel to Italy to testify. His status as a political refugee had expired during the 3 years he spent in prison, and Egypt had placed him on a no-travel list (Hennion, 2007; Whitlock, 2005).

The Question of Torture. Compounding the criticism of the U.S. policy of extraordinary rendition, the world recoiled at the mistreatment of prisoners at the Abu Ghraib prison in Iraq when the photographic evidence became public in April 2004. Prison conditions at the U.S. naval base at Guantanamo, Cuba, also elicited international protest and criticism. The International Red Cross and international human rights groups argued that requiring Guantanamo detainees to maintain stressful positions, endure sleep deprivation, remain confined in cells without light for long periods, and be subjected to water boarding (a practice in which water from a bucket is poured down the throat of a blindfolded person to simulate drowning) were, in the words of the International Committee of the Red Cross, "an intentional system of cruel, unusual, and degrading treatment and a form of torture" (McCoy, 2006, p. 157).

The confinement of Masri and others extraordinarily rendered was far worse than the confinement of most prisoners at Abu Ghraib and Guantanamo. The report of the Council of Europe, chief watchdog for human rights in Europe, found that these prisoners never saw natural light—a lightbulb was their sole source of light, and its intermittent use disoriented prisoners from any sense of time; their cells were kept frigid or hot, alternatively; loud music or noise was their constant companion; and they were often shackled in the cell for "long, painful periods" (Marty, 2007, p. 53). A report of the International Red Cross concluded that prisoners held in the CIA's secret prisons were kept and questioned under highly abusive conditions (Shrader, 2007).

The CIA had been conducting these detention practices covertly since the early 1950s (McCoy, 2006). On the eve of the cold war, the U.S. intelligence agencies, fearing that the Soviet Union had an upper hand in psychological warfare, conducted experiments and research to determine the best ways to break down a person's resistance in interrogation. The research led to the adoption of practices such as isolation, sleep deprivation, sensory deprivation, and the others described in the Council of Europe report (Marty, 2007, p. 53; McCoy, 2006, pp. 7–11). These practices did not constitute torture according to the United States and were condoned officially when the United States ratified the UN Convention against Torture. The convention prohibited psychological torture, including the use of mind-altering drugs and imminent death threats, as the corollary of physical torture. By narrowly defining psychological torture, however, the CIA could still employ

(Continued)

(Continued)

methods of psychological coercion, such as sensory deprivation, self-inflicted pain from imposed stressful positions, isolation, and sleep deprivation, without explicitly violating U.S. law or its interpretation of the terms of the UN Convention against Torture (Mayer 2005; McCoy, 2006, p. 157).

The Department of Justice, at least temporarily, went even further than the CIA in restricting the definition of what constituted physical torture. In August 2002, the Department of Justice and the White House legal counsel suggested that the UN Convention permitted torture up to the point of severe pain akin to organ failure, serious physical injury, or death. Even in instances that reached or passed these thresholds, the Department of Justice maintained that if the intent of the interrogator was to gather information rather than to inflict mental or physical pain, it was not torture (McCoy, 2006, pp. 121–124). Thus, official U.S. policy permitted the use of extraordinary rendition and the coercive acts that accompanied it in cases such as Masri's; such acts did not fall within the parameters of mental and physical torture as defined by the United States.

These interpretations stirred controversy within the Bush administration. The State Department legal adviser opined that the new definitions and policies would make those implementing them subject to charges for violations of the UN Convention and the president subject to charges of war crimes (Mayer, 2005). Even within the CIA some officials objected to the changed practices, including the use of extraordinary rendition. They argued that the use of so-called black sites, secret prisons set up by the CIA in foreign countries for the purpose of retaining and interrogating suspected terrorists, violated the culture of the CIA and was not as effective as other methods of information gathering. Supporters of the new policies cited the possibility of a second imminent series of terrorist attacks, arguing that extraordinary means were necessary to prevent such attacks from recurring (Mayer, 2006; Priest, 2005a). A Harvard University study examined the need for "highly coercive interrogation" in the war on terrorism. It concluded that the United States needed to employ methods greater than ordinary police interrogation but short of forms of torture explicitly forbidden by U.S. laws and treaties (Heymann & Kayyem, 2005, pp. 1–9; PBS, 2005).

What came to be known as the Jack Bauer, or ticking-bomb, scenario seemed to offer a legitimate, and perhaps necessary, reason for resorting to physical torture when a terrorist had information of an imminent plot. Jack Bauer, the hero of the Fox network television action drama *24*, had 24 hours to foil a terrorist plot and used torture to do so. Opponents of extraordinary rendition countered that ticking-bomb scenarios were rare and did not apply to cases such as Masri's. Masri and others like him were detained and interrogated, some would say tortured, not for the information they had but to determine if they had information. Finally, some within the Federal Bureau of Investigations (FBI) who opposed the new practices argued that interrogations based on trust and a relationship provided more and better information than those based on torture (Mayer, 2005; McCoy, 2006). Tortured detainees sometimes provide false information just to stop the pain. One proponent of highly coercive interrogation acknowledged that the Jack Bauer scenario was unlikely but could not simply be wished away (Kayyem, 2005). Her assertion alluded to what became known as the 1% solution. Formulated by Vice President Dick Cheney, the policy asserted a strong preference for action over analysis. If analysis suggested a 1% chance of a threat being carried out, the United States had to respond as if the threat were a certainty (Suskind, 2006, p. 62). Response to a perceived threat became a top priority, as exemplified by the cases of extraordinary rendition. Masri's abduction was indicative of how low the bar of perceived threat could be set.

The White House and the Department of Justice also tangled with the Pentagon about the revised definitions of torture. Senior law officers of all branches of the military pointed out that the new interpretations of torture and the policies they permitted violated the Military Code of Justice and the Geneva Conventions and could subject military interrogators to criminal proceedings. When the proposals became official, a group of military lawyers unofficially visited the head of the Human Rights Committee of the New York Bar Association. The delegates urged the committee "to challenge the Bush administration about its standards for detention and interrogation" (McCoy, 2006, p. 131); thus, they attempted to enlist allies outside the government to continue the fight they had waged unsuccessfully from inside the government (Mayer, 2006; McCoy, 2006, pp. 128–131).

A Covert Operation Becomes Public. After disclosure and criticism of U.S. policies at Guantanamo surfaced, the clandestine operation of extraordinary rendition came to light in November 2005. Dana Priest, with information supplied by a source within the CIA, reported in the *Washington Post* that extraordinary rendition was part of a larger policy that included "secret prisons" operated by the CIA in eight countries. The story detailed the policy by which suspected terrorists, such as Masri, were abducted in one country; brought to black sites; held as "ghost detainees," incommunicado, without any records of imprisonment and without acknowledgment by any government; and tortured by all but U.S. standards (Priest, 2005a).

In the wake of these reports, the European Parliament set up a temporary committee on extraordinary rendition. One of the committee's tasks was to judge the validity of reports of ghost detainees and their subjection to cruel, inhumane or degrading treatment or torture (Marty, 2007) in violation of fundamental European and international rights. The committee also sought to determine whether European Union nations were complicit in any of these matters—either inadvertently, such as through the use of a sovereign nation's airspace without its knowledge, or deliberately, such as through assistance with the abduction or transport of detainees or the hosting of a black site.

On December 5, 2005, only a month after breaking the secret-prisons story, the *Washington Post* gave details of the Masri case (Priest, 2005b). The next day, the American Civil Liberties Union (ACLU) filed suit against the CIA on behalf of Masri in U.S federal court. The suit contended that George Tenet and other CIA agents violated U.S. and universal human rights laws when they authorized and carried out Masri's abduction. "The CIA's policy of extraordinary rendition is a clear violation of universal human rights protections. . . . Snatching Mr. El-Masri off the street and hiding him away in a secret prison was illegal under American and international law. Keeping him imprisoned after his innocence was established was immoral by any standard" (American Civil Liberties Union, 2005). Masri had modest goals for his legal action: "I am asking the American government to admit its mistakes and to apologize for my treatment. Throughout my time in the prison, I asked to be brought before a court but was refused. Now I am hoping that an American court will say very clearly that what happened to me was illegal and cannot be done to others" (American Civil Liberties Union, 2005). Masri had intended to attend the press conference announcing the suit but was refused entrance into the country after his plane arrived, and he was sent back to Germany on the next available plane. Immigration officials gave no reason for their action.

(Continued)

(Continued)

The United States Does Not Torture. Masri's front-page story broke at an inauspicious time for Secretary of State Condoleezza Rice, who was preparing to leave for a trip to Europe to mend fences over the reports of the month before. Now complete details of an instance of extraordinary rendition would precede her.

In light of public concern and investigations, Rice (2005) issued a formal statement about U.S. policy. She stressed the difficulties that the new form of conflict, global terrorism, placed on the first and oldest duty of any government—to protect its citizens. "The captured terrorists of the 21st century do not fit easily into traditional systems of criminal or military justice, which were designed for different needs. We have to adapt." Indeed, a cornerstone of the new policy of interrogation included a classification of unlawful enemy combatants who did not fall under the Geneva Conventions governing responsibilities toward soldiers and civilians during war. Nor did these enemy combatants enjoy the protection of U.S. laws. Rice thus echoed the opinion of the Department of Justice that international terrorism was "a category of behavior not covered by the legal system" and that "historically, there were people so bad that they were not given protection of the laws" and did not deserve them (Mayer, 2005). Rice explained that the war against terrorism had many forms, including conventional military and intelligence forms, which required the cooperation of intelligence services of other nations. It also had many fronts, such as Iraq and Afghanistan, and areas "where governments cannot take effective action, including where the terrorists cannot in practice be reached by the ordinary processes of law."

Rendition, Rice (2005) maintained, was permissible under international law; consistent with the responsibilities of government to protect its citizens, and a well-established practice. "For decades, the United States and other countries have used 'renditions' to transport terrorist suspects from the country where they were captured to their home country or to other countries where they can be questioned, held, or brought to justice."

Certainly since the mid-1990s, the CIA had conducted extraordinary renditions. In the aftermath of the 1993 bombing of the World Trade Center, the CIA encountered frustration in handling suspects. Granting them due process under U.S. trial procedures risked revealing too much about CIA methods of investigation, informants, and the cooperation of foreign nations, which preferred anonymity in clandestine investigations. One CIA agent involved in these investigations complained, "We were turning into voyeurs. We knew where these people were, but we couldn't capture them because we had nowhere to take them." The CIA realized it needed to collaborate with another country and gained the cooperation of Egypt (Mayer, 2005). After 9/11, extraordinary rendition increased greatly. What had been a very targeted policy became more widespread.

In her defense of rendition in which she touched on precedents for it and suggested its proven success, Rice (2005) reiterated eight times that the United States did not torture rendered individuals or condone the use of torture. She invoked the U.S. Constitution, laws, and treaties, including the UN Convention against Torture, as prohibiting physical and psychological torture and gave assurances that the U.S. policy of rendition operated within those parameters. Before rendering a detainee for interrogation, she explained, the United States acquired assurances that the country to which a prisoner was sent would comply with the bans against torture. Rice reminded people that democratic governments face tough choices in balancing the traditional practices of democracy, such as respect for the rights of the accused, while simultaneously striving to ensure the physical safety of their citizens: "Debate in and among democracies is natural and healthy. I hope that that debate also includes a healthy regard for the responsibilities of governments to protect their citizens."

Rescinding Extraordinary Rendition. Indeed, the debate ensued immediately. Human Rights Watch challenged the accuracy of Rice's remarks. This international nongovernmental organization (NGO) monitors human rights issues in different nations and advocates for compliance with the highest standards of international agreements relating to human rights. Rice's statement, as the group parsed it, had not denied the existence of secret prisons and skirted the torture issue. Claiming that the United States did not transport detainees "for the purpose" of interrogation using torture did not mean that detainees were not tortured at the sites where the United States took them. Certainly, the countries that the United States selected for detention of those subjected to extraordinary rendition had reputations for human rights violations, including the torture and mistreatment of prisoners. This made it likely that rendered prisoners would be tortured, assurances to the contrary notwithstanding. For example, the State Department's annual country-by-country report on human rights described the prison system in Afghanistan, where Masri was rendered, as "poor." The report cited accounts of other secret or informal detention centers in the country where prisoners "were reportedly beaten, tortured, and denied adequate food" (U.S. Department of State, 2005). Ironically, the State Department depended on the work of international NGOs such as Human Rights Watch and Amnesty International for the information used in its report.

Human Rights Watch also explained that Rice's assurances of compliance with the UN Convention against Torture had to be viewed in light of the Bush administration's own definition of torture. The administration's definition differed from more widely accepted definitions of torture in that it excluded most views of psychological torture and did not apply to interrogations of non-Americans abroad, even in cases where such persons were in U.S. custody (Human Rights Watch, 2005). Human Rights Watch suggested that Masri's case, other cases of extraordinary rendition, and some of the events that occurred at Abu Ghraib and Guantanamo all pointed to new government policies that condoned the use of torture.

These policies began to erode with the publication of graphic photographic evidence of the torture of Iraqi prisoners at Abu Ghraib, rising criticism of the treatment of detainees at Guantanamo, and international legal action against U.S. officials for their part in extraordinary rendition. The Department of Justice rescinded its expanded definition of physical torture. In September 2006, President Bush—under continuing pressure from human rights advocates, Congress, European governments, and members of the Republican Party—acknowledged the past use of secret prisons and indicated that all U.S.-held detainees had been transferred to Guantanamo so that the prisons were now empty. He insisted that interrogation "procedures were designed to be safe, to comply with our laws, our Constitution, and our treaty obligations. . . . The procedures were tough, and they were safe, and lawful, and necessary" (BBC, 2006).

Members of the president's own party hoped to insulate the United States from mounting charges of human rights violations by passing legislation banning torture, as defined by the U.S. Army in its Military Code of Conduct, and establishing military tribunals to hear cases of unlawful

(Continued)

(Continued)

enemy combatants detained at Guantanamo. After some discussion, the president reached a compromise with Congress and key Republican leaders in which he agreed to such legislation. When he subsequently signed it into law, however, he explained that the law would not encroach upon his powers as commander in chief and his responsibility "of protecting the American people from further terrorist attacks." Bush asserted that he could invoke those powers as president, thereby effectively bypassing the law. The administration had used this same premise to defend its earlier legitimation of expansive methods of torture. Thus, the president not only repeated what Secretary Rice had offered as the basis for the U.S. policy of extraordinary rendition but went even further by citing his constitutional authority as commander in chief as a justification for ignoring the law's ban on torture (Savage, 2006).

In the midst of all this, Masri's case made its way through the federal courts. The government presented arguments in May 2006 stating that this unprecedented lawsuit would harm national security by exposing state secrets and, therefore, should be dismissed. The judge agreed with the government. On March 2, 2007, the U.S. Fourth Circuit Court of Appeals upheld that decision. On May 30, 2007, the ACLU petitioned the U.S. Supreme Court to review Masri's case. The appeal would test how far the government could use state secrets to avoid a trial in which it was charged with criminal action. Worldwide knowledge of Masri's treatment and the government's official acknowledgment of the rendition policy brought attention to his case; however, the Court refused to hear it. Masri was in court for other matters as well, including his assault of a vocational training instructor in January 2007 and his arrest in May 2007 on suspicion of arson at a wholesale market. His supporters attributed his alleged actions to the psychological torture he had suffered and his inability to get redress from the U.S. or German governments (Hennion, 2007; Marty, 2007, p. 58).

Masri's experience may have represented only one incident in a global effort to hinder terrorism and punish terrorists. Nevertheless, his case focused attention on the practices of extraordinary rendition and torture and contributed to the national and international debate about the use of such practices by the U.S. government.

Concepts of Political Change

The change of extraordinary rendition, though far more dramatic than most political change, provides a useful case to examine change in the political context. It brings front and center the distinguishing characteristic of the political context— the use of force and coercion. From there the other theoretical concepts of leadership take on meanings uniquely hewn to the political context. In this chapter, we examine the means-ends relationship of change. It often occasions a conflict of evil means for good ends and unintended consequences. The best assurance of a strong bond of means and ends comes with a combination of modal and end values. These include values and transactional and transforming leadership, both of which are discussed in other chapters of this book. They take on unique meaning in the political context because of two other leadership concepts—the ethics of responsibility and folly. These are absent from other chapters in the book and perhaps illustrate how leadership concepts most common to the political context can inform other contexts. Most of the time, the influence is in the other direction.

Field

Change occurs within a field of collaborative and conflicting organizations and individual actors. For example, in the case study detailed in this chapter, Human Rights Watch and the Department of State collaborated in compiling the annual report on terror nation by nation but clashed regarding Rice's justifications of extraordinary rendition and denials of the use of torture in interrogations of rendered prisoners. An analysis of leadership examines the influence of the actions taken by leaders and followers opposed to and supportive of the same or related changes.

Four analytical frames emphasize this network of influence, rather than a specific leader: Kurt Lewin's field theory, Gunnar Myrdal's principle of cumulative effect, Margaret Wheatley's work on systems (Hickman & Couto, 2006, pp. 160–168), and Ronald Heifetz's concept of adaptive work.

Kurt Lewin's (1951) field theory espouses that effective change requires understanding "the totality of coexisting facts which are conceived as mutually interdependent" (p. 240). Lewin, a psychologist, concerned himself with individual and group behavior, including change. He contributed action research to the field of problem-centered scholarship. Problem solving, like effective change, requires placing a problem within a system or field containing as many relevant and interdependent elements as possible. Within this field, each individual becomes his or her own dynamic field with interdependent parts, including "life spaces" of family, work, worship, and other groups. People take positive and negative influences from their experiences that shape their identity and help explain their behavior. Lewin advocated assembling all the relevant, mutually independent factors to explain social phenomena, such as leadership and change.

Consider extraordinary rendition through the lens of field theory. Some administration officials disagreed with the political change leading to the use of extraordinary rendition, and they used the press to voice their criticism anonymously. Press reports set off a chain of checks and balances. Congress passed legislation to establish the lawful boundaries of new forms of force within the rendition policy. The judicial branch gave individuals and advocacy groups access to contest the constitutionality of rendition. Political leaders of different nations disagreed regarding the legality of rendition. The rendition policy implied the authority of one country to seize citizens or legal residents within the sovereign boundaries of another country and transport them to a third country for interrogation. Opposition to rendition increased when international NGOs and supranational government bodies, such as the European Parliament and the United Nations, undertook investigations that revealed these interrogations often entailed torture.

Some unusual circumstances came together at the beginning of Masri's ordeal. The CIA agent who first approved Masri's detention on New Year's Eve was low on the chain of command but anxious to play a part in the war on terror. She had been left in charge so other staff members could have the holiday off of work. The CIA's system of rewards and sanctions provided her, and later her superiors, the incentive to detain Masri and render him for interrogation despite a lack of clear evidence (Priest, 2005b). Field theory would point to all of these circumstances as key factors in the development of Masri's case.

Gunnar Myrdal's (1944) principle of cumulative effect provides another way of analyzing Masri's case. Myrdal began with the notion of a system in stable equilibrium and rejected it as inadequate to provide a "dynamic analysis of the process of change in social relations" (p. 1065). The static equilibrium of a system is merely a starting point for exploring the balance of opposing forces. In the simplest of systems comprising only two opposing elements, a change in one brings about a change in the other, which in turn brings on more change. The changes may be subtle enough to appear stable in what is actually a constant state of adjustment. Most systems, however, comprise many interrelated elements, making them far more complex. Even the simplest system with two opposing elements becomes complex given the composites of each element.

Myrdal (1944) proposed a principle of cumulation to explain change within a system of dynamic social causation. Change accumulates as one change brings on another change, and the elements of a system and their composites, or subsystems, represent a second form of cumulation. Assuming an initial static state of balanced forces, Myrdal states the following principle:

> *Any change in any one of . . . [its] factors, independent of the way in which it is brought about, will, by the aggregate weight of the cumulative effects running back and forth between them all, start the whole system moving* in one direction or the other as the case may be, with a speed depending upon the original push and the functions of causal interrelation within the system. (p. 1067)

Myrdal (1944) explained that the final effects of the cumulative process may greatly accelerate after the original push. Once the practice of extraordinary rendition increased post-9/11, adverse consequences cascaded as Myrdal suggested they would in a field of interrelated parts. "The process of change will continue without a new balance in sight," he wrote (p. 1066). This happens largely because the system in which any change occurs is far more complicated than it appears. Every element of the system interrelates with every other element, and every element has its peculiarities and irregularities (p. 1068).

Margaret Wheatley's work (1992, 2007) bridged the field theory of Lewin and the cumulative principle of Myrdal. Wheatley explained that physics introduced field theory to explain gravity, electromagnetism, and relativity. These three fields are similar in that they are "unseen structures, occupying space and becoming known to us through their effects." The space of fields, much like their time, is not empty but "a cornucopia of invisible but powerfully effective structure" (Wheatley, 1992, p. 49). Like Wheatley, Lewin and Myrdal suggested that to understand human behavior and social change one needs to recognize that time and space are not empty and begin to fill in their invisible, but effective, structure.

Wheatley (1992) elaborated on the consequence of this conception of field for leadership. The idea that leaders have vision, set goals, and then marshal their own energy and that of others to achieve these goals is a Newtonian view of change focused on a prime mover and a mechanistic concept of change. Although partially true, this Newtonian focus overlooks the complex fields of cumulative interactions across time and space in which all of this takes place. Better, Wheatley argued, to think about organizational culture and the deliberate and intentional formation of fields that reinforce the values and goals of an organization and fill its spaces and history with coherent messages (pp. 52–57).

Ronald Heifetz (2007) implicitly used the concept of field in his conceptualization of leadership as adaptive work. He defined leadership as the work of mobilizing people's adaptive capacity to tackle tough problems and thrive. Meeting adaptive challenges, known as adaptive work, comprises the basic unit of leadership. Heifetz borrowed the concept of "thriving" from evolutionary biology, in which a successful adaptation preserves essential DNA—the accumulated wisdom of generations; rearranges, reregulates, or discards the DNA that no longer serves the current need; and innovates to develop capacity that enables the organism to thrive in new, challenging environments. A successful adaptation enables a living system to incorporate the best aspects from its past with some enterprising changes to ensure its success in the future.

Mediating Incremental Change

The intricate complexity and interdependency of factors within the field of any political change limit the amount of change possible. The prospect of sustainability most often occurs with incremental, rather than sweeping, change, unless a great deal of effort is made to include the input of as many stakeholders as possible.

These considerations of field also necessitate what Max Weber called considerations of balance and proportion. How do Americans adapt to the threat of terrorism without forfeiting their commitment to human rights? Such questions entail a fundamental rethinking of authority and power as means rather than ends, Heifetz (1994) suggested. The use of coercion cannot be justified solely by the desire to achieve a goal, such as national security, however important that goal may be; rather, those employing coercion must be willing to accept responsibility for the consequences of their actions if they hope to justify them.

After 5 years in which numerous revelations about extraordinary rendition came to light, President Bush faced overwhelming public opinion that the policy represented an unsustainable adaptation to a changed environment characterized by the threat of terrorism. This suggests that change comes best in incremental, rather than large, amounts. Adam Yarmolinsky (2007), a lawyer and an academician who held several high-level government and university positions, proposed that operating at a reasonably high level in any organization, public or private, is really like being in charge of an engine:

> Between keeping the machine from running down for lack of fuel or seizing up for lack of oil, there is seldom, if ever, a time to think about where it is going. You have to jump on the train while the train is moving, and you have to figure out which way it is moving. It may be moving backwards with respect to what you want but forward with what else is happening in the world. (p. 46)

Certainly the Masri case exemplifies the complexity to which Yarmolinsky referred. Extraordinary rendition may have moved the acquisition of information about terrorism forward, but it sent diplomatic relations backward. Agreements at the highest levels of the U.S., German, and Italian governments were undermined when local prosecutors and courts in Germany and Italy treated CIA actions connected to the policy of extraordinary rendition as criminal acts rather than national security secrets. Likewise, the Bush administration faced criticism from Republicans and Democrats alike over the policy.

Yarmolinsky's (2007) comparison of change efforts to the path taken by a locomotive differs from other scholars' conceptualization of change. Locomotives run on linear tracks. It's useful, therefore, to remember that any locomotive is a component of a system of moving parts going in different directions on set paths. When the extraordinary rendition policy moved forward, it sent other parts of the international and national political systems moving down paths fated for a collision unless adjustments to speed and direction could be made. Even presidents can't hold the locomotive's throttle wide open and send a train hurtling down a determined path without risking a wreck or, as historian Barbara Tuchman (1984) said, folly.

Concepts of Political Leadership

A government must provide its citizenry with security from physical harm if it is to be effective and maintain political order. At times this may require waging war against another government and using force and violence against groups and, in the case of extraordinary rendition, individuals. In his profound essay "Politics as a Vocation," Weber (1946) defined the state in terms of violence: "a human community that (successfully) claims *the monopoly of the legitimate use of physical force within a given territory*" (p. 78). At its root, political change, like all politics, "means striving to share power or striving to influence the distribution of power, either among states or among groups within a state" (p. 78). Part of the authority of the state comes from establishing the legitimacy of its power so that it does not have to resort to using the physical force on which its power rests. Weber combined these definitional elements in powerful sociological terms: "The state is a relation of men dominating men, a relation supported by means of a legitimate (i.e., considered to be legitimate) violence" (p. 78). This does not preclude the role of deliberation. To the contrary, in a democracy the line between legitimate and illegitimate violence is most often determined by deliberation. Nor is the state the only political association—families, workplaces, places of worship, churches, and other institutions are all characterized by politics, including formal and informal mechanisms of legitimate and illegitimate forms of force. The state's claim, however, supersedes all the rest.

Government claims a monopoly on legitimate violence to ensure compliance with its demands and to limit the use of force and violence in other contexts. Other organizations and actors may use force (e.g., when a bouncer physically ejects a patron from a restaurant), but they must do so within the legal framework established by the government. Clearly, actors in the private sector are greatly restricted in terms of the kind of force they are permitted to use as compared to actors in the public sector. The power to coerce increases as the level of government increases, being much greater on the national level than on the local level. Likewise, the forms of coercion increase with ascension through government levels, moving from policing and security at the local level to armed battle at the national level. Some government officials may even legitimately and lawfully take a human life, as in cases of capital punishment or war. Similarly, as political authority becomes more democratic, deliberation becomes more inclusive: witness the post-Aristotelian abolition of slavery and the political participation of women. Social stratification certainly remains even in democratic societies, but, in general, democratic political leadership leans toward the reduction of such stratification and toward the reduction of violence based on stratification—witness laws against violence toward women.

Yet the question Weber (1946) asked remains: If we must do harm to others, how do we legitimate it? How do we strike the right balance between competing values—such as social order versus individual rights or, in the Masri case, national security versus the rights of an individual suspected of terrorism?

Values

That question brings us to the heart of leadership and change in any context: values. From 1995 to 1998, the Kellogg Foundation supported a series of forums and discussions about the state and future of the study of leadership. James MacGregor Burns hosted these discussions, which were coordinated by the Burns Academy of Leadership at the University of Maryland and the Jepson School of Leadership Studies at the University of Richmond, and about 50 leadership studies scholars participated in them. Two central points emerged from the discussions:

- Leadership has common tasks—change, conflict, and collaboration.
- Leadership has distinguishing elements—values, initiative, inclusiveness, and creativity—that may be seen in leadership in any context.

Values suffuse the common elements of leadership—change, conflict, and collaboration. How leadership deals with these common elements varies depending on the values of a group or its leadership. For example, values affect initiative (which kind of change to undertake and when to undertake it) and inclusiveness (who should participate in the change process and who should benefit from the change). Creativity has constituent elements: critical thinking, vision, communication, and reflective practice. All of these variables constitute the common elements of leadership as shown in Table 7.1.

Clarity about values offers a starting point for understanding initiative and inclusiveness. Creativity remains the outlier, but even so, values play a part in determining which creative tactics and strategies are appropriate and what emphasis should be placed on humor and other moral resources in the conduct of change, conflict, and collaboration.

Figure 7.1 presents a further refinement of the original Kellogg Leadership Study Group model. It begins to explain how values can drive a person to initiate change and how change can impinge on values and consequently drive people to take

TABLE 7.1 Common Elements of Leadership

Distinguishing Elements of Leadership	Change	Conflict	Collaboration
Values			
Initiative			
Inclusiveness			
Creativity			

FIGURE 7.1 The Common and Distinguishing Elements of Leadership

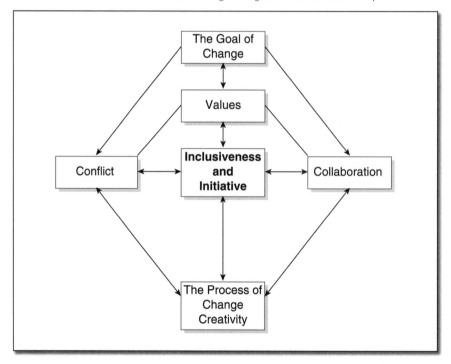

initiative. Change brings conflict and collaboration, both of which have reflexive relationships with inclusiveness and initiative. Values affect leaders' decisions about which people to include or exclude in the change process and which people to include or exclude from the benefits of the intended change. Similarly, creativity affects and is affected by conflict and collaboration. Figure 7.1 suggests that creativity affects *who* is included in leadership efforts and *when* initiative begins, both of which influence the nature of conflict and collaboration.

If only the study and conduct of leadership were as simple as a model comprising straight lines and boxes! Moving leadership from a model depicted on a printed page to actual day-to-day experience entails moving from an inanimate, two-dimensional chart to a dynamic system of interrelated parts and subsystems in a state of constant change without clear boundaries—a fractal. To think that one can understand leadership as a set of categories with fixed points and relations, such as in Figure 7.1, or as a list of generalizations, such as the one just given, would undermine the dynamic nature of leadership as it is experienced. Using a grid to analyze the universe, for example, may leave one without any sense of the dynamic, ever-changing nature of the universe. Likewise, the grids from Table 7.1 and Figure 7.1 serve as only a temporary, static representation of the ever-changing reality of leadership. Even so, the static framework suggests the elements around which any dynamic system will organize itself and those that effective leadership will use.

Figure 7.2 captures the dynamic nature of leadership. It includes the same factors as Table 7.1 and Figure 7.1 but attempts to illustrate a more fluid, ever-changing environment held together by the energy of its interrelated parts, analogous to the activity at the subatomic level of matter. At the core of this dynamic model of leadership reside values and related components that distinguish one form of leadership from another. Change, conflict, and collaboration travel around this core in a pattern that can be specified but not predicted. These leadership elements have their own interrelationships and are held in orbit by values, inclusiveness, initiative, and creativity.

The clarity about values as the central element of change in any context invites the question, what values? What groups and individuals share common values in this leadership effort and would be willing to form alliances in conflicts over change? In the political context, this conflict over values may entail the legitimacy and wisdom of forceful coercion to promote one set of values over another.

FIGURE 7.2   The Quantum of Leadership

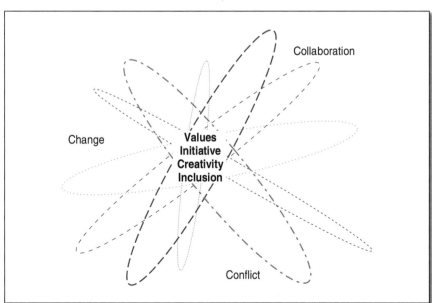

In the Masri case, the conflicting values, in broadest terms, were national security against terrorist attacks and the human rights of those suspected of terrorist planning. On the one hand, these values may be considered absolute ends, but in practice they have limits. The administration's effort to imprison and to permit others to interrogate terrorist suspects with enhanced coercive techniques, if not torture, met almost universal criticism for their violation of human rights. On the other hand, it is quite clear, as Rice (2005) pointed out, that the value of human rights cannot be permitted to jeopardize national security by protecting the rights of those with information vital to national security to remain silent. The task then is not to choose between competing values but how to pursue one without abandoning the other.

The Ethic of Responsibility

Weber (1946) addressed the difficulty of this choice and brought it to stage center of political leadership. He contrasted an ethic of absolute or ultimate ends and an ethic of responsibility. Taken alone, the emphasis on passion, ideals, and cause in politics—whether national security or human rights—could support extremism. The decisive distinctions between them are a consideration of consequences of action and proportionality. The ethos of cause, an absolute value, risks becoming extremism without an ethos of responsible compromise and proportionate action.

The ethic of ultimate ends focuses on intention, whereas the ethic of responsibility focuses on the foreseeable adverse consequences of one's actions (Weber, 1946, pp. 119–120). "The believer in an ethic of ultimate ends feels 'responsible' only for seeing to it that the flame of pure intentions is not squelched; for example, the flame of protesting against the injustice of the social order" (p. 121). Thus, suicide bombers may see their action as a means to protest injustice and to inspire others to similar protest with no attention to the real and human consequences of that action to others.

The responsible ethic focuses on adverse consequences. It seeks and examines all foreseeable consequences of an action and assumes responsibility for them. One consequence not foreseen that posed a difficult problem for the administration was that of an innocent person being rendered. When faced with this consequence, the highest ranking officials of the CIA and the State Department took a month to decide what to do. Tenet's initial idea, reverse rendition, would pretend that Masri had never been rendered a complete abdication of the ethics of responsibility. Eventually, the United States chose a middle path. It took responsibility for Masri's treatment but only to the German government and asked its assistance to deny this adverse consequence of its policy.

In terms of the second feature of an ethics of responsibility, extraordinary rendition seemed more proportionate than measures that the United Nations, strongly backed by the Clinton administration, took against the regime of Saddam Hussein. The UN Food and Agricultural Organization estimated that 567,000 Iraqi children younger than 5 years of age had died between 1990 and 1995 because of sanctions. The United States opposed lifting those sanctions. On the television magazine program *60 Minutes*, reporter Leslie Stahl asked Madeleine Albright, ambassador to the United Nations and future secretary of State, if the effort to topple Saddam Hussein was worth that price. Albright, echoing Weber's observation that good things might come from evil, replied, "I think this is a very hard choice, but the price—we think the price is worth it." She apologized for that remark in her memoirs (Richman, 2003). Although rendition received much more press coverage than the deaths of Iraqi children, it took and disrupted far fewer lives. A few errors in extraordinary rendition, such as Masri, might be considered collateral damage—a regrettable but unavoidable consequence of a legitimate battle tactic in the war on terrorism—and far less reprehensible than the policy consequences of the deaths of thousands of children.

In political terms, however, extraordinary rendition had more adverse consequences. Internationally, the United States had allied with nations with reputations for torture of prisoners and other violations of human rights. At the same time, it kept allies with reputations for respect of human rights at arms length with its refusal to cooperate in those governments' investigations of extraordinary rendition of its citizens or residents. Thus, the United States impugned the sovereignty of those nations. Extraordinary rendition differed from the UN sanctions on Iraq, in part because of the allies it had in each policy. In addition, these U.S. policies eroded its moral standing to criticize other nations for doing the same. When Iran seized four Americans in 2007, for example, the parallels between its actions and the United States' extraordinary rendition left the Bush administration hampered in its protest of Iranian action (Greenberg, 2007). World support for the U.S. war on terror slipped from 2002 to 2005 (Pew Global Attitudes Project, 2005), in each of the 16 nations polled, except for 1 in which the support was already low—17%. The favorable opinion of the United States also declined over this same period (PBS, 2007). At the same time within the United States, polls indicated that Americans who thought the country was heading in the right direction dropped from 70% to 30% (Polling Report, n.d.). The Bush administration insisted that extraordinary rendition had thwarted terrorist plots and its effectiveness outweighed the criticism the United States received about its regard for human rights.

Behind this calculation or proportions of adverse and beneficial consequences, other matters of proportion can be found. The numbers of extraordinary renditions jumped dramatically after 9/11. Rather than rendering individuals whose guilt was well documented and in most cases decided in absentia by a court, the CIA now rendered people like Masri on the suspicion of terrorism. In the disproportionate emphasis on gathering information for national security, it seemingly never occurred to policy makers what to do with innocent people who had been rendered after questioning them.

Good Ends and Wrong Means

The coin of ethics of responsibility has another side, however. The nature of the state, a relationship of legitimate violence, may require pursuing good ends (national security) through "morally dubious means or at least dangerous ones" (extraordinary rendition) with evil consequences. This brings Weber (1946) back to his lamentable premise that "the decisive means for politics is violence" (p. 121) to which he added that in the experience of the irrationality of the world good consequences may come from evil means and evil consequences from good means. "The world is governed by demons and . . . he who lets himself in for politics, that is, for power and force as means, contracts with diabolical powers" precisely because of this irrationality of the world (p. 123).

As Weber (1946) explained about the ethics of absolutes, the ethics of responsibility runs the same risk if disproportionately pursued as an absolute value:

> He who seeks the salvation of the soul, of his own and of others, should not seek it along the avenue of politics, for the quite different tasks of politics can only be solved by violence. . . . Everything that is striven for through political action operating with violent means and following an ethic of responsibility endangers the "salvation of the soul." (p. 126)

Is one then left with dueling ethics? Weber (1946) seems to throw up his hands, sadly concluding, "From no ethics in the world can it be concluded when and to what extent the ethically good purpose 'justifies' the ethically dangerous means and ramifications" (p. 121).

Transforming and Transactional Leadership

Perhaps one can resolve this value conflict by putting the ethics of responsibility and absolutes in more familiar terms of transactional and transforming leadership. Burns (1978) associates the first with modal values—honesty, integrity, trust, empathy, and other values that permit people to engage in the transactions of everyday life with some confidence. Transforming leadership he associates with end values—liberty, justice—and, in the context of this discussion, human rights and security from physical harm. Modal values share much in common with the ethos of responsibility, which assesses the possible consequences of a particular change to achieve some end value. End values share much in common with the ethos of ultimate ends, which focuses on the goal to be achieved. Weber (1946) called for some sense of proportion between intended changes and ensuing consequences. Perhaps then, the responsible pursuit of transforming leadership goals also requires a portion of transactional leadership modal values. Without such temperance, the end most surely might come to justify the means whenever the state is powerful enough to justify its violence in terms of values, such as social order.

The Masri case invites reconsideration of transforming and transactional leadership. Often they are seen as dichotomies (Burns, 2007), but clearly they entail the fusion of modal values—the stuff of transactional leadership—and end values—the material of transforming. When the pursuit of end values—such as national security—cannot be done with modal values—such as honesty, integrity, trust, truthfulness, accountability, and openness—it may indicate inauthentic transforming leadership or what others have called the dark side of charismatic leadership (Yukl, 1998, pp. 311–314). This suggests further that although leadership is always moral action, sometimes it may engage in immoral action. This brings us back to the "ends justifying the means" principle that Weber (1946) made central to political leadership. Clearly, however, when the means entails secrecy, even after they are made public, it undermines the credibility of claims to legitimate coercive force.

On balance then, the ethics of absolutes and responsibility require political leadership to cling to a cause—the purpose to which politics, power, and violence are a means—but to act responsibly. The latter requires examining foreseeable consequences, forgoing disproportionate actions even in pursuit of a cause, and remaining in touch with the adverse consequences of action. The political vocation is transforming, in James MacGregor Burns's (1978) terms, because the responsible pursuit of ultimate ends is the only means to discover what is possible.

Folly

Without proportion and a balance of absolute and responsible ethics, political leaders run the risk of folly—the lengthy pursuit of policies that run counter to their self-interest. Barbara Tuchman (1984) carefully outlined the characteristics of folly: "wooden headedness," which removes reason from political leadership and in its place substitutes wishful thinking; the use of fixed and biased notions; and the refusal or inability to learn from experience. The decision to bring the wooden horse left by the Greeks at the city gates of Troy presents an archetype of folly (pp. 36–49) further illustrated by the Papacy on the eve of the Reformation, the British government on the eve of the American Revolution, and the U.S. government in Vietnam. The adverse consequences of folly, a failure of the ethics of responsibility, in the political realm almost always exceeds folly in other contexts by dramatic proportions.

The strategic and tactical effectiveness of the war in Iraq and other parts of the war on terrorism will be discussed for decades, but the strategic and tactical effectiveness of torture has already been debated for centuries. Ulpian, a third century Roman jurist, argued that the strong can resist torture and the weak will say anything to end their pain (McCoy, 2006, p. 203). Torture may be effective when carried out on a large scale. In 1957, for example, the French government destroyed the urban underground resistance in Algiers by rounding up 30% to 40% of all men in the Casbah section, interrogating them, torturing some of them, and summarily executing 3,000 of them. The United States replicated the French methods of torture, interrogation, and murder in Vietnam with Project Phoenix. William Colby, later head of the CIA and in 1971 in charge of Project Phoenix, testified to a House subcommittee that the project had killed 20,587 Vietcong suspects in the previous 3 years. This and other action drained U.S. support from its war in Vietnam (McCoy, 2006, pp. 196–198).

The "success" of large-scale torture against terror comes at very high political costs to the broader war efforts and indeed the loss of legitimacy for governments themselves. The French in Algeria and the United States in Vietnam are clear examples. British tactics in Northern Ireland brought rebuke from the European Human Rights Commission. Israeli torture of Palestinian prisoners brought its own recommendation against physical torture in 1987 and against all abuse in 1999. The shocking revelations of conditions, including torture, in the U.S.-maintained Abu Ghraib prison of Iraq brought universal condemnation. Efforts to skirt U.S. law and international accords, such as the prison for unlawful combatants at Guantanamo Base in Cuba, have brought rebukes from other nations, international government agencies, international NGOs, national human rights advocates, and the U.S. Supreme Court (Intelligence Science Board, 2007).

The high costs of a policy of torture include the shadow that torture casts over the legitimacy of information gained through individual instances of torture. Thus, confessions gained by torture are routinely discarded by courts in democratic nations. As the U.S. military war tribunal arrangements—constructed with the war powers of the president—got started, its first case ended with a guilty plea of an Australian citizen. Although a powerful legitimating factor in most cases, the extraordinary rendition and allegations of torture of David Hicks strained the credibility of a guilty verdict among Australian citizens. His case became a major problem for the Australian government, an ally of the Bush administration's war on terrorism's policies. His and other cases embroiled the tribunals, an effort to provide some legitimacy to extraordinary rendition and to counter allegations of torture, in endless rounds of quarrels about the legitimacy of confessions, the nature of torture, and the rules of process as well as the question of the innocence or guilt of the persons on trial.

If individual torture is ineffective and mass torture brings pyrrhic victories at best, why do governments persist in their practice as the United States most recently did or at the very least appeared to do so? Critics of the use of torture point out that it may serve a symbolic function, giving people a false sense that they have control over threats to their safety (McCoy, 2006, p. 207). This touches on the much larger issue of political leadership as symbolic action and the myth and ritual surrounding it (Edelman, 1971). Our case contains several instances of symbolic action including the signing ceremony for the bill to eliminate torture even as the signing statement undermined its authority.

Change Practices

The leadership practices of change in the political context resemble those in other contexts. They include signalizing, or pointing out changes and problems in the environment that need to be addressed. Robert Tucker's (1995) work on this concept resembles Heifetz's (1994) concept of adaptive work. But for every effort to signal a problem, there are other efforts to dismiss or define differently the same problem. In addition, every effort to signal a problem competes with efforts to signal other problems. Thus, the question becomes why does one signalizing effort prevail over another? For any signalizing effort to succeed it must have legitimacy and appeal to some form of authority. In addition, the individual or group effectively signaling the problem balances voice—the attempt to address an objectionable set of affairs—with the threat of leaving it and loyalty that exceeds it. A formal set of checks and balances most clearly distinguishes change within the political context, although they may be found, at least informally, in all contexts.

Signalizing

Political leadership, according to Tucker (1995), includes both constituted and nonconstituted leaders, namely, those with formal authority and power and those without it. Both types of leaders must define societal problems, prescribe actions or policies to correct or deal with these problems, and line up support for their problem analysis and prescription (p. xii). Political problems arise when situations "take on meaning in relation to a political community's purpose and concerns" (p. 49). Some leaders act sooner than others to explain the meaning of events in light of government values. Political problems are often characterized by a community's competing values. The Masri case, for example, was characterized by a conflict between national security and human rights. The application in Chapter 5 pitted a homeowners association's concern for the integrity of a neighborhood against an advocacy group's proposal for housing for mentally retarded adults in the neighborhood.

Heifetz (1994) built on Tucker's ideas that political leadership signals, or identifies, political-problem situations. Heifetz referred to this as adaptive work that requires mobilizing the resources of a group to address whatever problem the group faces. Both Tucker and Heifetz included nonconstituted actors, or those without formal authority, in their frameworks of political leadership; by doing so, they looked beyond the concept of authority and power over (Weber's primary emphasis) others to concepts of sharing power with others and granting power to others to work for change:

> By using different units of analysis for leadership and authority, i.e., work and power, and thereby uncoupling them, we can then analyze what we commonly observe: that people lead—i.e., mobilize progress on challenges demanding new adaptations for the social system to thrive—both with and without authority at the same time. Moreover, the various forms of power, from coercive to inspirational, remain useful in various contexts in the practice of leadership. (Heifetz, 2007, pp. 34–35)

The Masri case comprised a number of constituted actors, not the least of which was the Bush administration, which signaled the security risk to U.S. citizens regarding the threat of terrorist attacks. Dealing with terrorists, a new type of enemy, required adaptive work. The U.S. and German governments signaled their agreement, at least in the Masri case, that in the interest of ensuring national security, they would preserve the secrecy associated with extraordinary rendition. Congress signaled its intolerance of torture as a tactic in the war on terror and pressed the White House to approve legislation outlawing torture. Although the president signed this legislation, he signaled that the war powers granted him by the Constitution gave him the authority to approve the use of enhanced interrogations if he deemed them necessary to preserve the security of the nation.

Other constituted actors signaled their concern that extraordinary rendition posed a risk to human rights. Opposition parties in all western European countries wanted to know if their governments had cooperated in rendition flights. If, for example, the United States approved a rendition flight that used a country's airspace without the knowledge and cooperation of that country's government, it would constitute a violation of national sovereignty. If, on the other hand, a country's government was complicit in permitting rendition flights, opposition parties could challenge their country's government for violating international treaties banning the use of torture or complicity in its use.

Not all debate occurred at the national level, however. Local courts in Munich, Germany, for example, signalized their willingness to pursue criminal charges against U.S. CIA officers. Back in the United States, Congress and the federal courts signaled their own concerns about the enhanced interrogation methods employed in extraordinary renditions and at Abu Ghraib and Guantanamo Bay. Many believed these methods violated U.S. values of human rights and U.S. policies banning physical torture.

Another set of actors, including the United Nations and the European Parliament, occupy a place between constituted and nonconstituted authorities. The European Parliament responded to Priest's (2005a, 2005b) reports in the *Washington Post* by launching hearings. The UN set a higher standard for treatment of prisoners than did the United States and considered some of the tactics employed by the United States to be torture. Although both the European Parliament and the UN were constituted authorities, neither had the power to make the United States halt the practices of interrogation it had adopted in its war on terrorism.

Nonconstituted actors, such as Human Rights Watch and the ACLU, also featured in the Masri case. Both organizations contested the U.S. government's assertions about extraordinary rendition and invoked standards for which constituted actors should be held responsible. Whereas the U.S. government insisted on the primacy of its responsibility to protect its citizens, these nonconstituted actors extolled human rights and the laws and treaties that protected them. Indeed, Human Rights Watch and the ACLU suggested that lacking some ethic of responsibility, the United States could become much like other nations notorious for their human rights violations. Masri himself expressed that concern: "I have very bad feelings [about the United States]. I think it's just like in the Arab countries: arresting people, treating them inhumanly and less than that, and with no rights and no laws" (Priest, 2005b).

Legitimizing

The process of signalizing provides reasons for, or challenges to, the legitimacy of a particular change effort (Tucker, 1995, pp. 79–85). The Masri case illuminates this contest over legitimacy particularly well. It entails the state's fundamental, distinctive claim to legitimacy in its use of violent coercion. Weber (1946) offered three sources of legitimate authority:

- The eternal yesterday of tradition—traditional.
- Extraordinary and personal gifts of grace—charismatic.
- Legality premised on the validity of legal statute and functional competence premised on rationally created rules—legal. (pp. 78–79)

Unlike Weber's sources of legitimate authority, the changes in extraordinary rendition and torture policies reflected charisma of purpose, defined as a dedication to a powerful purpose that motivates people to take action. This suggests Gill Hickman's (2004) concept of invisible leadership, albeit in a distinct form. The lack of visibility resulted from the effort to make and keep the new policies a secret. Even after the policies came to light, the administration and the courts invoked national security as a reason for not disclosing details of Masri's abduction and detention. Clearly, acts of terrorism had changed the environment. The clandestine nature of the policies created to deal with this new and challenging environment ultimately undermined the legitimacy of the policies. Even the charisma of purpose—national security in this case—could not extend legitimate authority to extraordinary rendition given its violation of human rights, which were protected by other sources of legitimate authority.

Several appeals to tradition as legitimating authority characterized the Masri case. Secretary Rice and President Bush appealed to the authority of the eternal past in grounding extraordinary rendition in the fundamental responsibility of the government to protect its citizens from harm. Rice invoked precedent for the policy in the Lincoln administration. Because the Confederacy relied on slaves to aid its war effort, Lincoln decided to use the war powers granted the president by the Constitution to proclaim the emancipation of slaves in the Confederate states. He also used his war powers to suspend the right to habeas corpus for those who impeded enlistment in the Union Army or thwarted Union war efforts. His use of those powers served as a powerful precedent on which the Bush administration called. In her initial response to newspaper accounts of the Masri case, Rice (2005) argued that the war on terrorism "challenges traditional norms and precedents of previous conflicts," but she insisted that the new and changed legal standards adhered to traditional values. Thus, the administration cited authority from the past to break with traditional authoritative practices of the past.

Most of the efforts to legitimate extraordinary rendition involved the legal realm. The administration denied claims of torture by using a controversial definition of torture that was based on the legal opinions of the Department of Justice, the guidelines from the U.S. Military Code of Conduct, and the U.S. reservations to the UN Convention against Torture. Rice also assured the public that the United States did not render a prisoner without first getting an assurance that neither physical nor psychological torture would be employed. When Congress voted to ban torture, Bush invoked his constitutional war powers as president.

Those opposed to extraordinary rendition rebutted these legitimations by offering their own appeals to one or another form of legal authority. For example, the European Parliament invoked its own statutes on torture. Human Rights Watch refuted the accuracy of the precedents Rice invoked. The press raised questions about the extent of the president's war-power authority, citing limitations set by the U.S. Supreme Court. Opponents of extraordinary rendition also insisted that the Geneva Accords and the UN Convention against Torture applied despite the administration's denial of their authority. Lower courts in Germany and Italy treated cases of extraordinary rendition as crimes of abduction.

Exit, Voice, and Loyalty

Sometimes situations arise in which constituted actors move beyond their customary realm of authority in their efforts to change policies and practices. Albert O. Hirschman (1970) called this *voice*—"any attempt at all to change . . . an objectionable state of affairs" (p. 30). He contrasted *voice* with *exit*, whereby a person chooses to leave an unsatisfactory state of affairs, and *loyalty*, whereby a person chooses to remain in one. Thus, a person might exercise the exit option by resigning from a position because he or she disagrees with policy changes, or the person might exercise the loyalty option by remaining in a position of authority despite disagreeing with policy changes.

Hirschman (1970) argued that voice is essential to the vitality of organizations but is successful only in the context of an appropriate mix of exit and loyalty. For example, criticism voiced at the time of resignation, or exit, has less influence within an organization than criticism voiced in conjunction with the threat of resignation. Similarly, criticism of a change has power beyond the authority of a constituted position when it comes from a loyal member of the organization. Exit without voice provides no feedback, and loyalty without voice acquiesces to the decline of an organization. Thus, optimal change requires a balance of all three strategies.

As described earlier in this chapter, U.S. military lawyers voiced their opposition to the new, more restricted definition of torture offered by the Department of Justice. Some CIA officials opposed the new policy based on the law, the precedent of organizational culture and practice, and efficacy. By expressing their objections, these lawyers and CIA officials demonstrated voice rather than exit or loyalty. After the policies on torture were approved, a group of military lawyers visited members of an advocacy group and encouraged them to continue opposition to the new policies. CIA officials leaked information about extraordinary rendition to the *Washington Post*. A person accused of whistle-blowing denied the charge but was fired anyway.

Instances of an effective balance of voice, exit, and loyalty also stand out in Masri's case. Republican Party leaders in the U.S. Senate criticized enhanced interrogation methods at Abu Ghraib and Guantanamo. They succeeded in passing new legislation precisely because they threatened to exit, which would have led to the override of a presidential veto, and because they were known for their loyalty as members of the president's political party who were ordinarily supportive of his policies. Masri himself provided another instance of effective voice. He chose to voice his narrative in the courts rather than remain silent out of loyalty to his national government.

Checks and Balances

These instances of effective voice point to another element of change unique to the political context: checks and balances. Most democratic political systems use checks and balances to reduce the risk of a constituted actor exceeding his or her authority and causing a governmental train wreck.

The framers of the U.S. Constitution were students of history and government and were not unfamiliar with power. They embraced the challenge of constructing a government and tried to incorporate every imaginable safeguard to protect against many of the same risks Weber (1946) associated with political leadership. The framers agreed that political authority in the United States would not be based on tradition as the aristocracies and monarchies of Europe were. Nor did they want charisma to determine political authority; they deliberately created firewalls to divide authority among branches of government so that no one person could hold sway over the entire government. They instituted a cumbersome presidential election system precisely to protect the office of the presidency from a charismatic individual (Couto, 2002). They achieved a balanced Congress by modeling the Senate after an oligarchy and the House after a representative government. Finally, suspicious of a military that could resort to violence to achieve its ends, the framers placed a civilian, the president, as commander in chief of the armed forces of the new country. The result was political leadership premised on Weber's third source of legitimate political authority: a legal framework of rationally created rules (Weber, 1946, pp. 78–79). The new government would be ruled by law; no individual, regardless of political position, would be above the law.

The framers not only divided government, but they also limited its power. During the early 19th century, Alexis de Tocqueville remarked on the unique role of voluntary associations in the U.S. democracy. The limits placed on government left a vacuum in meeting public needs that nongovernmental bodies filled. The government was limited not only by its accountability to laws but also by its accountability to a public informed by media outlets. The First Amendment to the Constitution enshrined these limits on government by assuring freedom of the press and of citizens' right to assemble and associate.

The framers' system of checks and balances among constituted authority was evident in the Masri case. The federal courts provided Masri a venue to hold the U.S. government accountable for his extraordinary rendition. The court refused to hear the case, ruling that the government's right to maintain secrecy in matters of national security policy superseded Masri's right to a trial. Masri's lawyers appealed that decision unsuccessfully to the U.S. Supreme Court. Congress passed legislation effectively banning extraordinary rendition. President Bush, facing a likely veto override, bowed to congressional will, but only after invoking his constitutional war powers as a check and balance against congressional power.

The Masri case also highlighted checks and balances in the international context. Local governments in Germany and Italy took action to make extraordinary rendition a crime even though these nations' national governments did not. Supranational and international bodies, such as the European Parliament and the United Nations, asserted their higher standards for the treatment of prisoners and their more encompassing ban on torture. Nonconstituted actors also served as checks and balances. The *Washington Post* articles brought to light what had been a secret program of the U.S. government. NGOs such as Human Rights Watch, the International Red Cross, and the ACLU sought to change the policy of extraordinary rendition by writing reports, influencing policy makers, and taking court action.

Conclusion

The many groups in the Masri case each had its narrative to signal the challenge to each of their "purposes and concerns" and the legitimacy of extraordinary rendition. The effectiveness of narrative depends on finding a venue for it, which the system of checks and balances, including constituted and nonconstituted actors, provides. As with any change efforts, these actors and their narratives compete and collaborate in a complex field in interdependent and interrelated ways. Yarmolinsky (2007) imagined that the complexity of this field exceeds the imagination of most newcomers to the realm of political change:

> It comes as an unpleasant surprise to people fresh in leadership positions to discover that they cannot give orders and expect them to be obeyed. . . . The dilemma is that leadership is a joint enterprise. One cannot lead without the cooperation of others. . . . The leader is a mediator, a moderator, someone who adjusts the facts of change and the intransigent facts of organizations and institutions. (pp. 46–47)

Secrecy may circumvent some of opposition and simple bureaucratic inertia to which Yarmolinsky referred. But sustainable political change requires the combination of transforming and modal values, such as openness. In a democratic system with many venues to express voice and narratives of adaptive work and many actors to do so, it becomes all the more likely that no political change will endure without the balance of passion, values, and responsibility of which Weber (1946) spoke. Thus we come back to a point made earlier: that transforming or charismatic leadership without modal values—in this case transparency—falls short of the proper balance of passion, values, and responsibility that Weber used as a measure for political leadership. Those policies that endure without such a balance and combination of transforming and modal values are likely to result in folly, as Tuchman (1984) described.

Perhaps more than other context, leadership for change in politics requires patience for a long, deliberative process that involves compromise. Weber (1946) concluded his essay on the vocation of politics with this caution that links to the ethics of ultimate ends and responsibility with the mix of passion, responsibility, and proportion:

> Politics is a strong and slow boring of hard boards. It takes both passion and perspective. Certainly all historical experience confirms the truth—that man would not have attained the possible unless time and again he had reached out for the impossible. . . . This is necessary right now, or else men will not be able to attain even that which is possible today. (p. 128)

Holding on to passion and perspective requires leadership, according to Weber, and heroism because hope to attain important values—security or human rights— might crumble in light of opposition from the other. Some have the capacity to hold fast when things crumble and the world seems "too stupid or too base" for what they offer. Yet our only hope for political leadership rests with the willingness of people, who may be neither leaders nor heroes, to act responsibly for the seeming impossible while sadly mindful that effort may only provide a measure of what is possible, not what is needed or necessary.

Thus, we deal in our own time and in our own way with the enduring questions of political leadership. How does leadership harmonize conflicting values? How do political authorities use their power in a manner that seems legitimate and thus maintains their power rather than undermines it? How do we deal with differences among people? Do we make them into castelike categories or do we remain mindful of the human qualities and rights of all people? How do we balance the rights of others and the threats that they may pose to our security? And last, how do we decide these matters and who should be included or excluded from their deliberation?

Application and Reflection

Application

To Hear or Not to Hear

No one could remember the last time that the United States Supreme Court had reversed itself in such a short period of time. In April, the Court had declined to review a decision of an appellate court that ruled that persons held at Guantanamo Bay did not have a right to challenge their detention in U.S. courts. This supported the Bush administration's

(Continued)

(Continued)

position that non-U.S. citizens detained outside of the United States do not have access to the U.S. court system. Now, 2 months later, the court agreed to review the decision in the fall term, probably in December. Experts could not recall such a reversal in decades (Glaberson, 2007).

The central legal question was and remains whether or not "enemy combatants" can be held indefinitely without the right of habeas corpus—that is, review by a court to determine the legality of the detention. A Republican majority in Congress sided with the president and passed legislation to establish military tribunals that would pass judgment on the legality of the detention of any and all of the 375 detainees at Guantanamo. That legislation also barred U.S. courts from hearing habeas corpus suits filed by the detainees. One issue in the case was whether or not Congress exceeded its constitutional authority in this legislation. The Constitution permits the suspension of the right to a habeas corpus hearing at times of "rebellion or invasion." Another issue was the fairness of the military tribunals that determine the status of detainees as enemy combatants. In the closed hearings, detainees are not permitted lawyers, do not see all the evidence against them, and may have confessions and other incriminating statements held against them, even though these statements come from conditions most international bodies consider mental and physical torture. One military lawyer found the military hearings to be haphazard and under pressure from commanding officers to determine the prisoners as enemy combatants and thus legally detained. His affidavit listing his conclusions was part of the motion to reconsider, which the Court granted.

The Court had ruled twice against the government's detention policies at Guantanamo by narrow margins. In April, it refused to hear a case that upheld the constitutionality of Congress's last effort to establish hearings for Guantanamo detainees while still denying them access to federal courts. The Court took the very narrow grounds that the decision in that case had not yet been appealed to the full Appeals Court for the District of Columbia. In reversing itself, the Court signaled that it thought the case could not wait. Apparently, one judge had changed his mind in the 2-month interval between decisions.

REFLECTION

Imagine that you are law clerks for the nine Supreme Court justices; imagine yourselves alone in the lunch room of the Supreme Court building.

- Discuss why you think the judge might have changed his mind.

- What is the delicate balance of order and rights, security and legal protections at play?

- What is the field in which the Court is an actor? How are the actions of the judges of the court acts of political leadership?

- What is the role of the courts in attaining the deliberation that Aristotle thought was essential in democracy?

- What is the role of the courts in the system of checks and balances to safeguard the state from acts of illegitimate coercion?

- Would you have voted to hear the case or wait for the full Appellate Court to make its decision?

- When and if the case reaches the Supreme Court, what do you think its decision should be? Why?

References

American Civil Liberties Union. (2005, December 6). *ACLU files landmark lawsuit challenging CIA's "extraordinary rendition" of innocent man.* Retrieved March 12, 2007, from http://www.aclu.org/natsec/emergpowers/22207prs20051206.html

Arar Commission. (2006). *Commission of inquiry into the actions of Canadian officials in relation to Maher Arar.* Retrieved February 3, 2007, from http://www.ararcommission.ca/

BBC. (2006, September 7). *Bush's secret prisons.* Retrieved June 14, 2007, from http://news.bbc.co.uk/1/hi/world/americas/5322954.stm

Burns, J. M. (1978). *Leadership.* New York: Harper& Row.

Burns, J. M. (2007). Foreword. In R. A. Couto (Ed.), *Reflections on leadership* (pp. v–viii). Lanham, MD: University Press of America.

Couto, R. A. (2002). Dear Publius: Reflections on the Founding Fathers and charismatic leadership. In B. J. Avolio & F. Yammarino (Eds.), *Transformational and charismatic leadership: The road ahead* (pp. 95–108). Oxford, UK: Elsevier Science.

Edelman, M. (1971). *Politics as symbolic action: Mass arousal and quiescence.* Chicago: Markam.

Glaberson, W. (2007, June 30). In shift, justices agree to review detainees' case. *The New York Times.* Retrieved February 25, 2009, from http://www.nytimes.com/2007/06/30/washington/30scotus.html?pagewanted=print

Greenberg, K. J. (2007). *Blowback, detainee-style: The plight of American prisoners in Iran.* Retrieved June 18, 2007, from http://www.truthout.org/docs_2006/061807F.shtml

Heifetz, R. A. (1994). *Leadership without easy answers.* Cambridge, MA: Belknap Press.

Heifetz, R. A. (2007). The scholarly/practical challenge of leadership. In R. A. Couto (Ed.), *Reflections on leadership* (pp. 31–44). Lanham, MD: University Press of America.

Hennion, C. (2007, June 7). Kidnapped by the CIA—Tortured in Egypt. *Le Monde.* Retrieved February 3, 2007, from http://www.truthout.org/docs_2006/061207G.shtml

Heymann, P. B., & Kayyem, J. N. (2005). *Preserving security and democratic freedoms in the war on terrorism.* Cambridge, MA: MIT Press.

Hickman, G. R. (2004). Invisible leadership. In J. M. Burns, G. Goethals, & G. Sorenson (Eds.), *Encyclopedia of leadership* (pp. 75–54). Thousand Oaks, CA: Sage.

Hickman, G., & Couto, R. A. (2006). Causality, change and leadership. In G. R. Goethals & G. L. J. Sorenson (Eds.), *The quest for a general theory of leadership* (pp. 152–187). Northampton, MA: Edward Elgar.

Hirschman, A. O. (1970). *Exit, voice, and loyalty: Responses to decline in firms, organizations, and states.* Cambridge, MA: Harvard University Press.

Human Rights Watch. (2005). *U.S.: Rice miscasts policy on torture.* Retrieved February 12, 2007, from http://hrw.org/english/docs/2005/12/05/usint12147.htm

Intelligence Science Board. (2007). *Educing information—Interrogation: Science and art.* Washington, DC: National Defense Intelligence College Press. Retrieved March 23, 2007, from http://www.fas.org/irp/dni/educing.pdf

Kayyem, J. (2005, October 18). *The question of torture.* Retrieved March 23, 2007, http://www.pbs.org/wgbh/pages/frontline/torture/justify/

Lewin, K. (1951). *Field theory in social science: Selected theoretical papers.* New York: Harper.

Marty, D. (2007). *Secret detentions and illegal transfers of detainees involving Council of Europe member states: Second report. Committee on Legal Affairs and Human Rights Parliamentary Assembly Council of Europe.* Retrieved February 25, 2009, from http://assembly.coe.int/CommitteeDocs/2007/EMarty_20070608_NoEmbargo.pdf

Mattern, M. (2006). *Putting ideas to work: A practical introduction to political thought.* New York: Rowman & Littlefield.

Mayer, J. (2005, February 14). Outsourcing torture: The secret history of America's "extraordinary rendition" program. *The New Yorker.* Retrieved June 5, 2007, from http://www.newyorker.com/archive/2005/02/14/050214fa_fact6

Mayer, J. (2006, February 27). The memo: How an internal effort to ban the abuse and torture of detainees was thwarted. *The New Yorker.* Retrieved June 5, 2007, from http://www.newyorker.com/archive/2006/02/27/060227fa_fact

McCoy, A. W. (2006). *A question of torture: CIA interrogation from the Cold War to the war on terror.* New York: Henry Holt.

Myrdal, G. (1944). *An American dilemma: The Negro problem and modern democracy.* New York: Harper & Row.

PBS. (2005, October 18). *The torture question.* Retrieved June 5, 2007, from http://www.pbs.org/wgbh/pages/frontline/torture/justify/

PBS. (2007, April 6). *What does the world think of us?.* Retrieved June 5, 2007, from http://www.pbs.org/now/shows/314/opinions-of-us.html

Pew Global Attitudes Project. (2005). *U.S. image up slightly, but still negative.* Retrieved June 6, 2007, from http://pewglobal.org/reports/display.php?PageID=803

Polling Report. (n.d.). *Right track, wrong track.* Retrieved June, 2007, from http://www.pollingreport.com/right.htm

Priest, D. (2005a, November 2). CIA holds terror suspects in secret prisons: Debate is growing within agency about legality and morality of overseas system set up after 9/11. *The Washington Post,* pp. A1ff.

Priest, D. (2005b, December 4). Wrongful imprisonment: Anatomy of a CIA mistake. German citizen released after months in "rendition." *The Washington Post,* pp. A1ff.

Rice, C. (2005). *Remarks upon her departure for Europe.* Retrieved February 22, 2007, from http://www.state.gov/secretary/rm/2005/57602.htm

Richman, S. (2003). *Albright "apologizes."* Retrieved May 23, 2007, from http://www.fff.org/comment/com0311c.asp

Savage, C. (2006, January 4). Bush could bypass new torture ban: Waiver right is reserved. *The Boston Globe.* Retrieved June 5, 2007, from http://www.boston.com/news/nation/washington/articles/2006/01/04/bush_could_bypass_new_torture_ban/

Shrader, K. (2007, March 20). Red Cross says detainees reported abuse. *Guardian Unlimited.* Retrieved March 25, 2007, from http://www.guardian.co.uk/worldlatest/story/0,,-6495382,00.html

Suskind, R. (2006). *The one percent doctrine: Deep inside America's pursuit of its enemies since 9/11.* New York: Simon & Schuster.

Tuchman, B.W. (1984). *The march of folly: From Troy to Vietnam.* New York: Ballantine Books.

Tucker, R. C. (1995). *Politics as leadership* (Rev. ed.). Columbia: University of Missouri Press.

U.S. Department of State. (2005). *Human rights.* Retrieved March 12, 2007, http://www.state.gov/g/drl/rls/hrrpt/

Weber, M. (1946). "Politics as a vocation." In H. H. Gerth & C. W. Mills (Eds.), *From Max Weber: Essays in sociology* (pp. 77–128). New York: Oxford University Press.

Wheatley, M. J. (1992). *Leadership and the new science: Learning about organization from an orderly universe.* San Francisco: Berrett-Koehler.

Wheatley, M. J. (2007). A new paradigm for a new leadership. In R. Couto (Ed.), *Reflections on leadership* (pp. 105–115). Lanham, MD: University Press of America.

Whitlock, C. (2005, December 6). CIA Ruse is said to have damaged probe in Milan. *The Washington Post.* Retrieved March 20, 2007, from http://www.washingtonpost.com/wp-dyn/content/article/2005/12/04/AR2005120400885.html

Yarmolinsky, A. (2007). The challenge of change in leadership. In R. Couto (Ed.), *Reflections on leadership* (pp. 45–51). Lanham, MD: University Press of America.

Yukl, G. (1998). *Leadership in organizations* (4th ed.). Upper Saddle River, NJ: Prentice Hall.

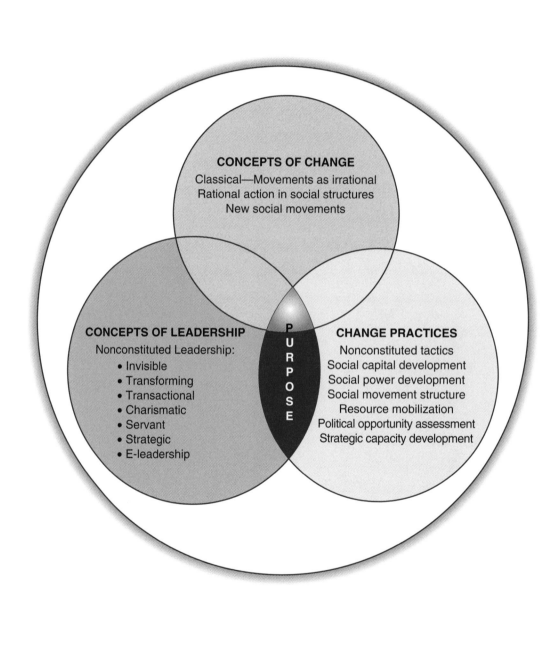

CONCEPTS OF CHANGE
Classical—Movements as irrational
Rational action in social structures
New social movements

CONCEPTS OF LEADERSHIP
Nonconstituted Leadership:
- Invisible
- Transforming
- Transactional
- Charismatic
- Servant
- Strategic
- E-leadership

PURPOSE

CHANGE PRACTICES
Nonconstituted tactics
Social capital development
Social power development
Social movement structure
Resource mobilization
Political opportunity assessment
Strategic capacity development

CHAPTER 8

Social Change Context

Introduction

The term "social change" or "social movement"[1] evokes images of people marching en masse on a capital mall or public square in support or protest of a significant social issue. Indeed, this depiction represents the pinnacle of many social movements, especially in the 1960s and 1970s. Initiating a social movement may seem to be a daunting and improbable task to the average person. However, social change often begins with local initiatives in one or more communities and then spreads across multiple communities, states, and countries based on the importance of the cause to many people. With the advent of the Internet, social change initiatives can spread across the globe rapidly, although the actual change or outcome generally takes place more slowly. Social movements often start with the efforts of people who are not larger than life at the movement's inception.

Roberta Garner (1997) defined social movements as "collectivities engaged in noninstitutionalized discourses and practices aimed at changing the existing condition of society" (p. 1). Social movements are deliberate, explicit, relatively long term, and collective. As social movements grow, they gain members and leadership structures that often result in social movement organizations with familiar names, such as the National Organization for Women (NOW), Greenpeace, National Council of La Raza, the Christian Coalition of America, and the World Rainforest Movement.

The Purpose of Social Change

Groups initiate and sustain social movements to give voice to a specific cause to correct injustices, counter or resist social conditions, or pursue and create new

EDITOR'S NOTE: This chapter draws from Roberta Garner's (1997) comprehensive introduction, "Fifty Years of Social Movement Theory: An Interpretation," to identify and explain major theories of social movements.

possibilities in society that established leaders and institutions have disregarded or inadequately addressed. The focus and theories of social movements have changed over time from the classical period to movements of the 1960s and 1970s to the current period of new social movements (NSMs). The change vignette in this chapter, in contrast to the case in Chapter 1 from the early civil rights movement, highlights a new social movement using the experience of Barbara Kirby, the mother of a son with Asperger syndrome. It describes a social change initiative within the health consumer movement, specifically focused on the mental health community.

Change Vignette

OASIS: An Initiative in the Mental Health Consumer Movement

Our son was eight years old in 1993 when we first heard the term Asperger Syndrome. We hadn't heard it from any of the score of professionals we had turned to for help throughout the years when we wondered and worried about his particular difficulties and differences. Instead, a friend who knew something about autism had the courage to hand us a copy of a relatively new publication, *Autism and Asperger Syndrome* by Uta Frith, and say, "Please read this. It reminds me of your son."

When I put down the book, I knew I had found an explanation that finally made sense. It helped me to understand that what was happening to my son and to our family wasn't his fault or the fault of my parenting—as so many people, professionals, friends, and family members had so hurtfully suggested. He was not a "bad" child and we were not "bad" parents.

I would like to say that when I finally learned the news, I hit the ground running. But that would be a lie. What really happened is I hit the ground with a huge splat. I can't ever remember being so frightened. My son, whom I loved more than anything in the world, had a problem that could not be fixed even if I would only relax, stop hovering, discipline him properly, stop trying to be his friend and act like a mother, pay more attention, pay less attention, spank him—or follow any of the other "helpful" suggestions offered to me by well-meaning professionals, family, and friends. Certainly none of them ever suggested that my son's problems stemmed from a neurological disorder about which no more than a handful of people around the world knew anything.

Though I'll never forget the pain of those comments, I've learned that there was nothing in my advisors' personal experience that could have allowed them to understand that my son's behaviors were anything other than the result of incompetence—ours at parenting and his at being a "good" boy. They simply did not know. As I soon learned, there was a world of "experts" out there who knew just about as much. Or as little.

You would think that finding a name for our son's behaviors would translate into finding some help and answers. But you would be wrong. Our son's doctor had never heard of Asperger Syndrome, neither the library nor the bookstore had a book on it, the local autism group had "heard" of it but did not have any information, and when I called local hospitals, they told me that the condition was rare and they had never seen a child with the diagnosis. How was this possible?

The realization that we were alone with this disorder, diagnosis, whatever it was, induced a level of fear and frustration that after all these years I still cannot explain. Perhaps it's something only another parent in exactly the same position can understand. Even today, when I open up the OASIS message board and see a post titled "Help! Just Got DX," I feel that ache inside, as if the world had ended. And for most of us, for a day, a week, a year, it feels that way. But it also goes on.

In 1994, about six months after we'd first heard the term, the American Psychiatric Association officially listed Asperger Syndrome in the *Diagnostic and Statistical Manual of Mental Disorders, Fourth Edition* (DSM-IV), its diagnostic bible. Doctors agreed that AS was the best diagnostic "fit" for our son. Still, they had no idea what we should do. Once again, we were alone. Six months later we arranged for our son to have a full psychoeducational evaluation; the psychologist suspected Asperger Syndrome. Three months after that, an appointment with a pediatric neurologist confirmed the diagnosis. However, the most any of these professionals could offer were vague, general suggestions and a pat on the back with a reminder that it was not our fault.

My son's teachers were more than willing to help, but they were also in the dark. After all, they weren't trained to deal with students like him. Looking back, I am amazed at how hard they worked at understanding and supporting my son. Still, I cried—and I continued to cry for a very, very long time.

One evening, on a whim, I decided to sign on to America Online, then a relatively new service. I knew nothing about our new home computer, and about all I could do with it was play solitaire and Tetris. I'd never heard of e-mail, I didn't know what a Web site was, and the Internet was someplace much too "scary" for a nontechnical stay-at-home mom like me.

After signing on, I found my way to the disability forums and posted messages asking if anyone had heard of Asperger Syndrome. Within a day, I'd received a message from a woman named Judy, who told me that she had a son who was diagnosed with AS and that I was not alone. One other mother, one other child in the world. I was overjoyed! I spent literally the next two days reading through message boards, leaving messages, and sending and answering e-mail. Finally! I'd found a few other families who understood.

Over the next several months, I was invited to join a small e-mail group for parents of children with a variety of pervasive developmental disorders. At the same time, I met another mother online, and we began collecting names of other AS families, with the goal of convincing AOL that there were enough interested people to open a chat room specifically for Asperger Syndrome. After several months, the AS families formed their own group. We shared what few resources were available at the time. Most important, we shared support and understanding.

In the fall of 1995, I approached the University of Delaware, where my husband is a faculty member, to ask if they would be willing to donate server space so I could automate the e-mail list. They generously agreed to do so and offered me space on their server for the list and for a Web page. I was thrilled—and terrified. I had no idea how to make a Web page, and at that time there were no programs that automatically formatted Web sites. Fortunately, Ted Whaley, who is the parent of a child diagnosed with hyperlexia and who had set up a Web site for the AHA (American Hyperlexia Association), came to the rescue. With his guidance and a copy of *HTML for Dummies*, the Asperger Syndrome Resources Web site was launched in December 1995. It was renamed OASIS (Online Asperger Syndrome Information and Support) several months later, in 1996.

(Continued)

(Continued)

OASIS and the new e-mail group (as-support) quickly became the central meeting place for families whose children were diagnosed with Asperger Syndrome. Any information on AS and related diagnoses, including conferences, parenting ideas, support services, educational resources, and laws were shared among members and eventually placed on the Web site. By 1998, I'd added a public message board forum and in the summer of 1999 opened the private and moderated OASIS message board and chat room support forum. (At the time of publication of this book, the OASIS site will have been visited more than a million times, and the current active membership of the OASIS forums is well over five thousand families.)

The further you delve into the world of autism, the more you are struck by the fact that virtually every organization, research project, support group, piece of legislation, program, and innovation was created by or initially financed by parents of children with autism. It is the parents of children with AS and related disorders and the individuals with autism spectrum diagnoses who have led the way. Today, thanks in no small part to the Internet, parents of AS children and adults with AS are building local and national support networks throughout the country and the world. And in the process, they are changing what it means to have AS and autism.

SOURCE: From "Introduction" by Barbara L. Kirby. In *The OASIS Guide to Asperger Syndrome: Advice, Support, Insight, and Inspiration* by Patricia Romanowski Bashe and Barbara L. Kirby. Copyright © 2005 by PAR Bookworks, Ltd., and Barbara L. Kirby. By permission of Random House, Inc. Published by Crown Publishers.

Concepts of Social Change

The OASIS vignette describes one of several social change initiatives within the health consumer movement. This section provides a brief overview of social movement theories and concepts in an attempt to place new social movements and the OASIS vignette in perspective.

First Period: Classical—Movements as Irrational

Garner (1997) divided social movements into three broad historical and intellectual periods. Scholars characterize the first or classical period, from 1945 to 1960, as negative and irrational. This was the era of Nazism, fascism, Stalinism, race riots, lynchings, and McCarthyism. Classical theorists explained the pathological and destructive behavior of this period using theories from psychoanalysis, social psychology, collective behavior, mass society, and status politics (Garner, 1997, p. 7). They perceived the underlying ideologies of the classical era as fueled by individual personality characteristics and irrational collective behavior. Researchers associated movement behavior with authoritarian tendencies and intolerant attitudes and actions.

Second Period: Rational Action Within Structural Constraints

During the second period, from the early 1960s to the mid-1970s, sociologists began to regard social movements as positive and rational action within the structural constraints of social movement organizations (SMOs). SMOs created structure—"a set of limiting conditions on individual action" (Garner, 1997, p. 19). Movements—including the civil rights movement, national liberation or decolonization movements, student movements, and, later, the farm worker movement and the women's movement—aimed to reform or transform oppressive social institutions and constructs (Garner, 1997, pp. 17–18). Many government programs emerged in response to social movements in this period, such as the welfare state in Europe and the Great Society and War on Poverty programs in the United States.

Theorists shifted their attention away from individual motivations and personality to studies of SMOs—their participants and resources, internal structure, goals, professionalization (use of movement professionals and experts), and environments, including political opportunity structure, political culture, and dynamics of movements and countermovements. Several concepts emerged in succession: (1) Structural strain focused on the interrelationship between existing problems in society unattended by established institutions and the formation of movements to address them; (2) resource mobilization focused on the ability of social movement organizations to assemble human, fiscal, and media resources and take rational actions at politically appropriate times; and (3) structural Marxism focused less on reform and more on revolutionary movements to replace capitalism, class structures, and, later, global markets and nation-states, among other existing social structures or constructs (Garner, 1997, pp. 21–30).

Third Period: New Social Movements

New social movements (NSMs) emerged in the third period, from the 1970s to the present. Social movements of the 1960s and 1970s encountered problems sustaining their success as they experienced former coalitions falling apart and economic and social structures shifting to postindustrialization with its service and information economy (Garner, 1997 pp. 30–33). Government is no longer seen as the primary force that could be on the side of working people by legitimatizing unions, regulating the private sector, providing social services, and expanding the welfare state (Garner, 1997, p. 34). These movements incorporate new categories of activists across various segments of society who focus on a wider range of social issues and open-ended processes. Previous social movements appealed to—and recruited from—support bases that were identified by their preexisting, relatively stable demographic characteristics (e.g., disenfranchised African Americans in the South prior to the civil rights movements). Members of NSMs are not easily identifiable by such demographic factors.

New social movements center on ideology and identity (or identity politics). Ideology is "the belief system of a movement" (Garner, 1997, p. 11), and, unlike social movements of the first period, NSM belief systems embody collective thought or ideas rather than beliefs rooted in individual personality. Ideology is a defining element of NSMs and stimulates movements and countermovements on the Left and the Right. Movements on the Left include environmentalism, gay rights activism, urban grassroots mobilization, women's and human rights initiatives, and new antiwar activism. On the Right, movements and countermovements form a large, loosely coherent conservative front that focuses on matters such as pro-life, religious fundamentalism, political conservatism, and an aggregation of single-issue constituencies (e.g., antitax or anti-gun-control groups) among other issues (Garner, 1997, pp. 34–35).

Collective identity in NSMs is socially constructed from ongoing processes of discourse and social interaction that often form and articulate ideology. Schneider and Somers (2006) indicated, "Actors in a social movement are signifying agents actively engaged in the development of meaning for others in an interactivist manner, making these collective frames of meaning the result of a negotiated, shared process" (p. 359). Theorists perceive these processes in NSMs as "causing identity" (Garner, 1997 p. 45). In other words, members form their identity as a group through discourse and interaction concerning their particular set of beliefs.

Social movements bring about change in society through the exercise of social power. By extrapolating from Speer and Hughey's (1995) definition, social power or empowerment may be conceptualized as the ability of a community (or social movement) organization to reward or punish targets, control topics in public debates, and shape how residents and public officials think about their community or society (p. 732). Community and social movements become empowered when they have the capacity to exercise these instruments of social power (p. 732).

The health consumer movement typifies many new social movements. OASIS and other mental health organizations are part of a widespread health consumer movement that extends nationally and globally. Allsop, Jones, and Baggott (2004) explained that the health consumer movement developed from experiences in the personal and intimate aspects of individual lives: "People are drawn into new social movements because they feel marginalized by dominant social practices" (p. 738). Certainly, this was the case with Barbara Kirby as she attempted to find a diagnosis for her son's condition and then desperately sought information, treatment, and support. This kind of NSM enhances participants' positive sense of self within a group that shares their experiences and perceptions. Stories and descriptions of personal experiences, like Kirby's, help people explain life events, rebuild identities, and develop plans for collective action.

Members of the mental health consumer movement came together over the Internet and in face-to-face meetings where they used their newfound social power to propel the movement into action. According to a government report, mental health researchers define empowerment as "gaining control over one's life in influencing the organizational and societal structures in which one lives" (Segal et al., as cited in U.S. Department of Health and Human Services, 1999, p. 95). Mental health consumer organizations, such as the National Alliance on Mental Illness (NAMI), Autism Society of America (ASA), and OASIS, establish self-help groups, advocate for legislation, and become involved in mental health service agencies and research (U.S. Department of Health and Human Services, 1999, p. 95). As a result, empowerment derived from the collective actions of consumer and family organizations has contributed greatly to the transformation of mental health services.

Concepts and theories of change in NSMs are still in a relatively early stage of development. Though NSMs differ from previous movements, Garner (1997) argued that they still retain some of the theories of the first and second periods (p. 46). Social psychological perspectives on collective identities and belief systems from the first period can apply in new ways to NSMs that facilitate micromobilization (smaller scale processes in contrast to mass movement) initiated by individuals or small groups. Theories of social movement organizations, resource mobilization, and political opportunity structure from the first and second period remain viable in NSMs. Accordingly, this chapter draws on social movement theories from all three periods.

Concepts of Social Change Leadership

Nonconstituted Leadership: Leadership Without Formal Authority

Initiatives for social change usually begin with nonconstituted leadership, a broad category of leadership that functions without the formal authority of constituted leadership (the power and authority granted to elected political officials or appointed organizational officers) (Tucker, 1995, p. 7). Nonconstituted leaders or activists may also be described as tags—"leaders without authority but with great influence in their communities" (Schneider & Somers, 2006, p. 359). This form of leadership responds when constituted leadership in political, civic, government, private, or religious sectors fail to recognize social issues that require action. Individuals may assume nonconstituted leadership roles voluntarily, or others may implore certain individuals to lead based on their passion and personal commitment to a social goal. They find or initiate opportunities to bring their issue to the attention of other like-minded individuals, the broader community, and constituted leaders who have the authority to change conditions or institutions.

Nonconstituted actors draw on various concepts of leadership to generate social change—invisible, transforming, transactional, charismatic, servant, and e-leadership (see definitions in Chapters 2 and 3). Both constituted and nonconstituted actors use these concepts of leadership, although their source of power differs. Nonconstituted leaders and participants exercise leadership using social power, whereas constituted actors use formal authority.

Invisible Leadership

Nonconstituted leaders and participants often use invisible leadership to achieve their social change goals. Participants, like those in the health consumer movement, are most often attracted to the leadership process and to each other based on charisma of purpose, a perceived opportunity to act, and their individual agency.

Barbara Kirby and other members of the health consumer movement took action because of a passionate commitment to the purpose of improving the lives of individuals and their families who struggle with mental health issues. Although her cause began with a desperate search for information and resources to support her son's Asperger syndrome diagnoses, it quickly broadened to encompass as many individuals as possible seeking help and involvement in initiatives concerning Asperger's and the broader sphere of autism and mental health.

Invisible leadership incorporates shared leadership processes in which peers lead and influence each other to achieve group goals, including decisions about who among them can or should provide visible leadership on behalf of the group. Leadership is broadly distributed among group members and often is not fully visible to or recognized by nonmembers of the group. This does not mean that leaders are not important or that there are no leaders involved in significant roles. Instead, it means that most people involved in invisible leadership come to the process with a sense of collective efficacy and identity and that they are already motivated to take the necessary actions to bring about change.

For example, Jo Ann Robinson's (Robinson, 1987) account of the Montgomery, Alabama, bus boycott maintains that "the city's black congregations were quite intelligent on the matter and were planning to support the one-day boycott with or without their ministers' leadership" (p. 53). Once the city's Black ministers recognized that the people—their congregants—were determined to stage this protest, they decided it was time for them to "catch up with the masses" (Robinson, 1987, p. 53). The leaders who became visible in this process did so within the framework of a collective or collaborative process. The ministers formed an interdenominational group offering their leadership to the boycott efforts and held a meeting at the Dexter Avenue Baptist Church, where Dr. Martin Luther King Jr. was the minister. They failed to select one person to lead the boycott at that meeting; instead, they waited to see if the 1-day boycott would be successful. "When the ministers realized that the one-day boycott was going to be successful . . . they met again, and Dr. Martin Luther King Jr. *agreed to accept* the leadership post" (italics added; Robinson, 1987, p. 56).

During the civil rights movement, the public recognized the visible leadership of Dr. Martin Luther King Jr., but few people outside the group knew that the invisible leadership of Jo Ann Robinson and the Women's Political Council (WPC) organized and launched the Montgomery bus boycott (Robinson, 1987, p. xv). Robinson worked diligently throughout the boycott and civil rights movement but chose to remain behind the scenes to protect the historically Black state university where she worked from political and economic retribution. Many years later, through the coaxing of political scientist David Garrow, Robinson wrote her account of the bus boycott.

Transforming and Transactional Leadership

Transforming leadership is one of the most widely cited theories with regard to creating social and political change—what James MacGregor Burns (1978) called "real intended change" (p. 413). Transforming leadership "occurs when one or more persons engage with others in such a way that leaders and followers raise one another to higher levels of motivation and morality" (p. 20). Burns (1978) explained that transforming leaders engage in collective purpose linked to social change, with the ultimate objective of achieving goals that enhance the well-being of human existence (p. 3). This explanation captures the intent of many social movements. Transforming leadership ultimately becomes moral in that it raises the level of human conduct and ethical aspiration of both the leader and the led, and thus it has a transforming effect on both (p. 20). Gary Yukl (2006) noted, "Transforming leadership appeals to the moral values of followers in an attempt to raise their consciousness about ethical issues and to mobilize their energy and resources to reform institutions" (p. 249).

Burns (2003) differentiated transforming leadership from transactional leadership, which is a "practical give-and-take leadership" used for "expedient, high level brokerage" (p. 23). Transactional leadership is an essential and valuable form of leadership, although it does not (and perhaps is not intended to) generate transformational change. Burns contended that transforming leadership causes "a metamorphosis in form or structure, a change in the very condition or nature of a thing, a change into another substance, a radical change in outward form or inner character" (p. 24).

Participants or followers play an important role in bringing about social and political transformation, and they become empowered by the process. However, Burns (2003) emphasized that leaders have a distinct function. Their purpose is to "take the initiative in mobilizing people for participation in the process of change, encouraging a sense of collective identity and collective efficacy, which in turn brings stronger feelings of self-worth and self-efficacy" (p. 25).

Both constituted and nonconstituted leaders can exercise transforming leadership. Burns (1978, 2003) often drew his examples from constituted transforming leaders, such as Franklin D. Roosevelt and Winston Churchill, and nonconstituted transforming leaders, such as Eleanor Roosevelt and Gandhi. The essential purpose for transforming leaders is to enhance the well-being of human existence by bringing about real, intended change in social and political systems and structures.

Charismatic Leadership

Scholars continually grapple with the question, is charismatic leadership essential to the creation of major social change or social movements? Certainly, there have been many prominent charismatic leaders involved in social change, and there have been many scholarly studies devoted to the topic. Whether charismatic leaders are essential to social change has not been fully established.

Burns (2003) argued that charismatic leadership "at best is a confusing and undemocratic form of leadership," and "at worst, it is a type of tyranny" (p. 27). He believed that pure charismatic leaders hinder mutual empowerment between leaders and followers because followers become so loyal and fallible that they can have limited impact on the leader (Burns, 2003, p. 27). Burns concurred, in spite of his apprehension, with David A. Nadler and Michael L. Tushman (1990) that the strongest components of charismatic leadership are envisioning, energizing, and enabling, especially when the effect is to liberate and empower followers (Burns, 2003, p. 27). As noted in extensive research about charismatic leadership (Bass, 1985; Conger & Kanungo, 1987; House, 1977; Howell, 1988; Howell & Avolio, 1992; Weber & Parsons, 1947), the most positive and effective charismatic leaders can be distinguished by the following features: an inspiring vision that builds a particular kind of image of the future in the hearts and minds of participants, highly developed rhetorical skills, an engaging personalized style of leadership (Hughes, Ginnett, & Curphy, 2006, p. 412), and an ethical foundation that guides their motivation and actions.

Servant Leadership

Servant leadership frequently plays an essential role in social change, especially in the context of SMOs and social institutions. Greenleaf (1977) identified the role of institutions in society—churches, universities, and businesses—as servants of the people:

> If a better society is to be built, one that is more just and more loving, one that provides greater creative opportunity for its people, then the most open course is to *raise both the capacity to serve and the very performance as servant* of existing major institutions by new regenerative forces operating within them. (p. 62, italics in original)

Though Greenleaf (1977) was referring to existing institutions in society, the purpose of many SMOs and their leaders seems to fit his concept of servant institutions. These SMOs generate awareness of specific social issues on behalf of the people they serve (e.g., health care consumers) and induce major institutions to change to provide more just, inclusive, and caring service. Organizations such as the National Alliance on Mental Illness and the Autism Society of America are servant organizations for mental health care consumers, and they serve as advocates that persuade major institutions in society to recognize and care for the needs of these individuals. They stimulate major institutions to become more responsive and effective servant leaders for mental health consumers.

Strategic Leadership

Strategic leadership is a critical capability in SMOs. SMOs do not focus on the same competitive, profit-driven environmental factors as businesses; still, they need leadership that can adapt movement organizations to complex forces in the political and social environment, especially the actions and reactions of other actors (see the discussion of political opportunity structure later in this chapter). Marshall Ganz (2005) warned that "in settings in which rules, resources, and interests are emergent—such as social movements—strategy has more in common with creative thinking" (p. 215). As a result, strategic leaders or actors must generate imaginative approaches and processes to adapt the organization to conditions in the environment and reach its intended goals.

The promotion and use of self-help groups by the mental health consumer movement was an innovative approach and a fundamental departure from previous approaches that were wholly dependent on government and private mental health agencies and professionals. "Self help is predicated on the belief that individuals who share the same health problem can help themselves and each other to cope with their condition" (U.S. Department of Health and Human Services, 1999, p. 94). Consumers ran many of the initial self-help programs independently. This strategy empowered consumers and restructured mainstream mental health services to incorporate consumer groups, programs, and positions. The mental health consumer movement used its collective power to affect public policy, funding, service delivery and evaluation, and research.

E-Leadership

The founding of Online Asperger Syndrome Information and Support by Barbara Kirby provides a fitting example of e-leadership in a NSM. Using her contacts at the University of Delaware, Kirby launched the OASIS Web site on the university's server, which became the central meeting place for families whose children were diagnosed with Asperger syndrome. She indicated in the opening vignette that "today, *thanks in no small part to the Internet*, parents of AS are building local and national support networks throughout the country and the world. And in the process, they are changing what it means to have AS and autism" (Bashe & Kirby, 2005, p. 4, italics added).

Advanced information technology makes it feasible and cost effective to launch NSMs that bring together people worldwide around social change issues of importance to millions of individuals. Because virtual activism is such a major phenomenon in global NSMs, this topic is explored in greater depth in Chapter 9.

Social Change Practices

New social movements on the Right and Left use nonconstituted practices to generate action on behalf of their social issues. NSMs use a combination of old and new social change practices that include nonconstituted tactics, social movement structure, resource mobilization, assessment of political opportunity structure, social capital development, social power or empowerment, and advocacy. These practices, together with the concepts of change and leadership described earlier, provide the momentum for many social change initiatives.

Nonconstituted Tactics

Nonconstituted actors draw attention to social issues through a process of signaling—"the activity of apprising [constituted] leaders of circumstances that appear meaningful enough to merit diagnosis and policy response" (Tucker, 1995, p. 31). Mass media plays a major role in signaling by bringing attention to social issues and allowing the voices of concerned individuals to be heard. Sometimes crises or disasters, such as Hurricane Katrina, draw the media to the problem. At other times, leaders or activists on behalf of a cause plan events, including rallies or protests, to gain media attention. In contrast to social movements of earlier eras, technology provides a direct means for individuals to signalize quickly to large audiences using the Internet. Social activists use advanced Internet technology to manage the timing, presentation, and content of their message, rather than relying solely on the media to signalize their issues to local, national, or international communities.

Leaders and participants in NSMs draw on multiple tactics to propel change as greater numbers of people become aware of social problems or issues. According to Robert Tucker (1995), these nonconstituted tactics entail the following strategies:

- diagnosing or defining situations and problems, often in new ways that individuals, groups, and organizations with formal authority fail to define or recognize;
- proposing a course of collective action to meet the situation as defined;
- seeking support of others for their views of what the situation is and what should be done about it;
- devising proposals for change;
- attracting people to the movement based on persuasive influence of the previous factors;
- organizing to exert pressure on constituted leaders, organizations, and institutions to address the problem through formal processes; and
- initiating sociopolitical action and participation such as protesting, lobbying, using legal recourses, voting, and advocating for new public policy. (pp. 31, 85–86)

The mental health consumer movement and other NSMs use these nonconstituted tactics, such as activists in the community context (Chapter 5), to signalize issues, propose solutions, and advocate for change in public awareness programs, public policy, and appropriations for mental health. Like leadership in the community context, social change leadership makes use of social capital development, social power or empowerment, and advocacy as change practices.

Social change initiatives call for the development of social capital to succeed. Leaders and participants in social movements develop social networks, such as the self-help groups described earlier, along with norms of reciprocity and trustworthiness by finding or attracting others who share similar experiences or ideologies and connecting them in electronic and face-to-face communities. Barbara Kirby began OASIS, as did the founders of NAMI and other mental health consumer groups, by searching for and connecting with others like her who were struggling in near isolation with mental health concerns in their families. The social ties that develop through these connections make social networks possible and allow people to join together in support of each other and the change that they seek.

Once movements develop social networks, they can frame issues and mobilize networks using the group's social power or empowerment to influence decisions and actions of constituted leaders and institutions. Speer and Hughey's (1995) guiding principles of social power emphasize that social power is only realized through organization, built on the strength of interpersonal relationships, and grounded in a dialectic of action and reflection (pp. 732–733). These principles anchor the development and use of social power in four organizing practices—assessment, research, action, and reflection:

- Assessment is the process through which critical issues affecting a community are identified and defined by organizations. Assessment is conducted one on one and face to face so that the conversations connect individuals to facilitate dialogue and enhance relationships.
- Research, like the participatory action research discussed in Chapter 5, provides information on issues such as which resources exist to address an issue, how these resources are transferred, and which organization or institution controls the resources capable of addressing a specific issue. Research uncovers the ways allocation of resources affects an issue and how organizational entities or players exercise social power around an issue.
- Action in a community (or social) change context is a collective attempt to exercise social power developed through organization. Actions are planned public events that bring together large numbers of people, as well as the media, public officials, and other organizations concerned with the issue. This entails both strategy development and organizational mobilization for action with the intent to uncover contradictions between the expressed values of constituted leaders or entities and their actual practices, policies, or funding priorities.
- Reflection allows members to consider how the organization evolved through the organizing cycle. Participants examine the effectiveness of implemented strategies, discuss lessons learned, identify emerging leadership, consider how social power was demonstrated, and calculate future directions for the organization. (pp. 734–735)

While Speer and Hughey (1995) discovered these principles and practices of social power in a community organizing setting, social change activists can scale and adapt them to the needs of a social movements context.

Advocacy for social change, as indicated in Chapter 5, consists of organized actions to "highlight ignored and suppressed critical issues, influence public attitudes, and promote the enactment and implementation of laws and public policies that turn visions of 'what should be' in a just, decent society into reality" (Cohen, de la Vega, & Watson, 2001, p. 8). Research helps social change activists prepare for advocacy by identifying decision makers or constituted leaders who can effect change for specific social issues and assess strategies and tactics to persuade these actors to support change initiatives.

Social change groups and organizations shape their advocacy approach to fit the specific social change initiative, but many similarities exist across organizations. Advocacy by members of the NAMI "provides a key voice for state and federal public and private-sector policies that facilitate research, end discrimination, reduce barriers to successful life in the community and promote timely, comprehensive and effective mental health services and supports."

NAMI researches and distributes an advocacy toolkit on their Web site and conducts advocacy training throughout the United States for members and groups that want to influence legislators to pass bills and appropriate funding for mental health–related issues. The toolkit includes information on the legislative process, sample legislation from various states, letters to legislators and governors, fact sheets, and sample editorials, among other information. The main objective of NAMI's advocacy efforts is to improve the lives of people living with mental illness.

Advocacy often entails persuading members of the public and constituted leaders to change their minds about the views or positions they hold on core issues in the movement. Howard Gardner's (2004) research proposed seven "levers" that work in concert to bring about a change of mind in individuals:

1. *Reason* (Cognitive)—A rational approach involves identifying relevant factors, weighing each in turn, and making an overall assessment. It can be logic (use of argument), the use of analogies, or the creation of taxonomies.

2. *Research* (Cognitive)—Research is the collection of relevant data. It can be formal (scientific with statistical tests) or informal research. It need only entail the identification of relevant cases and a judgment about whether they warrant a change of mind.

3. *Resonance* (Affective)—The view, idea, or perspective feels right to an individual, seems to fit the current situation, and convinces the person that further considerations are superfluous. The fit may follow reason and research or may be at an unconscious level. Resonance may also involve the relationship to the mind changer; for example, an individual may feel that the mind changer is reliable or worthy of respect. Rhetoric is also a principle vehicle for changing minds. Rhetoric works best when it encompasses tight logic, draws on relevant research, and resonates with an audience.

4. *Redescriptions* (Representational redescriptions)—A change of mind is convincing if it is represented in a number of different forms, where these forms reinforce one another.

5. *Resources and rewards*—A mind change is more likely to occur when considerable resources can be drawn on: positive reinforcement. Individuals are being rewarded for one course of action instead of another.

6. *Real-world events*—An event occurs in the broader society that affects many individuals, not just those who are contemplating a mind change (e.g., wars, hurricanes, terrorist attacks, economic depressions, eras of peace and prosperity, availability of medical treatments to prevent illness or lengthen life, ascendancy of a benign leader, group, or political party) (p. 17).

7. *Resistances*—It is difficult to change one's mind as the years pass. People develop strong views and perspectives that are resistant to change. A mind change is most likely to occur when the first six factors operate in consort and the resistances are relatively weak. Conversely, mind changing is unlikely to occur when the resistances are strong, and the other factors do not point strongly in one direction (pp. 15–18).

Actors in the mental health consumer movement use many of these levers consciously or instinctively to influence mind changes among constituted leaders.

Additionally, the success of many consumer-run, self-help services resulted in leaders and professionals in mental health service agencies changing their minds concerning the value of consumer involvement in these agencies as volunteers, employees, consumer liaisons, and group leaders. These results can serve as incentives for movement participants to incorporate these levers intentionally into advocacy initiatives.

Social Movement Structure

Movements for social change typically create structure to implement their initiatives effectively as they expand and gain momentum. Social change leaders and participants often form SMOs to provide both structure and resources through the power of an organized group focused on a common goal. These organizations become acting units of the movement to reach certain constituencies and assemble participants (Garner, 1997, p. 22). As illustrated in the mental health consumer movement, organizations like OASIS and NAMI reach and assemble their constituencies and mobilize other key resources to help them carry out the aims of their social change.

SMOs are organizations at their core. Leaders and participants in NSM organizations use many of the practices in the organizational context—such as environmental scanning and strategic planning, scenario building and planning, e-practices, stages of praxis, and collective or collaborative practices that include institutionalized leadership and change practices, organizational learning, shared power, and ethical practices (see descriptions in Chapter 4). Even so, context does matter, and therefore the focus, emphasis, and content of their practices differ from other organizations, especially in the areas of resource mobilization and political opportunity structure.

Resource Mobilization

Resource mobilization remains a critical function of NSM organizations. Leaders and participants seek, assemble, and use needed resources to run the organization and advance their initiatives. These resources include time and energy of human resources (people), money, elite sponsorship, technology, media support, favorable public opinion (Garner, 1997, pp. 20, 23), social capital, and social power. Additionally, SMOs recruit technical experts to assist with functions such as fundraising, strategic planning, resource management, technology, political advocacy, and media relations.

Resource mobilization scholars in an earlier period assumed that social movements depended almost exclusively on the resources of elites or sponsors external to the movement. These external elites and sponsors were most often identified as "church groups, foundations, organized labor, and the federal government" (McAdam, 1982, pp. 22). Doug McAdam emphasized that resource mobilization scholars discounted the importance and influence of an essential internal resource—the movement's mass base (p. 29). Far from being resource deficient, this mass base of human resources used its social capital and empowerment to generate unparalleled movements for change. This does not imply that external elites and other resources are not important; still, movement participants represent one of the most essential assets of social movements.

Political Opportunity Structure

A critical factor in social movement activity is political opportunity structure—conditions in mainstream institutional politics or policies that either enhance or inhibit prospects for social movement participants to take action (Meyer & Minkoff, 2004, p. 1457). Political opportunity structure exists in the context of a society's larger political environment, which encompasses forces and institutions that operate for or against a movement, including the political culture, dynamics of other movements (that function as competitors, cooperatives, or coalitions), countermovements or cultures of resistance, actions of constituted leaders, and the exercise of or restraint from social control through sanctions (Gardner, 1997, p. 24).

Political opportunities such as presidential attention to the issues of a movement provide incentives for people to undertake collective action through protesting or forming SMOs (Meyer & Minkoff, 2004, p. 1457). On the other hand, the uncertainty of congressional turnover may diminish or discourage collective action. Political and social analyses, analogous to environmental scanning, combined with strategy development can assist social movement actors in identifying and pursuing political opportunities.

Development of Strategic Capacity

Marshall Ganz (2005) argued that SMOs need to develop strategic capacity among its actors to increase the movement's chance of success in the face of powerful institutions and leaders. He described strategic capacity in social movements as a function of the motivation of actors or leaders, access to salient knowledge, and the quality of heuristic or imaginative processes actors employ in their deliberations (p. 216). Ganz discerned that the motivation of social movement leaders or actors derives from intrinsic sources based on the "meaningfulness of the work" combined with the actors' identity with the work and its values as a vocation; in turn, this vocation infuses the actors' lives with meaning (p. 219).

Salient knowledge entails the mastery of skills (how to strategize), access to information about how to work in a specific setting or domain—that is, knowledge of political opportunity structure, constituencies, opponents, and other actors—and regular feedback (Ganz, 2005; McAdam, 1982; Speer & Hughey, 1995). Heuristic processes involve actors' ability to see problems in a new way, reframe information, and innovate or imagine new solutions (Ganz, 2005; Tucker, 1995). SMOs can facilitate these processes by engaging a team of actors with diverse perspectives and fostering divergent thinking and minority expression (Ganz, 2005, p. 221).

Strategic capacity may account for why one SMO makes better use of the same opportunity or resources than another, why one set of actors does a better job of framing social change issues than another, how actors with fewer resources can prevail over those with more resources, or why one set of actors exercises agency better than others with regard to cultural, political, or economic structures (Ganz, 2005, pp. 211–212). SMOs can develop or enhance the strategic capacity of a team of actors or leaders by seeking and attracting individuals who are motivated by the meaningfulness of the movement's work, possess or are able to acquire salient knowledge quickly, and bring diverse perspectives to the group.

Conclusion

Social change requires nonconstituted leadership and practices to address issues in society that have been underrepresented or overlooked by institutions and leaders with formal authority. In the absence of formal authority, social change actors use social capital and social power to initiate movements, form organizations, mobilize resources, and bring about change in public policy, funding, and programs. Social movements rely on collective or collaborative leadership and practices that use the talents and resources of all members.

NSMs have emerged in postmodern societies that embody groups and issues unlike movements in the past. Although the period of NSMs is still unfolding, emergent patterns suggest that the prevailing themes of this period focus on ideology and collective identities represented by social concerns of groups on the Right and the Left. NSMs, such as the mental health consumer movement, emerge from experiences in deeply personal aspects of people's lives. Others represent countermovements or communities of resistance such as anti-gun-control or antiabortion movements. Regardless of the issue, social movements continue to provide an essential means of influencing constituted leaders and institutions to change conditions in society.

Application and Reflection

Application

The Fatherhood Movement: Can It Reduce the Number of Fatherless Children?

By Kathy Koch

Introduction

Thirty years of high divorce rates and rising birth rates among unwed mothers have left the United States a nation of fatherless households. More than a third of American children don't live with their biological fathers, and 17 million don't live with any fathers at all. Of those, about 40% haven't seen their fathers in a year. As the nation prepares to honor fathers on June 18, child-development experts are hoping a growing nonpartisan, multiracial, "responsible fatherhood" movement, dedicated to reconnecting estranged dads with their kids, will help increase fathers' involvement in their kids' lives. But some question whether having fathers involved in children's lives is essential, while others say that some of the movement's goals—such as promoting marriage and joint custody—will hurt mothers.

Overview

To understand the burgeoning fatherhood movement, talk to Thomas Fulford, a recovering crack addict and ex-con. Fulford has gotten his life back together and is reunited with his

(Continued)

(Continued)

two sons and says the Institute for Responsible Fatherhood and Family Revitalization made it possible.

"My relationship with them has really blossomed," says Fulford, 48, who was divorced from the boys' mother when they were youngsters. "We have a working, loving relationship. We're upfront with each other," he says of the boys, now 20 and 22, who came to live with him last year after he finished serving time for bank robbery.

But it's not easy. "They are learning things that they should have learned from me 10 or 15 years ago," he says, "but we're still dancing around, getting to know each other."

Recently remarried, Fulford says, "All of this happened because I'm living the risk-free lifestyle that the institute promotes."

The institute is part of a fast-growing coalition of groups dedicated to reversing America's high rate of fatherlessness—the "single greatest social problem plaguing our nation today," according to Sen. Joseph I. Lieberman, D-Conn.[1]

More than one-third of the nation's 71 million children don't live with their biological fathers, and 17 million don't live with any father at all. And about 40% of those children haven't seen their fathers in a year, according to the National Fatherhood Initiative (NFI), in Gaithersburg, Md.

"Court and school officials report that many children do not even know what to put in the 'Father's Name' blank on printed forms," David Blankenhorn, president of the Institute for American Values, wrote in his 1995 book *Fatherless America*.[2]

The fragile coalition of racially and politically diverse groups spawned by the fatherhood movement includes conservative pro-marriage groups like Blankenhorn's, fathers'-rights groups working on the child-custody and child-support concerns of mostly middle-class divorced fathers and more liberal organizations helping low-income fathers reconnect with their children.

Judging by the rapid growth of the movement, it has tapped into a sore spot in the nation's psyche. "There's a greater awareness today that children are better off when they have both dad and mom around," says David L. Levy, co-founder and president of the Children's Rights Council. "When we started in 1985, for a long time we were the lone voice in the wilderness. No one else was talking about the importance of both parents in a child's life."

Now it seems everyone is talking—and writing—about it. Amazon.com's database lists 85 books about fatherhood. Literally dozens of Web sites are now dedicated to fatherhood issues, including at least one for stay-at-home dads. And pro-fatherhood events like the 1995 Million Man March and the 1997 Promise Keepers rally have filled entire stadiums.

The movement has also caught the attention of legislators on both sides of the aisle. With broad bipartisan support, the House last November passed the Fathers Count Act, which would provide millions of dollars to groups promoting responsible fatherhood. A similar measure pending in the Senate also has bipartisan support. Meanwhile, political leaders like Democratic Vice President Al Gore and former Republican Vice President Dan Quayle have championed the movement.

"What's incredible is the breadth of bipartisan agreement that this movement has been able to generate," says NFI President Wade Horn.

He points to a policy statement issued last Father's Day by 50 scholars, community leaders and reformers—black and white—as evidence of a new consensus developing around issues that once fostered deep divisions along racial and political lines. The document called for a nationwide effort to reduce fatherlessness in black America, where 70% of all babies today are born to unwed mothers.[3]

The statement grew out of a 1998 conference—sponsored by the Morehouse Research Institute in Atlanta and the conservative Institute for American Values—on "fragile families." Fragile families are formed when young, low-income, poorly educated and unmarried parents have a child.

Many black communities with fragile families, the statement said, have become "radically fatherless." In 1990, it said, about 4.5 million U.S. children—nearly 80% of them African-American—lived in predominantly fatherless neighborhoods, in which more than half of all households were headed by single women.

The statement noted that while a higher percentage of black babies are born out of wedlock, by far the largest number born each year are white. One in three white births are now to unmarried mothers, a figure that has been steadily rising. Among all races, unmarried births have increased 1,000% since 1946.[4]

"Father absence is not a uniquely African-American problem," said the Morehouse statement. "It is an American problem that crosses racial, ethnic and class lines. All across the United States, fathers are quietly disappearing from the lives of children."

In addition to unwed parenthood, skyrocketing divorce rates also are fueling the fatherlessness epidemic. Today more than half of all marriages end in divorce, compared with about 15% in 1960.[5]

While they tackle the problem in different ways, fatherhood groups agree on one thing: Fatherlessness has reached crisis proportions in the United States, and the effects on children are devastating. For instance, according to senior Heritage Foundation research fellow Robert Rector:

- Almost 75% of children of single mothers will experience poverty before they turn 11, compared with only 20% of children raised with two parents at home.
- Sixty percent of convicted rapists, 72% of teen murderers and 70% of long-term prison inmates are males who grew up without fathers.
- Fatherless children are suspended from school, drop out, commit suicide and are abused or neglected significantly more often than children raised in two-parent households.
- Children of single mothers get involved in substance abuse, sexual promiscuity and teen pregnancy more than kids with fathers at home.

But because members of the movement disagree, sometimes heatedly, about how to fix the problem, the result is an uneasy alliance between the left and right. Conservatives generally see the problem as a lack of marriage, while the left sees it as a lack of money. Conservatives say the answer is to attack rising illegitimacy and divorce rates by encouraging matrimony, reforming welfare, making divorce harder to obtain and changing cultural norms about extramarital sex and unwed parenthood. Liberals say fatherlessness will be eliminated only by spending more money on job training and improved educational opportunities for economically marginalized fathers.

"Marriage is most fragile in communities where men can't get and keep jobs," says Scott Coltrane, a sociology professor at the University of California at Riverside and author of *The Family Man*.

A third segment of the movement—divorced fathers—wants to change divorce, child-support and child-custody rules that it says discourage fathers from staying involved in their children's lives.

"Certainly there are deadbeats, but there are also the pushed away, the forced away and the dead broke," Levy says.

(Continued)

(Continued)

Meanwhile, women's advocates suspect the motives of fathers'-rights groups like Fathers Manifesto, which supports sole father custody in all cases and the repeal of women's right to vote.

"From what they've said on their Web sites, they do not have the best interest of children at heart," says Kim Gandy, executive vice president of the National Organization for Women (NOW). "They are all about bashing women. It is beyond the pale."

Horn disavows the Fathers Manifesto group, particularly some of its statistics about damage done to children raised by single mothers. "We have nothing whatsoever to do with them," he says. "They are a bunch of misogynists who don't have any problem making up false statistics to support their rhetoric."

As Congress and advocacy groups grapple with the fatherlessness crisis, here is one of the questions they are asking: Are fathers essential for raising healthy, well-adjusted children?

The American Psychological Association (APA) unleashed a firestorm among conservatives last June when it published "Deconstructing the Essential Father," a study by two clinical psychologists at Yeshiva University Medical School in Bronx, N.Y. Authors Louise B. Silverstein and Carl F. Auerbach concluded that raising a healthy child hinges on the quality and reliability of the parents' relationship with the child.

If that relationship is strong, they wrote, it doesn't matter whether the parenting is by the mother, the father, two moms, two dads, a grandmother or caregivers with no biological relationship to the child.[6]

"The traditional family is one way of parenting, but there are other equally good ways," Auerbach said. "We do think kids need parents, as many parents as possible. We just don't think it even has to be one biological parent."[7]

Other academics agree. Coltrane calls the "uncritical acceptance" of the theory that the fathers are essential and irreplaceable in the lives of their children "the most alarming trend I see today." Two parents are better than one only if those parents are doing good parenting, he says.

"But [fatherhood advocates] argue that even an emotionally remote father is enough to improve a child's outcome," he continues. "Children need regularity, care and love. That can be provided by two mothers or two fathers. There's nothing built into our genes that requires the participation of men."

Silverstein and Auerbach also criticized fatherhood advocates' claim that dozens of sociological studies prove unequivocally that fatherlessness is the root cause of urban decay, societal violence, teenage pregnancy and poor school performance. Their interpretation of the data is a "dramatic oversimplification of the complex relations between father presence and social problems," the authors wrote.

"We don't really know what is causing the problems," Coltrane says. "There could be a self-selection bias in those studies." Many of the social problems cited by the fatherhood advocates are more related to class, poverty and residential situation, he points out.

Phil and Carolyn Cowan, psychology professors at the University of California at Berkeley, say their own study of 200 divorced families showed that the quality of a child's relationships with his parents and the parents' relationship with each other determine the child's academic, social and emotional outcomes. "Just having a father in the house is not in and of itself the controlling factor," Carolyn Cowan says.

Moreover, when studies control for poverty, only about 5 to 12% of single-parent children have an increased risk of trouble at home or school, says Phil Cowan, a senior researcher at the Council on Contemporary Families. "If there isn't a father in the home, it is still possible for the child to grow up well," he says. "It may increase his odds of having problems, but it doesn't guarantee it."

And while children from divorced households have adjustment problems, so do children who remain in high-conflict married households, he points out. "At least 20 different studies, including our own, show that kids in high-conflict households are more depressed, more aggressive and do worse academically than their peers," Phil Cowan says. "There's lots of research like that, which the [fatherhood] folks are just not citing."

"Kids in all kinds of families have all kinds of problems," says Pepper Schwartz, a sociology professor at the University of Washington, "just as kids from all kinds of families do well." In fact, she says, several studies show that children living in one- or two-parent gay or lesbian households are "no different from children in heterosexual households, in terms of their sociability or their acting-out behavior, their grades or rates of delinquency."

Indeed, fatherhood advocates contend, legitimizing gay and lesbian parenting arrangements was Silverstein and Auerbach's real agenda.

"For radically divergent concepts of the family, such as those espoused by homosexual activists, to be considered 'legitimate,' it must first be shown that neither mothers nor fathers are essential to successful families," wrote Timothy J. Dailey, a senior analyst at the conservative Family Research Council (FRC), in response to the APA article. He listed dozens of studies showing that the authors' key assertions were "insupportable by the weight of evidence."

"I think the authors hate marriage," Horn says. "They want to deconstruct society in a way that marriage doesn't matter." He calls the Silverstein-Auerbach report "intellectually frivolous and insubstantial." The authors "completely distorted the empirical literature" about the impact of fatherlessness on children's lives, polarizing what until then had been an extraordinarily non-polarized issue, he says.

Horn angrily denounces what he calls "ivory tower, limousine liberals, who live in gated communities offering theories about society, while consigning large segments of the population to live in communities devastated by the consequences of those theories."

He continues, "I would pay [Silverstein and Auerbach's] rent for them to live for six months in a one-room apartment in a public-housing complex where 90% of the households are unmarried."

Furthermore, the Institute for American Values' Blankenhorn contends, Silverstein and Auerbach ignored 30 years of research showing that children growing up without an involved mother and an involved father are likely to exhibit "just about every negative indicator you can think of." Publicizing that research—and changing attitudes about fatherlessness—have been the primary achievements of the fatherhood movement, he says.

"Fathers make irreplaceable contributions to the well-being of their children," Blankenhorn adds. "That's the one thought that binds all these diverse fatherhood groups together."

Notes

1. Lieberman's statement was made July 14, 1999, at a press conference as the Responsible Fatherhood Act was being introduced in the Senate.

2. David Blankenhorn, *Fatherless America* (1995), p. 10.

3. "Turning the Corner on Father Absence in Black America," Morehouse Research Institute and the Institute for American Values (1999).

(Continued)

(Continued)

4. Robert Rector, "Out-of-Wedlock Childbearing and Paternal Absence: Trends and Social Effects," *Heritage Foundation,* July 7, 1999.

5. Ibid.

6. Louise B. Silverstein and Carl F. Auerbach, "Deconstructing the Essential Father," *American Psychologist,* June 1999, pp. 397–407.

7. Quoted by Joan Lowy, "Dad? Who Needs Him? Support of Non-traditional Families Sends Religious Right into a Tizzy," *Arizona Republic,* August 29, 1999.

SOURCE: From "Fatherhood Movement," by Kathy Koch, 2000, *CQ Researcher, 10,* pp. 473–478. Copyright © 2002 CQ Press, a division of Sage Publications, Inc. By permission of The CQ Researcher.

REFLECTION

- What aspects of the fatherhood movement correspond to the characteristics of new social movements?

- How does this movement differ from movements in the first and second period?

- Considering the disagreements among members of the movement, how do they establish an agenda for advocacy and action?

- Koch (2000) raised two additional questions in the full article on the fatherhood movement:

  ○ Should government policies encourage marriage and discourage divorce to decrease fatherlessness in America?

  ○ Should joint custody be assumed as the preferred arrangement in divorces involving children?

  ○ How would you respond to these questions? What kinds of public policies would you advocate? What opposition do you expect to encounter to your policy proposals?

Note

1. The terms *social change* and *social movements* are used interchangeably in this chapter even though social movements may be considered a subcategory of social change.

References

Allsop, J., Jones, K., & Baggott, R. (2004). Health consumer groups in the UK: A new social movement? *Sociology of Health and Illness, 26,* 737–756.

Bashe, P. R., & Kirby, B. L. (2005). *The OASIS guide to Asperger syndrome: Advice, support, insight, and inspiration.* New York: Crown Publishers.

Bass, B. M. (1985). *Leadership and performance beyond expectations.* New York: Free Press.

Burns, J. M. (1978). *Leadership.* New York: Harper & Row.

Burns, J. M. (2003). *Transforming leadership: A new pursuit of happiness.* New York: Atlantic Monthly Press.

Cohen, D., de la Vega, R., & Watson, G. (2001). *Advocacy for social justice: A global action and reflection guide.* Bloomfield, CT: Kumarian Press.

Conger, J. A., & Kanungo, R. N. (1987). Toward a behavioral theory of charismatic leadership in organizational settings. *Academy of Management Review, 12,* 637–647.

Ganz, M. (2005). Why David sometimes wins: Strategic capacity in social movements. In D. M. Messick & R. M. Kramer (Ed.), *The psychology of leadership: New perspectives and research* (pp. 209–238). Mahwah, NJ: Lawrence Erlbaum.

Gardner, H. (2004). *Changing minds: The art and science of changing our own and other people's minds.* Boston: Harvard Business School Press.

Garner, R. (1997). Fifty years of social movement theory: An interpretation. In R. T. Garner & J. Tenuto (Eds.), *Social movement theory and research: An annotated bibliographical guide* (pp. 1–48). Lanham, MD: Scarecrow Press.

Greenleaf, R. K. (1977). *Servant leadership: A journey into the nature of legitimate power and greatness.* New York: Paulist Press.

House, R. J. (1977). A 1976 theory of charismatic leadership. In J. G. Hunt & L. L. Larson (Eds.), *Leadership: The cutting edge* (pp. 189–207). Carbondale: Southern Illinois University Press.

Howell, J. M. (1988). Two faces of charisma: Socialized and personalized leadership in organizations. In J. A. Conger & R. N. Kanungo (Eds.), *Charismatic leadership: The elusive factor in organizational effectiveness* (pp. 213–236). San Francisco: Jossey-Bass.

Howell, J. M., & Avolio, B. J. (1992). The ethics of charismatic leadership: Submission or liberation? *Academy of Management Executive, 6*(2), 43–54.

Hughes, R. L., Ginnett, R. C., & Curphy, G. J. (2006). *Leadership: Enhancing the lessons of experience* (5th ed.). Boston: McGraw-Hill/Irwin.

Koch, K. (2000, June 2). Fatherhood movement. *CQ Researcher, 10,* 473–496. Retrieved August 7, 2008, from CQ Researcher Online, http://newman.richmond.edu:2271/cqresearcher/cqresrre2000060200

McAdam, D. (1982). *Political process and the development of black insurgency, 1930–1970.* Chicago: University of Chicago Press.

Meyer, D. S., & Minkoff, D. C. (2004). Conceptualizing political opportunity. *Social Forces, 82,* 1457–1492.

Nadler, D. A., & Tushman, M. L. (1990). Beyond the charismatic leader: Leadership and organizational change. *California Management Review, 32*(2), 77–98.

National Alliance on Mental Illness. (n.d.). *Factsheet.* Retrieved July 30, 2008, from http://www.nami.org/Template.cfm?Section=About_NAMI&Template=/ContentManagement/ContentDisplay.cfm&ContentID=58580

Robinson, J. A. G. (1987). *The Montgomery bus boycott and the women who started it: The memoir of Jo Ann Gibson Robinson.* Knoxville: University of Tennessee Press.

Schneider, M., & Somers, M. (2006). Organizations as complex adaptive systems: Implications of complexity theory for leadership research. *Leadership Quarterly, 17,* 351–365.

Speer, P. W., & Hughey, J. (1995). Community organizing: An ecological route to empowerment and power. *American Journal of Community Psychology, 23,* 729–748.

Tucker, R. C. (1995). *Politics as leadership* (rev. ed.). Columbia: University of Missouri Press.

U.S. Department of Health and Human Services. (1999). *Mental health: A report of the surgeon general.* Rockville, MD: Author.

Weber, M., & Parsons, T. (1947). *The theory of social and economic organization.* New York: Free Press.

Yukl, G. A. (2006). *Leadership in organizations* (6th ed.). Upper Saddle River, NJ: Pearson/Prentice Hall.

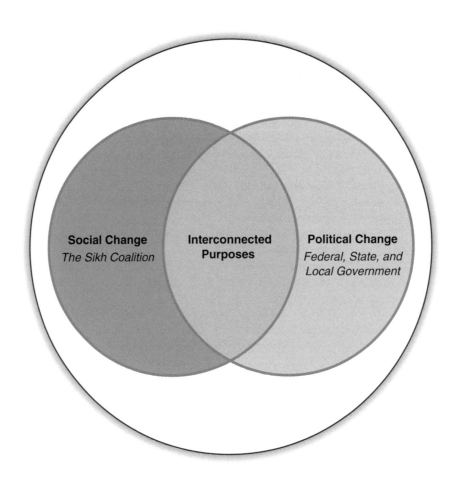

CHAPTER 9

Crossing Political and Social Contexts

Introduction

Social and political contexts have a symbiotic relationship in the implementation of social change. Some movements require more political action to achieve results than others, as the examples illustrate in Chapter 8. When nonconstituted leaders and participants pursue social change with the intent of influencing political action, these movements are designated sociopolitical (Tucker, 1995, pp. 75–76). The intent of actors in these sociopolitical movements is to institutionalize social change—in some cases by replacing one group of political actors with another to pursue the politics of change and in others by influencing the enactment of public policy in support of the movement's aims. For instance, the early civil rights movement, the disability movement, and the women's movement would have had limited effect in society without corresponding public policy and Supreme Court actions that institutionalized these changes.

This chapter presents a vignette about the Sikh Coalition, which was formed after the tragedies of 9/11. The coalition's initiatives demonstrate their efforts in a rights-focused movement to influence constituted leaders in political/governmental and legal systems to correct injustices by influencing new public policy and government procedures and using legal action to enforce existing laws.

Vignette

The Sikh Coalition

The Coalition Is Born. The Sikh Coalition was born in the aftermath of bigotry, violence and discrimination against the city's Sikh population following the terrorist attacks of 9/11, 2001. We

(Continued)

(Continued)

began as a volunteer effort on the night of 9/11, 2001, when an elderly Sikh and two teenagers were violently attacked in Richmond Hill, Queens in "reprisal" attacks by fellow Americans. The group that became the Sikh Coalition issued a press release the next day under the organizational title "Coalition of Sikh Organizations of New York" condemning the terrorist attacks and calling on police to better protect our neighborhoods.

Anticipating that more hate crimes and bias attacks were to come, the group in New York City, which labeled itself "The Coalition of Sikh Organizations," initiated a program to send press releases to the media on 9/11th and began creating press kits [to] enable communities across the country to organize at a grass roots level. With the aid of some activists in Chicago, a website was set up by September 12 to record the occurrence of hate crimes across the country, a chat board, and resources for the media. Other activists from various metropolitan cities across North America joined the initiative and a virtual Coalition emerged.

Within a 2-week time period, the Coalition developed affiliations in Toronto, Boston, Washington DC, Chicago, Houston, Seattle, San Francisco, and Los Angeles. A synergetic energy propelled these groups into an impetus for change. The Coalition worked with the US Justice Department to battle hate crimes and get directives published by the Department of Transportation to combat profiling at airports. Simultaneously, a contingent was dedicated to working with the media in educating the public across North America through print articles and television coverage.

On October 18, 2001, the Sikh Coalition formally incorporated and began operating as a volunteer led organization of concerned Sikhs across the country since no national civil rights–focused Sikh organization existed until the Sikh Coalition was formed. By October 25, 2001, the newly formed Sikh Coalition had its first major victory, persuading the United States Senate to pass a resolution the Coalition had drafted recognizing Sikh-Americans and condemning hate crimes against Sikhs and other minorities.

Since our inception, we have used all available means to tackle the discrimination our community faces. We have often used a combination of education, government advocacy, community organizing and where necessary, legal action to protect our community's civil rights.

Our Development. For 3 years after 9/11 we remained a volunteer organization with a core group of 15 mostly young Sikhs who devoted anywhere from 10 to 30 hours per week working to protect our community.

In September 2003, we hired our first staff member, Amardeep Singh as our Legal Director. In March 2004, we opened our first office in New York City, situated perfectly between our core constituencies in Queens and northern New Jersey. At present, with grant assistance from the New York Foundation, Mehtab Kaur is our Community Advocate. Amardeep Singh has been promoted to Executive Director, Manbeena Kaur is our Operations Manager, and Harsimran Kaur is our Staff Attorney.

Since 9/11, 2001, our work to humanize our community has been difficult given the predominant association in this city and country of the turban and beard with terrorism. We have provided direct legal services to 71 victims of hate crimes, 29 victims of airport profiling, and 21 Sikhs who were prosecuted for carrying the kirpan, a Sikh article of faith. Over 70% of these cases come from New York; the rest are selectively chosen from around the country when victims requesting assistance have no other means of support.

In the 5 years of our existence, we have forced two of the city's largest agencies to accept Sikhs for the quality of their work rather than their appearance and the city's police department to recognize that Sikhs when pushed will demand that their police department protect them like all other citizens. Our reputation around the country continues to grow.

In addition, over the past 2 years, our organization has worked with a member of the New York City Council to develop a package of two post-9/11 discrimination bills, Intro 576, which would require the city of New York to create a plan to mitigate backlash violence against Sikhs, Arabs, Muslims, and South Asians in case of an event that would precipitate such violence, and Intro 577, which would ban discrimination on the basis of religious garb in New York City uniformed agencies. Together, these two bills are a huge step forward in our community's effort to force government to respond to our concerns. They mark the first time a city, state, or federal legislature has ever introduced a bill drafted by the Sikh community to address a concern affecting the Sikh community.

SOURCE: From "History," by The Sikh Coalition. Copyright © 2002–2007 by The Sikh Coalition. By permission of The Sikh Coalition. Retrieved October 31, 2008, from http://www.sikhcoalition.org/History.asp

Concepts of Political and Social Change

Field

The backdrop to 9/11 helps place the Sikh Coalition's origin in the context of interdependent influences of field (see Chapters 1 and 5). Anti-American sentiments had been brewing in places around the world in a struggle that Benjamin Barber (1995) referred to as *Jihad vs. McWorld.* Six years prior to the 9/11 attack, Barber described colliding forces that played a role in the terrorist attacks on the United States:

> Jihad forges communities of blood rooted in exclusion and hatred, communities that slight democracy in favor of tyrannical paternalism or consensual tribalism. McWorld forges global markets rooted in consumption and profit, leaving to an untrustworthy, if not altogether fictitious, invisible hand issues of public interest and common good that once might have been nurtured by democratic citizenries and their watchful governments. . . . Jihad pursues a bloody politics of identity, McWorld a bloodless economics of profit. (pp. 7–8)

These influences of field, among others, contributed to the backdrop of the 9/11 attack, with Jihad representing the terrorists and McWorld representing transnational capitalism emanating from the United States.

The Sikh community was no stranger to discrimination in U.S. cities prior to 9/11. American citizens who are members of the Sikh community were already being identified as "different" from the majority due to outward symbols of their religious traditions, such as turbans and beards. Encounters with discrimination were evident in the bandanas some Sikhs kept readily available to cover and disguise their turbans in cases where threats were imminent. But on 9/11, threats to members of the Sikh community became threats of violence or death. Amardeep Singh, executive director of the Sikh Coalition, told documentary filmmaker Valerie Kaur (2005), in *Divided We Fall, Americans in the Aftermath,* his story of 9/11, when he was rushing home to his family in New Jersey from Washington, D.C.:

> My mom was able to reach me about an hour and a half out of DC. The first thing she says to me is, "Do you have your bandana in the car?" I said, "I have

it in the car." I knew why she was asking. She said, "Put it on." I said, "I'm not putting it on." She started crying and said, "You're in danger." I said, "I understand that I'm in danger. But I'm not putting it on." Then my fiancé called me and she started crying too. And she said, "Put on the bandana." I said, "I'm not putting on the bandana."

In fact, there was every reason for Singh's family to be fearful. Sikhs, along with other innocent Americans of Arab, Middle Eastern, and South Asian or Muslim decent, were being targeted as terrorists. An elderly Sikh and two teenagers were attacked, as indicated in the vignette, on the night of 9/11. For a number of people in the Sikh community the situation reached a threshold (see Chapter 1) where the perceived benefits of taking action simply exceeded the perceived costs. That same night, the Sikh Coalition was born out of the tragedy of these violent attacks.

Structural Strain and the Development of a Movement

Within a month following 9/11 at least 200 hate crimes were directed toward Sikhs, and crimes such as these continue (Lampman, 2001; Merida, 2001; Ritter, 2002). Bullying and harassment in public schools persist against Sikh children despite constant efforts by Sikhs to educate the larger community and urge school official to stop the aggressive behavior (Chan, 2007; Ruiz, 2008). Newspapers continue to report incidents of Sikhs facing job discrimination and harassment in employment. After 9/11, one Sikh transit worker filed suit in the Brooklyn Federal Court after being told by New York's Metropolitan Transit Authority (MTA) that he needed to remove his turban. Several other workers filed complaints with the Equal Employment Opportunity Commission (EEOC) when they were instructed to wear turbans branded with the MTA's logo (Armstrong, 2005).

After 9/11, the U.S. Transportation Security Administration (TSA) created further problems for those who wear turbans in its implementation of air travel security procedures. The screening procedures gave TSA screeners the authority to compel travelers to remove their turbans or have screeners pat them down (Constable & Wilber, 2007; Wilson, 2007). The coalition cited several concerns about the TSA policy:

> TSA guidance on the new policy specifically lists the turban as an example of headwear that can be subjected to secondary screening at the discretion of screeners; the new procedure should be made public so that air travelers subjected to them understand their rights while traveling; TSA giving screeners personal discretion on applying the procedure could lead to religious profiling; and the new procedures were created without consulting any Sikh organizations to determine if safety concerns could be met without compromising religious freedom. (Wilson, 2007, p. 3)

These civil rights violations, in turn, contributed to structural strain—the interrelationship between existing problems in society unattended by established institutions and the formation of movements to address them. The coalition challenged established political actors at local, state, and federal levels to resolve these injustices.

Sikhs began a movement throughout the United States that in many ways parallel the civil rights movements of the second period (see Chapter 8). Like the previous civil rights movements, Sikhs belong to a preexisting, identifiable, and established demographic in which their human and civil rights have been violated by fellow citizens and some local, state, and federal institutions. These violations spurred social action by Sikh Coalition volunteers.

Concepts of Political and Social Leadership

Interrelated Leadership

The coalition was formed by nonconstituted leaders, citizen volunteers who became citizen leaders, in response to the attacks on the Sikh community and civil rights violations. A movement formed and is currently sustained through invisible leadership—that is, leadership that motivates individuals to take action based on a passionate commitment to a common purpose—among affiliates across the country. In addition, coalition members act as servant leaders, who provide voluntary legal assistance to aggrieved Sikhs in their local and regional areas.

Coalition activists needed the cooperation and involvement of constituted leaders, in conjunction with their own involvement, to achieve their goals. The coalition sought justice and respect for Sikh citizens from public sector leaders in exchange for discontinuance of certain civic actions against government agencies (transactional leadership). In turn, government officials needed to work internally with their organizational constituency to develop and disseminate new public policy or regulation changes and, in some cases, change behavior. These changes would require adaptive work within the government for purposes such as influencing other lawmakers to support bills on behalf of the Sikh community or to bring Sikh representatives into the organization to collaborate on developing new security procedures.

Interconnected Values and the Ethic of Responsibility

The values of the Sikh Coalition emerge from the Sikh culture and religion—devotion, remembrance of God at all times, truthful living, equality between all human beings, social justice—while emphatically denouncing superstitions and blind rituals (Sikh Coalition, n.d., Sikhism section, paragraph 1), along with comparable American values of liberty, equality, and justice. As Richard Couto discussed in Chapter 7, values affect leadership in significant ways.

Values suffuse the common elements of leadership—change, conflict, and collaboration. How leadership deals with these common elements will vary depending upon the values of a group or its leadership. For example, values affect initiative (what kind of change to undertake and when to undertake it) and inclusiveness (who should participate in the change process and who should benefit from the change). . . . Clarity about values offers a starting point for understanding initiative and inclusiveness.

Sikh and American values guided the initiation and founding of the coalition and continue to provide the foundation for its civil and human rights advocacy.

The rights claims of the Sikh community relate directly to the moral obligation of constituted government leaders to uphold values evident in the U.S. Constitution and the Declaration of Independence.

In the aftermath of 9/11, values of equality and justice collided with the volatile emotions of many people who had limited or no knowledge about Sikh or Muslim Americans' religious traditions and Americans of Arab, Middle Eastern, and South Asian descent. As a result, the ethic of responsibility for government and political leaders at all levels required consideration of the consequences of action (or lack of action) and proportionality. Yet lawful U.S. citizens from Sikh and other communities were frequently and disproportionately subjected to treatment as suspects of terrorism by some government employees and average citizens, or they were victimized by the inaction of officials to educate themselves and fully protect members of the Sikh community.

Change Practices Across Political and Social Contexts

Signalizing, Voice, and Mobilization

As indicated in the vignette, nonconstituted Sikh leaders began drawing attention to the problem of reprisal attacks by fellow Americans on 9/11. The activists issued press releases condemning the terrorist attacks and calling on police to provide better protection for their neighborhoods. They gave voice to the situation by drawing media attention to the acts of reprisal, and they continue to voice objections concerning injustice toward Sikhs through rallies, protests, letter-writing campaigns, and court cases.

The Sikh Coalition's 21st century version of a civil rights movement has one advantage that previous movements did not have—the Internet. The Internet provided an immediate means of resource mobilization by allowing movement initiators in New York to work with colleagues in Chicago to create a Web site the day after 9/11 and to develop affiliations in Toronto, Boston, Washington, D.C., Chicago, Houston, Seattle, San Francisco, and Los Angeles within 2 weeks.

The coalition used virtual activism to disseminate information and pair aggrieved community members with volunteer attorneys in various regions of the country. It operated on the Internet without paid staff until 2003, when the organization hired its first staff member. Their virtual movement organization allowed the coalition to establish an immediate presence, organize quickly, and operate inexpensively. By 2004, it also established a physical location, making it a hybrid ("clicks and bricks") social movement organization. The addition of a physical location and staff lends further credibility and trust to the coalition that some online-only organizations may lack.

Advocacy

Advocacy, as indicated in Chapter 5, is critical to the ability of a movement to highlight critical issues, influence public attitudes, and promote the enactment and implementation of laws and public policies. The Sikh Coalition's commitment to advocacy on behalf of its citizens is apparent in their mission statement:

We pursue our mission by:

- Providing direct legal services to persons whose civil or human rights are violated;
- Advocating for law and policies that are respectful of fundamental rights;
- Promoting appreciation for diversity through education; and
- Fostering civic engagement in order to promote local community empowerment. (Sikh Coalition, n.d., Mission section, paragraph 2)

Additionally, advocacy is one of four program areas in the organization. The coalition's advocacy agenda was carried out solely by volunteers for several years, and today its small staff is still largely supplemented by individuals who volunteer their time and expertise to the organization's affiliates throughout the country.

Linking Social and Legitimate Power

Sikh Coalition members exercise their social power—the ability to reward or punish targets, control what gets talked about in public debates, and shape how residents and public officials think about their community—in ways that gain the attention and cooperation of constituted leaders. Constituted leaders, in turn, exercise legitimate authority to institutionalize the social change sought by community members. Constituted leaders have responded to the coalition's pressures and appeals in several ways.

- U.S. Senate leaders worked with Coalition leaders to pass a Senate Resolution (S. Con. Res. 74) "Condemning bigotry and violence against Sikh-Americans in the wake of terrorist attacks in New York City and Washington, D.C. on 9/11, 2001";
- Transportation Security Administration officials and Sikh representatives collaborated to develop new security screening procedures that apply to all religious head coverings at U.S. airports;
- The Sikh Coalition worked with a member of the New York City Council to develop two bills to protect Sikh citizens from discrimination and violence;
- The U.S. Attorney General met with Coalition leaders to discuss issues facing the Sikh community and reiterated the commitment of the Department of Justice—as well as his personal commitment—to continue regular engagement with religious communities in the United States; and
- The Chancellor of New York City's Department of Education pledged to work with the Coalition on an ongoing basis to make schools safe for Sikh children. (Sikh Coalition, n.d., Advocacy section)

But even with these efforts, hate crimes, bullying in schools, employment discrimination, and "flying while Sikh" rights violations continue. These rights violations exist in the United States and in other places around the world, most prominently in the United Kingdom and Canada. The work between the Sikh Coalition and authorized public leaders has resulted in policy and procedure changes that have moved the Sikh community's cause forward. Still, there is considerable work to be done.

Conclusion

The Sikh Coalition vignette helps demonstrate the interdependent relationship between social movement and political contexts, especially with regard to rights-focused movements. Coalition activists signaled rights violations and harassment of Sikhs to the media in the aftermath of 9/11. They quickly developed a movement structure, mobilized resources using the Internet, and later established a physical location and staff. The movement created a structural strain in societal institutions that required a response from constituted leaders at various levels of government. Coalition and public sector leaders continue to work together to institutionalize change and protect the rights of the Sikh community.

References

Armstrong, J. R. (2005, July 16). Five Sikhs sue MTA over its turban rule. *New York Daily News*. Retrieved October 30, 2008, from http://www.nydailynews.com/news/2005/07/16/2005-07-16_5_sikhs_sue_mta_over_its_turban_rule.html

Barber, B. R. (1995). *Jihad vs. McWorld: How globalism and tribalism are reshaping the world*. New York: Ballantine.

Chan, E. (2007, June 6). Harassment ordeal of Boro's Sikh kids. *New York Daily News*. Retrieved October 30, 2008, from http://newman.richmond.edu:2435/us/lnacademic/search/homesubmitForm.do

Constable, P., & Wilber, D.Q. (2007, September 9). Turban searches rile Sikh community: Rule change gives airport workers wider leeway in screening headgear. *The Washington Post*. Retrieved October 31, 2008, from http://www.washingtonpost.com/wp-dyn/content/article/2007/09/08/AR2007090801606.html

Kaur, V. (2005, October 8). *Into the whirlwind: Sikh coalition vs. New York City*. Retrieved October 29, 2008, from http://valariekaur.blogspot.com/2005/08/sikh-coalition-vs-new-york-city.html

Lampman, J. (2001, October 31). Under attack, Sikhs defend their religious liberties. *Christian Science Monitor*. Retrieved October 30, 2008, from http://www.csmonitor.com/2001/1031/p2s2-ussc.html%0A3

Merida, K. (2001, October 3). For "other" Americans, a new kind of terrorism. *The Washington Post*. Retrieved October 30, 2008, from http://www.washingtonpost.com/ac2/wp-dyn?pagename=article&node=&contentId=A61641-2001Oct3

Ritter, J. (2002, September 12). Hate crimes born out of tragedy added victims. *USA Today*. Retrieved October 30, 2008, from http://www.beliefnet.com/News/2002/09/Hate-Crimes-Born-Out-Of-Tragedy-Added-Victims.aspx?print=true

Ruiz, A. (2008, June 11). Battling hate in our schools. *New York Daily News*. Retrieved October 30, 2008, from http://www.nydailynews.com/ny_local/2008/06/11/2008-06-11_battling_hate_in_our_schools.html

The Sikh Coalition. (n.d.). *Sikhism*. Retrieved March 3, 2009, from http://www.sikhcoalition.org/SikhismGlance.asp

Tucker, R. C. (1995). *Politics as leadership* (rev. ed.). Columbia: University of Missouri Press.

Wilson, B. (2007, August 29). Sikhs blast TSA for forcing new turban removal procedures. *Aviation Daily*, *396*(42). Retrieved October 31, 2008, from http://newman.richmond.edu:2435/us/lnacademic/search/homesubmitForm.do

PART V

Leading Global Change

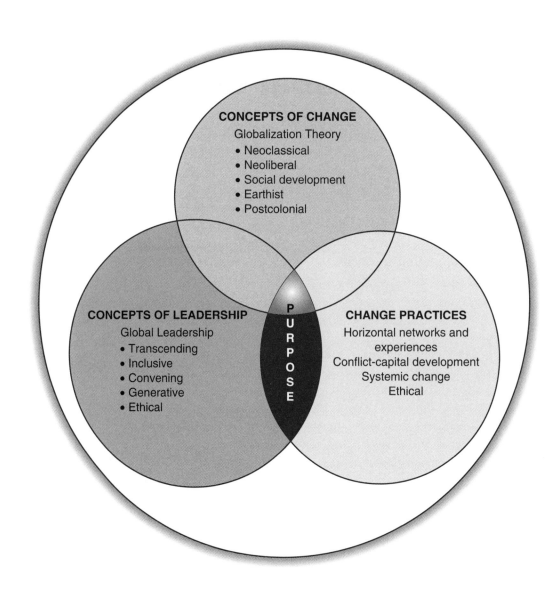

CONCEPTS OF CHANGE
Globalization Theory
- Neoclassical
- Neoliberal
- Social development
- Earthist
- Postcolonial

CONCEPTS OF LEADERSHIP
Global Leadership
- Transcending
- Inclusive
- Convening
- Generative
- Ethical

P U R P O S E

CHANGE PRACTICES
Horizontal networks and experiences
Conflict-capital development
Systemic change
Ethical

CHAPTER 10

Global Change Context

Rebecca Todd Peters and Gill Robinson Hickman

Introduction

Maggie Smith was born in Missouri but now lives in California. Last week she got help from Sanjay, a technician in India, when she called a support line for a problem that she was having with her computer. She bought her computer online from a company that had assembled it in Malaysia from parts manufactured in Mexico. The tag on the blouse she was wearing said it was made in Honduras but neglected to mention that the cotton was grown in China. She drives a Japanese car that was assembled in Kentucky, and her dinner consisted of food that traveled an average of 2,000 miles before it reached her table. If we spent more time with Maggie or almost any individual living in the First World today, it would be difficult to find anyone whose life was not thoroughly and completely integrated in the global economy. Although there is nothing particularly remarkable or unique about Maggie's experience, a snapshot of her day-to-day life highlights the remarkable shifts in the world community over the last 50 years, shifts that have redefined everyday life for some groups of people.

In contrast, Sara Mwambu still lives in the small village in Uganda where she was born. She is a subsistence farmer who gets up every day before dawn to care for her family by cooking, cleaning, washing, and dressing herself and her five children; tending to her vegetables; and fetching water, among other things. Although some of the family's clothes may be castoffs from more wealthy countries that reach them through aid agencies, most of the food, utensils, clothing, and other supplies in their life are produced by the family (usually, Sara) or are purchased locally. Sara does not have a computer, a telephone, or a car. Nevertheless, her world is also shaped by the changing global context of the world. For instance, increased floods and droughts (manifestations of global climate change) have destroyed Sara's crops more than once, compromising the food security of Sara's family. Another change is that, whereas Sara never received any formal education, her daughters are now in secondary school as a result of education initiatives supported by the World Bank.

The political and economic shifts that accompanied the end of the Second World War led to the rise of a new geopolitical landscape that included two major changes. The first change was the solidification of the Western and Eastern political "blocs" that came to be known respectively as the First World and the Second World. The second change was a growing concern with the economic development of newly independent nations in Africa and Latin America and, to a lesser extent, in Asia. The working assumption of the Western countries, or the First World, was that these former colonies needed to "develop" their assets and resources in ways that would make them more prosperous. The general consensus was that the best way for them to succeed was to emulate the industrial development model that had propelled the First World to economic success. These countries were referred to as "underdeveloped" or "developing" and also came to be known as the Third World. The most significant changes that have shaped the global economy and the context of global change have occurred in the last 60 years as business and political leaders have cooperated in the task of developing a more integrated global world.

The two scenarios discussed at the beginning of this chapter demonstrate three significant aspects of the context of global change that are important to highlight. First, differences in people's social locations (class, race, gender, nationality, etc.) translate into different experiences of the global changes that have taken place. Namely, Sara and Maggie are both affected by globalization and the changes that it has wrought in the world, but they experience those changes in very different ways. Second, differences in the way that people experience these shifts in the global context affect how they think about these changes and whether they experience them positively or negatively. Third, the global changes that have occurred in the last 60 years have resulted in both positive and negative shifts that are affecting the lives of everyone on the planet. Though it is true that Maggie has year-round access to fruits and vegetables from around the world, there has been a significant increase in the amount of greenhouse gases emitted in the production and transportation of food globally. Likewise, while Sara's girls are receiving an education, the long-term reliability of their food source is threatened by increased climate change that is directly related to the habits and lifestyles of people living in the First World.

Purpose of Global Change

The purpose of change in a global context is varied and multidimensional. As the world is increasingly drawn together through technology, ease of travel (for some), and global economic integration, people are increasingly attempting to address global problems, such as poverty, violence, disease, terrorism, intolerance, climate change, and health issues, as a global community. The idea that global change can be accomplished when humans work together to address large-scale problems that affect the quality of life for people across nations and cultures is the root of global change initiatives and programs such as the United Nation's Millennium

Development Goals and international agencies such as the World Bank and the World Health Organization, which work toward promoting coordinated strategies to address global problems.

This chapter uses one example of a global economic development project supported by the World Bank to examine the varieties of perspectives and interests that must be taken into account when working within a global context. In the story of the Chad-Cameroon pipeline, we show how different worldviews and perspectives cause people to think about the danger and value of the pipeline in different ways. At the root of these differences are different constituencies of people who hold different values and visions for what globalization might look like. Understanding these differences of perspective, values, and worldviews is a key aspect of effective leadership within a context of global change.

Change Vignette

Chad-Cameroon Pipeline

At the turn of the 21st century, Mabolo, a village of 13 mud huts in the central African rain forest, was one of the few places left in the world that could only be reached by foot. To get there, one had to follow a winding footpath that veered off a dirt road and passed through a maze of muddy hills and creeks on the way to the village. Few places remain untouched by the globalization processes that are transforming the world. Even remote Pygmy villages in Cameroon are seeing their way of life change in response to the changing world. For traditional nomadic hunting tribes, even the existence of the villages represents a significant lifestyle change as their attempts to adjust to a globalizing world over the last 50 years have included settling into villages. Here they grow cassava and yams to supplement the porcupines, rabbits, boars, and antelopes that have long been the mainstay of their diets. Living without electricity or running water and most assuredly living on less than the World Bank's $1.25 a day threshold for extreme poverty, these tribes represent the kind of people whom proponents of development are trying to reach. A recent development project jointly sponsored by the World Bank and several oil companies brought an oil pipeline through the hills nearby. The people who live in Mobolo and the surrounding villages are the Baka and Bakola populations in Cameroon. Some hope to get jobs from the pipeline. Others share 34-year-old Pierre Mbang's concern that "work is good, but the forest is our life. Work is good, but it will end." Numerous peasants live in villages surrounding the proposed pipeline route, and their voices and concerns regarding the environmental impact of the project, the proposed revenue-sharing development of their region, and the economic compensation for their land have not been adequately considered. Early in the process, local sources reported that military and government officials who visited towns and villages in the region threatened that anyone who opposed the pipeline would be summarily executed (Center for International Environmental Law, 2000). Life for all of the communities in the path of the oilfields or the pipeline itself has been transformed over the last few years as a $3.7 billion oil pipeline built by ExxonMobil, Chevron, and Malaysia's Petronas has snaked its way from oil reserves located in Chad through Cameroon on their way to the coast for export.

(Continued)

(Continued)

Chad is a landlocked country in central Africa that is ranked as one of the poorest countries in the world by the United Nations Human Development Report. In fact, in 2006 it was ranked 171 out of 177 countries according to its Human Development Index, or HDI. The HDI ranks countries according to three basic areas of human development—longevity and health of population, knowledge, and standard of living. The current life expectancy in Chad is 43 years, almost half Japan's life expectancy of 82 years (Human Development Report Office, 2006). Only 25% of the adult population is literate, and the average income is roughly $225 a year (Human Development Report Office, 2006; Sengupta, 2004).

Oil reserves were discovered in Chad 30 years ago, and discussions have been underway with the World Bank since 1995 regarding the development of an oil pipeline to access those reserves. The pipeline project represents an estimated 900 million barrels of oil, according to ExxonMobil's estimations, which will be extracted over a 25-year period. At current oil prices, ExxonMobil's 40% share of the profit stands to be about $9.8 billion.

In their words, the World Bank joined the negotiations to ensure that this will be "a development project rather than just an oil project." From the perspective of the World Bank, their 15% contribution (approximately $193 million) to the production costs of the pipeline buys them a substantial voice in determining how the oil will reach the market. The World Bank, which views its mission as the elimination of poverty through development, hopes to make a significant impact on the economy and living conditions of Chad. Toward that end the original agreement between the World Bank and the Chadian parliament earmarked 10% of the royalties and revenues for future generations; 80% of the remaining funds for education, health and social services, rural development, infrastructure, and environmental and water resource management; 5% for regional development in the oil-producing area; and 5% as discretionary funds (World Bank, 2000). Total revenue for Chad is anticipated to be about $2 billion and the expectation on the part of the World Bank was that this money would significantly improve the standard of living in this desperately poor country. Although this is an admirable goal, a variety of objections and concerns about the project have been raised over the years by nongovernmental organizations (NGOs) that are concerned about the viability and potential success of the project.

One of the most significant objections to the project has to do with the political instability in the region. Chad's involvement in a civil war for the first 30 years of its independence, from 1960–1990, is the primary reason this oil has not been exported already. The nonprofit Bank Information Center (BIC; 2000) that monitors the work of the World Bank and other International Financial Institutions reported that the pipeline has exacerbated conflicts between the largely Muslim government in the north and the Christian/Animist rebels in the south. Amnesty International and BIC reported two unexplained massacres of civilians in the oil-producing region, one in 1996 and the other in 1997, that killed 180 people combined.

Additional concerns that oil revenues would be used to arm and fund the military proved prescient when the president used $4.5 million from an initial $25 million signing bonus to secretly purchase weapons for the military in 2001 in direct violation of standing agreements with the World Bank and the International Monetary Fund. In August of 2006, President Idriss Deby ordered pipeline partners Chevron and Petronas to leave the country for tax nonpayment, a charge disputed by both companies. Some observers saw this move as part of Deby's attempts to renegotiate the pipeline contract with the World Bank to free up a larger percentage of the oil revenues to spend on beefing up the military and his security forces. Deby argued that he needs this freedom to adequately address the renewed civil unrest he faces in the east, which has been described as a second civil war. The porous borders between Chad and Sudan have meant that much of the conflict in Darfur has spilled over into neighboring Chad, and the Janjaweed forces reportedly have been attacking villages and eastern Chad since 2004. This kind of political instability makes it difficult to maintain the security of something as large as the oil fields and pipeline in the southern region. Transparency International has rated Chad as the most corrupt nation in the world, and Deby recently arranged to have the constitutional term limits for the office of the president removed as he faced the end of what should have been his second and final term of office.

Given that Chad and Cameroon are two of the poorest countries in the world, it is not surprising that social concerns are also a dominant factor in the debate over the pipeline. Questions and concerns about how the pipeline will affect the ability of local inhabitants to survive have been central to public debates. We have already discussed the threat to the remote Pygmy villages in Cameroon and their inhabitants who now number about 100,000 out of Cameroon's population of 14 million. But the livelihoods and well-being of many other communities in the pipeline's path are also threatened. Fertile land in the region was scarce even before the pipeline arrived, and many subsistence farmers and their families are finding their possibility for survival increasingly threatened by the expanding oil field development. The project is expanding because after the crews got into the fields they realized they were not going to be able to meet the original production goals. So they began expanding their drilling, and the original land-use estimates have expanded by 65%. The participation of the World Bank was intended to make sure that local residents would be compensated by the ExxonMobil consortium for any loss of land as a result of the pipeline project. Though efforts have been made to offer compensation, disputes over the valuation of the land, survey results, and land ownership have resulted in reports that the living conditions of many of the inhabitants of the region have been further immiserated since the pipeline came through. Furthermore, one-time cash compensation for the loss of farmland and fruit trees that provide food for local farmers and villagers is hardly an adequate solution to addressing the poverty of these two countries.

Obviously, any oil development project will also have its share of environmental concerns. In the case of this particular project, opponents have cited the threat to the wildlife, the threat of oil spills to drinking water and arable land, increased risk of drought, increased deforestation and loss of biodiversity, and concern for marine pollution along the Cameroonian coast as some of their primary concerns. Since completion of the project and the pumping of oil in 2003, one of the problems cited by local residents is the contamination of drinking water in the village wells. Madame M, a woman who lives in a village just north of Cameroon's capital, Yaounde, explained, "We used to have clean water, but since the oil pipeline was built all we have is pollution" (Horta & Djiriabe, 2007). The only source of water in her village is a small well located near the pipeline. The surface of the water is covered by a film of what appears to be grease. Other villagers agree that water contamination is a serious problem, and they complain of "skin rashes, stomach pains, and unknown ailments." A significant lack of dust control has also led to a decrease in the overall air quality as well as damage to crops. The dust causes visibility problems, eye infections, and

(Continued)

(Continued)

respiratory problems. The lack of an adequate health care infrastructure in the region means that many of these conditions are left untreated, further compromising the health of an already fragile people.

In December 2006, the World Bank completed a Project Implementation Completion Report, or ICR, which usually indicates the completion of World Bank involvement with a development project. The ICR assesses the actions of the borrowing government and whether or not a project achieved its stated development goals. The Environmental Defense Fund has produced its own report that characterizes the ICR as an incomprehensible and misleading report. In documenting both the current situation and the serious concerns about corruption, graft, and civil unrest in Chad, the EDF calls on the World Bank to remain actively engaged in working on the Chad-Cameroon pipeline project until the social, political, and environmental problems have been adequately addressed.

While participants in the pipeline debate are not engaged firsthand in a debate over globalization per se, globalization is exactly what is at stake. Now, that's not to say that the outcome of the Chad-Cameroon Petroleum Development and Pipeline Project will determine the future role of globalization in our society. It is instead to say that this pipeline project is emblematic of how globalization is being articulated, enacted, and experienced all over the world. Globalization is a historic phenomenon that incorporates economic, cultural, material, philosophical, and social aspects. Often globalization is reduced to an economic paradigm characterized by increased trade among nations and the creation of a single global economy. As we show in this chapter the neoliberal economic paradigm that this represents is a significant aspect of globalization, but we also demonstrate in the pipeline story that globalization extends far more broadly, touching on issues of culture, tradition, politics, work, values, the environment, human rights, consumerism, power, and a host of others. Leadership in the context of global change requires a deep understanding of the variety of ideologies, concerns, and experiences of all of the stakeholders involved.

Concepts of Global Change

The Chad-Cameroon pipeline and all its attendant controversies and complexities serves as an excellent example of the different voices, viewpoints, and experiences that pepper the globalization debates in the early 21st century. There are at least four major interests in the debates over the pipeline—the oil companies, the development community, NGOs, and local communities affected by the pipeline. These four groups have very different interests and values and significantly different levels of power and influence with regard to decision making about the pipeline project. These distinct voices correspond and help to illustrate four different theoretical positions regarding globalization—neoliberal, development, earthist, and postcolonial. Examining the positions and perspectives of different groups that correspond to these four theoretical positions help to illustrate how different communities understand and interpret the impacts of globalization.[1]

Although many people describe the context of global change as *globalization*, this term often implies a certain uniformity of definition or perspective that is too simplistic. There is not, in fact, a single theory of globalization but rather many ways that people understand, interpret, and respond to the global changes that are occurring in the world. In the opening figure, these different ways of thinking about and approaching global change are described as concepts of change. Here we examine the four theories of globalization that correspond to different constituencies and reflect different sets of values. We examine how these four theories correspond to various constituencies involved in the Chad-Cameroon pipeline debate.

Neoclassical Economics

The first two stakeholders in the pipeline are the oil companies and the development community. They represent the groups with the most money and political power in this scenario. Each of these groups works out of a distinct worldview that guides their analysis of the political, economic, and social realities of the African continent that affect the development of the pipeline project. The worldview of the oil companies can best be described as neoliberal, and the worldview of the development community most closely corresponds to a social equity approach (Johnston, 1998). These two worldviews also represent the two most widely held views of globalization that are competing for dominance in the political-economic sphere today. Although these two worldviews largely describe beliefs about how economies work, they share some basic assumptions about economics and anthropology that are rooted in their shared acceptance of neoclassical economic theory.

Neoclassical economics developed over a period of several hundred years. The classical economists Adam Smith and David Ricardo were early theorists who developed some of the foundational assumptions of the field of economics, including an emphasis on economic growth and the belief that the field of economics is an objective or scientific discipline. John Stuart Mill was another foundational classical economist who is attributed with the idea of *homo economicus*, or economic man. This term refers to the idea that consumers can primarily be understood as self-interested wealth maximizers who will make economic decisions based on what best promotes their own self-interest. Classical economics split in the 19th century between a group of theorists who emphasized the demand side of economics (marginalists) and a group who emphasized the supply side (classical). These two divergent approaches were brought together into what is known as the neoclassical synthesis, which emphasizes the examination of supply and demand as the lens through which to study economic behavior and practices. Although neoclassical economic theory continues to dominate contemporary approaches to economics, economic thought has again diverged into the two streams identified with the oil companies and the development community—namely, neoliberalism and social equity liberalism. These two worldviews share basic neoclassic economic assumptions, including an emphasis on economic growth, a belief that economics is a scientific discipline, and a basic anthropology that consumers are self-interested wealth maximizers. Although both groups promote growth and trade as essential aspects of economic health and wealth, they differ on their perspectives of what role governments should play in economic matters, and herein lies the greatest difference between these two approaches to globalization.

Neoliberalism

The term *neoliberalism* is widely used to refer to the economic ideology that has been driving global economic integration since the 1980s. Also known as laissez-faire, the Washington consensus, trickle-down or supply-side economics, and free market capitalism, neoliberal economic theory emphasizes three main policy goals—privatization, deregulation, and increased trade. Proponents of neoliberal ideology promote privatization on the grounds that markets are more efficient than governments at providing services. They seek deregulation based on the argument that governmental regulations inhibit economic growth, expansion, and trade. Supporters also promote trade liberalization based on Ricardo's law of comparative advantage. In short, this means that countries should focus on producing goods that they can produce most efficiently, and they should use those goods to trade on the market for all other necessities.

Neoliberalism was theorized most prominently by Milton Friedman and the Chicago school. It has become the dominant form of economic theory in the First World and thus has become synonymous with capitalism for many people. It is the driving ideology behind a variety of engines of big business as represented by the World Trade Organization (WTO), multinational (MNCs) and transnational corporations (TNCs), the Organization for Economic Co-operation and Development (OECD), and the International Chamber of Commerce (ICC) to name just a few. In short, these corporations and organizations are champions of the free market, and they promote growth and profits through increased external trade between nations. The neoliberal ideology is represented in the Chad-Cameroon pipeline scenario by ExxonMobil (U.S. based), Petronas (Malaysian based), and Chevron (U.S. based). Clearly, ExxonMobil's interest in the project is profit. As we already stated, ExxonMobil's share of the profit stands to be about $9.8 billion.

Social Development

The second stakeholder in the pipeline controversy is represented by the World Bank. By their own account, the World Bank entered into this project with the express intent of trying to ensure that this project would promote human development rather than function purely in an extractive and exploitative fashion. From the perspective of economic theory, this worldview is influenced by the work of John Maynard Keynes, who argued that there are compelling reasons why the state should intervene in the market. Keynes advocated two roles for government that contradict the laissez-faire model of neoliberalism. First, it is sometimes necessary for the government to step in and stimulate the economy when private enterprise fails to do so. This can happen through public works programs or interest rate changes from a central bank. Second, financial supports for the poor, such as unemployment aide or food assistance, can also function to stimulate the economy because a higher percentage of the poor's income is spent on basic needs. This means that governmental funds that are used to support the poor are highly likely to reenter the economy and function to stimulate needed growth. Countries that follow a Keynesian or social equity liberal model of economic theory generally affirm that governments have a responsibility to ensure the basic health and safety of their citizens and that this includes the implementation of certain social safety nets, such as unemployment, health care, care for the elderly and disabled, and other programs that support marginalized populations.

Whereas the development community includes a number of different approaches to the practice of development, the development approach that corresponds more closely to the social equity model of globalization is a subset of the development community that has come to value social development as a way to identify aspects of globalization and development theory that should be front and center in theory and practice. The people who share this perspective largely work in agencies, institutions, and NGOs that approach the project of development from the holistic perspective of attending to a variety of aspects of people's lives, including education, health, and community life in addition to the traditional development emphasis on economic growth. This approach to development—which moves beyond a strictly economic analysis of the problem of poverty—is known as the capability approach to development and is most closely associated with the work of economists Amartya Sen and Martha Nussbaum. The capability approach moves beyond a traditional developmental focus on procuring the "basic" necessities of life for people who live in poverty, traditionally defined as food, clothing, and shelter, to include a broader interpretation of what things are necessary to allow people to flourish. Poverty is seen as depriving people of the basic fundamentals or capacities necessary to exercise freedom. From this worldview, people's need for employment, safe and healthy workplaces, access to education and job training, health care, and self-governance are all included in a more holistic understanding of development work as creating the capacity for human well-being. The development community is represented by organizations like the World Bank, the United States Agency for International Development (USAID), the United Nations International Children's Emergency Fund (UNICEF), and the United Nations Conference on Environment and Development (UNCED), among others.

The World Bank is the major development player in the pipeline story. The World Bank felt that their influence on the political and economic stages would allow them to play a major role in shaping the oil pipeline project in ways that would contribute to the social development of the people living in Chad, one of the poorest countries in the world.[2] Though the World Bank did have a significant hand in developing the agreements that earmarked the majority of the oil revenues for social development, they proved not to have the political power necessary to force the Chadian government to keep up their end of the bargain. In 2006, President Deby violated the original intent of the World Bank agreements by redefining priority sectors for development to include military expenditures (Horta, Nguiffo, & Djiraibe, 2007). This allowed Deby to divert funds to support continued military buildup and eventually forced a renegotiation of the original agreement with the World Bank to include a reduction of oil revenues to be used for poverty alleviation among other changes.

Earthist

Whereas the two dominant approaches to globalization in the world today emerged out of economic theories about growth and trade, important and distinctive voices in the globalization debate argued that people need to broaden their worldviews beyond a narrow focus on economic growth to include questions of sustainability and culture. These voices are often found in a variety of civil society organizations. In the case of the Chad-Cameroon pipeline, these voices are strongest in the presence of a variety of NGOs that have opposed the pipeline, organizations that can roughly be described as sharing a basic concern for a growing grassroots principle alternately called globalization from below, bioregional model, and localization. This principle is rooted in the belief that local communities need to once again become the center of economic, cultural, and social activity rather than continuing the trend of recent decades toward transnational corporations and what has been termed the *McDonaldization* of culture (Ritzer, 1996).

A number of NGOs have been involved in protesting the oil pipeline project, including the Center for International Environmental Law (CIEL), Environmental Defense, Amnesty International, CILONG (a coordinating body of NGOs in Chad), and EIRENE (a Chadian-based NGO). Objections of NGOs to the proposed pipeline project fall into three main categories—environmental, social, and political. The environmental concerns include the threat to wildlife, the threat of oil spills to drinking water and arable land, increased risk of drought, increased deforestation and loss of biodiversity, and concern for marine pollution along the Camaroonian coast (Onishi, 2000). These concerns must be viewed in light of the region's experience with oil pipelines in recent years. In neighboring Nigeria, official figures indicate that more than 2,000 women, men, and children have died in pipeline explosions in the last 2 years. These explosions are not a result of accidents but rather a result of robbery as organized rings of thieves, frequently escorted by corrupt military officials, siphon large quantities of oil into waiting trucks. In addition to the environmental damage of the resultant leaks in the pipeline, the oil spills attract desperately poor local villagers to the site in attempts to gather oil to sell on the black market. Invariably, these are the people who are killed by the explosions (Onishi, 2000).

The NGOs that protest the pipeline based on environmental concerns share elements of a worldview that can largely be described as earthist (Cobb, 1999). An earthist worldview moves beyond the narrow concerns of economic growth as the solution to poverty and focuses on a broader attention to the sustainability of human practices in the world. It is rooted in an anthropology that understands humans as neither separate from nor higher than the rest of the natural world. Humanity's impact on the earth and its systems is of primary concern for people who hold an earthist worldview, and development projects such as the pipeline are seen through a lens in which the environmental risks often outweigh the economic potential of such a project. In the case of the Chad-Cameroon pipeline, in addition to the health problems associated with the lack of dust control and clean water in the pipeline region and serious problems with erosion, mosquitoes, and toxic waste, the project has generated a far larger ecological footprint than was originally projected.

Postcolonial

In addition to the environmental concerns expressed by many NGOs, there are also social and political concerns that have played a significant role in the debate over the pipeline. Social concerns center around the potential effects that the pipeline poses to numerous people in villages and communities in the pipeline's path, including a number of indigenous Pygmy communities. Politically speaking, Chad and Cameroon are both extremely unstable countries that lack transparency and have histories of violent civil conflict and unrest. Significant concerns have been raised that oil revenues will be used to arm and fund the military. These social and political concerns are closely related to a fourth worldview labeled postcolonial (Peters, 2004). Although NGOs are often the public face of these concerns, these organizations often represent the most vulnerable and marginalized stakeholders in the debate—the poor and indigenous communities living in the areas of Chad and Cameroon—the area that the pipeline will affect. Because the poor are often illiterate, unable to speak the languages of the globalization dialogues, and lacking in formal education, the postcolonial perspective is largely represented by those who stand in solidarity with the poor, those who work with and advocate for the poor.

This position is referred to as postcolonial because it represents a worldview that reflects a historical consciousness that is highly critical of the exploitation of countries in the developing world by their colonizers. During the colonial era, most colonized states were not only governed politically by their colonizers, but their natural resources (gold, minerals, crops, etc.) were also exploited to build up the wealth of the colonizing powers. Although many countries, including many in Africa, gained political independence in the 1950s and 60s, the postcolonial worldview describes the successive neoliberal and development policies of the developed world as a continuation of the exploitation of the colonial era and even refers to the dominant model of economic globalization as neocolonialism. From a postcolonial perspective, the Chad-Cameroon pipeline is another example of the plundering of African resources to make money for people and corporations in the developed world. This belief is reinforced by the political and social repercussions of the pipeline project in which the Chadian government has used part of its revenues to arm its military and local communities that are suffering from loss of livelihood due to significant loss of cropland. Although it is true that the ExxonMobil consortium paid compensation for land lost to the pipeline project, serious questions have been raised about whether the compensation was adequate to cover the loss of land and whether the entitled landowners even received the compensation.

Other Perspectives

Although these four theories of globalization help to elucidate the conflicts inherent in the Chad-Cameroon pipeline controversy, they do not explain the actions, behavior, or worldviews of all of the significant actors and stakeholders. The fifth significant stakeholder in this debate are the governments of Chad and Cameroon. Because Chad is the primary government involved in the pipeline negotiations, we focus on their actions. Although the four theories of globalization previously presented can be useful in helping to understand how different stakeholders in a situation of global conflict understand and approach a particular problem, as the Chadian government illustrates, not all stakeholders fall neatly into one of these categories. As we showed with other areas of Africa (e.g., Rwanda/Burundi, Darfur), situations of dire poverty can combine with greed and hunger for power to exacerbate previously dormant ethnic and religious tensions. Chad's close proximity to Rwanda, Burundi, and Sudan; its long history of civil war; and the profound poverty of a population that primarily survives on subsistence agriculture have led to a political situation that is driven by graft, greed, and power, and civil war and ethnic conflict remain legitimate threats. President Deby's recent success at altering the constitution to eliminate term limits does not bode well for Chad's fragile attempts at democracy and peace. This case study highlights the inherent difficulty and unpredictability that undergird many international global change contexts. It also highlights the weaknesses of international financial institutions such as the World Bank that have no firm mechanism for enforcement of agreements. Although money and credit ratings can be used as financial tools to pressure governments, lack of transparency and corruption remain significant obstacles in global political and economic arenas.

Concepts of Global Leadership

The term *global leadership* has become a part of daily media commentary and casual conversation. Yet there is a relative dearth of global leadership theory. Most likely, this conceptual void exists because developing a theory or theories of global leadership requires truly interdisciplinary work among scholars and practitioners in fields such as leadership studies, sociology, international relations, political science, communication, international business, applied ethics, social psychology, and cultural anthropology, among other areas. No single field is likely to have the capacity to put forward theories that encompass the dimensions of leadership in transnational, transcultural, and trans-sector environments.

Global leadership theorists need to assemble ideas that appear instinctively incompatible—ideas that include dual and even incongruous perspectives. The Chad-Cameroon pipeline serves to illustrate this point. It encompasses an array of global actors and issues in a situation where the parties do not coexist geographically, culturally, socially, or politically, and they have little or no social capital on which to build. Although this chapter does not propose a theory of global leadership, it presents several potential components of global leadership for cross-boundary situations such as the Chad-Cameroon pipeline. As shown in Figure 10.1, these components include transcending, inclusive, convening, generative, and ethical elements of global leadership.

FIGURE 10.1 Possible Components of Global Leadership

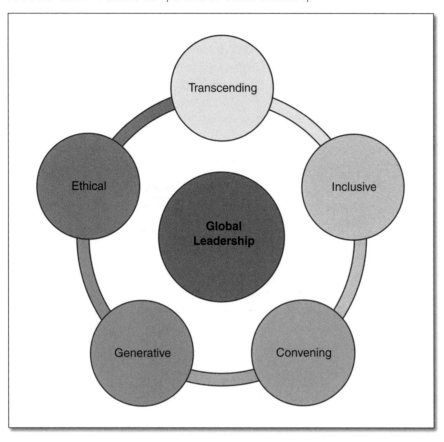

Transcending Components

The works of Howard Gardner (1995) and Nancy Adler (1997) offer a point of departure for identifying components of global leadership. Adler (1997) contended that most current leadership theories are domestic theories masquerading as universal theories that typically incorporate U.S. and male perspectives; even when these theories are not U.S. based, they still represent the domestic perspective of a specific culture or country (p. 174). Adler instead made the following proposal:

Global leadership theory, unlike its domestic counterpart, is concerned with the interaction of people and ideas among cultures, rather than with either the efficacy of particular leadership styles within the leader's home country or with the comparison of leadership approaches among leaders from various countries—each of whose domain is limited to issues and people within their own cultural environment. A fundamental distinction is that global leadership is neither domestic nor multidomestic: it *focuses on cross-cultural interaction* rather than on either single-culture description or multi-country comparison. (italics added; p. 175)

Adler (1997) supported her premise by referencing Gardner's (1995) study in *Leading Minds*, where he concluded that transnational leadership is "the form [of leadership] that goes beyond the nation-state and seeks to address all human beings" (p. 20). Accordingly, global leadership relies on transcending components— factors that enhance the ability of participants to work across multiple sectors, cultures, and countries. Gardner's examination of leadership that goes beyond nation-states illuminated several potential transcending components, including a systems perspective, an appeal to common humanity, broadened identity and vision, and the use of stories, among others.

A Systems Perspective

Situations like the one in the Chad-Cameroon pipeline vignette point to the need for global leadership to employ a systems perspective—that is, to see the vast array of causes and effects that make up a situation in contrast to seeing problems in disjointed, linear, or simplistic ways (see discussion in Chapter 1). Circumstances described in the vignette at the beginning of this chapter demonstrate how transnational business and finance, transnational politics, and transcultural groups intersect in a global arena to affect economic development, political stability, social development, and environmental sustainability. These consequences show how change in one situation (e.g., creating jobs and revenue through the oil pipeline project) operates interdependently to create positive, negative, and unintended consequences (e.g., polluting drinking water, reducing farmland, decreasing biodiversity) in other circumstances. Global leadership in the pipeline case must address multiple human, economic, and environmental dynamics involving the oil companies, development organizations, affected communities, environmental conditions, and governments to deal with problems on this scale.

Appeal to Common Humanity

An appeal to common humanity within and across boundaries, perspectives, and worldviews is another transcending component of global leadership. Gardner (1995) contended that individuals involved in global leadership engage in cross-boundary experiences that enable them to recognize that what members of the global audience or constituency have in common "is only that which is most fundamentally human to each individual. . . . They must communicate in terms of what is commonsense and commonplace for people worldwide; they therefore must communicate in the most fundamental terms of humanity" (p. 12; see also Adler, 1997, p. 177).

Mahatma Gandhi and later Martin Luther King, Jr. were able to convey to people across their respective countries and across the world that subjugation of another human group was morally wrong and that "members of the species must learn to face one another as equals, unafraid" (Gardner, 1995, p. 277). These appeals to the common humanity among people spurred individuals from different walks of life to join together for change that enriches the quality of life for others and themselves.

Broadened Identity and Vision

The appeal to common humanity is connected to one more transcending component—cultivating a broadened identity and vision. Actors involved in global leadership help participants and larger constituencies tap into their common humanity by shaping an expanded identity beyond a single culture, country, or context. Gandhi's statement that "we are all, first and foremost, human beings and we must relate to one another on that naked basis" (Gardner, 1995, p. 283) served to broaden a sense of identity across groups and nations, colonizers and colonists. Using this broadened identity, leaders shape a vision that has meaning for people's lives and work around the world (Gardner, 1995, p. 288; Adler, 1997, pp. 175–176). Gandhi used the broadened identity of being, first, human beings to help people envision a new way of leading change, which demonstrates "that it is possible to resist injustice in a way that is honorable, does not involve counterattack, and may even bring about resolutions that empower all concerned" (Gardner, 1995, p. 275).

Use of Stories

Often participants in global leadership appeal to common humanity and evoke a broadened identity through their capacity to transmit and embody stories. Gardner (1995) stressed that transnational leaders achieve effectiveness through the stories they tell and embody (p. 9). These stories reflect their authentic experiences across boundaries and their understanding of the common humanity embedded in these experiences. They tell stories "about themselves and their groups, about where they were coming from and where they were headed, about what was to be feared, struggled against, and dreamed about" (Gardner, 1995, p. 15). These illustrations of past struggles and future states can cultivate an image in the minds and hearts of listeners that transforms possibilities for change from abstract ideas to concrete images of attainable realities.

The Global Leadership Process

What do these transcendent components of global leadership mean in relation to the process of global leadership? Adler (1997) combined ideas from two scholarly works to describe "a process by which members of . . . [the world community] are empowered to work together synergistically toward a common vision and common goals . . . [resulting in an] improve[ment in] the quality of life" on and for the planet (Hollander, 1985, as cited in Adler, 1997, p. 174; see also Astin & Leland 1991, p. 8).

The process of global leadership involves participants in the hard work of addressing cross-sector, transcultural, transnational issues like those surrounding the Chad-Cameroon pipeline. As a result, the process compels participants to focus on two seemingly conflicting elements at the same time—transcending and inclusive components of global leadership. Participants must transcend sector, culture, and nation-state boundaries while including the differing perspectives and worldviews of the people involved. The challenge for leadership throughout the process is to keep participants focused on the core of what it means to be human, while helping them understand and draw on the heterogeneity of actors and stakeholders affected by the process.

Inclusive Components

Though global leadership crosses multiple terrains, it is not simply a blending of humanity, cultures, sectors, and national identities. The Chad-Cameroon pipeline vignette suggests that global leadership incorporates inclusive components that represent the unique and varied aspects of people and issues in the change process. An underlying assumption of these inclusive components is that the human community has a greater chance of understanding the key issues, engaging in creative or innovative work, and creating effective, sustainable change by involving heterogeneous stakeholders in a mutual problem-solving arena. In this section, we examine several aspects of difference that are often present in a global leadership process.

Different Sectors and Stakeholders

Actors in the pipeline vignette represent different sectors of society, including business, development agencies, NGOs, and government. These sectors bring diverse contributions, perspectives, and expectations to the Chad-Cameroon situation, and their inclusion in a global leadership process is critical to the outcome. These sectors "encompass multiple stakeholders," which have a stake—a claim of some sort such as ownership, legal or moral rights, an investment, or a bond (Waddock, 2006, pp. 7–8)—that links them to the purpose. The pipeline vignette involves an array of stakeholders, including oil companies Exxon, Chevron, and Petronas; international financial institutions, including the World Bank and the International Monetary Fund; community members represented by the NGOs CILONG and EIRENE; environmental activists, such as the Environmental Defense Fund and the CIEL; and the governments of Chad and Cameroon. Each set of actors has a unique stake in the situation that must be addressed, rather than simply blended, in the process.

Different Cultures and Perspectives

Another inclusive component of global leadership focuses on multiple cultures. Culture is generally understood as the shared experiences of a group of people that are learned and transmitted through language, beliefs, values, practices, norms, symbols, and traditions, among other factors. How do multiple cultures interact in a global leadership context? Researchers in leadership studies know little about how different cultures interact in global leadership settings such as the Chad-Cameroon pipeline scenario. Much of the contemporary research in leadership studies on culture and leadership has been conducted in the context of organizations (companies) situated in different national cultures (Goldsmith, Greenberg, Robertson & Hu-Chan, 2003; Hofstede, 1980, 2001; House, Hanges, Javidan, Dorfman & Gupta, 2004). The research does not specifically address situations where actors from various cultures and contexts come together to work on interconnected problems. These studies focus on how culture, and in some cases subculture, affects organizational leadership (managers) in different countries—stimulated no doubt by the growth of transnational business.

Information from these studies provides insights into organizational leadership in different cultures. Geert Hofstede's (1980, 2001) study of different national cultures collected data from 116,000 respondents working in subsidiaries of one multinational company in more than 50 countries. He identified five main dimensions on which country cultures vary: power distance; uncertainty avoidance; individualism versus collectivism; masculinity versus femininity; and long-term versus short-term orientation (Hofstede, 2001, p. 29). Hofstede (2001) emphasized that culture is extremely stable over time and change comes primarily from the outside "in the form of forces of nature or forces of human beings: trade, conquest, economical or political dominance, and technological breakthroughs" (p. 34).

The Global Leadership and Organizational Behavior Effectiveness (GLOBE) study conducted by Robert House et al. (2004) surveyed 17,000 managers in more than 950 organizations in 62 countries.[3] They grouped the countries into 10 clustered regions of the world—Latin Europe, Anglo, Nordic Europe, Germanic Europe, Eastern Europe, Latin America, Middle East, Sub-Saharan Africa, Southern Asia, and Confucian Asia. Building on the work of Hofstede and others, they developed nine dimensions on which cultures differ:

Uncertainty avoidance—the extent to which members of an organization or society strive to avoid uncertainty by relying on established social norms, rituals, and bureaucratic practices;

Power distance—the degree to which members of an organization or society expect and agree that power should be stratified and concentrated at higher levels of an organization;

Institutional collectivism—the degree to which organizational and societal institutional practices encourage and reward collective distribution of resources and collective action;

In-group collectivism—the degree to which individuals express pride, loyalty, and cohesiveness in their organizations and families;

Gender egalitarianism—the degree to which an organization or a society minimizes gender role differences while promoting gender equality;

Assertiveness—the degree to which individuals in organizations or societies are assertive, confrontational, and aggressive in social relationships;

Future orientation—the degree to which individuals in organizations or societies engage in future-oriented behaviors such as planning, investing in the future, and delaying individual or collective gratification;

Performance orientation—the degree to which an organization or society encourages and rewards group members for performance improvement and excellence; and

Humane orientation—the degree to which individuals in organizations or societies encourage and reward individuals in organizations for being fair, altruistic, friendly, generous, caring, and kind to others. (pp. 11–13)

On the basis of the country clusters in the GLOBE study, the Chad-Cameroon situation involves actors primarily from the regions of sub-Saharan Africa (NGOs representing the people's interest, national governments), Anglo (economic development agencies, two oil companies, an environmental NGO), and southern Asia (one oil company). Actors in a global leadership process would need a basic understanding of the various cultures of these representatives. Table 10.1 uses data from the GLOBE study to indicate the cultural practices (what people actually do) and values (what people believe should be done) of the representatives from the three regions in the pipeline vignette.

TABLE 10.1 Comparison of Cultural Dimensions in the Chad-Cameroon Pipeline Vignette

Cultural Dimension	Sub-Saharan Africa		Anglo		Southern Asia	
	Practices (As is)	Values (Should be)	Practices (As is)	Values (Should be)	Practices (As is)	Values (Should be)
Performance Orientation	Mid-Score	Mid-Score	High	Mid-Score	Mid-Score	Mid-Score
Assertiveness	Mid-Score	Mid-Score	Mid-Score	Mid-Score	Mid-Score	High
Future Orientation	Mid-Score	High	Mid-Score	Mid-Score	Mid-Score	High
Humane Orientation	High	Mid-Score	Mid-Score	Mid-Score	High	Mid-Score
Institutional Collectivism	Mid-Score	Mid-Score	Mid-Score	Low	Mid-Score	High
In-Group Collectivism	Mid-Score	Mid-Score	Low	High	High	Mid-Score
Gender Egalitarianism	Mid-Score	Mid-Score	Mid-Score	High	Mid-Score	Low
Power Distance	Mid-Score	Mid-Score	Mid-Score	Mid-Score	Mid-Score	Mid-Score
Uncertainty Avoidance	Mid-Score	High	Mid-Score	Low	Mid-Score	High

SOURCE: Adapted from House, R. J., Hanges, P. J., Javidan, M., Dorfman, P. W., & Gupta, V. (Eds.), *Culture, Leadership, and Organizations: The GLOBE Study of 62 Societies,* pp. 193–194, copyright © 2004, Sage Publications, Inc. Reprinted with permission.

The ratings of representatives, according to the table, vary most in their "practices" of in-group collectivism, whereas their "values" vary most in the areas of gender egalitarianism and institutional collectivism. Representatives from these regions scored their practices in the same range on six cultural dimensions—assertiveness, future orientation, institutional collectivism, gender egalitarianism, and power distance—yet their values differed on all but two of the six dimensions (assertiveness and power distance). Still, it is difficult to know based on the GLOBE study how practices and values interact in situations where participants from these cultures come together in a joint endeavor.

The GLOBE study is one of the largest and most ambitious studies to date on culture and leadership. It has made a substantial scholarly contribution to the field and highlighted the considerable range of research that still remains. It is hoped that future studies will examine whether these cultural dimensions or some dimensions yet to be discovered are the most authentic and fitting ones for the study of culture and leadership within and across organizations, communities, political arenas, and other contexts. The studies will also need to examine other kinds of leaders and participants (from NGOs, government and politics, religion, and communities) in cross-cultural settings. Researchers in the GLOBE study and other projects realized that their work is a beginning step toward a larger agenda. Dorfman and House (2004) acknowledged the "ultimate destination is to validate a cross-level integrated theory specifying the relationship among culture and societal, organizational, and leadership effectiveness" (p. 66). Current studies of culture and leadership make it clear that cultural distinctions must be understood, acknowledged, and included in global leadership processes to resolve problems or generate new methods and outcomes.

Different Gender Perspectives

In the global arena, leadership appears to emphasize more cooperative, participative, interactional, and relational styles based on deep personal relationships (Adler, 1997, p. 185). Adler's study of global leadership pointed out that women and many non-American male leaders display patterns and trends that seem especially useful for leadership in the 21st century. These patterns, which are generally seen as feminine in North America, often reflect both male and female styles in other parts of the world and in global leadership settings:

> Not surprisingly, relational skills (labeled by anthropologists as particularism and by North Americans as typically feminine) outperform the seemingly more objective approach of following the same rules with everyone (labeled as universalism by anthropologists and as typically male by North Americans). (p. 186)

Women leaders in the study used processes that seem increasingly significant for global leadership by men and women. They include incorporating and symbolizing people's aspirations for hope, change, and unity; focusing on vision, mission, or cause rather than hierarchical status; and developing broad-based support as a basis of power (Adler, 1997, pp. 187–189).

National culture does not seem to play the role in selection of women leaders that people might suspect. Countries led by the 37 women[4] in Adler's (1997) study represented six of the major world religions, including 4 women prime ministers from predominantly Muslim countries and some from the world's largest and smallest countries, richest and poorest countries, and the most socially and economically advantaged and disadvantaged countries (p. 187). Seemingly female-friendly countries, where women have equal rights, do not elect a higher proportion of women presidents and prime ministers, and in the business sector, companies that select women for senior leadership positions do not always implement the most female-friendly policies (Adler, 1997, p. 187). These occurrences may reflect differences identified previously in the GLOBE study between cultural practices (what people actually do) and cultural values (what people believe should be done).

There is still limited information on how the trends and patterns in Adler's (1997) study and others intersect when men and women come together in global leadership processes. Like studies of culture, there is a need for more research and theory building on global leadership processes that involve men and women.

Different Religious Perspectives

Participants in global leadership processes often come from different religious traditions that help shape their perspectives, worldviews, and identity. Inclusion of religious diversity (beliefs, traditions, practices, dress, and speech) in global leadership fosters what Douglas Hicks (2003) referred to as respectful pluralism (pp. 159–160). Hicks identified several moral claims of respectful pluralism that assert the following: all persons possess an inviolable human dignity, every human being deserves to be accorded respect, and all human beings possess equal dignity and thus deserve equal respect (p. 167). Respectful pluralism allows people to communicate—on their own terms—across religious, spiritual, and moral divides; provides freedom for them to draw on their religiously based ideas and symbols as they work; and allows them to explain their beliefs and describe how these beliefs affect the way they approach work (p. 165).

Though Hicks (2003) describes respectful pluralism in the context of workplaces, it seems to apply equally to global leadership processes in which differing religious perspectives converge. It provides a framework for understanding and promoting interactions among diverse participants in global leadership processes. It requires leadership that enables the development of pluralism among participants by deliberately creating environments that promote active engagement and a convergence of meaningful relationships among diverse people (pp. 184–185).

Convening Components

Global leadership calls for convening components to bring together stakeholders from multiple sectors, cultures, and countries to work toward problem solving, innovation, or outcomes that benefit all parties. Convening components of global leadership include the power to invite and attract parties to the process and the assurance of fairness in the process.

Power to Invite and Attract Parties

Adler's (1997) description of global leadership makes only a vague reference to power. She mentioned that members of the world community are empowered to work together, but there is no indication of the source of their empowerment or how it operates (p. 174).

The power to invite and attract parties is an initiating leadership function that stems from both formal authority and nonconstituted sources. Organizational and political actors draw power and authority from their constituted positions and institutions, whereas actors from NGOs and activist groups rely more heavily on social power and credibility to represent affected communities and the environment. Whether global leaders hold official positions of authority or work as nonconstituted change leaders, their diverse experiences and range of contacts often allow them to work through nontraditional or "extragovernmental" channels (Gardner, 1995, p. 283). By convening cross-boundary groups, they create new forms and methods of working or generate new structures using these nontraditional channels and experiences (Gardner, 1995, p. 268).

In a cross-boundary situation like the Chad-Cameroon pipeline, either set of actors has a source of power that permits them to invite participants and convene a global leadership process. They would each need to assess whether their singular power to convene is sufficient for the situation or whether they should convene in partnership with one or more groups of actors. Though the pipeline vignette does not conclude with any group convening the collective stakeholders, it would be feasible for one or more actors to initiate change by inviting the parties into a global leadership process.

Assurance of Fairness in the Process

Assurance of fairness in the process is another convening component. In addition to their apparent stake in the situation, participants may be willing to accept an invitation to join a global leadership process if they perceive that the process is fair. Conveners that do not have a stake or predisposition regarding an issue could serve as fair facilitators of processes with diverse participants. A third party with high credibility and no predisposition toward one side or another could also facilitate or mediate a fair process with diverse participants, whether or not the convener is a party in the situation (Carlson, 2006, p. 58). Diverse stakeholders are more willing to join and remain engaged in a process when participants are invited to a neutral or safe meeting place; the convener or facilitator is impartial and frames the issues in an unbiased way; no party is dominant, and each one can discuss, listen, and ask questions; parties demonstrate ongoing commitment to the process; and participants keep working to consider options and work toward viable solutions (Carlson, 2006, p. 59).

Generative Components

Generative components emerge from global leadership that facilitates interaction among participants across boundaries of difference for the purpose of creative problem solving or innovation. One generative component that can emerge from global leadership is conflict capital. Conflict capital (akin to other forms of capital) is a resource that results from discovering, understanding, and making use of differences among participants or stakeholders (Hickman, 1998, p. 408).

Conflict can contain the substance of remarkable problem solving, creativity, and innovation, as well as divisiveness and harm. Developing conflict capital requires a process that allows participants to discover the perspectives and humanity of each group—how participants see an issue or problem, what stake participants have in the situation, and what participants hope to gain from engaging in the process. Conflict capital can only develop and accrue, however, if and when the parties can be persuaded to come together. As a result, an initial generative component of global leadership is cultivation of participant readiness for collective engagement. Other generative components of global leadership entail discovery of the root cause of conflict, mediator perspective taking, adaptive work, and new public diplomacy.

Cultivation of Participant Readiness

Some types of conflict require parties to engage in considerable work prior to meeting. In situations such as ethnic conflict, where positions appear nearly intractable, global leadership aimed toward conflict resolution or conflict transformation must cultivate participant readiness and persuade stakeholders that there are members of the other groups "to whom it is worth talking" (Ross, 2000, p. 1002). Marc Ross (2000) offered two hypotheses concerning conflict in these conditions: "(1) that until key preconditions are met, competing groups are unlikely to make effective progress towards an agreement; and (2) that the development of cooperation between small groups in local settings can produce changes which spill over and produce s shift in the larger conflict" (p. 1003).

Ross (2000) identified six theories of practice pertinent to conflict resolutions in seemingly intractable ethnic conflict: community relations, principled negotiation, human needs, psychoanalytically rooted identity, intercultural miscommunications, and conflict transformation. Although there are differences among these theories, they all share several common elements—involving the parties in conflict in the resolutions; emphasizing the significance of the process, not just the outcomes of conflict resolution; allowing parties in a conflict to conceptualize and own the outcome; and recognizing conflict resolution as a long-term process involving both pre- and postsettlement tasks (pp. 1027–1028).

Discovery of Underlying Causes of Conflict

Global leadership requires a process of comprehensive discovery to unravel the underlying causes of conflict. Without this discovery, conflicting parties ultimately find it difficult to fully recognize the situations or issues that led to their conflict or to gain perspective on how to work toward a potential solution. Frances Stewart (2002) demonstrated this point in her analysis of the root causes of violent conflict in developing countries. She pointed out major cultural and economic root causes of war in these situations that need to be fully illuminated.

Stewart (2002) explained that groups of people who fight together see themselves as belonging to the same cultural group and fight to maintain their cultural autonomy. They attribute the war to "primordial" ethnic passions, which make the conflict seem intractable. Global leadership processes become more feasible when certain cultural factors can be disentangled based on the points Stewart enumerated:

- Individuals may be born into certain cultures; however, cultures are constructed and chosen, and many people have multiple identities;
- Many identities that seem so strong in certain areas of the world today were actually invented by colonial powers for administrative purposes and have only weak links to a group's pre-colonial history;
- The boundaries of these identities are generally fluid and have been described as "fuzzy" sets; and
- In wars, political leaders may deliberately rework historical memories to engender or strengthen these cultural identities in the competition for power and resources. (p. 342)

Stewart (2002) cited four economic hypotheses that contribute to understanding the factors that predispose groups to intrastate wars—group motivation, private motivation, failure of the social contract, and environmental degradation:

- *Group motivation hypothesis*—Based on the idea of horizontal inequalities (resentments inspired by group differences), group resentments often lead to war when there is a disparity between groups in the distribution and exercise of political and economic power. In these cases, relatively deprived groups are likely to seek (or be persuaded by their leaders to seek) redress, and relatively privileged groups may be motivated to fight to protect their privilege from deprived groups. Horizontal inequalities are most likely to lead to conflict when they are substantial, consistent, and increasing over time.

- *Private motivation hypothesis*—This is commonly known as the greed hypothesis, where individuals with relatively few opportunities to prosper are motivated to fight because of the perceived benefits of war, such as employment as soldiers (especially for uneducated young men) or opportunities to loot, profiteer from shortage and aid, and trade in drugs, diamonds, and other commodities. In a study of the greed hypothesis, researchers found that greater male education to the higher secondary level reduced the risk of war.

- *Failure of the social contract*—Conflict occurs when government fails to live up to its hypothetical social contract with citizens to deliver services and provide reasonable economic conditions. The social contract breaks down as poverty rates rise and services worsen. Research shows that the incidence of conflict is higher among countries with low per capita incomes, life expectancy, and economic growth.

- *Green war hypothesis*—This hypothesis indicates that people fight when environmental degradation (decrease in water supply or falling agricultural productivity) becomes a source of poverty. Though this hypothesis does not purport that people fight to secure environmental riches, evidence is contradictory. It seems that both environmental poverty and resource riches can be associated with conflict. (p. 344)

The Chad-Cameroon pipeline vignette illustrates many of these interconnected issues. Discovering the root cause of conflict provides critical information and guidance for global leadership processes and initiatives. These insights help actors in multistakeholder forums focus on the fundamental problems that require policy and resource development so that sustainable solutions can be identified and implemented.

Mediator Perspective Taking

Once parties agree to convene in a global forum, leadership must involve them in a process of genuine engagement and participation. Mark Gerzon (2006) contended that in multistakeholder situations the mediator represents a leadership perspective that transforms differences into opportunities by serving as a steward of the whole rather than an owner of the parts (p. 6). This leadership approach places conflict at the center of the process so that participants or stakeholders understand differing perspectives and use these differences to generate original solutions. Mediators "lead through conflict" to enable participants to understand differences beyond superficial levels and to deal with their complexity and scope honestly and creatively (p. 4). The mediator approach does not require actors in the process to be conflict-resolution professionals. Instead, it provides a mediator perspective for leading in cross-boundary settings and incorporates practices to implement this approach. These practices are outlined in the Global Change Practices section in this chapter.

Adaptive Work

Often, conflict in global settings stems from perceived or real differences in the values of stakeholders. Ronald Heifetz (1994) explained that adaptive work (described in Chapter 5) "consists of the learning required to address conflicts in the values people hold, or to diminish the gap between the values people stand for and the reality they face" (p. 22). Leadership mobilizes participants from different sectors, cultures, and countries to engage in the adaptive work required to address or lessen the gap between value conflicts among individuals. Success is influenced by the openness of participants to diverse and even competing value perspectives and their willingness to use creative tensions and conflict to generate new knowledge, approaches, and outcomes.

New Public Diplomacy

Emerging scholarship in the field of new public diplomacy (NPD) may provide insight into global leadership and change in world affairs. Eytan Gilboa (2008) defined new public diplomacy as follows:

> the interactivity between states and nonstate actors; utilization of "soft power" [acting through cooperation rather than coercion based on the attractiveness of a nation's values, culture, and policies], two-way communication, strategic public diplomacy [using scientific knowledge and methods of public opinion research], media framing, information management; PR, nation branding, self-presentation, and e-image; domestication of foreign policy; and addressing both short- and long-term issues. (p. 58)

This new attention to public diplomacy is a result of revolutions in three areas: communication technologies (the Internet and global broadcast networks); politics (involvement of nonstate actors, such as NGOs, civil society groups, and individuals in political processes); and international relations (change in the goals and means of foreign policy through such techniques as communication, education, and persuasion) (Gilboa, 2008, p. 56). Gilboa contended that "favorable image and reputation around the world, achieved through attraction and persuasion," have become more important in international relations than outcomes acquired through military and economic means (p. 56). Conflict is an ever-present factor in this process; however, NPD provides a greater opportunity for the development of generative conflict or conflict capital over hard power (military and economic) responses to conflict.

The search for a theory of NPD has much in common with the search for global leadership theory because both involve processes among state and nonstate actors across multiple sectors, cultures, and countries. Gilboa (2008) suggested that a multidisciplinary approach involving researchers and practitioners is needed to develop a coherent theory. Conceivably, the work of researchers and practitioners in NPD and leadership studies could prove mutually beneficial in the search for new frameworks.

Ethical Component

An essential challenge for the study of leadership is to determine what morally good and effective leadership entails (Ciulla, 2004, p. 18). Ethics in a global leadership context, like other contexts, involves working out the rights and obligations individuals have and share with others—that is, setting standards and making decisions based on what ought to be done in regard to those we work with and serve (see definition in Chapter 1). In a global leadership context, however, individuals from different sectors, cultures, and countries must work out these rights and obligations together while attempting to solve cross-boundary problems or generate new approaches and outcomes. Obviously, there are no simple answers to this complex challenge.

Robin Attfield (2006) proposed that one feature of a global ethic must be cosmopolitanism (p. 5). There are two interlinked strands in the notion of cosmopolitanism, as identified by Kwame Appiah (2006):

One is the idea that we have obligations to others, obligations that stretch beyond those to whom we are related by the ties of kith and kind, or even the more formal ties of a shared citizenship. The other is that we take seriously the value not just of human life but of particular human lives, which means taking an interest in the practices and beliefs that lend them significance. People are different, the cosmopolitan knows, and there is much to learn from differences. Because there are so many human possibilities worth exploring, we neither expect nor desire that every person or every society should converge on a single mode of life. (p. xv)

Cosmopolitanism is neither a new nor an undisputed concept. It dates back to "the Cynics of the fourth century B.C., who first coined the expression cosmopolitan, 'citizen of the cosmos'" (Appiah, 2006, p. xiv). Later, Voltaire expressed the ideal cosmopolitan as follows:

[one who regards] all the people of the earth as so many branches of a single family, and the universe as a state, of which they, with innumerable other rational beings, are citizens, promoting together under the general laws of nature the perfection of the whole, while each in his own fashion is busy about his own well-being. (Voltaire, as quoted in Appiah, 2006, p. xv)

Appiah (2006) warned, "There is a sense in which cosmopolitanism is the name not of the solution but of the challenge" (p. xv). Attfield (2006) outlined a global ethic she called "cosmopolitan consequentialism and global cooperation." This ethic incorporates cosmopolitanism, described previously; adds a biocentric perspective that "locates value in whatever is good in human and nonhuman lives"; includes a form of consequentialism (described by Attfield as total view practice-consequentialism), by which individuals assess the moral consequences of their actions, including foreseeable consequences (i.e., results or outcomes that individuals could have anticipated) and foreseeable omissions (i.e., results of inaction or lack of action that individuals could have anticipated); and entails cooperation among actors in matters of global problem solving or governance (Attfield, 2006, pp. 12–13, 16).

Working through the challenge of cosmopolitanism and other possible contributions to a global ethic might begin and evolve through a process of discourse (described in Chapter 1). Discourse in a global setting provides space for articulation of different narratives of practice, beliefs, values, cultures, and identities, among other factors. Dialogue is used in this process to create thoughtful exchange and interaction, make assumptions explicit, generate mutual understanding, and take action with regard to the issues and problems for which the group is assembled. The process is intended to foster a spirit of inquiry and reflective questioning in a setting where, according to Seyla Benhabib (2005), participants honor norms of egalitarian reciprocity (equal respect and consideration of all persons), voluntary self-ascription (ability to assert or claim one's own identity and culture), and freedom of exit and association (autonomy to depart or separate) (p. 756). Continued work by scholars and practitioners on ethics in these deeply plural settings will be central to the development of good and effective leadership in a global context.

Global Leadership and Theory Building

There are many questions to explore. How is global leadership initiated, by whom, and for what purpose? What is the relationship between or among the people in the process—are they leaders and followers (participants) or an assembly of leaders with a convener or moderator? How are parties motivated to come to the process or work together? Do the goals or visions of global leadership need to be common goals or can parties have differentiated goals and work together on the interconnected components? What constitutes an improvement in the quality of life from the perspective of the group and the people who might be affected? What effect does global leadership have on duly authorized governments and their constituents?

It seems that leadership in the global arena encompasses multiple forms of leadership and many types of leaders—leaders as initiators, leaders as conveners, leaders as the creators of transcending vision and moral direction, leaders as advocates for inclusion and facilitators of respectful pluralism, and leaders as mediators, collaborators, and guiding forces for adaptive work and public diplomacy. These and many other forms comprise the collective expressions of global leadership. All participants in the process are vitally important, and their capabilities as leaders and participants are essential at different points in the process. Some move in and out of leader and participant roles, whereas others maintain consistent roles throughout the process. These dynamics frame the course of inquiry into global leadership theory and practice.

Global Change Practices

Much more has been written about global change and leadership practices than about global leadership theory—especially with regard to multinational companies and multilateral partnerships. Even so, there is no set of practices generally agreed on by contributors to the subject. In this section, we identify several current practices in the literature that may well contribute to leading change in global settings.

Horizontal Networks and Experiences

Chapter 5 discussed horizontal networks in relation to community change. Adler (1997) identified the use of horizontal networks and experiences as vital preparation for global leadership in her study of women global leaders. She observed that "transferring across organizations, sectors of society, and areas of the world allows leaders to develop alternative perspectives and an understanding of context that is almost impossible to acquire within a single setting" (p. 190). Gardner's (1995) work indicates that transnational leaders often acquire experience that facilitates their global leadership while living or working in diverse geographic locations and cultures, and leaders draw ideas and viewpoints from a range of heterogeneous contacts (p. 287).

Global leaders gain and use alternative perspectives and diverse experiences that increase their capacity to engage in and understand different communities and domains. Joanne Ciulla (2005) indicated that out of 179 heads of state more than 45% of these world leaders were educated in countries other than their own. She captured the idea of leadership informed by building horizontal networks and experiences in a concept called bridge leaders. Ciulla (2000) characterized bridge leaders as "those who leave their cultures for some significant time. They live, go to school, or travel in another culture or cultures, then return home and become leaders or take on leadership positions" (p. 27). She hypothesized that bridge leaders may broaden their moral repertoires through exposure to other cultures and experiences that allow them to bridge between their culture's value systems and others to create a third way of understanding the world and approaching problems (Ciulla, 2000, pp. 27–28). Because this research is ongoing, it is too early to draw conclusions about whether bridge experiences broaden the moral repertoires of these heads of state. However, it is apparent that many global leaders see value in cross-cultural experiences and seek opportunities to immerse themselves in new cultural settings outside their local community or nation-state.

Conflict-Capital Development

Conflict capital, as described previously, may develop in processes where participants work to understand differences and use them to lead change in a global context. Adaptive, collaborative, and mediator practices, among others, are examples of processes with the potential for building conflict capital.

Adaptive Practices

Heifetz (1994) identified several adaptive practices for leadership processes where value conflicts arise as participants attempt to accommodate the values they hold to the reality of actual situations. He identified five principles for leadership:

1. *Identify the adaptive challenge.* Diagnose the situation in light of the values at stake, and unbundle the issues that come with it.

2. *Keep the level of distress within a tolerable range for doing adaptive work.* To use the pressure cooker analogy, keep the heat up without blowing up the vessel.

3. *Focus attention on ripening issues and not on stress-reducing distractions.* Identify which issues can currently engage attention; and while directing attention to them, counteract work avoidance mechanisms like denial, scapegoating, externalizing the enemy, pretending the problem is technical, or attacking individuals rather than issues.

4. *Give the work back to people, but at a rate they can stand.* Place and develop responsibility by putting the pressure on the people with the problem.

5. *Protect voices of leadership without authority.* [In situations where individuals leading the process have formal authority], give cover to those who raise hard questions and generate distress—people who point to the internal contradictions of the society. These individuals often will have latitude to provoke rethinking that authorities do not have. (p. 128)

Collaborative Practices

Collaboration "is a process through which parties who see different aspects of a problem can constructively explore their differences and search for solutions that go beyond their own limited vision of what is possible" (Gray, 1998, p. 467).

Global problems typically fit the characteristics of problems for which collaborative models are appropriate:

- The problems are ill-defined, or there is disagreement about how they should be defined.
- Several stakeholders have a vested interest in the problems and are interdependent.
- These stakeholders are not necessarily identified a priori or organized in any systematic way.
- There may be a disparity of power or resources for dealing with the problems among the stakeholders.
- Stakeholders may have different levels of expertise and different access to information about the problems.
- The problems are often characterized by technical complexity and scientific uncertainty.
- Differing perspectives on the problems often lead to adversarial relationships among the stakeholders.
- Incremental or unilateral efforts to deal with the problems typically produce less than satisfactory solutions.
- Existing processes for addressing the problems have proved insufficient and many even exacerbate them. (Gray, 1998, p. 472)

Participants involved in collaboration join such processes if they believe they can benefit from taking part and they have confidence that their interest will be presented, heard, and understood; that the process is protected, often by a third party, from cooptation or lack of fairness; and that the process is structured so participants own the process and outcomes (Gray, 1998, pp. 478–479). Once participants join the process, collaboration focuses participants' attention on the vital ways problems or issues interconnect in a situation. This focus on interdependence challenges participants to recognize why they need to engage each other in a problem-solving or innovation process; for this reason, interdependence is a fundamental component of collaboration.

Collaboration emerges as a function of the participants' engagement in the process and empowers them to create and own the process and outcomes. Barbara Gray (1998) described the outcome of collaboration as "weaving together of multiple and diverse viewpoints into a mosaic replete with new insights and directions for action agreed on by all the stakeholders" (p. 474). However, Gray acknowledged that collaboration is not amenable to all situations, especially in cases where parties are unwilling or unable to engage each other in this manner. Concerns about possible cooptation, distributional disputes, and lack of fairness may prevent parties from coming together unless these issues can be dispelled prior to initiating the collaboration process.

Mediator Practices

Gerzon (2006) synthesized his and other colleagues' mediator practices into eight tools for leading through conflict:

1. *Integral vision:* committing ourselves to hold all sides of the conflict, in all their complexity, in our minds—and in our hearts.

2. *Systems thinking:* identifying all (or as many as possible) of the significant elements related to the conflict situation and understanding the relationships between these elements.

3. *Presence:* applying all our mental, emotional, and spiritual resources to witnessing the conflict of which we are now a part.

4. *Inquiry:* asking questions that elicit essential information about the conflict that is vital to understanding how to transform it.

5. *Conscious conversation:* becoming aware of our full range of choices about how we speak and listen.

6. *Dialogue:* communicating in order to catalyze the human capacity for bridging and innovation.

7. *Bridging:* building partnerships and alliances that cross the borders that divide an organization or a community.

8. *Innovation:* fostering social or entrepreneurial breakthroughs that create new options for moving through conflicts. (p. 7)

The challenge for actors in the change process is to create "a vision of what is possible"—that is, to imagine a situation where the conflict has been transformed—then hold on to that vision throughout the process (Gerzon, 2006, p. 225). The result of leading in this manner could well produce substantial conflict capital.

Systemic Change

Peter Senge and colleagues (Senge, Lichtenstein, Kaeufer, Bradbury, & Carroll, 2007) conducted research focused on several change initiatives where cross-sector groups sought collaborative solutions to sustainability issues (social and ecological imbalances created by globalization). Researchers found three interconnected types of work involved in collaboration for systemic change—conceptual, making sense of complex issues; relational, far-reaching, unorchestrated dialogue for thinking, learning, and asking questions together; and action driven, building new change initiatives together (p. 45). Senge et al. (2007) summarized the lessons learned from work in these three areas. Lessons from the conceptual work include the following:

- Build community through thinking together and sharing. When conceptual frameworks are developed collaboratively, the process builds community and fosters more extended application and testing;
- Achieve simplicity without reduction. Clarity must not come at the expense of oversimplification and trivialization of complex issues. (p. 47)

Lessons from the relational work include the following:

- Dialogue groups emerge from deep question and longings. Participants shape their collective futures in "conversations that matter" while recognizing and engaging powerful questions seriously in a spirit of dialogue and joint exploration;
- Nurturing relational space can be systematic and purposeful. Provide free space for participants to simply explore what emerges and encourage them to bring specific methods to the group (personal check-ins or basic principles of dialogue) out of which initiatives will self-organize;
- Once it is recognized and legitimized, deepening relational space also infuses results-oriented work. Effective relational work encourages diverging conversations, asks difficult questions and helps confront dysfunctional practices and attitudes—practices that benefit action-oriented work. (pp. 48–49)

Lessons from the action-oriented work include the following:

- It can take significant time to bring together the diversity of players needed for effective collaborative action. A common principle for all system-change processes is that the people who are present should represent all aspects and stakeholders of the processes;
- Systems thinking is essential for change, but it also can be messy and uncomfortable. Systems thinking can help to clarify interdependencies and complex change dynamics; and, at the same time, seeing systems *together* means allowing for different, sometimes conflicting views;
- Radical methods are needed for collaborative action work. New approaches for organizing complex change processes and for large scale dialogue like the World Café—a process for leading collaborative dialogue and knowledge sharing, particularly for large groups—will also be needed. (pp. 50–51)

The practices that foster collaborative work for systemic change seem promising for actors involved in leading global change similar to the sustainability initiative portrayed by Senge and colleagues (2007). Specifically, these practices appear to support the potential components of global leadership described earlier, including transcending, inclusive, and generative elements.

Ethical Practices

Three practices relate to Attfield's (2006) proposed global ethic of cosmopolitan consequentialism and global cooperation—reciprocal care, harmony with nature and sustainability, and scenario building. First, reciprocal care—to create communities where every person matters and each person's welfare and dignity is respected and supported (see Chapter 4)—seems most relevant to the moral framework of cosmopolitanism. Allen et al. (1998) designated several leadership practices to implement reciprocal care:

- developing trusting relationships;
- attending to the well-being (basic needs and human rights) of others and providing opportunities for them to sustain themselves;
- supporting basic freedom for others and providing opportunities for them to maintain freedom for themselves; and
- maintaining opportunities for people to make choices for themselves that are not harmful to others, and honoring the choices they make. (p. 57)

In a global context, these leadership practices seemingly support a cosmopolitan ethic in which each person is of equal moral concern and should be taken equally into account.

The second practice—promoting harmony with nature and thereby providing sustainability for future generations (Allen et al., 1998, p. 56)—relates to Attfield's (2006) moral concern for a biocentric perspective that values the good in human and nonhuman lives including the lives of future generations. The following specific components are included in this practice:

- understanding the interdependent relationship between human and natural systems and working to enhance their viability;
- practicing "enoughness" (bigger or more is not always better);
- achieving balance in emotional, spiritual, and physical aspects of life;
- using a long-term perspective thereby creating viability for current and future generations;
- generating and supporting systems thinking (wholistic thinking) as a basis for action;
- facilitating self-organizing, self-regulating, and self-renewing systems;
- using natural conflict to foster growth and change;
- recognizing and promoting the spiritual connectedness of all life; and
- generating and sustaining peace among ourselves and aiding peace efforts globally. (Allen et al., 1998, p. 56)

The third practice, scenario building, relates to Attfield's (2006) consequentialism component, particularly with regard to foreseeable consequences and foreseeable omissions. As indicated in Chapter 4, scenario building is a practice championed by Schwartz (1996) to help actors in leadership processes use information gathered from scanning the environment (physical and human) to construct probable situations and outcomes. Participants identify central questions, rank and weigh environmental forces and uncertainties that are most significant to the questions, and plot several probable scenarios. Actors make decisions and take action based on early indicators of movement toward or away from a desirable scenario, while keeping plans flexible and adjustable. Among other things, this practice is intended to identify and respond to foreseeable consequences and omissions.

Risks and Side Effects of Boundary Crossing

Jens Martens (2007) explained that boundary-crossing initiatives and global partnerships among government, business, and civil society are held up as a way of achieving what governments and organizations such as the United Nations cannot manage alone (p. 4). However, he offered several cautions about potential risks and side effects of these relationships. Global leaders and stakeholders from all sectors can benefit from carefully examining these issues even though Martens directed his advice to UN officials:

- *Growing influence of the business sector in the political discourse and agenda setting.* Critics fear that partnership initiatives allow transnational corporations and their interest groups growing influence over agenda setting and political decision making by governments.
- *Risks to reputation: choosing the wrong partner.* This can have ethical repercussions for participants in the group if one partner is accused of violating environmental, social, or human rights standards.
- *Distorting competition and the pretence of representativeness.* When public-private partnerships grant exclusive rights for certain projects to the private partners, these companies receive advantages over others in opening up markets, gaining access to governments, and enhancing their image. Representativeness can be distorted if the initiating partners, rather than the respective stakeholder groups, nominate representatives to the body.
- *Proliferation of partnership initiatives and fragmentation of global governance.* The explosive growth in partnerships can lead to isolated solutions, which are poorly coordinated and contribute to the institutional weakening of other transnational governance organizations.
- *Unstable financing—a threat to the sufficient provision of public goods.* If the provision of public goods becomes increasingly privatized, governments will become dependent on voluntary and ultimately unpredictable channels of financing through benevolent individuals.

- *Dubious complementarity—governments escape responsibility.* Instead of considering partnership initiatives as complementary to intergovernmental processes, they are often promoted as replacements for intergovernmental agreements.
- *Selectivity in partnerships—governance gaps remain.* If partnerships only select and focus on fixing problems that can result in relatively quick wins (i.e., vaccination programs), long-term structural problems such as building up a health system or overcoming gender inequality are only peripherally touched.
- *Trends toward elite models of global governance—weakening of representative democracy.* The special political and legal position occupied legitimately by public bodies (governments and parliaments) are set aside or compromised when partnerships give all participating actors equal rights. (pp. 5–6)

These cautions do not suggest that global initiatives and partnerships should be discontinued. They do imply that considerable work needs to be done to develop and assess systematic approaches to these initiatives and that criteria need to be established to "ensure that long-term interests of the public are not damaged by the particular partnership initiative" (Martens, 2007, p. 6).

Conclusion

The Chad-Cameroon pipeline vignette is a poignant example of the challenges inherent in leading global change. It demonstrates how different concepts and practices of economic development and change shape circumstances and alter lives in a global context. The pipeline vignette further illustrates how different perspectives and worldviews cause people to think about and experience the problems and opportunities of global development initiatives in different ways. The worldviews of stakeholders influence their understanding of religion, politics, economics, and social interactions in ways that significantly affect how they define problems and identify possible solutions. The purpose of leadership in this context is to help the human community work together to address large-scale issues that affect the quality of life for people across nations and cultures.

Currently, actors from multiple sectors, cultures, and nations are meeting, partnering, and conflicting in this ever-changing, boundary-crossing environment. Though there is much promise in the global arena, there are many unanswered questions and problems. How does leadership function to address "the whole" in situations like the Chad-Cameroon pipeline vignette? In others words, what kind of leadership is required to understand the connections among issues surrounding the problems and what actions are needed to initiate and convene the stakeholders? What kind of leadership is required to understand the consequences of inaction? If stakeholders do convene, what leadership processes should the group use to ensure that all stakeholders are represented to define the problem, build relationships, address conflict, and find solutions? These and other questions signal a stimulating era ahead for scholars and practitioners of global leadership. The work is just beginning despite the fact that global initiatives and partnerships continue to flourish.

Application and Reflection

Looming Water Crisis:
Is the World Running Out of Water?

By Peter Behr

Introduction

In the past decade drought has marched across much of the globe, hitting China, the Mediterranean, southeast Australia and the U.S. Sun Belt. The amount of water used by humans has tripled since 1950, and irrigated cropland has doubled. About one-fifth of the world's population lacks sufficient water, a figure that could reach 40% by 2025 by some estimates, in part because of growing world economies. In the poorest societies more than a billion people lack access to clean water, and dirty water kills 5,000 children—enough to fill 12 jumbo jets—every day. By century's end drought is expected to spread across half the Earth's land surface due to climate change, causing hunger and higher food prices. The United Nations says it would cost an extra $10 billion or more annually to provide clean water and sanitation for all. Some recommend privatizing water supplies, while others suggest that charging more for water to encourage conservation would help to avoid future crises.

Overview

As 2007 came to a close, the steady drumbeat of headlines about China's worst drought in a half-century affirmed Prime Minister Wen Jiabao's earlier warning that the crisis threatens "the survival of the Chinese nation."[1]

The alarming developments included:

- The drying up of 133 reservoirs in burgeoning Guangdong Province, leaving a quarter of a million people facing water shortages.[2]
- The lowest levels since 1866 on portions of the Yangtze River, restricting barge and ship traffic and reducing hydroelectric output on China's largest river, even as pollution from 9,000 industrial plants along its course jeopardizes drinking water supplies.[3]
- Near-record low levels in vast Lake Poyang, restricting water supplies for 100,000 people.[4]

"My house used to be by the side of the lake," villager Yu Wenchang told the Xinhua News Agency. "Now I have to go over a dozen kilometers away to get to the lake water."[5]

Similar woes are being reported across the globe, as one of the worst decades of drought on record afflicts rich and poor nations alike. While scientists hedge their conclusions about whether long-term climate change is causing the dry spell, many warn that Earth's gradual warming trend unquestionably poses a growing threat to water supplies and food

(Continued)

(Continued)

production in arid regions. Already, population growth and economic expansion are straining water supplies in many places, particularly in the poorest nations. But despite an unending series of international water conferences—attended by thousands of experts—no consensus has emerged on how to make adequate clean water available to all people in affordable, environmentally sustainable ways.[6]

A fifth of the world's population—1.2 billion people—live in areas experiencing "physical water scarcity," or insufficient supplies for everyone's demands, according to a 2006 study by the International Water Management Institute that draws on the work of 700 scientists and experts. Another 1 billion face "economic scarcity," in which "human capacity or financial resources" cannot provide adequate water, the report found.[7]

While drought and expanding populations visibly affect the world's lakes and rivers, a less-visible problem also threatens water supplies. Accelerated pumping of groundwater for irrigation is depleting underground aquifers faster than they can be refreshed in densely populated areas of North China, India and Mexico. And land and water resources there and beyond are being degraded through erosion, pollution, salination, nutrient depletion and seawater intrusion, according to the institute.

A United Nations task force on water predicted that by 2025, 3 billion people will face "water stress" conditions, lacking enough water to meet all human and environmental needs.[8] By that time, there will be 63 major river basins with populations of at least 10 million, of which 47 are either already water-stressed, will become stressed or will experience a significant deterioration in water supply, according to a separate study by the World Resources Institute incorporating the U.N. data.[9]

As water depletion accelerates, drought is undermining nature's capacity to replenish this essential resource, punishing the planet's midsection—from eastern Australia and northern China through the Middle East and sub-Saharan Africa to the U.S. Sun Belt, the Great Plains and northern Mexico.

In the United States, chronic alarms over depleted water resources in the Southwestern states have spread to the Southeast. The water level in giant Lake Sidney Lanier outside Atlanta has dropped about a dozen feet in this decade, causing an intense struggle among Georgia and neighboring Alabama and Florida over rights to the lake's diminished flows.[10]

And drought conditions worldwide are likely to worsen as the effects of climate change are felt, many scientists warn.[11] Climate change is expected to expand and intensify drought in traditionally dry regions and disrupt water flows from the world's mountain snowcaps and glaciers.

Finally, a new threat to global water supplies has emerged: terrorism. "The chance that terrorists will strike at water systems is real," said Peter H. Gleick, president of the Pacific Institute for Studies in Development, Environment and Security in Oakland, Calif.[12] Modern public water systems are designed to protect users from biological agents and toxins, but deliberate contamination by terrorists could kill or sicken thousands, he said. Since the Sept. 11, 2001, terrorist attacks most major U.S. cities have sent the federal government confidential reports on the vulnerability of local water supplies, and the Environmental Protection Agency's (EPA) Water Sentinel Initiative is designing a water-contamination warning system.[13]

Perhaps the grimmest long-range prediction on water availability was issued by the Met Office Hadley Centre for Climate Prediction and Research in London. Using supercomputer modeling, the center projected that if current trends continue, by this century's end drought will have spread across half the Earth's land surface due to climate change, threatening millions of lives. Moreover, "extreme drought"—which makes traditional agriculture virtually impossible—will affect about a third of the planet, according to the group's November 2006 report.

"Even though (globally) total rainfall will increase as the climate warms, the proportion of land in drought is projected to rise throughout the 21st century," the report said.[14]

"There's almost no aspect of life in the developing countries that these predictions don't undermine—the ability to grow food, the ability to have a safe sanitation system, the availability of water," said Andrew Simms, policy director of the liberal London-based New Economics Foundation.[15] The consequences will be most dire for the planet's poorest inhabitants, he added. "For hundreds of millions of people for whom getting through the day is already a struggle, this is going to push them over the precipice."

Access to safe, fresh water separates the well off—who can treat water as if it were air—from the world's poorest, who hoard it like gold. In the United States, the average consumer uses nearly 160 gallons of water per day, summoned by the twist of a faucet. In much of Africa, women often trudge for hours to and from wells, carrying the two to five gallons per person used by the typical person in sub-Saharan Africa.[16]

But the lack of clean water is not only inconvenient. It can also be deadly. Each year 1.8 million children—5,000 per day—die from waterborne illnesses such as diarrhea, according to the United Nations. "That's equivalent to 12 full jumbo jets crashing every day," said U.N. water expert Brian Appleton. "If 12 full jumbo jets were crashing every day, the world would want to do something about it—they would want to find out why it was happening."[17]

Policymakers are trying various ways to solve the global water challenge, including contracting with private firms to operate urban water and sanitary systems, adopting new conservation technologies, enacting multination pacts to manage regional watersheds and increasing funds for water projects in the world's poorest regions. Water experts advocate "environmental flow" policies—the release of enough water from dams to sustain the environment of rivers, wetlands and underground aquifers.[18]

And their efforts seem to be paying off—at least in some areas. Between 1990 and 2002, more than 1 billion people in the developing world gained access to fresh water and basic sanitation. But because of population growth, the total number of people still lacking safe water remained more than a billion, and there was no change in the number lacking basic sanitation.[19]

In 2003, the U.N. General Assembly designated the period from 2005 to 2015 as the International Decade for Action on "Water for Life." And the U.N.'s new Millennium Development Goals include a campaign to cut in half by 2015 the proportion of people without sustainable access to safe drinking water and basic sanitation—at a cost of more than $10 billion per year.[20] Currently, governments and international agencies like the U.N. and World Bank provide only $4 billion a year in aid for water and sanitation projects.[21]

(Continued)

(Continued)

"We will see these issues play out silently: dry rivers, dead deltas, destocked fisheries, depleted springs and wells," wrote Margaret Carley-Carlson, chairwoman of the Global Water Partnership in Stockholm, and M. S. Swaminathan, president of the Pugwash Conferences on Science and World Affairs in Chennai, India.[22] "We will also see famine; increased and sometimes violent competition for water, especially within states; more migration; and environmental devastation with fires, dust, and new plagues and blights."

Averting that future will require fundamental changes in governmental policies and human practices governing the use, conservation, and value of water, experts agree.

As water experts and policymakers discuss how to conserve and protect future water supplies, here are some of the questions they are debating:

Are We Running Out of Water?

Amid the growing alarm about water shortages, water expert Frank Rijsberman offers a contrarian perspective. "The world is far from running out of water," he says. "There is land and human resources and water enough to grow food and provide drinking water for everyone."[23]

The issue is how efficiently water is used, says Rijsberman, former director of the International Water Management Institute in Colombo, Sri Lanka. Every year, about 110,000 cubic kilometers of rain falls on Earth's surface, of which humans withdraw just over 3%—about 3,700 cubic kilometers—from rivers and groundwater to use in cities, industries and farming. About 40,000 cubic kilometers flows into rivers and is absorbed into groundwater, and the rest evaporates.

Much of the water used by humans is returned to watersheds as wastewater, farm runoff or discharges from energy and industrial plants, with only a small fraction used for drinking and cooking.[24] Irrigation claims 70% of total water withdrawals, 22% is used by industry and the rest goes for homes, personal and municipal uses.[25]

Water isn't running out everywhere, said Canadian journalist Marq de Villiers, author of *Water: The Fate of Our Most Precious Resource.* "It's only running out in places where it's needed most. It's an allocation, supply, and management problem."[26]

It's also a demand problem: Over the past half century, millions of people have migrated from colder, wetter, northern climates to warmer, drier, southern locales such as the American Southwest or southern France, putting new pressure on those expanding "Sun Belt" communities to build irrigation systems, tap into groundwater supplies, or rechannel large amounts of river water.

Experts agree that the world should not be facing an overall water-scarcity crisis. But water supplies in much of Africa, parts of China, southern Europe, northern Mexico and the American Southwest and high plains aren't meeting demand, and climate change may be accelerating the problem, the experts say.[27] The issues add up to what the World Commission on Water calls the "gloomy arithmetic of water."[28]

In addition, man has transformed most of the world's great rivers. For example, the Danube—Central Europe's "lifeline"—has been dredged, deepened, straightened, channelized, and obstructed by dams and fishing weirs. It is now "a manufactured waterway," says de Villiers, with more than a third of its volume withdrawn for human use, compared to an average of about 10% for other rivers.[29]

Pollution is also reducing the world's supply of potable water. In Asia, many rivers "are dead or dying," according to Rijsberman. The Musi River near India's Hyderabad technology center has become "a dwindling black wastewater stream," he writes. "[Y]et the cows that produce the curd and the dairy products for Hyderabad are bathing in that black and stinking water."[30] In China, 265 billion gallons of raw sewage is dumped into the Yangtze River every year.[31]

The depletion and despoiling of the world's reservoirs, rivers and watersheds also contribute to the problem. During the 20th century, more than half the wetlands in parts of Australia, Europe, New Zealand and North America were destroyed by population growth and development. The loss of wetlands increases water runoff, which exacerbates flooding, reduces the replenishment of aquifers and leaves rivers and lakes more vulnerable to pollution.[32]

Aquifers—the immense storehouses of water found beneath the Earth's surface—are the largest and fastest-growing source of irrigation water. Depleting those underground rivers will have deleterious effects on the 40% of the planet's agricultural output that relies on irrigation from groundwater.[33] Experts say some of that water—which dates back to past ice ages—would take eons to refresh but is being consumed in less than a century.

"Large areas of China, South Asia and the Middle East are now maintaining irrigation through unsustainable mining of groundwater or over-extraction from rivers," said the U.N. "Human Development Report 2006."[34] The problem is widespread in Mexico, India and Russia, as well, although precise data are not available for many countries.[35]

In his seminal 1986 book *Cadillac Desert*, the late Marc Reisner warned about the long-term effects of water policies in the Western United States, including the depletion of the giant Ogallala Aquifer, which runs southward from South Dakota to Texas. It has two distinctions, he wrote, "one of being the largest discrete aquifer in the world, the other of being the fastest-disappearing aquifer in the world."[36]

In the 1930s a farmer on the Great Plains could raise a few gallons per minute from the Ogallala, using a windmill-driven pump. After the New Deal brought electricity to the region and oil and gas discoveries provided plenty of cheap fuel, electric pumps raised 800 gallons per minute.

"All of a sudden, irrigation became very energy and labor-efficient. You turn on the switch and let it run," says Robert M. Hirsch, associate director for water at the U.S. Geological Survey. "There was an explosion of irrigated agriculture, particularly on the high plains, and in California."

In 1937, West Texas had 1,116 irrigation wells. Thirty years later it had 27,983. By 1977, Texas was withdrawing 11 billion gallons of groundwater a day to grow corn, cotton and other crops in what once had been part of the Great American Desert, Reisner wrote.[37]

Now, experts say the Ogallala—a resource that could have lasted hundreds of years—will be virtually depleted within the lifetimes of today's farmers.

(Continued)

(Continued)

Yet during the optimism and opportunism that characterized development of the modern American West, worries about future water supplies evaporated. "What are you going to do with all that water?" the late Felix Sparks, former head of the Colorado Water Conservation Board, asked in the mid-1980s. "When we use it up, we'll just have to get water from somewhere else." But today, "somewhere else" is not an answer, say authors Robin Clarke, editor of climate publications for the United Nations and World Meteorological Organization, and environmental author Jannet King. The co-authors of *The Water Atlas* insist water must be considered a finite resource.[38]

Should Water Be Privatized?

In 2000, street fighting broke out between government forces and political activists, rural cocoa farmers and residents of shantytowns on the hilly outskirts of Cochabamba—Bolivia's third-largest city. The dispute was over privatization of the city's water supplies.

The year before, Cochabamba had turned its water and sanitation system over to Aguas del Tunari, a coalition of multinational and Bolivian water and engineering corporations whose biggest stakeholder was Bechtel Corp., based in San Francisco.[39] This was the high-water mark of a global, pro-market movement toward deregulation and privatization of state-owned monopolies in water, electricity and other services.[40] The World Bank and other international lenders had been supporting privatization strategies in hopes that investments and better management by private industry would help bring water and sanitation to more than a billion poor people whose governments couldn't or wouldn't do the job.

But Cochabamba's privatization included a costly dam and pipeline to import more water, which required sharp rate increases starting at 35%. Some customers' water bills doubled. Farmers outside the city, who had enjoyed free water, suddenly had to pay. The city erupted in protest, the water company's officials fled and their contract was rescinded.[41] The government reclaimed the water operations, and Cochabamba became a rallying cry against privatization and globalization for the political left.

Elsewhere, however, corporate involvement in water and sanitation system operations has not ceased. Veolia Water, a subsidiary of the French firm Veolia Environment SA—the world's largest water-services firm—signed a $3.8 billion, 30-year contract in 2007 to supply drinking water to 3 million residents of the Chinese river port city of Tianjin. Since 1997, Veolia has signed more than 20 water and sanitation contracts in China, and supplies more than 110 million people in 57 countries worldwide.[42]

These projects, and smaller-scale versions in poorer nations, suggest that while the inflamed debate over water privatization continues, threats of water scarcity and climate change may help accelerate the search for private sector support. The percentage of the world's population served at some level by private firms has grown from 5% in 1999 to 11%—or 707 million people—in 2007, according to *Pinsent Masons Water Yearbook*, a widely consulted summary of private-sector water projects.[43]

Opponents of privatization argue that safe drinking water and adequate sanitation are essential human rights, obligating governments to provide them at affordable rates or free if necessary. "If it's a human need, it can be delivered by the private sector on a for-profit basis. If it's a human right, that's different," says Canadian anti-globalization activist Maude Barlow, co-author of *Blue Gold: The Battle Against Corporate Theft of the World's Water.* "You can't really charge for a human right; you can't trade it or deny it to someone because they don't have money."[44]

Bringing in private firms to run water and sewer operations does not make the services more efficient or affordable, opponents also argue, but forces the poor to pay for corporate profits, shareholder dividends and high executive salaries. "The efficiencies don't happen," asserts Wenonah Hauter, executive director of Food and Water Watch, a Washington anti-globalization group. "The companies simply lay off staff members until they don't have enough people to take care of the infrastructure. And they raise rates. We've seen this all over the world." Last year Hauter's organization issued a study claiming privatized water operations in California, Illinois, Wisconsin, and New York charged more for water than comparable publicly owned systems.[45]

Privatization advocates dispute Hauter's claims, and facts to settle the issue are illusive. A 2005 survey by the AEI-Brookings Center for Regulatory studies found "no systematic empirical evidence comparing public and private water systems in the United States."[46]

A study by the Inter-American Development Bank of water rates in Colombia said prices charged by privatized systems were not significantly different from those charged by public systems.[47] And privatization appears to have improved water quality in urban areas but not in rural communities, said the study. After privatization began, water bills for the poor rose about 10% but declined for the wealthy, reflecting a scaling back in government subsidies to poorer consumers. Similar shifts occurred in both privatized and non-privatized cities.[48]

In central cities, water-rate subsidies tend to favor the wealthy and middle classes, who are usually connected to municipal water systems, while the poor often are not, says American journalist Diane Raines Ward, author of *Water Wars: Drought, Flood, Folly, and the Politics of Thirst.* And by keeping water rates artificially low, utilities typically collect only about a third of their actual costs, so they don't raise enough money to expand pipelines to unserved poor neighborhoods, she says.[49]

The rural poor or those living in urban slums often must haul water home from public wells or buy it from independent merchants—delivered by truck or burro—at much higher prices. In Cairo, Egypt, for instance, the poor pay 40 times the real cost of delivery; in Karachi, Pakistan, the figure is 83 times; and in parts of Haiti, 100 times, Ward says.

In the years since Cochabamba galvanized the left against privatizing water, privatization has declined in Latin America and sub-Saharan Africa but increased in Europe and Asia, according to the *Water Yearbook.*[50] The average contract size also has diminished since the 1990s, it said, due to a trend away from mega-contracts with multinational water companies in favor of "local and possibly less contentious contracts."[51]

A U.N.-sponsored analysis cites Chile and parts of Colombia among the successful examples of collaborative water and sanitation services. In Cartagena, Colombia's fifth-largest city, the local government retains control of the pipes and facilities and raises

(Continued)

(Continued)

investment capital, but a private firm runs the service. Today, nearly all the city's residents have water in their homes, up from only one-quarter in 1995.[52] Chile's water program offers subsidies to the poorest households, guaranteeing an essential minimum of supply of up to 4,000 gallons per month. Deliveries are monitored to limit cheating, and every household must have a water meter to verify usage.[53]

Experts say the political problems of water privatization cannot be managed without effective government regulation and consumer involvement at all levels. Both elements were missing in Cochabamba but are present in Chile, the U.N. report says.[54]

Will Water Scarcity Lead to Conflicts?

In 1995 Ismail Serageldin, a World Bank vice president, predicted that "the wars of the next century will be over water."[55]

The reality has been different thus far. "Water resources are rarely the sole source of conflict, and indeed, water is frequently a source of cooperation," writes Gleick, of the Pacific Institute for Studies in Development, Environment and Security, in the new edition of *The World's Water 2006–2007.*[56] The survey of reported conflicts over water in the past 50 years, compiled by Oregon State University researchers, found 37 cases of violence between nations, all but seven in the Middle East.[57]

In 1964, Israel opened its massive National Water Carrier canal to carry water from the Sea of Galilee and the Jordan River to its farms and cities. Syria retaliated to maintain its access to the Jordan by starting two canals to divert Jordan flows for its uses. Skirmishes by military units and raids by the newly established al-Fatah forces escalated until Israeli air strikes halted the diversion projects. By then, Israel and the Arab League were on the road to the Six-Day War of 1967.[58]

"The attacks by Syria, Egypt, and Jordan that eventually followed had many causes, but water remained a priority for both sides," says author Ward.[59]

Still, more than 200 water treaties have been negotiated peacefully over the past half-century. The Partition of India in 1947, for instance, could have led to war between India and newly created Pakistan over control of the mighty Indus River basin. Instead, the two nations were brought together with World Bank support over a perilous decade of negotiations, signing the Indus Water Treaty in 1960. Three rivers were given to Pakistan, and three to India, with a stream of international financial support for dams and canals in both countries. Even when war raged between the two nations in later years, they never attacked water infrastructure.[60]

"Most peoples and even nations are hesitant to deny life's most basic necessity to others," Ward wrote. Two modern exceptions occurred during the Bosnian War (1992–1996), when Serbs "lay waiting to shoot men, women and children arriving at riverbanks or taps around Sarajevo carrying buckets or bottles," and during Saddam Hussein's regime in Iraq, when he diverted the lower waters of the Tigris and Euphrates rivers to destroy the homes and livelihood of the Marsh Arabs.[61]

Except for such instances, cooperation over water resources is common today, even if sometimes grudging and incomplete, says Undala Alam, a professor and specialist in water diplomacy at Britain's Cranfield University. "Turkey was releasing water for Syria and Iraq;

the Nile countries are preparing projects jointly to develop the river; the Niger countries have a shared vision for the basin's development, and the Zambezi countries are working within the Southern African Development Community," she notes.[62]

But analysts warn that growing stress on water supplies, coupled with the impact of climate change, will create combustible conditions in the coming years that will undermine collaboration over water.

There is plenty of precedence for the concern, notes Gleick, who describes the history of violence over fresh water as "long and distressing."[63] The latest volume of *The World's Water* lists 22 pages of historical water conflicts—beginning in about 1700 B.C. with the Sumerians' efforts to dam the Tigris River to block retreating rebels.

In the future, climate change is expected to extend and intensify drought in Earth's driest regions and disrupt normal water flows from mountain snowcaps in Europe, North America and Central Asia. "Climate change has the potential to exacerbate tensions over water as precipitation patterns change, declining by as much as 60% in some areas," warned a recent report by a panel of retired U.S. generals and admirals convened by CNA, a think tank with longstanding ties to the military. "The potential for escalating tensions, economic disruption and armed conflict is great," said the report, "National Security and the Threat of Climate Change."[64]

On the simplest level, the report said, climate change "has the potential to create sustained natural and humanitarian disasters on a scale far beyond those we see today." Already, it said, Darfur, Ethiopia, Eritrea, Somalia, Angola, Nigeria, Cameroon and Western Sahara have all been hit hard by tensions that can be traced in part to environmental causes.[65] If the drought continues, the report said, more people will leave their homelands, increasing migration pressures within Africa and into Europe.[66]

The impact will be especially acute in the Middle East, where about two-thirds of the inhabitants depend on water sources outside their borders. Water remains a potential flashpoint between the Israelis and Palestinians, who lack established rights to the Jordan River and receive only about 10% of the water used by Israel's West Bank settlers.[67] "Only Egypt, Iran, and Turkey have abundant fresh water resources," the CNA report said.

The military advisers urged the United States to take a stronger national and international role in stabilizing climate change and to create global partnerships to help less-developed nations confront climate impacts.[68]

Currently, there is only a weak international foundation for water collaboration, according to the U.N. Human Development report. While a 1997 U.N. convention lays out principles for cooperation, only 14 nations have signed it, and it has no workable enforcement mechanism. In 55 years, the International Court of Justice has decided only one case involving international rivers.[69]

It is possible, however, that as the awareness of climate impacts on water supplies deepens, so will the urgency for governments to respond. "Unlike the challenges that we are used to dealing with, these will come upon us extremely slowly, but come they will, and they will be grinding and inexorable," said former Vice Adm. Richard H. Truly, a former astronaut who headed the U.S. National Aeronautics and Space Administration (NASA) and served as a CNA consultant.[70] "They will affect every nation, and all simultaneously."

(Continued)

(Continued)

Notes

1. Charles C. Mann, "The Rise of Big Water," *Vanity Fair*, May 2007; Reuters, "China Drought Threatens Water Supply for Millions," March 28, 2007.

2. Xinhua News Agency, "Drought Leaves Nearly 250,000 Short of Drinking Water in Guangdong," *People's Daily Online*, December 13, 2007, http://english.people.com.cn/90001/90776/6320617.html.

3. Jonathan Watts, "Dry, Polluted, Plagued by Rats: The Crisis in China's Greatest Yangtze River," *The Guardian* (Britain), January 17, 2008, http://chinaview.wordpress.com/category/environment/drought/.

4. Xinhua News Agency, "Climate Change Blamed as Drought Hits 100,000 at China's Largest Freshwater Lake," *People's Daily Online*, December 14, 2007, http://english.people.com.cn/90001/90776/6321329.html.

5. Chris O'Brien, "Global Warming Hits China," *Forbes.com*, January 6, 2008, www.forbes.com/opinions/2008/01/04/poyanglake-china-oped-cx_cob_0106poyang.html.

6. Peter H. Gleick, "Time to Rethink Large International Water Meetings," *The World's Water 2006–2007* (Island Press) 182; www.worldwater.org/.

7. David Molden, "Summary," in *Water for Food, Water for Life: A Comprehensive Assessment of Water Management in Agriculture*, ed. David Molden, 10 (International Water Management Institute); www.iwmi.cgiar.org/assessment/files_new/synthesis/Summary_SynthesisBook.pdf.

8. See United Nations Development Programme, "Summary," in *Human Development Report 2006: Beyond Scarcity: Power, Poverty and the Global Water Crisis,*" ed. United Nations Development Programme, 26, http://hdr.undp.org/en/media/hdr2006_english_summary.pdf.

9. Carmen Revenga and others, "Executive Summary," in *Pilot Analysis of Global Ecosystems: Freshwater Systems*, ed. World Resources Institute, 4, 26 (World Resources Institute, 2000), www.wri.org/publication/pilot-analysis-global-ecosystemsfreshwater-systems.

10. Stacy Shelton, "Lake Lanier Hits Lowest Point Since Its Construction," *The Atlanta-Journal Constitution*, November 19, 2007, www.ajc.com/metro/content/metro/stories/2007/11/19/lanierlowweb_1120.html?cxntlid=homepage_tab_newstab; for background, see Mary H. Cooper, "Water Shortages," *CQ Researcher*, August 1, 2003, 649–672.

11. M. Falkenmark and others, "On the Verge of a New Water Scarcity: A Call for Good Governance and Human Ingenuity," in *Stockholm International Water Institute (SIWI) Policy Brief*, 2007, 17; for background, see Colin Woodard, "Curbing Climate Change," CQ *Global Researcher*, February 2007, 27–50.

12. "Water and Terrorism," in *The World's Water* 2006–2007, op. cit., 1.

13. Environmental Protection Agency, "Water Sentinel Initiative," ww.epa.gov/watersecurity/pubs/water_sentinel_factsheet.pdf.

14. Met Office Hadley Centre, "Effects of Climate Change in Developing Countries," November 2006, 2–3, www.metoffice.gov.uk/research/hadleycentre/pubs/brochures/COP12.pdf; Michael McCarthy, "The Century of Drought," *The Independent* (London), October 4, 2006, 1.

15. McCarthy, ibid., 1.

16. World Water Council.

17. Quoted in "Billions Without Clean Water," March 14, 2000, BBC, http://news.bbc.co.uk/2/hi/676064.stm.

18.   David Katz, "Going with the Flow," *The World's Water 2006–2007*, op. cit., 30–39.

19.   Data Table 5, Access to Water Supply and Sanitation by Region, *The World's Water 2006–2007*, op. cit., 258.

20.   "Synthesis of the 4th World Water Forum," August 2006, 23–24, www.worldwaterforum4 .org.mx/files/report/SynthesisoftheForum.pdf; for background on Millennium Development Goals, see www.un.org/millenniumgoals and "U.N. Fact Sheet on Water and Sanitation," 2006, www.un.org/ waterforlifedecade/factsheet.html.

21.   "Human Development Report 2006," op. cit., 8, http://hdr.undp.org/en/reports/global/hdr2006/.

22.   Australian Broadcasting Corporation, "Issues in Science and Technology," transcript, September 22, 2007.

23.   Frank Rijsberman, Charlotte Fraiture, and David Molden, "Water Scarcity: The Food Factor," in *Issues in Science and Technology*, June 22, 2007.

24.   Ibid.

25.   Sharon P. Nappier, Robert S. Lawrence, and Kellogg J. Schwab, "Dangerous Waters," *Natural History*, November 2007, 48.

26.   Marq de Villiers, *Water: The Fate of Our Most Precious Resource* (1999), 267.

27.   "World Hit by Water Shortage," *Birmingham Post*, August 21, 2006, 10, http://icbirmingham .icnetwork.co.uk/birminghampost/news/tm_method=full%26objectid=17597105%26siteid= 50002-name_page.html.

28.   "Water Resources Sector Strategy, Strategic Directions for World Bank Engagement," World Bank, 2004, 5, www-wds.worldbank.org/external/default/WDSContentServer/WDSP/IB/2004/06/01/ 000090341_20040601150257/Rendered/PDF/28114.pdf.

29.   de Villiers, op. cit., 176–177.

30.   Frank R. Rijsberman, "1st Asia-Pacific Water Summit," *MaximsNews Network*, October 8, 2007, www.abc.net.au/7.30/content/2006/s1716766.htm.

31.   Diane Raines Ward, *Water Wars: Drought, Flood, Folly and the Politics of Thirst* (2002), 171.

32.   Nappier et al., op. cit.

33.   "Human Development Report," op. cit., 176; see also Meena Palaniappan, Emily Lee, and Andrea Samulon, "Environmental Justice and Water," *The World's Water 2006–2007*, op. cit., 125.

34.   "Human Development Report," ibid.

35.   Palaniappan et al., op. cit.

36.   Marc Reisner, *Cadillac Desert, the American West and its Disappearing Water* (1986), 10.

37.   Ibid., 437.

38.   Ibid., 10–11; see also Robin Clarke and Jannet King, *The Water Atlas* (2004).

39.   "Approaches to Private Participation in Water Services," *World Bank*, 2006, 213.

40.   Daniel Yergin and Joseph Stanislaw, *Commanding Heights: The Battle for the World Economy* (2004).

41.   Juan Forero, "Multinational Is Ousted, but Local Ills Persist," *The New York Times*, December 15, 2005, 1; see also Public Citizen, "Water Privatization Case Study: Cochabamba, Bolivia," 1–2, www.tradewatch.org/documents/Bolivia_(PDF).PDF; and Bechtel Corporation, "Cochabamba and the Aquas del Tunari Consortium," www.bechtel.com/assets/files/PDF/Cochabambafacts0305.pdf.

42.   Xinhua News Agency, "European Environment Giant Veolia to Increase Investment in China to $2.5 Billion by 2013," November 1, 2007.

(Continued)

(Continued)

43. *Pinsent Masons Water Yearbook 2007–2008*, xii, www.pinsentmasons.com/media/1976627452.pdf.

44. Quoted in Jeff Fleischer, "Blue Gold: An Interview with Maude Barlow," *Mother Jones*, January 14, 2005, www.motherjones.com/news/qa/2005/01/maude_barlow.html.

45. "Economic Failures of Private Water Systems," *Food and Water Watch*, December 2007, www.foodandwaterwatch.org/water/waterprivatization/usa/Public_vs_Private.pdf.

46. Scott Wallsten and Katrina Kosec, "Public or Private Drinking Water?" *AEI-Brookings Joint Center for Regulatory Studies*, March 2005, 2, 7, www.reg-markets.org/publications/abstract.php?pid=919.

47. Felipe Barrera-Osorio and Mauricio Olivera, "Does Society Win or Lose as a Result of Privatization?" in Inter-American Development Bank, Research Network Working Paper #R-525, March 2007, 19.

48. Ibid., 21.

49. Ward, op. cit., 206–207.

50. *Pinsent Masons Water Yearbook,* op. cit., 3.

51. Ibid., 5.

52. Paul Constance, "The Day that Water Ran Uphill," ed. IDB America, Inter-American Development Bank, December 9, 2007, www.iadb.org/idbamerica/index.cfm?thisid=3909&lanid=1.

53. "Human Development Report," op. cit., 92.

54. Ibid., 179; Ward, op. cit., 210.

55. Malcolm Scully, "The Politics of Running Out of Water," *The Chronicle of Higher Education*, November 17, 2000.

56. Peter H. Gleick, "Environment and Security," *The World's Water 2006–2007*, op. cit., 189.

57. "Human Development Report," op. cit., 221.

58. Benny Morris, *Righteous Victims* (2001), 303–304.

59. Ward, op. cit., 174.

60. Ibid., 85.

61. Ibid., 192.

62. Undala Alam, letter to the *Financial Times*, April 1, 2006, 6; see also www.transboundarywaters.orst.edu/publications/related_research/Alam1998.pdf.

63. Gleick, "Environment and Security," op. cit., 189.

64. CNA Corporation, *Security and the Threat of Climate Change* (2007), 3, http://securityandclimate.cna.org/.

65. Ibid., 20.

66. Ibid., 22.

67. "Human Development Report," op. cit., 216; Clarke and King, op. cit., 79.

68. Ibid., 47.

69. "Human Development Report," op. cit., 218.

70. CNA, op. cit., 14.

REFLECTION

- Is clean water a human right, a public good, or a commodity?

- How would you respond to the three questions raised in "The Looming Water Crisis?"
  - ○ Are we running out of water?
  - ○ Should water be privatized?
  - ○ Will water scarcity lead to conflict?

- What factors or arguments influenced your answers?

- Should there be a World Water Summit?
  - ○ If not, how would you address the issues concerning water across regional and nation-state boundaries?
  - ○ If so, who should convene the summit and what source of power would they use?
    - – Who should be invited and why?
    - – Using a systems perspective, how might the members define the problem and the change they seek?
    - – What concepts of change would be most appropriate?
    - – What kind of leadership would the summit require?
    - – What change practices should they use?

Notes

1. For a more detailed analysis of these four theories of globalization, see Rebecca Todd Peters's book *In Search of the Good Life: The Ethics of Globalization* (2004).

2. The most recent Human Development Report published by the UN ranked Chad as 167 out of 174 countries. Not incidentally, all seven countries that ranked lower than Chad are also in Africa.

3. House et al. (2004) acknowledged that views of the importance and value of leadership vary across cultures, even to the extent that some national cultures are skeptical of leaders and the concept of leadership while others embrace and even romanticize leadership (p. 5).

4. By 2008, a total of 57 women from 45 countries had served as prime minister, president, or chancellor (see the listing at the Web site for Equal Representation in Government and Democracy at http://www.ergd.org/Premiers.htm).

References

Adler, N. J. (1997). Global leadership: Women leaders. *Management International Review,* *37*(1), 171–196.

Allen, K. E., Bordas, J., Hickman, G. R., Matusak, L. R., Sorenson, G. J., & Whitmire, K. J. (1998). Leadership in the 21st century. In B. Kellerman (Ed.), *Rethinking leadership: Kellogg leadership studies project 1994–1997* (pp. 41–62). College Park: MD: James MacGregor Burns Academy of Leadership.

Appiah, K. A. (2006). *Cosmopolitanism: Ethics in a world of strangers.* New York: W. W. Norton.

Astin, H. S.,& Leland, C. (1991). *Women of influence, women of vision.* San Francisco: Jossey-Bass.

Attfield, R. (2006). The shape of a global ethic. *Philosophy and Social Criticism, 32*(1), 5–19.

Bank Information Center. (2000). *Project alert #2: Chad-Cameroon pipeline project.* Retrieved October 8, 2007, from http://www.bicusa.org/africa/ppa_chad1.htm

Behr, P. (2008). Looming water crisis. *CQ Global Researcher, 2,* 27–56. Retrieved October 9, 2008, from http://newman.richmond.edu:2271/globalresearcher/cqrglobal2008020000

Benhabib, S. (2005). Beyond interventionism and indifference: Culture, deliberation and pluralism. *Philosophy and Social Criticism, 31,* 753–771.

Carlson, C. (2006). Using political power to convene. *National Civic Review, 95*(3), 57–60.

Center for International Environmental Law. (2000, May 30). *Press release.* Retrieved October 8, 2007, from http://www.ciel.org/Ifi/pressreleasechadcam.html

Ciulla, J. B. (2000). Bridge leaders. In B. Kellerman & L. R. Matusak (Eds.), *Cutting edge leadership* (pp. 25–28). College Park, MD: James MacGregor Burns Academy of Leadership.

Ciulla, J. B. (Ed.). (2004). *Ethics, the heart of leadership* (2nd ed.). Westport, CT: Praeger.

Ciulla, J. B. (2005). Bridge leaders. Unpublished raw data prepared for the World Economic Forum in Davos, Switzerland.

Cobb, J. B., Jr. (1999). *An earthist challenge to economism: A theological critique of the World Bank.* London: Macmillan.

Dorfman, P. W., & House, R. J. (2004). Cultural influences on organizational leadership: Literature review, theoretical rationale, and globe project goals. In R. J. House, P. J. Hanges, M. Javidan, P. W. Dorfman, & V. Gupta (Eds.), *Culture, leadership, and organizations: The globe study of 62 societies* (pp. 51–73). Thousand Oaks, CA: Sage.

Gardner, H. (1995). *Leading minds: An anatomy of leadership.* New York: BasicBooks.

Gerzon, M. (2006). *Leading through conflict: How successful leaders transform differences into opportunity.* Boston: Harvard Business School Press.

Gilboa, E. (2008). Searching for a theory of public diplomacy. *Annals of the American Academy of Political and Social Science, 616,* 55–77.

Goldsmith, M., Greenberg, C. L., Robertson, A., & Hu-Chan, M. (2003). *Global leadership: The next generation.* Upper Saddle River, NJ: Prentice Hall.

Gray, B. (1998). Collaboration: The constructive management of differences. In G. R. Hickman, (Ed.), *Leading organizations: Perspectives for a new era* (pp. 467–479). Thousand Oaks, CA: Sage.

Heifetz, R. 1994. *Leadership without easy answers.* Cambridge, MA: Belknap Press.

Hickman, G. R. (Ed.). (1998). *Leading organizations: Perspectives for a new era.* Thousand Oaks, CA: Sage.

Hicks, D. (2003). *Religion and the workplace.* Cambridge, UK: Cambridge University Press.

Hofstede, G. H. (1980). *Culture's consequences: International differences in work-related values.* Beverly Hills, CA: Sage.

Hofstede, G. H. (2001). *Culture's consequences: Comparing values, behaviors, institutions, and organizations across nations* (2nd ed.). Thousand Oaks, CA: Sage.

Horta, K., & Djiriabe, D. (2007, January 17). Trouble in the pipeline. *The Guardian.* Retrieved March 4, 2009, from http://www.guardian.co.uk/environment/2007/jan/17/energy.society

Horta, K., Nguiffo, S., & Djiraibe, D. (2007). *The Chad-Cameroon oil and pipeline project: A project non-completion.* Retrieved October 8, 2007, from http://www.environmentaldefense.org/documents/6282_ChadCameroon-Non-Completion.pdf

House, R. J., Hanges, P. J., Javidan, M., Dorfman, P. W., & Gupta, V. (Eds.). (2004). *Culture, leadership, and organizations: The globe study of 62 societies.* Thousand Oaks, CA: Sage.

Human Development Report Office. (2006). *United Nations Human Development Report 2006.* Retrieved July 20, 2007, from http://origin-hdr.undp.org/hdr2006/statistics/countries/country_fact_sheets/cty_fs_TCD.html

Johnston, C. (1998). *The wealth or health of nations: Transforming capitalism from within.* Cleveland, OH: Pilgrim Press.

Martens, J. (2007). *Multistakeholder partnerships—Future models of multilateralism?* (Occasional Paper No. 29). Berlin: Friedrich-Ebert-Stiftung.

Onishi, N. (2000, August 11). In the Oil-Rich Nigeria Delta, Deep Poverty and Grim Fires. *New York Times,* pp. A1, 8.

Peters, R. T. (2004). *In search of the good life: The ethics of globalization.* New York: Continuum.

Ritzer, G. (1996). *The McDonaldization of society: An investigation into the changing character of contemporary social life.* Thousand Oaks, CA: Pine Forge Press.

Ross, M. H. (2000). Creating the conditions for peacemaking: Theories of practice in ethnic conflict resolution. *Ethnic and Racial Studies, 23,* 1002–1034.

Schwartz, P. (1996). *The art of the long view: Paths to strategic insight for yourself and your company.* New York: Currency Doubleday.

Senge, P., Lichtenstein, B. B., Kaeufer, K., Bradbury, H., & Carroll, J. S. (2007). Collaborating for systemic change. *MIT Sloan Management Review, 48*(2), 44–53.

Sengupta, S. (2004, February 18). The making of an African petrostate. *New York Times.* Retrieved March 10, 2009 from http://query.nytimes.com/gst/fullpage.html?res=9B04EFDF123DF93BA25751C0A9629C8B63&sec=&spon=&pagewanted=1

Stewart, F. (2002). Root causes of violent conflict in developing countries. *BMJ, 324,* 342–345.

Waddock, S. (2006). *Leading corporate citizens: Vision, values, value-added* (2nd ed.). New York: McGraw-Hill.

World Bank. (2000, June 6). *World Bank group approves support for Chad-Cameroon petroleum development and pipeline project* [Press release]. Retrieved October 8, 2007, from http://www.esso.com/Chadenglish/PA/Newsroom/TD_NewsRelease_060600.asp

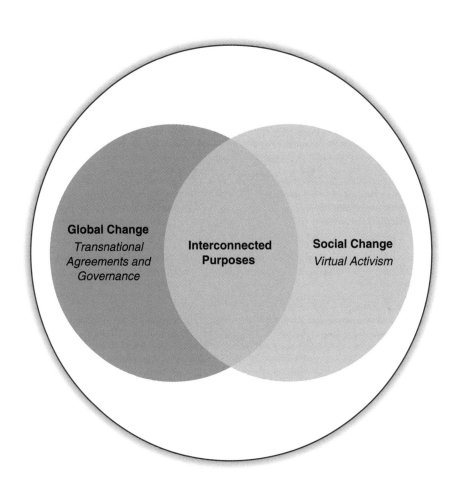

CHAPTER 11

Crossing Global and Social Contexts

Virtual Activism in Transnational Dotcauses, E-Movements, and Internet Nongovernmental Organizations

Introduction

Each context—organizational, community, political, and social movement—has changed dramatically as a result of the instant, low-cost, and expansive reach of the Internet and other forms of technology. The Internet's capacity has allowed individuals and organizations to reach current and potential clients and customers globally, to unite and galvanize communities, to make government more accessible, to bring political campaigns directly to the people, and to unite activists for and against social causes throughout the world. This chapter focuses on the use of the Internet to effect global or transnational social change. The Internet has changed the way nongovernmental organizations (NGOs) and movement activists meet, mobilize, and carry out social change, and perhaps this and other forms of technology have changed the nature and type of leadership involved in civil society worldwide.

Virtual Activists, Virtual Causes

Groups engaged in global Internet activism are known by several names including dotcauses, Internet NGOs, and e-movements. Most fit the definition of dotcauses provided by John Clark and Nuno Themudo (2006):

Dotcauses are political networks, which mobilize support for social causes primarily (but not necessarily exclusively) through the Internet. The dotcause is the civil society equivalent of the "dotcom" organization in the business world (i.e., a commercial organization, such as Amazon.com, which relies primarily on its Internet presence to undertake its core business). Similarly, dotcauses rely on the Internet to undertake their core activities. Without the Internet they would not exist or would not exist in anything like their current form. (p. 52)

As a collective, dotcauses or e-movements comprise advocacy networks that are "bound together by shared values, a common discourse, and dense exchanges of information and services" (Clark & Themudo, 2006, p. 52). In the global arena, these collectives are referred to as transnational advocacy networks (TANs). They engage in advocacy and activism on behalf of citizens whose interests are often unrecognized or underrepresented in transnational agreements and global governance.

The purpose of virtual causes and TANs is as varied as the organizations themselves. Some organizations, such as the International Campaign to Ban Landmines (ICBL), International Animal Rescue (IAR), and Defense for Children International (DCI), advocate for singular global causes. Other causes focus on the antiglobalization or global justice movement to counter what their members perceive as the negative effects large multinational corporations have on the global community. Examples of these organizations include Peoples Global Action, ATTAC, Third World Network, and One World.Net, among numerous others.

This chapter uses a commentary by Ann Florini (2004) to examine aspects of civil society activism in the global arena, and then places virtual activism within this context. The commentary also raises important issues about the accountability and transparency of transnational NGOs.

Change Vignette

Is Global Civil Society a Good Thing?

Tanks in the streets of Seattle in 1999. Molotov cocktails in Prague in 2000. Gunfire in Genoa in 2001. A hundred thousand people gathering every winter in a World Social Forum to talk about how to improve the world. Global agreements on everything from human rights protections to banning weapons systems. Fifteen million people on the streets in cities around the world on a single day in 2003 to protest the Iraq war. These headlines reflect the rise of a force now so potent in world affairs that the *New York Times* has referred to it as "the second superpower." It is the power of civil society, that ill-defined, amorphous realm of human associations that are not family or government or profit-seeking business.

But does the rising power of civil society augur good or ill? Is the world to be rendered just and prosperous by hordes of concerned citizens banding together to demand, and create, a better world? Or will the fragile progress toward democracy around the globe be undermined by unelected, unaccountable extremists? Few in democratic societies dispute the right of citizens to come together in peaceful associations to pursue common purposes. But governments, corporate leaders, and pundits are raising alarms about just how well organized and powerful some parts of civil society are becoming.

They particularly fear the formalized part of civil society: non-governmental organizations (NGOs), which are legally recognized entities able to do such things as hire staff and open bank accounts. It is the NGOs that organize the massive street protests seen around most meetings of world leaders. NGOs led the global campaign that resulted in a widespread ban on landmines, over the objections of such major powers as the United States. NGOs lead campaigns targeting corporations they accuse of harming the environment or mistreating workers, campaigns that sometimes cause share prices to plunge.

The influence of NGOs is hardly new in world affairs. NGOs drove the international anti-slavery campaign starting more than two centuries ago and since then have weighed in on every major question of their day, from war and peace to environmental degradation to the rights of indigenous peoples. But two things have changed of late. The sheer number of NGOs is skyrocketing in most parts of the world. And those NGOs are becoming ever more effective at linking up across borders to pursue transnational agendas.

As they become more powerful, their role faces increasing scrutiny. At the United Nations, Secretary-General Kofi Annan has assembled a high-level panel led by former Brazilian president Fernando Henrique Cardoso to conduct a sweeping assessment of interactions between the UN and civil society organizations. Within the U.S., long a proponent of citizen activism in other countries, an anti-NGO backlash has emerged. A Washington think tank has launched an NGO-monitoring project that describes the activities of such groups as Amnesty International and Greenpeace as a threat to democracy. The U.S. Agency for International Development, which gives much of its funding for development and relief projects to NGOs, told several such recipients that they were not allowed to speak to the media. Others were threatened with loss of funding if they were unwilling to conform to Bush administration foreign and domestic policy.

Some of this backlash just represents the efforts of the powerful to squash rivals and critics. Some reflects legitimate concerns about the terms on which various groups get to influence the rules that run the world. But in either case, the fight is likely to intensify because this greatly enhanced power of NGOs is here to stay.

In part, this is because globalization has created new battlegrounds over what rules (on everything from trade to Internet regulation to protecting endangered species) will govern the world. As governments get together to come up with those rules, NGOs flock to the meetings, determined to ensure that their views are heard. The series of UN conferences that began in the 1970s were meant primarily to draw governments together to consider how to deal with global issues. But as it turned out, the most important role of the conferences was to provide a focal point around which global civil society could coalesce. Non-governmental groups appeared in force at the 1972 UN Conference on the Human Environment, with accredited NGOs outnumbering governmental delegations two to one. Over the next 25 years, the UN hosted more than a dozen enormous conferences on everything from food to population to the role of women. Each stimulated a flurry of networking among the non-governmental groups working on the issues.

(Continued)

(Continued)

And information technology has linked those groups together into powerful networks of the socially concerned. Activist groups have always relied on information technologies to get their messages out and mobilize citizens. The Western social movements of the 1960s were transformed by television. A few mentions on the evening news could do much of what previously required massive organizing. This had been somewhat true in the age of print, but visuals proved much more compelling. The effects were national because television at that time was a national medium. But the Internet and e-mail are free of such geographical constraints, enabling networks to incorporate a vastly greater range of people than ever before possible. The massive protests against the Iraq war were pulled together in weeks, coordinated via e-mail list serves and Web sites.

In addition, thanks to higher levels of education and material standards of living, more and more people from all parts of the world have entered the middle class, with the skills and leisure time to participate in civil society. And once they start, they tend to keep going. Movements and coalitions often recruit their members from existing organizations that serve a different purpose. Churches were the springboard of both the early American women's movement and the more recent civil rights movement. But we seem to be reaching a self-sustaining cascade, as so many people are involved in some form of civil society organization in so many parts of the world that vast numbers are available for recruitment.

As democratic ideals spread, governments are finding themselves under pressure to allow citizens to form NGOs. The U.S. used to be unusual in making it fairly easy for organizations to establish themselves. But after the Cold War ended, central and eastern European countries found themselves overwhelmed with Western funds to support the creation of NGOs, along with strongly worded advice about the necessity of allowing citizens to organize themselves. Even Asia, where many governments strictly regulate which organizations can be legally registered or allowed to exist at all, is seeing change. In 1998, Japan abolished onerous regulations that had, among other things, required would-be NGOs to have 300 million yen (about $3 million) in "basic capital" permanently in the bank.

Most NGOs have nowhere near $3 million. But some have considerably more, and all have to raise funds from somewhere. That money general [*sic*] comes from three sources: governments (which are the largest contributors, especially to non-profit service providers like hospitals, educational institutions and various charities), voluntary contributions from individuals, corporations and foundations, and fees charged for services rendered. And there may soon be a lot more money available. In the world's rich countries, the next 50 years will witness a huge transfer of wealth from one generation to the next, totaling well over $10 trillion for the U.S. alone. Since bequests often provide a means for channeling large amounts of money from private hands to NGOs, a fair chunk of this money may go to support civil society. The examples of Bill Gates, George Soros and Ted Turner, whose donations are in the hundreds of millions, or billions, of dollars, may spur other members of the world's growing group of extremely wealthy individuals to follow suit.

In short, it seems likely that the explosion of NGO activism around the world is still in its infancy. Globalization will continue to create targets of opportunity. More and more people will be able and willing to participate. Information technology will continue to lower the costs of staying connected to distant regions. Money, while not plentiful, will be available. And governments will accommodate the growing pressures for civil society participation by providing the legal conditions under which these groups can exist, and perhaps even flourish.

So is this a good thing? The world of NGO-watchers resounds these days with criticisms about the lack of accountability of the self-appointed do-gooders inhabiting the NGO community. These unelected guardians of the global public good, the critics say, claim to speak for the world but in fact speak only for themselves. The so-called "anti-globalization" movement comes in for the harshest criticism, dismissed as ill-informed Northern do-gooders or wild-eyed anti-capitalist anarchists, who either don't know or don't care that their campaigns against global economic integration will hurt the very poor they claim to want to help.

For the most part, this is a bum rap. Few oppose global integration per se. Instead, they are "globalization's critics"—people who object to specific consequences of certain global rules, or to the political processes by which globalization is being governed, or both. It is a broad, loose-knit collection of NGOs, labor unions, church groups and other associations from both rich and poor countries—so broad that many of its participants, rejecting the "anti-globalization" label but unable to come up with an accurate replacement, simply call it "the Movement."

The Movement arose because many of the activists whose primary concerns are local and national have come to believe that the roots of their problems lie at the global level. Those concerned with national environmental protection or labor rights must pay attention to global trade rules that affect domestic regulations. Those concerned with national economic development can hardly ignore the implications of International Monetary Fund conditionality or financial volatility. Yes, there are plenty of participants more interested in street theater than in serious substance, but many of the groups are well-informed and deeply concerned with the substance of global issues. And the violent fringe is just that, a tiny minority widely resented by the much larger number of peaceful protestors.

Although the attacks on globalization's critics are often unfair, there are real and important questions about the newfound global power of NGOs. NGOs are powerful to the degree they can persuade others (government officials, corporate leaders, voters, consumers) to act. They are primarily conveyers of information and opinions. But not all are motivated by the pursuit of truth, justice, and equity. Some are little more than front groups for various concealed interests. There's a whole lexicon of pejorative terms for such groups: GONGOs (governmental NGOs), BONGOs (business NGOs), QUANGOs (quasi-NGOs) and, my personal favorite, MANGOs (Mafia-front NGOs). A good case can be made for a new term: TANGOs, describing the "charitable" groups that channel money to terrorists.

But the existence of bad groups does not mean that NGOs as a whole should be restricted. The good ones, who far outnumber the bad, do a great deal of good for the world. Without NGOs, there would be little pressure to stop governments from torturing citizens, devastating the environment, or caving in to corporate pressures to design the rules of globalization to favor corporate interests. Without NGOs, many of the pressing issues now on the global agenda, from human rights to the inequities of global trade rules to ozone depletion, would never have received much attention.

(Continued)

(Continued)

The way to deal with NGOs isn't to attack them all as somehow illegitimate. Instead, NGOs should be required to demonstrate the same transparency they regularly demand of governments and corporations. Good NGOs are already recognizing that their growing role carries with it new responsibilities for public accountability. Through such initiatives as the Humanitarian Accountability Partnership (http://www.hapinternational.org/en/), the British-based organization AccountAbility (http://www.accountability.org.uk/) and the Global Reporting Initiative (http://www.globalreporting.org/), NGOs are trying to come up with ways to hold themselves to the same standards they are demanding of others. That is a huge first step, but it needs to go much farther [*sic*]. Those who have designated themselves the guardians of a global public interest must now make it much easier for others to watch them. The public whose interests they adamantly claim to defend has the right to see what they are up to in the public's name.

SOURCE: From "Is Global Civil Society a Good Thing?" by A. Florini, 2004, *New Perspectives Quarterly, 21*(2), pp. 72–76. Copyright © 2004 by New Perspectives Quarterly. By permission of Wiley-Blackwell.

Concepts of Virtual Change

Florini (2004) asked, "Is global civil society a good thing? She concluded that the majority of NGOs "do a great deal of good for the world," though there are some bad groups in the mix, and she asserted that NGOs must meet the same standards of accountability they demand of others. In her commentary, Florini acknowledged the substantial impact of the Internet and other information technology on collective action in civil society; however, she did not examine virtual activism or virtual change initiatives per se. Are global dotcauses or e-movements a good thing? What change and leadership concepts do they employ and what practices do they use? In the remaining sections, we focus on several of these questions.

Transnational Advocacy and Activism in Cyberspace

The role and influence of transnational advocacy networks have increased exponentially with the advent of information technology. Advocacy, as explained in Chapters 5 and 8 by Cohen, De la Vega, and Watson (2001), consists of organized actions to highlight ignored and suppressed critical issues, influence public attitudes, and promote the enactment and implementation of laws and public policies. However, information technology allows transnational NGOs to signalize and attract many more potential advocates to an issue or cause globally than traditional communication methods through the use of their Internet presence, and they create a hyperlinked network of organizations that share their concern and advocacy agenda about a particular issue. These hyperlinks help form transnational advocacy networks in cyberspace that "connect websites much as social relations connect agents in real space" (Carpenter, 2007, p. 113). Their advocacy plans and process can then be loosely or closely coordinated to achieve their aims.

Virtual activism is a relatively recent phenomenon. Many dotcauses did not exist before 1995, and many came into being after 2001 (Clark & Themudo, 2006, p. 52). Like their business counterparts, dotcauses exist as *clicks only* and as hybrids known as *clicks and bricks*. Dotcauses that are clicks exist solely on the Internet and have no physical address, whereas hybrids, or clicks and bricks, have both an Internet and a physical presence. Even in the case of hybrids, their Internet presence fosters a considerable amount of their activism.

Virtual activism involves concerted actions for change by dotcauses and e-movements that can range from raising funds online to organizing rallies and demonstrations online that take place at physical sites such as the ones mentioned in Florini's (2004) commentary to staging "virtual sit-ins," also known as engaging in *hacktivism*—a type of cyber-civil disobedience used in social or political protest to disrupt a target's Web site by overloading it with requests or searches for a period of time (Slambrouck, 1999, p. 3). TANs direct their actions toward specific targets or organizations whose social or political policies they want to influence, and their actions have often resulted in substantive change on behalf of citizens or affected groups.

Cultural Framing and Online Identity

Cultural framing refers to the development or existence of shared understanding and meaning among people in a movement or dotcause—a shared awareness of the issue or cause, and a shared view of the world and themselves (Clark & Themudo, 2006, p. 63). This shared understanding and meaning help to create a collective identity (see Chapter 8) and provide the basis for collective action.

Dotcauses or e-movements have developed online media outlets that provide alternative news, analyses, and information that are different from representations in mainstream media. These online outlets allow dotcauses to communicate their own cultural framing without the filtering of traditional media.

The cultural framing and direct communication of alternative perspectives have contributed to greater ideological pluralism, "giving transnational voice to many previously unheard groups," especially with regard to diverse grievances "ranging from worry about job security, corporate greed, Third World debt, and HIV/AIDS, to concerns of cultural takeover, and environmental destruction" associated with the antiglobal capitalist movement (Clark & Themudo, 2006, p. 64). Given the diverse range of issues and constituencies encompassed broadly under problems related to globalization, the Movement has had a difficult time proposing a unifying alternative. TANs are in search of a unifying frame for their diverse constituency that promotes a movement for the world they want rather than a movement against the world they do not want. John Clark and Nuno Themudo (2006) indicated that the World Social Forum (WSF) and the International Forum on Globalization are creating greater unity in the Movement toward agreement on desirable components of the world that activists are seeking (p. 64).

Global Social Contract Formation

The idea of a social contract between government and its citizens about the rights and responsibilities of the parties to each other has long been an established component within nation-states. Yet Baogang He and Hannah Murphy (2007) contended that the neoliberal economic paradigm (described in Chapter 10) "has increased the power of the private sector and has weakened the social contract between citizens and their governments" (p. 709). They argued that the decline of the social contract within nation-states and the delegation of several areas of policy making to international organizations have caused NGO activists and scholars to call for a global social contract that promotes social justice and equitable development.

By compiling several definitions, He and Murphy (2007) suggested that "a global social contract is a political and moral principle for international agreements and for governing the conduct of all actors in the international arena" (p. 711). Their construct incorporates three core elements:

- A global social contract is *global*: that is, it recognizes that citizens in developed, developing, and underdeveloped nations are interdependent, and ought to be regarded as important contracting parties;
- A global social contract embodies *social justice*, meaning that adequate social protection and the principle of equality should be incorporated into international agreements; and
- A global social contract is the *democratic process* undertaken in constructing the agreement. (He & Murphy, 2007, p. 711, italics in original)

The role of transnational dotcauses and other NGOs is to serve as representatives of the third sector (civil society) and work with government and the private sector to help construct a global social contract.

Concepts of Virtual Leadership

Leadership of Online Activism

As scholars begin to study leadership of online TANs and NGOs, they are discovering a different kind of leadership emerging than the leadership in face-to-face activism. A study conducted by Alan Schussman and Jennifer Earl (2004) on leadership in the strategic voting movement (also known as Nader-trading) found that, contrary to studies of movement leadership in previous periods, prior activism experience was not the sole or best indicator of the kinds of individuals that became online leaders (p. 440). They examined Web site content from 19 strategic voting movement sites and conducted interviews with site creators from 13 of those sites. The researchers found that many of the e-movement entrepreneurs or founders (9 of 13) were more likely to have strong technological experience (as Web masters, concept designers, computer scientists, or information technology professionals) and little or no prior activist experience, whereas only 5 of the 13 individuals had high levels of prior activist experience (e.g., participation in protest campaigns and fundraising for political or civil rights issues), and 4 of the 13 had little or no technological experience (pp. 448–450).

Schussman and Earl's (2004) study provides insights into leadership of online activism in several areas:

- *Leadership expectations*—Leadership of online activism seems to be less hampered by traditional expectations from members of social movement organizations for leaders to use different styles that meet members' needs. Instead, the desire for different styles of leadership is replaced by users' preferences for certain kinds of technologies and implementation approaches—that is, the choices offered on a Web site or by different kinds of Web sites present users with variations that suit their needs and preferences, much like variations in leadership styles.
- *Size of leadership team and costs*—Reduced labor and capital costs of sites founded by technological experts resulted in a significant reduction in size of the organizing group, whereas sites founded by individuals with limited technological expertise and more activism experience resulted in larger teams or organizing groups. The site with the largest organizing group (a hired professional team) was founded by an individual with no activist or technological expertise.
- *Conceptual frames for organizing and problem solving*—Different paths to leadership of online social activism (i.e., through technological experience, political experience, a combination of technological and political experience, or no experience in either area) lead to different models of problem solving, different ways of organizing politically oriented activity, and different levels of knowledge about the role and capacity of technology.
- *Paths to online leadership*—Technically savvy individuals with limited activism experience seem to be drawn to leadership of online activism "because of their ability to imagine problems in a technically informed manner" and not their actual programming skills, whereas individuals with considerable activism experience and limited technical savvy seem to be drawn to leadership of online activism because of prior socialization and experience in the activist community, and a few individuals come to online leadership with a combination of activism experience and technical expertise (pp. 456–458).

There are many questions for future research based on this and other studies of online leadership of dotcauses or e-movements. Does the expert knowledge and use of communication technology change the nature and type of leadership involved in activism? What are the advantages and consequences of group size on leadership of online activism, especially considering some sites are run by only one or two individuals? Which paths or types of preparation for online leadership are most effective for advancing social and political activism? How are problems framed and solved differently through technically informed means than through face-to-face approaches?

Leadership Structure, Power, and Roles

The leadership structure of dotcauses or e-movements is often based on equalitarian networks and organized using collegial principles with limited or no hierarchy. "The Movement celebrates equality, not hierarchy; followers are urged to be leaders, to think for themselves, and to act as they choose" (Clark & Themudo, 2006, p. 67). Bureaucracy and hierarchical structures are impractical in most e-movements because their membership base is dispersed and events or campaigns are frequently staffed by volunteers. These leadership structures function through voluntary, reciprocal, and horizontal patterns of communication and exchange (Keck & Sikkink, as cited in Custard, 2007, p. 7).

Power is broadly distributed in many e-movements or dotcauses. In some dotcauses, membership alone gives individuals the right to participate and the power to make decisions. Members may organize events and campaigns that reflect the basic purpose and mission or platform of the dotcause. Even though the distinguishing feature of dotcauses is that they would not exist without the Internet, many dotcauses organize face-to-face events, such as meetings or conferences, protests, and affinity groups, or encourage their members to form their own chapters, branches, or franchises (Clark & Themudo, 2006, p. 63).

The aversion of dotcause founders to traditional concepts of power and leadership present both opportunities and challenges for e-movements. Dotcause founders are reluctant to be seen as leaders or spokespersons because of their grassroots or populist philosophy of social activism (Clark & Themudo, 2006, p. 67). Dotcause structures support the citizen's use of her or his own agency to bring about change. Their approach is the opposite of traditional leader-centric models that typify many Western concepts of leadership.

In their effort to distance themselves from leader-centric models of positional authority, dotcause founders may have overlooked the value of having leadership roles to facilitate organizational functioning and effectiveness. Roles structure behavior (in terms of who is responsible for what functions) and determine the "part" that members take in groups or organizations, but they are not fixed, and they do not need to be relegated to one person or an elite group. Members can move in and out of different roles within a dotcause or between various dotcauses or TANs. Establishing leadership roles (not positions) may be vital for helping dotcauses engender trust and credibility or generate support and raise funds. Implementing leadership roles may help dotcauses work between and among the many grassroots movements within the Movement to provide greater coherence among advocacy agendas and goals on a global scale. Clark and Themudo (2006) summarized the impending issue for dotcauses:

> Many Movement proponents are trying to present an alternative political project but have not yet succeeded . . . it is too early to say whether the Movement will indeed lead to the emergence of a global democracy "from below" or disintegrate through lack of unity in purpose. (p. 68)

Access, Culture, and the Digital Divide

Transnational advocacy networks and NGOs strive to embrace the causes of groups around the world. Yet dotcauses and e-movements remain unavailable to many segments of the global population. Custard (2007) contended that "to achieve a true global civil society, greater efforts need to be made to incorporate marginalized voices and facilitate true intercultural understanding" (p. 4).

One of the difficult challenges for dotcause or e-movement leadership is bridging the access, cultural, and digital divide between North-South, urban-rural, rich-poor, young-old, minority-majority groups, powerful-disenfranchised, and educated-uneducated, among other categories. Only about 21.9% of the world's population has access to the Internet (Internet World Stats, 2008). This lack of access excludes many individuals and organizations from bringing their causes to the forefront and initiating or participating in e-movements. Their voices and perspectives "reside outside the network" (Custard, 2007, p. 20). Still others are excluded because of their lack of education and ability to read, which inhibits their capacity to use the computer, and an inability to communicate in a major international language (typically English, French, or Spanish). These factors create the very problem that movement activists endeavor to resolve—creating a power hierarchy of the privileged and wealthy over the disadvantaged and poor.

TANs must negotiate the challenges of intercultural communication and interface online. Custard (2007) pointed out that little work has been done on how diverse cultures in TANs interact, negotiate meaning, or identify and overcome potential bias in participation (p. 17). To include the diversity of voices and perspectives that currently reside outside the network, she suggested that NGOs need to engage with the communities they intend to serve because these NGOs are often the only advocates with access to technology and TANs. This process of engagement "includes participatory acts of collaboration and negotiation to determine needs and shape solutions at physical locations that then needs to be 'translated' onto the network" (Custard, 2007, p. 20).

Virtual Change Practices

Establishing Virtual Presence and Identity

Dotcause or e-movement Web sites provide an opportunity for self-presentation and communication of philosophy, priorities, purpose, and social, political, and economic values. Web sites often provide the only representation of organizational identity; a number of dotcauses have no physical location or address. Words and images convey the organization's public identity and state its position on issues in an effort to attract members and visitors to the site.

The importance of a dotcause's virtual presence is illustrated by the International Campaign to Ban Landmines (ICBL). This dotcause mobilized people worldwide to eliminate the use of landmines, yet when their group was awarded the Nobel Peace Prize, they did not even have a bank account in which to deposit the prize money (Clark & Themudo, 2006, p. 52). An excerpt from ICBL's Web site and several dotcauses provide examples of how these movements develop their identity and presence online.

International Campaign to Ban Landmines

Who we are

- A network of more than 1,400 groups in over 90 countries, works locally, nationally and internationally to eradicate antipersonnel mines.
- Members include human rights, humanitarian, children, peace, disability, veterans, medical, humanitarian, mine action, development, arms control, religious, environmental and women's groups.

What we stand for
The campaign calls for:

- A worldwide ban on antipersonnel landmines
- Universal membership of the 1997 Mine Ban Treaty
- Support of the needs and rights of landmine survivors
- Demining and risk education to safeguard lives and livelihoods.

Our message can be summed up by the slogan: "Ban Mines! Clear Mines! Help the survivors!" (International Campaign to Ban Landmines, n.d.)

Third World Network

Third World Network (TWN) is an independent non-profit international network of organisations and individuals involved in issues relating to development, Third World and North-South affairs. . . . Its mission is to bring about a greater articulation of the needs and rights of peoples in the Third World, a fair distribution of world resources, and forms of development which are ecologically sustainable and fulfill human needs.

Its main objectives are: to conduct research on economic, social and environmental issues pertaining to the South; to publish books and magazines; to organise and participate in meetings and seminars; and to provide a platform representing broadly Southern interests and perspectives at international fora such as the UN Conferences and processes. (Third World Network, n.d.)

OneWorld.net

OneWorld aims to be the place global citizens turn to for news and views from around the world not covered in mainstream media; we are also a key hub that Americans use to find and interact with like-minded individuals and organizations from around the world.

To accomplish this mission, OneWorld has created a unique Web presence. OneWorld.net is an online media gateway for independently produced news on a host of issues that impact people worldwide. Built on sources from our global network, which includes nongovernmental organizations, development-oriented news services, foundations and research institutions, this unique Web space is both a search engine and online community for organizations and individuals seeking in-depth information or guidance on how to become involved in addressing challenges facing people worldwide. (OneWorld.net, n.d.)

Unrepresented Nations and People (UNPO)

The Unrepresented Nations and Peoples Organization (UNPO) is an international, nonviolent, and democratic membership organisation. Its members are indigenous peoples, minorities, and unrecognised or occupied territories who have joined together to protect and promote their human and cultural rights, to preserve their environments, and to find nonviolent solutions to conflicts which affect them.

Although the aspirations of UNPO Members differ greatly, they are all united by one shared condition—they are not adequately represented at major international fora, such as the United Nations. As a consequence, their opportunity to participate on the international stage is significantly limited, as is their ability to access and draw upon the support of the global bodies mandated to defend their rights, protect their environments, and mitigate the effects of conflict. (Unrepresented Nations and Peoples Organization, n.d.)

Virtual Mobilization and Political Opportunity Structure

Like social movements in the past, Internet activism relies on mobilization (to fuel their efforts; see Chapter 8), though much of the mobilization begins virtually. E-movements can serve as wholesalers or retailers for purposes of mobilization. Wholesalers coordinate a common global campaign strategy for activities such as protests in multiple geographic locations, whereas practical aspects of organizing take place at local or national levels (Clark & Themudo, 2006, pp. 61–62). They can attract hundreds of groups across multiple countries throughout the world. Retailers communicate directly with the public and provide space for supporters to become involved by conducting analysis, devising strategy, posting views and experiences, creating a blog, entering a chat room, or becoming an organizer (Clark & Themudo, 2006, p. 62).

The political opportunity structure (described in Chapter 8) can provide channels to advance social and political goals, and it can create barriers against raising issues and gaining access to power holders (Pudrovska & Ferree, 2004, p. 120). Dotcauses use political opportunities to further their cause and help identify the best location or level in the structure to mobilize and apply pressure (Clark & Themudo, 2006, p. 62). Major factors in opening political opportunities to TANs and dotcauses have been dwindling public trust and confidence in the ability of national governments and international governance organizations to manage the effects of globalization and to represent the interests of citizens and the environment in forums such as the World Trade Organization (WTO) (Clark & Themudo, 2006, p. 65). These factors have created political opportunities for online activists to use Web sites to provide alternative media and sources of information, organize major citizen protests, and voice civil society perspectives.

An organization's Internet presence and identity can play an important role in how the organization positions itself for transnational advocacy in the political opportunity structure. Pudrovska and Ferree's (2004) study of the European Women's Lobby (EWL), a transnational women's advocacy group, provides an example of how the group communicates its identity and presence on the Internet to make use of the European Union's (EU) political opportunity structure. The EU's wide range of legal and political institutions, such as the European Court of Justice and the European Parliament, provide a favorable opportunity structure for the EWL to advocate for women's rights and representation in the EU. Pudrovska and Ferree pointed out that the EWL receives political endorsement and resources from the European Commission of the EU (p. 134). As a result, the organization's self-presentation online illustrates how the EWL positions itself for transnational advocacy in the political opportunity structure:

> The European Women's Lobby aims at promoting women's rights and equality between women and men in the European Union. EWL is active in different areas such as women's economic and social position, women in decision-making, violence against women, women's diversity, etc. EWL works mainly with the institutions of the European Union: the European Parliament, the European Commission and the EU Council of Ministers. (European Women's Lobby, n.d.)

Pudrovska and Ferree (2004) analyzed 29 Web sites of international women's organizations and compared them to the EWL ($N = 30$). They examined the EWL's positioning in the transnational community of feminist activists and analyzed "how the words the EWL uses on its Web site construct a particular public identity for the group" (p. 126). The authors made the following findings:

- The EWL positions itself more narrowly as a European advocacy group and less globally than it might, particularly given that many groups in the United States reference it.
- The EWL's Web site avoids using the term *feminists* but frames women as active and organized and emphasizes agency, politics, law, and global sisterhood as themes.
- The EWL also does not engage as often in framing its concerns to include family or reproductive health, issues that fall outside the formal remit of the EU, than it does in mentioning the economy and other social problems, including violence against women.

- The EWL presents its Web site as actively engaging with a regulatory state that offers a market-led opportunity structure in which employment issues and legal/administrative strategies would dominate. (pp. 117, 133–136)

The agendas of other dotcauses or e-movements may not align as closely with a transnational organization's policy structure. However, they can take cues from the EWL's example of constructing its Web messages and social or political positions in a manner that allows its members to seize political opportunities.

Accountability and Legitimacy

Florini's (2004) commentary raises the issue of accountability and transparency in transnational NGOs. Because NGOs have stepped in to challenge globalization and interject citizen perspectives into global governance, they face closer scrutiny of their own legitimacy and accountability. Anton Vedder (2003) suggested that when NGOs are "exclusively active through the Internet (e.g., McSpotlight and Cokewatch), requirements of legitimacy and accountability run the risk of being easily pushed aside" (p. 54).

In response to criticisms that NGOs exaggerate their level of support and may represent only a minority of elites instead of civil society generally, He and Murphy (2007) contended that the value of NGOs is in their role as policy entrepreneurs, rather than as formal representatives (p. 713). The authors argued that NGOs help international organizations develop processes that create global social contracts and enhance the legitimacy and accountability of global governance.

Still, there are practices, especially by some virtual activists, that prompt critics to call for greater accountability. Dotcauses that use hacktivism or engage in strategic voting or Nader-trading carry out these activities at the margin of the law, while using virtuality to protect their anonymity (Clark & Themudo, 2006, p. 53). In addition, lack of face-to-face communication or sustained physical contact with members creates obstacles to identifying organizational constituencies and consequently makes accountability more difficult (Clark & Themudo, 2006, p. 54).

Vedder (2003) proposed that dotcauses use the very technologies that sustain their existence to bolster their accountability and legitimacy:

- They can use electronic means (email, websites, discussion panels, intranet) in order to raise the transparency of the organization and to involve people in their ideals, mission and work;
- ICT [information and communication technologies]—especially all kinds of Internet applications—offers all kinds of possibilities of interactivity with regard to the processing of information and the creation of awareness; and
- An archive with past performance records and a database with plans for the future—both of them publicly accessible on the website of the NGO—would already be a big step in the right direction. (pp. 53–54)

Florini (2004) added that good NGOs are already recognizing their responsibility for transparency and public accountability and are voluntarily participating in initiatives such as Humanitarian Accountability Partnerships and AccountAbility, among others.

Conclusion

Are global dotcauses or e-movements a good thing? Clark and Themudo (2006) suggested that "virtuality" generates a number of strengths and weaknesses. The benefits include little or no costs for startup and physical space; low cost for communication, printing, and publishing; use of egalitarian networks over hierarchical structure; and the ability to disseminate alternative opinions and information to a wide audience. Disadvantages include lack of face-to-face communications, which can hamper accountability and trust building; an ability to engage in anonymous disruptive activities; greater difficulty in reaching consensus on strategies and tactics; and limitations to access and participation by certain unrepresented groups (pp. 52–54).

Overall, dotcauses add a much needed voice and perspective from civil society to emerging global processes, agreements, and governance. Dotcauses help to foster unity within the Movement and perpetuate pluralism by avoiding strong hierarchical leadership both within networks and in the Movement; however, the emergence of dotcauses poses new dilemmas and challenges for groups such as traditional NGOs and trade unions about their collaboration and participation in the Movement (Clark & Themudo, 2006, pp. 67–69).

References

Carpenter, R. C. (2007). Setting the advocacy agenda: Theorizing issue emergence and nonemergence in transnational advocacy networks. *International Studies Quarterly, 51*, 99–120.

Clark, J. D., & Themudo, N. S. (2006). Linking the web and the street: Internet-based "dotcauses" and the "anti-globalization" movement. *World Development, 34*(1), 50–74.

Cohen, D., De la Vega, R., & Watson, G. (2001). *Advocacy for social justice: A global action and reflection guide.* Bloomfield, CT: Kumarian Press.

Custard, H. (2007, May). *The internet and global civil society: Communication and representation within transnational advocacy networks.* Paper presented at the annual meeting of the International Communication Association, San Francisco.

European Women's Lobby. (n.d.). *EWL.* Retrieved March 6, 2009, from http://www.women lobby.org/site/1Template1.asp?DocID=1&v1ID=&RevID=&namePage=&pageParent= &DocID_sousmenu=

Florini, A. (2004). Is global civil society a good thing? *New Perspectives Quarterly, 21*(2), 72–76.

He, B., & Murphy, H. (2007). Global social justice at the WTO? The role of NGOs in constructing global social contracts. *International Affairs, 83*, 707–727.

International Campaign to Ban Landmines. (n.d.). *What is the ICBL?* Retrieved March 6, 2009, from http://www.icbl.org/tools/faq/campaign/what_is_icbl

Internet World Stats. (2008). *Internet usage and population statistics.* Retrieved October 19, 2008, from http://www.internetworldstats.com/stats.htm

OneWorld.net. (n.d.). *How we work.* Retrieved March 6, 2009, from http://us.oneworld .net/about/how_we+work

Pudrovska, T., & Ferree, M. M. (2004). Global activism in "virtual space:" The European women's lobby in the network of transnational women's NGOs on the web. *Social Politics, 11,* 117–143.

Schussman, A., & Earl, J. (2004). From barricades to firewalls? Strategic voting and social movement leadership in the internet age. *Sociological Inquiry, 74,* 439–463.

Slambrouck, P. V. (1999). Newest tool for social protest: The Internet. *Christian Science Monitor.* Retrieved March 6, 2009, http://www.thehacktivist.com/archive/news/1999/ Newesttool-CSMonitor-1999.pdf

Third World Network. (n.d.). *Introduction.* Retrieved March 6, 2009, from http://twnside .org.sg/twnintro.htm

Unrepresented Nations and Peoples Organization. (n.d.). *Introduction.* Retrieved March 6, 2009, from http://www.unpo.org/content/view/7782/239/

Vedder, A. (2003). Internet NGOs: Legitimacy and accountability. *Electronic Government, Proceedings, 2739,* 49–54.

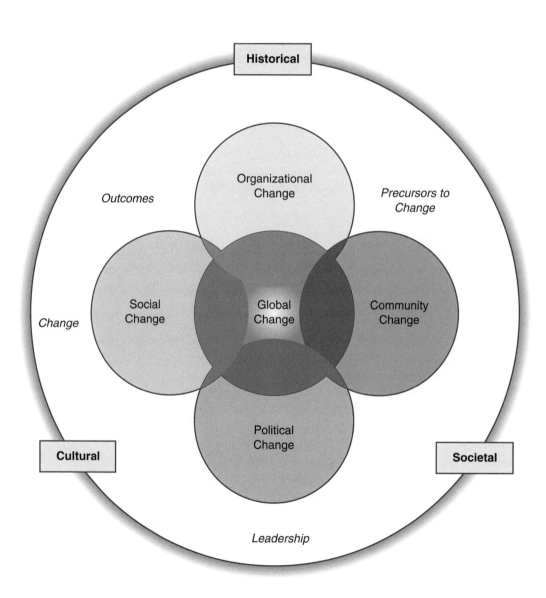

CHAPTER 12

Conclusion

Connecting Concepts and
Practices in Multiple Contexts

J ean Lipman-Blumen (1996) made the following projection at the end of the
20th century:

> All signs indicate that global *interdependence* is accelerating at a furious pace.
> Politically, economically, and environmentally, we are living in a world where
> leadership decisions anywhere now affect everything and everyone every-
> where. (p. 4, italics in original)

Now more than ever the effects of change can be seen reverberating across multiple contexts. The Venn diagram in the opening figure illustrates interdependence
among organizational, community, political, social, and global change. Examples of
interdependence between contexts in several chapters are highlighted in the
vignettes featuring microcredit to rural women, the Sikh Coalition, and the global
civil society.

Interdependence among contexts becomes even more apparent as one witnesses
examples such as the collapse of financial institutions and major companies that
fosters economic recession and a decline in the U.S. stock market, which in turn,
generate similar recessions and declines across the globe. Communities weaken and
crime rates soar as people experience job losses and housing foreclosures.

President Barack Obama, his team of advisors and cabinet members, and
members of Congress are called on to lead change—intentionally modify, alter, or
transform human social systems—with the purpose of financially reinforcing businesses, boosting the economy, and putting people back to work. To achieve change
of this magnitude, these actors may well consider many of the analytical and

contextual elements presented in the introductory chapters and examined throughout the book.

Table 12.1 reiterates these analytical and contextual elements and incorporates examples of concepts and practices of leading change that correspond to elements from preceding chapters. Long-term contextual forces of history, culture, and society (macroforces)—such as forming and restructuring nation-states with their diverse political and economic systems, cultures and ethnic groups, and societal norms and customs—promote and constrain change across and within immediate (micro)contexts. Immediate contexts influence the purpose, participants, source of authority, and affected groups in the change process. The vignettes throughout the text—about Technology Solutions (organizational); Citizens for the Responsible Destruction of Chemical Weapons (community); Extraordinary Rendition (political); OASIS/mental health consumer movement (social change/movements); and the Chad-Cameroon pipeline (global)—illustrate immediate contextual influences.

Examining precursors to change allows individuals in the change process to consider the field or totality of coexisting factors (causality), often dialectical, complex, and turbulent, that contribute to the change at hand and see them as an interdependent system. Individuals in the leadership process contemplate ethical issues and values along with potential consequences of taking one set of actions over another before moving forward (mindfulness). Actors in the Chad-Cameroon pipeline situation, for example, did not adequately consider the implications of change in one part of the system (building an oil pipeline) on the other parts (e.g., environmental impact, revenues used for military weapons rather than poverty relief) prior to beginning the project.

Participants in the leadership process must consider the social tensions and conditions that prompt change. For instance, a decline in the high-tech industry (conditions for change) contributed to a downturn in business for Technology Solutions and ultimately led to a reduction in profits and five rounds of layoffs. This situation exacerbated social tensions with regard to previously established relations between employees and senior managers. As a result, power relationships shifted from inclusive leadership to executive authority, and social capital among members declined. Even after the crisis subsided at Technology Solutions, a culture of resistance persisted among long-term employees.

Leadership can function as intended change, the cause of change, or the action for change in a particular process. In the vignette about Citizens for the Responsible Destruction of Chemical Weapons (CRDCW), all three functions of leadership were evident in the community's effort to keep a facility out of their area that posed an environmental threat. Community residents formed the CRDCW with the aim of producing teleological (purposeful) change. They used nonconstituted and convening leadership, expert advice, and systems thinking to lead intended change in Jefferson Township. Their use of social power along with invisible, generative, and transforming leadership and practices of signaling, resource mobilization, and advocacy led to the army's decision to issue stop-work orders to Perma-Fix (leadership as the cause of change and leadership as action for change).

Assessment of the outcomes of change entails a willingness by participants to evaluate intended consequences (anticipated change), unintended consequences (positive and negative outcomes that actors did not foresee), and the impact of these

TABLE 12.1 Analytical and Contextual Elements With Concepts and Practices of Leading Change

ANALYTICAL ELEMENTS	CONTEXTUAL ELEMENTS Historical Societal Cultural Organizational Community Political Social Global		
	Concepts of Change	Concepts of Leadership	Change Practices
Precursors to Change	**Examples**	**Examples**	**Examples**

Causality
 	
• Systems and field theory (interdependency, coexisting facts)
  ○ Subsystems
  ○ Patterns—fractals
• Dynamic social causation (cumulation)
• Invisible (unseen) structure (time, space, energy, uncertainty)
	• Field theory
	• Systems theory/change
	• Dialectical theory
	• Chaos and complexity theory
	• Turbulent environment
		• Ethical leadership/values
		• Transcending
			• Systems thinking
			• Scenario building/planning

Mindfulness • Critical reflection • Seeing total context • Consequences or costs	• Systems theory	• Tao leadership • Transcending • Ethical values	• Change of mind • Systems thinking • Scenario building/planning • Asset mapping • Appreciative inquiry
Change			
Social tensions • Identity and meaning • Resource availability and distribution • Power • Ethics	• Social movement theories—classical, rational, new social movements • Countermovements • Representation and participation • Social capital • Social power/empowerment • Legitimate/constituted power • Globalization theories	• Transcending • Inclusive • Ubuntu • Ethical leadership/ethics of responsibility	• Vertical and horizontal networks • Resource mobilization • Ethical practices • Cultures of resistance
Conditions for change • Climate • Timing • Threshold points	• Life cycle • Dialectical • Evolutionary	• Nonconstituted/citizens leadership • Legitimate/constituted • Strategic • Ethical leadership	• Signalizing • Political opportunity structure • Strategic planning

(Continued)

TABLE 12.1 (Continued)

CONTEXTUAL ELEMENTS Historical Societal Cultural Organizational Community Political Social Global			
ANALYTICAL ELEMENTS	**Concepts of Change**	**Concepts of Leadership**	**Change Practices**
Leadership	**Examples**	**Examples**	**Examples**
Leadership as intended change • Intentional and predictable • Unpredictable and unintentional	• Teleological theory • Systems theory/change • Social power/ empowerment • Global change theories	• Adaptive leadership/work • Transforming and transactional • Nonconstituted/ citizen • Legitimate/constituted • Convening • Ethic of responsibility • Ethical leadership	• Scenario building • Systems thinking • Expert advice • Stages of praxis • Incremental change
Leadership as the cause of change • Interdependent actors and influences • Direct influences and indirect influences	• Strategic change • Social power/ empowerment • Legitimate/ constituted power	• Charismatic leadership • Nonconstituted/ citizen leadership • Legitimate/ constituted leadership • Invisible leadership • Servant leadership • Folly	• Signalizing • Change of mind • Resource mobilization • Conflict capital development

Leadership as action for change
 	
• Purpose
• Coactors—leaders and participants
• Momentum or movement
   o Imagination and generativity
   o Communication and meaning making
   o Coaction
	• Teleological
	• Social movement theory
	• Social capital
	• Cultural framing and identity
		• Generative leadership
		• Shared leadership
		• Invisible leadership
		• Transforming
		• Transformational leadership
		• Transactional
		• E-leadership/virtual activism
		• Team leadership
		• Initiative, inclusiveness, creativity
		• Adaptive work
		• Nonconstituted/ citizen
		• Legitimate/ constituted
		• Ethical leadership
			• Voice
			• Collective/ collaborative approaches
			• Resource mobilization
			• Conflict capital
			• Appreciative inquiry
			• Advocacy
			• Discursive/dialogue
			• Participatory action research
			• Ethical practices

ANALYTICAL ELEMENTS	CONTEXTUAL ELEMENTS Historical Societal Cultural Organizational Community Political Social Global		
	Concepts of Change	Concepts of Leadership	Change Practices
Leadership	**Examples**	**Examples**	**Examples**

Outcomes
 	
• Assessment of
  outcomes
• Intended consequences
• Unintended
  consequences
• Impact on future
  events and change
	• Teleological theory
	• Systems
	  theory/change
	• Dialectical change
	• Field
	• Global change
	  theories
	• Countermovements
	• Social capital
	• Social power/
	  empowerment
	• Legitimate/
	  constituted power
		• Generative
		  leadership
		• Inclusive leadership
		• Convening
		  leadership
		• E-leadership/virtual
		  activism
		• Ethic of
		  responsibility
		• Ethical
		  leadership/values
		• Folly
			• Legitimizing
			• Conflict capital
			• Voice
			• Cultures of
			  resistance
			• Appreciative
			  inquiry
			• Ethical practices

outcomes on future events (an evaluation of how the past outcomes and actions affect future prospects for change). In the vignette involving extraordinary rendition, for instance, U.S. government officials needed to consider the ethics of responsibility, cultures of resistance, and effect of exposure by the media and nongovernmental organizations (NGOs) on the country's reputation with regard to cases such as Masri's and Abu Ghraib. An assessment of outcomes is essential to revising or establishing future policies and practices concerning extraordinary rendition.

The framework and content of this book bring together concepts of change, concepts of leadership, and change practices in an attempt to provide a more comprehensive approach to understanding and leading change in multiple contexts. There is more work to be done. Scholars and practitioners from various disciplines must contribute new and existing theories, research, and practices to this effort.

One of the most essential reasons for leadership is to bring about change in human conditions and systems. Throughout the years, people of the world have witnessed major injustices become moral victories, technological change connect people across the globe, and political change renew hope and inspire confidence worldwide; people have also seen the opposite outcome of change. Humanity can least afford the latter. Using concepts and practices of leading change, people have an opportunity to make a meaningful difference in the human condition and, in the words of James MacGregor Burns, bring about "real, intended change."

Reference

Lipman-Blumen, J. (1996). *The connective edge: Leading in an interdependent world.* San Francisco: Jossey-Bass.

Epilogue

Leading Intellectual Change: The Power of Ideas

James MacGregor Burns

Many a scholar of leadership may indulge in the dream that a sitting or prospective president would read just the right book about the job (ideally, of course, a book written by said scholar). My dream would be that President Obama—or at least one of his top advisers—would study this book.

Such a reader might note that above all it was the power of ideas—even more than specific policy proposals—that lifted Obama out of a galaxy of presidential candidates to win the Democratic nomination and then the presidency. The power of his ideas—far more than campaign funds—mobilized the millions of votes he needed to gain the White House.

Still, campaigning for votes is one thing; running a huge national government is many other things. *Leading Change in Multiple Contexts* captures the endless complexity of governing—the many dimensions and dilemmas of power, the unexpected ethical dilemmas, the need to use the techniques of both transforming and transactional leadership, and how the latter must ultimately serve and sustain the former.

In my own work, I have defined leadership as the mobilization of followers by political leaders who in turn empower the followers to become the new leaders, all of this tested by fundamental values long summarized—at least in the United States—as "life, liberty and the pursuit of happiness." This value-laden mobilization makes possible the kind of transforming leadership offered by a few outstanding presidents of the United States, from Thomas Jefferson to Franklin D. Roosevelt (FDR). Will Barack Obama be included some day in the galaxy of transforming leaders? Early on he showed in his brilliant campaign for the White House the power to bring to the polls tens of millions of voters, some of whom had never voted, at least for presidential candidates.

This mighty achievement, though, posed perhaps the harshest test for the new president. How can he perpetuate an "Obama majority" of enthusiasts and activists who will be voting for senators and members of Congress in 2010 and 2012? Many people have long been familiar with the drop-off of FDR or Reagan voters in subsequent Senate and House elections. But these elections may empower senators and members of Congress who can support or sap presidential power. All this in turn poses the question of how to organize and energize and even "institutionalize" the millions of Americans who voted for a presidential personality and not for a political party. Specifically, how will they vote in 2010 when the evocative name Barack Hussein Obama will not be on the ballot? The answer will depend in part on the sheer organizational skills of presidential and party leaders—but even more on the power of transforming ideas that can mobilize voters in congressional as well as presidential elections.

When it comes to governing, much of a new president's success in office will turn not only on his or her transforming leadership but also on day-to-day skills— in short, on transactional leadership. Perhaps the greatest virtue of Gill Hickman's work lies in its portrait of the sheer complexity of the federal government—even aside from the intricacies of county and city governments. To produce united action on the three levels of government and in the legislative and executive branches calls for bargaining and compromise in every level and branch of government. But how much of the needed energy and force of government is lost in the transactional leadership of concession and compromise?

Yes, U.S. citizens are still dominated by the checks and balances of the 1787 political system of government that they learned about as students in "Poly Sci 101" and in advanced treatments like *Leading Change in Multiple Contexts*. Citizens are still subject to the success and failures of political parties to mobilize support not only for candidates but also for party promises and platforms. Citizens are still aware of a constitutional amending process that makes major institutional change almost impossible. And, with this book, people are more aware than ever of the need in government not only for skillful brokers but also for inventiveness and creativity within the system.

President Obama, in short, and his successors will be 21st century leaders trying to govern through an 18th century constitutional system. Much will depend on the day-by-day resourcefulness of the managers of government; much will depend too on their knowledge of government drawn from fine studies like the present, with fresh ideas empowering the leadership of intellectual change.

Index

About the Author

Gill Robinson Hickman (PhD, University of Southern California) is currently a Professor of Leadership Studies in the Jepson School of Leadership Studies at the University of Richmond. Her previous experience includes founding Dean in the School of Health at California State University, acting Associate Dean at Virginia Commonwealth University, Professor of Public Administration, and Director of Human Resources for two organizations. She was also a founding partner in a small California retail business.

She has published two other books, titled *Leading Organizations: Perspectives for a New Era*, for Sage Publications, and *Managing Personnel in the Public Sector: A Shared Responsibility*, with Dalton Lee for Harcourt College Publishers. In addition, she has published a number of book chapters and articles on leadership studies. Her current research and book project with Dr. Georgia Sorenson is titled *The Power of Invisible Leadership* and examines leadership in settings where dedication to a powerful purpose is the motivating force for people to take action.

She was an invited presenter at the China Executive Leadership Academy Pudong (CELAP), Shanghai, China; the Leadership in Central Europe Conference at Palacky University in Olomouc, Czech Republic; the Salzburg Seminar in Salzburg, Austria; and the University of the Western Cape in South Africa. She has participated as a panel member at international conferences in Amsterdam, The Netherlands; Guadalajara, Mexico; and Vancouver and Toronto, Canada. At the Jepson School, she teaches courses on leading change, theories and models of leadership, leadership in organizations, and leadership in a diverse society.

About the Contributors

James MacGregor Burns (PhD, Harvard University) is a Pulitzer Prize–winning presidential biographer and a pioneer in the study of leadership. He is the Woodrow Wilson Professor of Government Emeritus at Williams College; Distinguished Leadership Scholar at the Academy of Leadership, which bears his name, at the University of Maryland; and a member of the American Academy of Arts and Sciences. Author of more than two dozen books, he has devoted his professional life to the study of leadership in various forms. In 1971, he won the Pulitzer Prize and the National Book Award for his biography *Roosevelt: Soldier of Freedom* (1970). His book *Leadership*, published in 1978, is still considered the seminal work in the field of leadership studies and is the basis of more than 400 doctoral dissertations. Among his most recent books are *Running Alone: Presidential Leadership from JFK to Bush II*, *Transforming Leadership*, and *Dead Center: Clinton-Gore Leadership*.

Richard A. Couto (PhD, University of Kentucky) is a senior scholar at the James MacGregor Burns Academy of Leadership at the University of Maryland. He has a background in practice and scholarship in community leadership. He directed the Center for Health Services at Vanderbilt University from 1975 to 1988 and has won several national awards, including a Kellogg National Fellowship for his work in support of community leadership in Appalachia and in rural, predominantly African American counties in western Tennessee. In 1991, he became a founding faculty member of the Jepson School of Leadership Studies at the University of Richmond. In 2002, he became a founding faculty member of Antioch University's PhD Program in Leadership and Change. His most recent books focus on community leadership, democratic theory and practice, a curriculum of courage for fearless thinking based on the achievements of Antioch College, and reflections on leadership, which commemorates the 25th anniversary of James MacGregor Burns's book *Leadership*.

Marti Goetz (MA, Wright State University) is a doctoral student in leadership and change at Antioch University. She is the executive director of Miami Valley In-Ovations, a nonprofit housing corporation serving people with developmental disabilities in southwest Ohio. She has worked to improve housing and services for this population throughout her career, helping to move people with developmental disabilities from state institutions to their own homes where they can participate fully in their communities.

Sarah Hippensteel Hall (MA, Antioch University Seattle) is Program Development Specialist at the Miami Conservancy District in Dayton, Ohio. She works with communities to build diverse partnerships and solve water quality challenges. Her research and scholarly interests include leadership in community-based organizations, empowerment, and participatory action research. She has presented at many national conferences. She is currently earning a doctorate in leadership and change at Antioch University.

Rebecca Todd Peters (PhD, Union Theological Seminary, New York) is Associate Professor of religious studies at Elon University. Her book *In Search of the Good Life: The Ethics of Globalization* (Continuum, 2004) won the 2003 Trinity Book Prize. She also coedited *Justice in the Making* (Westminster/John Knox, 2004); *Justice in a Global Economy: Strategies for Home, Community and World* (Westminster/John Knox, 2006); and *To Do Justice: A Guide for Progressive Christians* (Westminster/John Knox, 2008). In addition to teaching ethics courses in the Religious Studies department, she is a member of the Environmental Studies faculty and offers courses in the honors program and the women's and gender studies programs. Her research and teaching areas include economic and environmental ethics, sexuality issues, and reproductive concerns.